...rofessor, Department of War Studies, King's College London, UK

...is offers a powerful insight into the nature of ... Through careful archival research he shows how fascism ...iculated in various ways and in different forums for the duration of the Second World War. This wide-ranging and often startling book paves the way for scholars to show that British fascism was marked more by continuities than by breaks in the transition from war to postwar.

Dan Stone, *Professor of Modern History, Royal Holloway, University of London, UK*

Richard Griffiths seems to me to be presenting the collaborationist or Vichy England that would have emerged in the event of a successful German invasion in 1940. We always need to know about harmful cause-mongering, and it is very valuable to have this example of it.

David Pryce-Jones, *Senior Editor of* National Review *and author of* Unity Mitford: A Quest

WHAT DID YOU DO DURING THE WAR?

This book is a sequel to Richard Griffiths's two highly successful previous books on the British pro-Nazi Right, *Fellow Travellers of the Right: British Enthusiasts for Nazi Germany 1933–39*, and *Patriotism Perverted: Captain Ramsay, the Right Club and British Anti-Semitism 1939–1940*. It follows the fortunes of his protagonists after the arrests of May–June 1940, and charts their very varied reactions to the failure of their cause, while also looking at the possible reasons for the government's failure to detain prominent pro-Nazis from the higher strata of society.

Some of the pro-Nazis continued with their original views, and even undertook politically subversive activity, in Britain and in Germany. Others, finding that their pre-war balance between patriotism and pro-Nazism had now tipped firmly on the side of patriotism, fully supported the war effort, while still maintaining their old views privately. Other people found that events had made them change their views sincerely. And then there were those who, frightened by the prospect of detention or disgrace, tried to hide or even to deny their former views by a variety of subterfuges, including attacking former colleagues. This wide variety of reactions sheds new light on the equally wide range of reasons for their original admiration for Nazism, and also gives us some more general insight into what could be termed 'the psychology of failure'.

Richard Griffiths is an Emeritus Professor of King's College London, UK. One of his areas of specialisation is the European and British extreme Right, on which his major publications have been: *Marshal Pétain* (1970), *Fellow Travellers of the Right* (1980), *Patriotism Perverted* (1998) and *An Intelligent Person's Guide to Fascism* (2000).

Routledge Studies in Fascism and the Far Right
Series editors: Nigel Copsey, Teesside University, and Graham Macklin, Teesside University

This new book series focusses upon fascist, far-right-wing and right-wing politics within a historical context. Fascism falls within the far right, but the far right also extends to so-called 'radical-right populism'. Boundaries are not fixed and it is important not to overlook points of convergence and exchange with the mainstream right.

The series will include books with a broad thematic focus suitable for students and teachers. These will be available in hardback and paperback. It will also include more specialist books, aimed largely at subject specialists, which will appear in hardback and e-book format only.

Titles include:

Cultures of Post-War British Fascism
Nigel Copsey and John E. Richardson

France and Fascism
February 1934 and the dynamics of political crisis
Brian Jenkins and Chris Millington

Searching for Lord Haw-Haw
The political lives of William Joyce
Colin Holmes

Farming, Fascism and Ecology
A life of Jorian Jenks
Philip M. Coupland

Fascist in the Family
The tragedy of John Beckett MP
Francis Beckett

What Did You Do During The War?
The last throes of the British pro-Nazi Right, 1940–45
Richard Griffiths

WHAT DID YOU DO DURING THE WAR?

The last throes of the British pro-Nazi Right, 1940–45

Richard Griffiths

Routledge
Taylor & Francis Group

LONDON AND NEW YORK

First published 2017
by Routledge
2 Park Square, Milton Park, Abingdon, Oxon OX14 4RN

and by Routledge
711 Third Avenue, New York, NY 10017

Routledge is an imprint of the Taylor & Francis Group, an informa business

© 2017 Richard Griffiths

The right of Richard Griffiths to be identified as author of this work has been asserted by him in accordance with sections 77 and 78 of the Copyright, Designs and Patents Act 1988.

All rights reserved. No part of this book may be reprinted or reproduced or utilised in any form or by any electronic, mechanical, or other means, now known or hereafter invented, including photocopying and recording, or in any information storage or retrieval system, without permission in writing from the publishers.

Trademark notice: Product or corporate names may be trademarks or registered trademarks, and are used only for identification and explanation without intent to infringe.

British Library Cataloguing in Publication Data
A catalogue record for this book is available from the British Library

Library of Congress Cataloguing in Publication Data
Names: Griffiths, Richard, 1935– author. | Griffiths, Richard, 1935– Fellow travellers of the Right. | Griffiths, Richard, 1935– Patriotism perverted.
Title: What did you do during the war?: the last throes of the British pro-Nazi Right, 1940–45 | Richard Griffiths.
Description: Milton Park, Abingdon, Oxon; New York, NY: Routledge, 2017. | Series: Routledge studies in fascism and the far right |
Includes bibliographical references and index.
Identifiers: LCCN 2016013291| ISBN 9781138888968 (hardback) | ISBN 9781138888999 (pbk.) | ISBN 9781315712673 (e-book)
Subjects: LCSH: Great Britain–Politics and government–1936–1945. | World War, 1939–1945–Political aspects–Great Britain. | Right-wing extremists–Great Britain–History–20th century. | Nazis–Great Britain–History–20th century. | Fascists–Great Britain–History–20th century. | Failure (Psychology)–Political aspects–Great Britain–History–20th century. | Great Britain–Relations–Germany. | Germany–Relations–Great Britain.
Classification: LCC DA587.G75 2017 | DDC 320.53/3094109044–dc23
LC record available at https://lccn.loc.gov/2016013291

ISBN: 978-1-138-88896-8 (hbk)
ISBN: 978-1-138-88899-9 (pbk)
ISBN: 978-1-315-71267-3 (ebk)

Typeset in Bembo
By Out of House Publishing

For Tom, Millie, Dan, Giacomo, Bethan,
Annie and Alys

CONTENTS

List of illustrations   *xii*
Preface   *xiii*
Acknowledgements   *xv*
Abbreviations   *xviii*
Nomenclature   *xxi*

Introduction   1

Part I: Puncturing myths about the 'phoney war' period   **11**

1   To fight or not to fight: the myth of Mosley's patriotism   13

2   The reception of Bryant's *Unfinished Victory*: the myth of public unanimity against Nazi Germany in early 1940   33

Part II: Peace and war, high-mindedness and low connections: the Duke of Bedford and the peace movement   **57**

3   Evangelical anticapitalism: the strange case of the Duke of Bedford   59

4 'How can the Germans honestly be blamed?':
 The infiltration of the peace movement   74

Part III: Defence Regulation 18b and its after-effects   93

5 The watershed: the arrests of May–June 1940 and
 their aftermath   95

6 The re-emergence of extreme right-wing
 movements in Britain, 1940–5   111

Part IV: Renegades   139

7 'Long before 1939 I had become an admirer of
 the Nazi system': five British broadcasters for
 Nazi Germany   141

Part V: Pro-Nazism, patriotism, hatred, fear, remorse: the extraordinary variety of motives among former 'fellow travellers'   169

8 'Have you found many Lavals among your
 Galloway friends?': Wartime and post-war disputes
 between three former 'fellow travellers of the Right' 171

9 'I wrote a very full and strong letter to the
 King': two would-be negotiators   193

10 'The internment of a person of her social standing
 might give the public a wrong impression': the
 charmed lives of various 'pillars of society'   205

11 'His impetuous nature, obstinacy and flawed
 judgement': a bull in a china shop   221

12 'You know the Jewish racket as well as I do': the vagaries of the 'back-to-the-land' school	232
Part VI: Aftermath	**279**
13 'Change and decay in all around I see': further post-war decline	281
Conclusion	305
Appendix: Rogues' gallery	*312*
Bibliography	*333*
Index	*345*

ILLUSTRATIONS

1	Sir Oswald Mosley (Getty Images)	129
2	Sir Arthur Bryant (with Sir John Glubb Pasha) (Getty Images)	129
3	Captain and Mrs Ramsay at a society wedding (Getty Images)	130
4	Harry St John Philby (Getty Images)	131
5	Peveril Internment Camp, Isle of Man (Getty Images)	131
6	William Joyce (Getty Images)	132
7	Mrs Dorothy Eckersley (Getty Images)	133
8	General J.F.C. Fuller (Getty Images)	134
9	The 2nd Duke of Westminster, with Coco Chanel at the races (Getty Images)	135
10	Lord Redesdale giving away his daughter Deborah at her wartime wedding (Getty Images)	136
11	Captain George Lane-Fox Pitt-Rivers (Churchill Archives Centre, The Papers of George Henry Lane-Fox Pitt-Rivers)	137
12	Lord Sempill and Ernst Udet, the German flying ace (Getty Images)	138

PREFACE

How often, believing a task to have been completed, does one later begin to realise that there is much more to do! For me, this has been particularly true of my work on the British pro-Nazi and anti-Semitic Right. My first book on this subject, *Fellow Travellers of the Right: British Enthusiasts for Nazi Germany 1933–39* (1980), studied public opinion in the 1930s, mainly by using published sources. It provided a picture (surprising for the time, though much has been written on the subject since) of an inter-war Britain in which great sections of the public held and expressed opinions favourable to the Nazi regime – not just extremists, but also perfectly respectable citizens of apparently moderate views. This was not mere 'appeasement' of a foreign regime for reasons of national defence; it was whole-hearted approval of the Nazi internal regime. And, even more surprisingly, this approval seemed to grow as the Thirties progressed.

Having taken that book to the outbreak of war in September 1939, I thought my job had ended, as I believed there to have been little publicly expressed pro-Nazism thereafter – and the basis of my book had been the study of *public* expressions of pro-Nazi sympathies. So the last sentence of my 'Epilogue' ran: 'Our serious study of pro-German and pro-Nazi opinions in Great Britain has had, of necessity, to stop in 1939.' I was, of course, entirely wrong. As time went by, I was to find considerable evidence of pro-Nazi and anti-Semitic ideas and activity, both public and (mostly) private, in Britain during the 'phoney war' from September 1939 to May 1940. Various important documents came my way, and the discovery of the 'Red Book', the membership list of Captain Ramsay's secret society the Right Club, enabled me to follow up, via Home Office and MI5 files, the activities of many of its members. All this led me to produce, eighteen years later in 1998, a further book, *Patriotism Perverted: Captain Ramsay, the Right Club and British Anti-Semitism, 1939–40*. This book ended with the arrest of most right-wing extremists in May–June 1940; and I once again truly believed, at that point, that there was little further to say.

How wrong I was! Here I am, another eighteen years later, producing another book, this time mainly about the activities of a range of such people from 1940 to 1945 (though it also corrects certain presumptions about the period 1939–40). It is, however, a very different kind of book, in that it gives us, through their later vicissitudes after the failure of their cause, far greater insight into the various forms of motivation which had originally brought these people to pro-Nazism, and shows us the comparative strength or weakness of their original commitment. It is also, in a sense, a study of human reactions to failure. I had begun, some time ago, to realise that this was a fruitful area of study, and had already written several pieces which could become either articles or chapters of a book, when Craig Fowlie of Routledge contacted me out of the blue to find out if I had anything on the drawing-board. That concentrated my mind, and this book is the result.

It may well disappoint those who look for the trappings of conventional history. It is not about high politics, or the effect of actions upon world or national events; nor does it deal with important and influential strands of public opinion. Its remit is much more private. It deals with the reactions of specific individuals when under stress, and with the reasons that are thereby revealed about their previous actions; and, more generally, it is about the decline of an ethos that had permeated the society of the 1930s. The contrast between British post-war attitudes and the way people had behaved before the war has always been known; this study helps us to understand the process of that change.

Richard Griffiths

ACKNOWLEDGEMENTS

I am grateful to *Patterns of Prejudice* for permission to use material from my articles 'The reception of Bryant's *Unfinished Victory*: Insights into British Public Opinion in Early 1940' (*PoP*, 38, 1, March 2004, 18–36), and 'Antisemitic Obsessions: The Case of H.W. Wicks' (*PoP*, 48, 1, February 2014, 94–113); to the *Journal of Contemporary History* for permission to reproduce part of my article 'A Note on Mosley, the "Jewish War" and Conscientious Objection' (*JCH*, 40, 4, October 2005, 675–88); and to Ashgate Publishers for permission to reuse part of my chapter 'The Dangers of Definition: Post-facto Opinions on Rolf Gardiner's Attitudes towards Nazi Germany', in *Rolf Gardiner: Folk, Nature and Culture in Interwar Britain*, eds M. Jefferies and M. Tyldesley (Farnham: Ashgate, 2011, pp. 137–50).

My thanks are due to the following bodies and individuals for access to, and/or permission to quote from, the papers listed: the Trustees of the Liddell Hart Centre for Military Archives, King's College London (the papers of Sir Arthur Bryant, Captain Sir Basil Liddell Hart and Aubrey Lees); Hampshire Record Office and the 10th Earl of Portsmouth (the papers of the 9th Earl of Portsmouth); the Master and Fellows of Trinity College Cambridge (the papers of R.A. Butler); the Master and Fellows of Selwyn College Cambridge (the papers of H.W. Wicks); the Caird Archive and Library of the National Maritime Museum (the diaries of Admiral Sir Barry Domvile); His Grace the 10th Duke of Buccleuch (the letters of the 8th Duke of Buccleuch); the 2nd Earl of Stockton (the letters of Harold Macmillan); Mrs Rosalind Richards (the letters of Rolf Gardiner); Mrs Janet Henderson and the Estate of Hamish Henderson for permission to reproduce part of a poem by Hamish Henderson; and Ian Birchall and Laura Noszlopy for permission to quote from letters they have written to me. I am also grateful to Mr Edward Greene for giving me access to the papers of Ben Greene (of which in the event the relevant papers have in the meantime been used by Jeremy Lewis in his book on the Greene family). Thanks are also due to Getty Images and the Churchill Archives Centre for permission to include a number of illustrations. Every effort has been made to contact copyright holders, but in a small number of cases these efforts have been fruitless. In these cases, any copyright holder who may exist is asked to get in touch with the author.

For providing me with references for access to libraries and archives I would particularly like to thank Corelli Barnett and Theodore Zeldin. For first-hand information with regard to specific issues or people my thanks are due to Francis Beckett (John Beckett); Ivor Coats (Richard Findlay); Myles Eckersley (Peter and Dorothy Eckersley); Alasdair Ferguson (Admiral Sir Barry Domvile); the late Sir Michael Fraser (Sir Arthur Bryant); the late Sir Herbert Hart and Lady Hart (the Ben Greene case); the late Monsignor Alfred Gilbey (Francis Yeats-Brown); Robert Neild (R.A. Butler); the late Ben Pimlott (the Ben Greene post-war libel case); the late John Roberts (Rolf Gardiner); and John Spencer (H.W. Wicks).

I am indebted to many other people for information, advice or useful discussions, over a number of years. They include: Geoffrey Alderman, Bruce Anderson, Francis Beckett, Nicolas Bell, Ian Birchall, Vernon Bogdanor, Georgina Boyes, Robert Brotherton, Martin Ceadel, the late Owen Chadwick, the late Seweryn Chomet, Nigel Copsey, the late Maurice Cowling, Roger Eatwell, Aled Eirug, Michael Fahlbusch, Chris Flood, Julie Gottlieb, Dominic Griffiths, Patrick Ground, Colin Holmes, Caroline Jackson, Robert Jackson, Matthew Jefferies, Efraim Karsh, Tony Kushner, Anthony Lejeune, Thomas Linehan, Helder Macedo, Graham Macklin, Mike Mertens, Robert Neild, Scott Newton, Laura Noszlopy, Andrzej Olechnowicz, Richard Overy, Jan Palmowski, Hubert Picarda, Michael Pinto-Duschinsky, Mark Pitchford, David Pryce-Jones, David Renton, Andrew Roberts, the late Brian Simpson, Robert Skidelsky, Dai Smith, Peter Stead,

Dan Stone, Rob Stradling, Richard Thurlow, Errol Trzebinski, Mike Tyldesley, Philippe Vervaecke, Richard Vinen, the late Donald Cameron Watt, Hywel Williams and Yaakov Wise.

The books and articles that have been used in relation to this study are listed in the bibliography to each chapter. I would like to single out, however, those that have been of particular use: Martin Ceadel's *Pacifism in Britain 1914–1945*, and articles on the same subject by Mark Gilbert and David Lukowitz; Tony Kushner's *The Persistence of Prejudice*; Graham Macklin's *Very Deeply Dyed in Black*; Andrew Roberts's *Eminent Churchillians*; Brian Simpson's *In the Highest Degree Odious*; Dan Stone's *Breeding Superman* and *Responses to Nazism in Britain*; and Richard Thurlow's *Fascism in Britain*.

I have been greatly aided by the courteous and helpful staff of the National Archives, the British Library, Colindale Newspaper Library, the Wiener Library, the Liddell Hart Centre for Military Archives at King's College London, the Churchill Archives Centre, the National Maritime Museum, the Hampshire Record Office, the Royal Aeronautical Society, the Bodleian Library and Trinity College Cambridge Library. I would like particularly to thank Mark Paul of Getty Images, and Ceri Humphries of the Churchill Archive, for their great helpfulness. Very special thanks, too, are due to Barbara Rosenbaum at *Patterns of Prejudice*, and to Craig Fowlie and Emma Chappell, my editors at Routledge.

Finally, I would like to thank my wife Patricia and my daughter Hilary for their careful reading of my text and for their unfailingly useful suggestions.

ABBREVIATIONS

Archives, publishers and academic journals

BAK	Bundesarchiv, Koblenz
Bod.	Bodleian Library
CUP	Cambridge University Press
HRO	Hampshire Record Office
JCH	*Journal of Contemporary History*
LHCMA	Liddell Hart Centre for Military Archives, King's College London
NMM	The Caird Archive and Library, National Maritime Museum
PoP	*Patterns of Prejudice*
SCC	Selwyn College, Cambridge Library
TCC	Trinity College, Cambridge Library
TNA	The National Archives

Movements and other bodies, and their journals

AGF	Anglo-German Fellowship
BCAEC	British Council against European Commitments
BCCSE	British Council for a Christian Settlement in Europe
BF	British Fascists

Abbreviations **xix**

BNP	British National Party
BPP	British People's Party
BUF	British Union of Fascists (up to 1936)
BU	British Union (1936 onwards)
CRA	Constitutional Research Association
ENA	English Nationalist Association
FP	*The Free Press*
GR	*Gothic Ripples*
HDSE	Home Defence (Security) Executive
IFL	Imperial Fascist League
IP	*Information and Policy*
ILP	Independent Labour Party
LEL	League of Empire Loyalists
LRL	Liberty Restoration League
NA	Nationalist Association
NBBS	New British Broadcasting Service.
NFaV	National Front after Victory
NL	Nordic League
NP	*New Pioneer*
NSL	National Socialist League
PN	*Peace News*
PP	*People's Post*
PPIS	Peace and Progressive Information Service
PPU	Peace Pledge Union
QGEA	*Quarterly Gazette of the English Array*
RC	The Right Club
RRA	Rural Reconstruction Association
SA	Soil Association
SEA	Service for Economic Action
SRNS	*Springhead Ring News Sheet*
UBF	Union of British Freedom
UM	Union Movement
WAS	Women's Auxiliary Service
WPS	Women's Police Service

Newspapers

The abbreviations for these are given in the bibliographies of the chapters concerned.

Miscellaneous

DPP	Director of Public Prosecutions
DR 18B	Defence Regulation 18B
SOE	Special Operations Executive

NOMENCLATURE

Mosley's movement was called **'the British Union of Fascists' (BUF)** until 1936, when it was renamed 'the British Union of Fascists and National Socialists', commonly known as **'British Union' (BU)**. As far as possible, these two titles have been used correctly, according to the times being described.

'Fascist', with a capital letter, is here taken to refer to members either of the British Union of Fascists or of the Italian Fascist movement; **'fascist'**, without a capital letter, refers to people (and other movements) who had qualities that could be described as fascist, even though they were not members of specifically 'Fascist' movements.

INTRODUCTION

To understand what happened to the pro-Nazi Right in the period 1940–5, it will be necessary first to look back at their beginnings in the 1930s, and then at their activities from the outbreak of war to May 1940.

In the peacetime situation of the Thirties, there was no necessary contradiction between holding pro-Nazi views and being patriotic. Indeed, many of the enthusiasts for Nazi Germany were among the most patriotic of British citizens, who often figured prominently among those who were calling for national rearmament in the face of possible dangers. What distinguished them from their contemporaries was that they saw virtues in Nazism, saw Nazi Germany as a suitable ally for Britain and believed that those who denounced the German regime were either gravely misinformed, or possibly influenced by malign powers behind the scenes. (One must distinguish such people from the 'appeasers', many of whom had no admiration for Nazi Germany, though they were convinced of the need to 'appease' Germany in order to maintain peace.)

It is often forgotten just how many highly respectable people held pro-Nazi views. Looking back on the Thirties, the tendency has been to concentrate on the extremist, usually anti-Semitic, movements which espoused such beliefs – Mosley's British Union of Fascists and a host of lesser and sometimes even more extreme movements. But there was a far larger number of people of more moderate views who supported Germany's new 'experiment'. Some were convinced of the need for new, more dictatorial methods of government in order to combat the worldwide financial crisis, and admired what they saw as the 'German economic miracle'; some, given what they saw as the lack of leadership in successive British governments, admired Hitler's firm approach, and longed for a similar leader in Britain; some saw Nazi Germany as the only plausible defence against the Bolshevist threat; some saw Hitler as having 'restored self-confidence' to a nation that had been in decline; others, convinced of the Allies' guilt in relation to their treatment of Germany at Versailles, believed the rise of the Nazis to have been a natural result of this, and hoped that, as the regime settled in, it would become more moderate. All were convinced of the need to cultivate friendship with Germany, and of the dangers posed by what they saw as 'anti-German propaganda'. When they were faced by evidence of Nazi excesses, particularly the treatment of the Jews, all kinds of excuses came into play, in what I have called the 'but really' syndrome. 'Yes', such people would say, 'Nazi treatment of the Jews is deplorable. *But really*, we must not let such things stand in the way of the more important issues.' The Jewish question was not seen as important enough to detract from all the virtues and advantages of the Nazi regime.

Of course, there was also strong support for Nazi Germany among those who saw the regime's anti-Semitism as a positive advantage. As opposed to the 'fellow travellers' who have just been described, these people could be dubbed the 'extremists'. Various activist movements were the main spokesmen for their views. Often, members of these movements were convinced of a 'Jewish plot' to bring Britain and Germany to war. The argument ran as follows: the Jews had been running the capitalist system for their own profit. Hitler had successfully challenged that financial system, and had divested the Jews in Germany of their power. The Jews were now, through their financial resources and through their monopoly of the newspapers and the media, seeking to punish the Germans by persuading the democracies to fight against them. As war approached in the late Thirties, these views became even more extreme, and the myth of the 'Jewish War' dominated the debate.

It is worth describing, here, some of these movements, as their names will be recurring throughout this book, with many of the most prominent characters having belonged to one or more of them. There was, of course, Mosley's long-standing British Union of Fascists (known as British Union from 1936 onwards), of which so much has been written that there is little need to say much here. Of them all, it was the nearest approach to a mass movement. Membership had been in gradual decline from 1934 onwards, but its 'peace campaign', which came to a climax in 1938–9, caused the membership to grow considerably among all classes. The most loyal membership was, however, still to be found in those working-class areas (the East End, South-East Essex and certain Northern cities), where its anti-Semitic campaigns had their greatest effect.

Then there were the groups specifically concerned with Anglo-German Friendship, of which the most prominent were the Anglo-German Fellowship (AGF) and The Link. The AGF was a society of the 'great and the good', many of them businessmen who wished to maintain and improve commercial contacts with Germany. Major banks were represented in it, as were leading firms. Behind this facade, however, there was an enthusiasm for Nazi Germany that went far beyond these purely practical concerns. The AGF meetings were the occasion for much pro-Nazi propaganda, and the movement provided an umbrella for numerous pro-Nazi figures from other movements. It is, however, significant that many apparently moderate people in high positions in government, commerce and industry could belong to a body which clearly went over and beyond the mere desire for Anglo-German friendship. The Link, founded by Admiral Sir Barry Domvile, was another matter. Though its rank-and-file membership in various parts of the country may have believed it to be a fairly innocuous organisation, its leading members continually gave vent to violent pro-Nazi and anti-Semitic statements, in public meetings and in the pages of its magazine the *Anglo-German Review*; and the most successful branches, such as the Central London Branch (manned by the prominent anti-Semites H.T. Mills, chairman, Richard Findlay, vice-chairman, and Margaret Bothamley, secretary, and addressed at meetings not only by them, but among others by Captain Ramsay and General Fuller), were clearly extremist in tone.

There were also the movements whose main *raison d'être* was anti-Semitism, with pro-Nazism coming, as the Thirties progressed, as a natural concomitant. The most virulent of these were the Imperial Fascist League, the Nordic League and the Militant Christian Patriots. Occasionally a group with an apparently innocuous title would turn out to be as anti-Semitic as these. The best example of this was the Liberty Restoration League, chaired by the Duke of Wellington, of which the strongly anti-Semitic Captain Arthur Rogers was a prominent member. This was an association whose commitment to civil liberties masked its underlying anti-Semitism. Special Branch noted that it had close connections with the Nordic League, and that in the pre-war period Captain Rogers had regularly, at least once a month, met Captain Ramsay and other members of the NL 'to compare notes and exchange views, ... the two organisations [being] without doubt based on the same ideals' (TNA HO 144/21381/273).

As war approached, new movements emerged, and older movements changed their emphasis. In 1937 William Joyce and John Beckett, who had left British Union (BU), founded the National Socialist League, which was even more violently anti-Semitic than BU, and far more radical in its social policies. Meanwhile, the already existent 'back-to-the-land' movement the English Array (the successor to the 'English Mistery', discussed in Chapter 12), led by Lord Lymington, had been moving from its already strong reactionary and racist base to outright pro-Nazism, and Lymington's new venture, the journal *New Pioneer* (founded December 1938), was to be a prominent outlet for such opinions. In September 1938 Lymington had founded the British Council against European Commitments, in which he was joined by Joyce and Beckett, together with other prominent figures of the pro-Nazi Right. In April 1939 Lord Tavistock, together with Beckett and Ben Greene, founded the British People's Party, which was to play a major part, together with its offshoot the British Council for a Christian Settlement in Europe, in the first months of the war (and was to be revived in 1945).

One of the most important groups for our study is the Right Club, a secret society founded in May 1939 by Captain Archibald Maule

Ramsay MP. Its aims were to 'place opposition to [the Jewish menace] in the forefront of its activities' by co-ordinating the work of all the 'patriotic societies' through a Co-ordinating Committee chaired by the Duke of Wellington, to 'clear the Conservative Party of Jewish influence' and to 'avert war, which we considered to be mainly the work of Jewish intrigue centred in New York' (Ramsay, 1952: 103–4). The names on the Membership List were kept secret, apart from the Duke of Wellington and James Carlton Cross, a wealthy retired Lancashire mill-owner who was the father of the Conservative MP Ronald Cross (who served as a Minister under both Chamberlain and Churchill). In addition, the names of a few other members, such as Lord Sempill and Lord Ronald Graham, were known to MI5, either through indiscretions by RC members or through infiltration of the movement. Then in May 1940 the government gained possession of the full Membership List of the Right Club, though it did not reveal its contents publicly. After 1940 this Membership List was lost from sight, and it was not until 1990 that it was rediscovered (under circumstances described in Griffiths, 1998: 300–14). It was found to contain 235 names, some of them at first sight very surprising. Alongside a significant number of 'usual suspects' who were prominent in other extremist movements, there were also a large number of more 'respectable' names, including peers, Members of Parliament and scions of high society. Members' other right-wing affiliations were noted on the list, together with details of their subscriptions to the Right Club. The most important members were listed as either Wardens or Stewards. For a club with such aims, at such a time, the membership was amazing.

It has sometimes been suggested that some of those on the list may have been unaware of the nature of the Club. It is of course clear that those who joined in May–June 1939 would have been unaware at that stage of the treasonous activities which a minority, who continued the activities of the Club during the war, were to undertake. But even bearing that in mind, it is hard to believe that such people would have been unaware, in mid-1939, of Ramsay's publicly proclaimed anti-Semitic crusade. Some will have shared those views, and others, amid a welter of other views on which they found themselves in agreement with him – anti-Bolshevist, pro-Nazi, anti-war – would not necessarily have seen anti-Semitism as something to deter them from joining a movement which also stood for these other political attitudes. Indeed, further research into a great number of these named people has shown that even the most apparently respectable among them were imbued with opinions analogous to those of Ramsay (Griffiths, 1998: 128–64).

After September 1939 many Right Club members ceased activity. A 'rump' was left, who during the 'phoney war' undertook various subversive activities, and thereby gave the Right Club the reputation of a treasonous body. Before 1939, however, many of its members had had the usual mixture of patriotism and pro-Nazism, which when the war came meant that they had serious decisions to make.

At the outbreak of war, the tension between pro-Nazism and patriotism resolved itself in a variety of ways. Many 'fellow travellers' immediately volunteered for the Services. For some, as for example Sir Arnold Wilson MP (who volunteered as a rear-gunner, and was fatally shot down in May 1940), this involved realising that their previous views had been mistaken. For others, it was a question of patriotism having priority, but of their continuing in private to hold the same views, even though Germany was now the enemy and they were wholeheartedly committed to the defence of their country.

Meanwhile all kinds of other activities spurred on by pro-Nazism continued to exist. On an apparently respectable level, for example, a number of prominent people undertook various unofficial 'peace feelers' with Germany between September 1939 and May 1940 (the period known as the 'phoney war'), often through neutral countries, activities which were at times to cause considerable embarrassment to the British Government. It was, of course, in this period when the war was not impinging directly on the day-to-day existence of the majority of the people, hard for some people to believe that a return to peace was not possible. Others, while publicly hiding their feelings, continued privately to rail against the war and against the dark forces that had brought it about.

However, others continued in the same path as before, though by the nature of things their activities usually had to be far less public. Though the so-called 'patriotic societies' (apart from British Union and the British People's Party) publicly suspended operations at the outbreak of war, their members found various ways in which to continue their activities. Among other things, they infiltrated more respectable bodies such as the Peace Pledge Union.

Also, new groups, such as Norman Hay's 'Information and Policy', were formed to carry forward the baton. A number of bodies, such as what remained of Captain Ramsay's Right Club, undertook various subversive activities of a fairly innocuous kind at this stage. As for British Union, though Mosley was later to claim that he had given orders for his members to support the war effort, this was, as we shall see in Chapter 1, far from the truth. British Union remained a thorn in the flesh of the authorities, obstructing the war effort in various ways, but was allowed to remain in existence throughout the 'phoney war' period.

Behind the scenes, leaders of the various pro-Nazi groups – Mosley, Ramsay, Lymington, Domvile et al. – held private meetings with a view to collaboration against the war. Others, like the Marquess of Tavistock (the future Duke of Bedford), continued publicly to proclaim their opposition to the war, and their admiration for Hitler's achievements. All these activities were monitored closely by MI5 and Special Branch, though the Home Office's policy was still one of inaction on this front.

All this changed in May 1940. The invasion of the Low Countries and France had brought home the reality of war, and the present danger to Britain. The example of Holland seemed to point to the power of a subversive 'fifth column' to betray a country from within. It no longer seemed feasible to allow, in the interests of democratic freedom, those seeking to undermine the war effort to remain at large. Added to this, Churchill was now in charge. The catalyst was the arrest of the American Embassy code clerk Tyler Kent, and the revelation that he had been conveying confidential documents to members of the Right Club, together with the belief that such information was being passed on to the enemy. This was the awaited excuse for extensive arrests under Defence Regulation 18B. The first arrests were mainly of British Union members, but over the succeeding weeks many prominent members of other groups were added to the detainees. It appeared that the pro-Nazi efforts of the Right had come to an end.

However, this was not so. Right-wing activity continued on a number of fronts, at first discreetly and later more openly. As the DR 18B detainees were gradually released, this led to more concerted political activity at a certain level. Meanwhile, among those who had not been detained (for various reasons that will be discussed), there was a wide variety of reactions, from overt anti-war political activity to a genuine patriotic acceptance of the war effort (which was, however, often combined with the underlying beliefs which had originally led them to pro-Nazism), or to an actual re-evaluation, in some cases, of pre-war beliefs. Between these extremes there were many other attitudes, as the inner conflict between patriotism and ideology took its different forms. And there were also varying reactions to the danger of arrest, including the 'virtuous' denunciation of former associates and the denial of former activities. The variations are endless, and few generalisations are valid. One of the most interesting aspects of the situation is the discrepancy between some of these people's own later accounts of their activities and the evidence provided by contemporary documents, whether they be personal letters or reports from the Security Services.

This book aims at providing a picture of this wide and bewildering variety of reactions and motives. In assessing these reactions, it will naturally need to look at these individuals' previous history. Placing this side by side with their wartime activities provides some unexpected insights into both areas of their experience.

We start, however, by going back to the 'phoney war' period, 1939–40, with two chapters of new material, each of which punctures a well-established myth. In the first, Mosley's claim (on the basis of his wilful misrepresentation of contemporary documents) to have told his followers to back the war effort is seen to be false; and the movement's actual aims and activities in this period are examined in detail. In the second, the commonly-held belief that public reaction in early 1940 to Arthur Bryant's pro-Nazi and anti-Semitic book *Unfinished Victory* had been strongly adverse is shown to be wrong, as most reviews were strongly in favour of it and Bryant himself had no sense at this stage of public disapproval (though all was to change from the May 1940 watershed onwards). This undermines previous beliefs about the anti-Nazi nature of most public opinion in Britain in early 1940.

Introduction **9**

For the period from May 1940 onwards, in Parts II and III we first look at some of the more general aspects of the situation – the peace movement's involvement in, and infiltration by, pro-Nazism; the imprisonments from May 1940 onwards under Defence Regulation 18B and their lasting effects upon the detainees; and the various attempts by these people, throughout the rest of the war, to form new movements on the old model. In the process we also look closely at certain individuals who will recur in later chapters, from the Duke of Bedford to Ben Greene and Aubrey Lees.

Parts IV, V and VI are the nub of the book, in that they examine a series of individuals, and attempt to evaluate the reasons for their very varied reactions to their new situation. In Chapter 7 we study the wartime careers of a number of pre-war fascist sympathisers who broadcast for the Nazis from Germany. They are shown not only to differ widely in their motivation, but also to have later contrived skilfully, but unsuccessfully, to cover their tracks in various ways. In Chapter 8, we see the tangled relationship between three former 'fellow travellers of the Right', and the way in which they turned upon each other in self-justification. Chapter 9 looks at the cases of the would-be negotiators Lord Brocket and the Duke of Buccleuch, and their different reactions to the collapse of their hopes. Chapter 10 takes a number of those prominent people who evaded detention (attempting to assess the reasons for this), and studies their activities both before and during the war, and the relationship between their pre-war and wartime activities. Chapter 11 looks at one extraordinary and complicated case, that of Lord Sempill. Chapter 12 evaluates the very varied responses of the 'back-to-the land' school. Finally, Chapter 13 follows the careers in the post-war world of a number of those whom we have been studying. The appendix, 'Rogues' gallery', gives thumbnail accounts of a number of those figures who have played a part in the main text without being examined in depth there.

Wartime Britain has only too often mistakenly been believed to have provided a simple picture of the nation's single-minded patriotic determination to defeat the enemy. While there is much that is true in that picture, the actual situation was in fact far more complicated. This book will be attempting to give some account of the varied reactions of a number of members of the pre-war pro-Nazi Right to the new situation in which they now found themselves from mid-1940 onwards. In these reactions some showed their best side, at times taking surprising stances both during and after the war. Some did not. Others, for a variety of psychological, moral or pragmatic motives, fell between these two extremes. Throughout the book I have endeavoured to keep in mind Owen Chadwick's sage advice to historians, to try to get into the minds of their subjects, to attempt to understand their motives and to beware grafting onto them the presumptions produced by hindsight. This is what Owen said, in the closing paragraph of his inaugural lecture on appointment to the Cambridge Regius Chair of Modern History:

> St Augustine said you need to be a friend of a man before you understand him. So by analogy is our relation to men of the past, societies of the past, even documents in the archives. You may suspect, you ought to suspect them all as sure to mislead you vilely unless your critical sense is ever alert; but they do it (for the most part) by their inadvertence or partial vision. You need no white paint, you need to try to see things as they were. But you need to be inside their minds and to forget the future which they could not know, and to come towards them with the openness of mind, the readiness to listen, which a man gives to a friend.
>
> (Harrison, 2015)

Bibliography

Griffiths, Richard (1980), *Fellow Travellers of the Right: British Enthusiasts for Nazi Germany, 1933–39* (London: Constable).

Griffiths, Richard (1998), *Patriotism Perverted: Captain Ramsay, the Right Club and British Anti-Semitism, 1939–40* (London: Constable).

Harrison, Sir David (2015), Address at the funeral of the Revd Professor Owen Chadwick.

Ramsay, A.H.M. (1952), *The Nameless War* (London: The Britons Publishing Society).

PART I
Puncturing myths about the 'phoney war' period

PART 1

1

TO FIGHT OR NOT TO FIGHT

The myth of Mosley's patriotism

Some stories are so often repeated that they eventually become accepted as undisputed facts. Nowhere is this more true than in the literature dealing with Sir Oswald Mosley, much of which continues to rely heavily on, as Francis Beckett puts it, 'Mosley's own unsupported explanations of events' (Beckett, 1999: 219). This is partly because of the way in which, after the event, he succeeded in using truncated or misdated quotations from his own writings in order to justify his actions. A typical example of the continuing acceptance of Mosley's version of events by generations of commentators is the following statement, which makes the case that Mosley was wrongly arrested in May 1940:

> He had campaigned for peace, but publicly urged his members to fight once war was declared. At the beginning of September [1939] he had instructed them 'to do nothing to injure our country, or to help any other power, […] to obey [their] orders and in particular obey the rules of their service'.
>
> (Dalley, 1999: 241)

14 Puncturing myths about the 'phoney war'

The basis for these and similar assertions lies in a passage quoted by Mosley himself in his own memoirs. This was part of his 'Message to the members of British Union', which had been published in the movement's newspaper *Action* on 16 September 1939, but dated 1 September 1939. Once we look at it more closely, however, and relate it to the actions of Mosley and British Union (BU) during the next eight months, we see that he did the opposite of 'urging his members to fight once war was declared', and that the quotation in question, through its truncated nature, hides the fact that he never claimed, at the time, to be doing so. As he was later to quote it in *My Life* and elsewhere, the 1939 passage runs:

> To our members my message is plain and clear. Our country is involved in war. Therefore I ask you to do nothing to injure our country, or to help any other power. Our members should do what the law requires of them, and if they are members of any of the forces or services of the Crown, they should obey their orders, and, in particular, obey the rules of their service [...] We have said a hundred times that if the life of Britain were threatened we would fight again.
>
> (Mosley, 1968: 400)

This was to be repeated, in exactly the same form, by other apologists. Two questions need to be raised in relation to it. First, is this a correct account of Mosley's Message of 1 September? Secondly, does it accurately depict Mosley's wartime attitude, as shown by his and his movement's activities, and the advice to their members?

Is it a correct version? Though Mosley's version in his biography *My Life* does follow closely the text printed in the 16 September issue of *Action* (the BU newspaper), the first after the outbreak of war (the only change being that Mosley has inadvertently printed 'in particular' for 'in every particular'), the quotation is in fact very misleading. Mosley's Message had, by the time it appeared in *Action*, been so heavily censored that little of its original meaning remained, and it appeared as innocuous as Mosley was later to claim it to be. The full message had, however, been extensively distributed in its entirety to BU members, and to the movement's usual publication outlets. Its contents were perceived to be so subversive that in a written question in the House of Commons Brigadier-General Edward Spears MP asked the Home Secretary to 'consult the Director of Public Prosecutions as to the advisability of taking legal action against the author and publishers'. The DPP decided against prosecution not because he questioned the subversive nature of the content of the Message, but because it was dated (possibly pre-dated, for this reason) 1 September, which was before the outbreak of war, and could not therefore strictly be classed as seditious (TNA HO 144/21429).

What had aroused the ire of Spears? The full Message started with a depiction of the way in which the British public had been tricked into war by Jewish propaganda: 'The dope machine of Jewish finance deceived the people until Britain was involved in war in the interest of the Money Power which rules Britain through its Press and Parties.' More seriously, Mosley not only declared his own intention not to fight, but implicitly encouraged others to take the same attitude:

> We have said a hundred times that if the life of Britain were threatened we would fight again. But I am not offering to fight in the quarrel of Jewish finance, in a war from which Britain could withdraw at any moment she likes with her Empire intact and her people safe.

And he concluded: 'I am now concerned with only two simple facts. This war is no quarrel of the British people; this war is a quarrel of Jewish finance' (TNA HO 144/21429).

Only when we place the apparently innocuous version published by *Action* in its original context does it become clear that the passage later quoted by Mosley was in fact addressed only to those already in the Services: 'Our members should do what the law requires of them, and if they are members of any of the Forces or Services of the Crown …' As the Home Secretary Sir John Anderson was later to put it, 'Sir Oswald Mosley […] was too clever to put himself in the wrong by giving treasonable orders' (TNA CAB 65/7). And Mosley needed to be doubly careful on this score, given an article by A.P. Laurie which had appeared in *Action* on 2 September, the day before the outbreak of war. This article, addressed directly to the troops, had specifically preached desertion:

> Germany has committed the unforgivable sin of refusing to borrow money from the international financiers, and they must be punished. [...] The lust of the international financier for gold dripping with blood is not yet satisfied. Fools, why do you submit? [...] Why do you allow these fat bellied millionaires to send you out to kill and be killed by your brothers the Germans, who are good fellows? You must act quickly or you will be too late. Once war is declared, you are sheep in the pen, ready for the butcher's knife. You will be gagged, and not even allowed to cry out in protest before you die.

Mosley, then, specifically called on those already in the Services to obey orders. What the *Action* version left out was his instructions, immediately after that call, to *all other British Union members* (instructions so important that they were underlined – the only underlined passage in the whole Message):

> <u>But I ask all members who are free to carry on our work to take every opportunity within your power to awaken our people and to demand peace</u>.

(TNA HO 144/21429)

Furthermore, though those in the Armed Services were instructed to obey orders, the same was definitely not true, in practice, of the instructions given to those who joined civilian defence units. Indeed, from the first days of the war BU members were encouraged to join such bodies in order to spread propaganda within them. As Special Branch noted on 18 September:

> Unofficially, members (both male and female) are being encouraged to join the civilian defence units – Air Raid Precautions, Special Constabulary, Nursing Reserve, etc. – and to carry on the propaganda of the movement within these organisations.

(TNA HO 144/21429)

Of course, opposing the war was in itself legitimate, if done within the law, in the same way as the actions of the other peace movements in Britain, such as the Peace Pledge Union, were legitimate in themselves. Where Mosley's policy got onto more dangerous ground was in its strong support for Germany's case, in its distorted message as to the causes of the war, but above all in its advocacy of the refusal, by people who would otherwise have no objection of conscience to war in itself, to fight in a war that had, they believed, been brought about by the interests of Jewish finance. Only if the safety of Britain were actually threatened 'would we fight again' (and as we shall see, when the crunch appeared to have come in May 1940, even this promise went out of the window).

Practical instructions in relation to this policy of refusal to fight were soon developed in the first weeks of the war. On 16 October a circular letter signed by Neil Francis-Hawkins, Director-General of British Union, was sent to all branches. It read:

> Young men likely soon to be called up have addressed many questions to Headquarters upon their position. The position of the movement is as follows: We have always been willing to fight for our country if Britain or her Empire is threatened. In fact many of our members entered the Forces of the Crown before the War in case that ever threatened. Members who are in any of the Forces of the Crown have been advised to obey orders. All members have been asked to do nothing to injure the country and to obey the Law. Those of us who are now free under the Law to decide the matter for ourselves are not offering our services to fight in this War BECAUSE WE DO NOT CONSIDER THAT BRITAIN OR HER EMPIRE IS THREATENED. It is a matter for the individual conscience of young men who are now to be called up whether or not they exercise the right which the Law gives them of appearing before the Tribunal.
>
> (TNA HO 144/21429)

Accompanying this letter was a document of advice as to how to apply for the status of Conscientious Objector, while at the same time making it clear to the authorities that this did not mean that one would object to fighting in another kind of war, against another kind of enemy (the crucial passage was underlined):

> Applicant would begin by proving his sincere adherence to the creed of British Union, which is based upon belief in the British people and their national destiny. He would express his detestation of all international creeds which involve the nation in foreign quarrels of no concern to the British people.
>
> He would then express his willingness to serve his country in any ordinary war in defence of Britain or the British Empire, from whatsoever quarter attack might come. In this case, however, the Government has seen fit to publish as their war aims an ideological conflict to destroy the system of a foreign country. [...]
>
> Applicant should avoid long argument under what circumstances they would defend Britain from attack. [...]
>
> <u>The Applicant should maintain throughout that the onus for the creation of his conscientious objection rests with the Government, which has deliberately raised the ideological issue by making one of its principal war aims the destruction of the political system of another great nation.</u> [...]
>
> Religious grounds should be avoided, as they tend to confuse the main ideological contention. [...]
>
> (TNA HO 144/21429)

As Special Branch commented in the file containing this document, Francis-Hawkins's letter was 'so couched as to leave no doubt in the reader's mind that the leaders desire those of their followers who are of conscription age to refuse to serve'. The party's leaders were already 'very anxious to induce some young man to appear before a Tribunal, and make a test case'. It can never have been true, therefore, that Mosley 'publicly urged his members to fight once war was declared'. Indeed, as MI5 later stated:

> The outbreak of war brought about no change in the policy or outlook of British Union [...] For reasons which are obvious, Sir Oswald Mosley did not call upon his followers to perform

illegal acts. He did not call upon members of the Armed Forces to refuse to obey orders. But, short of committing illegal acts, everything was done to ensure that 'financial democracy dictated by Jewish interests' was not victorious and that world Fascism remained undefeated.

(TNA KV 2/886)

One wonders how hopeful the leaders were that such applications might be successful. Their tactic was probably that of causing chaos in the system, while advertising publicly the refusal to fight, and the idea of this being a 'Jewish War'. As a member of the Advisory Committee was later to state:

> One knows that so many members of the British Union did register as Conscientious Objectors, and that their attitude was that they were registering as part of the policy to upset the Government. […] There is a good deal of evidence in support of the view that those in the Party rather encouraged people so to register because it was a stick to beat the Government, […] with which to oppose the war policy.
>
> (TNA HO 283/63)

The movement continued to encourage this form of 'conscientious objection' throughout the following months. In *Action* on 4 January 1940 the BU supporter Hugh Ross Williamson praised the many young men who had been applying for exemption on these grounds, only to be thwarted by the Tribunals:

> Exemption can be claimed and, constitutionally, ought to be granted, if a man can show that he conscientiously objects to this war on *political* grounds. […] Those whom I have seen before the Tribunal at Cambridge are the very best (physically bravest) type of young man; and the great majority are in fact 'political objectors'.

This, and other contemporary accounts, make it clear that the policy outlined in the October Memorandum was being carried out by many young BU members, even though the tendency at the Tribunals was to conclude that theirs was 'not a conscientious objection to war but a Fascist objection to war' (TNA HO 283/63), and to refuse exemption. Such applications continued right up to the time of Mosley's detention in late May 1940, and were often reported in the newspapers. The last example we have, a typical one, is that of a certain Alfred Grahame Walker, aged 25, who appeared before Judge R.C. Essenleigh in Manchester on 22 May 1940:

> Describing himself as a National Socialist, but not a Nazi, [Walker] accused the British Government of 'a flagrant and unprovoked act of aggression by declaring war on Germany'. But he would be willing to defend this country if Germany committed an unprovoked aggression against her.
>
> (*Daily Despatch*, 23 May 1940)

In the heightened atmosphere of May 1940, when the success of the invasion of Holland and Belgium was being widely ascribed to an internal 'Fifth Column', the Judge gave a stern warning about Fifth Column activities, saying that 'those who are not with the Government now are against it' (*DD*, 23 May 1940).

An individual case: Derek Stuckey

The records of the Conscientious Objection Tribunals are not available, but we do have one fairly full account of the arguments put forward by such candidates for exemption. This is the case of Derek Stuckey, who, because of his prominence in British Union, and because of his other wartime activities, was detained on 2 June 1940. His comparative youth (he was 23 years old) made him one of the few prominent DR 18B detainees to have been of an age to put into practice the 'political conscientious objection' policy. The account of his interview with the Advisory Committee on 23 July 1940, while outlining his seditious wartime activities, also deals extensively with this issue, which the members clearly saw as being of great importance.

Stuckey had joined BU when at school at Radley. While reading Law at Oriel College, Oxford he became from 1936 vice-president of the OU National Socialist Club, and then in 1938 the secretary of the Federation of British University Fascist Associations. Within BU, in January 1939 he became the District Leader of the Combined British Universities, and in June 1939 District Inspector of the University Districts. On leaving university, he took up farming.

At the outbreak of war, a Special Branch report described him as 'an extremely clever and able propagandist, [...] indefatigable in his efforts to gain support to the Fascist movement'. He soon, in the wartime situation, began putting these qualities to work in earnest. In *Action* on 16 September he inserted an advertisement which ran as follows:

> Teachers. Will members and supporters among practising teachers, kindly communicate with D/I R. Stuckey, Box 803, *Action*.

This advertisement was carried by the journal for several weeks. To those answering it, Stuckey sent copies of Mosley's 1 September Message, 'for immediate distribution' in their schools, colleges or universities, together with a statement headed 'BRITISH UNION STUDENTS!'. The content of this statement was pretty strong stuff, calling for struggle in the streets of Britain, to produce a new regime:

> National Socialists, believing that the Youth of Britain should only fight in the vital interests of Britain, oppose this last suicidal venture of the lackeys of the Money Power. We have repeatedly stated that we shall always be willing to fight if Britain is attacked. Of our patriotism there can be no doubt. [...] Ridicule from misguided patriots, calumny and lies in the Jewish press, all these will cause temporary discomfort for true patriot Socialists. [...] Those of us who survive will see the rebirth of Britain through the National Socialist People's State. [...] Our destiny is the destiny of a great land – our war is the revolution of a great people: not a militaristic enterprise in a dubious quarrel but a struggle on the streets of Britain in the cause of the people of Britain. STUDENTS OF THE REVOLUTION, PREPARE YOURSELVES FOR THE DAY OF THE BRITISH

> UNION'S FINAL ADVANCE. LOYALTY TO MOSLEY AND LOYALTY TO BRITAIN AND HER PEOPLE ARE THE ONLY LOYALTIES.
>
> (TNA HO 144/21429)

On this basis the Advisory Committee 'deplored the type of activity to which he had lent himself since the outbreak of war'. They nevertheless recommended his release, believing that he could be trusted to take no further part in BU politics and could be of use to the war effort as a farmer. MI5 adhered to its original recommendation, however, stating that 'in view of his enthusiasm for the cause, we cannot place the hope in his future behaviour which is expressed by the Committee'. The Home Secretary took the MI5 view. His decision was, significantly, based on two main criteria: not just Stuckey's activities among teachers and schoolboys, but also 'his attempt to evade military service on false grounds' (TNA HO 283/63).

Discussion of Stuckey's 'conscientious objection' had taken up a large part of his interview with the Advisory Committee. Unlike most other BU objectors, Stuckey cited religious grounds; but when he was asked more about this, he defined his religion as follows: 'I put forward my religious views which govern my life. The whole thing that governs my actions is, is it in the interests of Britain? That is my religion.' When he was asked, 'That is not the ordinary meaning of religion, is it?', he replied 'No.' And, after a further long disquisition, he concluded: 'That is how I explain my objection. I do not consider it is in the interests of Britain to meddle about with foreign countries.'

Stuckey had clearly, while at Oxford, got into the habit of the 'It all depends on what you mean by …' argument. To the question 'Do you think that made you a conscientious objector', he replied 'Well, what is one's conscience?' Another short exchange is worth quoting:

Q. Do you wish Great Britain to defeat Germany in this war?
A. It is immaterial so long as Britain comes out of the war.
Q. Do you wish Great Britain to defeat Germany in this war?
A. 'Defeat' is a word which has not the same meaning as it used to have.

The myth of Mosley's patriotism

Q. Do you think that it is important that we should smash the Hitler regime?
A. I am just trying to discover the meaning of the word 'important'.

The nub of the discussion, however, centred around whether he could be brought to admit that he was not a true conscientious objector. The Committee homed in on BU's distinction between willingness to fight for Britain's defence and objection to fighting this war:

Q. Are you willing to be killed for the defence of Britain?
A. Yes, certainly.
Q. Then you do not for a moment think you are a conscientious objector, do you?
A. It is clearly only a matter of words.
Q. Well, you have been studying law for some years […].

He was asked whether he had read the Act [National Service (Armed Forces) Act 1939]: 'Yes'. Did he think he came within the definition of Conscientious Objector? He couldn't remember the words offhand. And so on, for a very long discussion, until at last he gave in:

Q. Then you do not suggest that you are a Conscientious Objector, do you?
A. Well, perhaps I am not.

Significantly, he also admitted that he 'did not think there would be a vast chance of that claim being upheld in court'.

Stuckey had asked his mother, Mrs Jarvis, to speak to the Committee on his behalf. Most of that interview consisted of questions about Stuckey's 'conscientious objection', and unfortunately Mrs Jarvis did not seem to realise the issues at stake, believing that it was necessary for her to assure the committee that her son would fight in any other cause, but not in this one. In so doing she must have confirmed the Committee in its views:

> I think what was at the back of my son's mind was this. He did not agree with the war in the first place. He thought it was rather a

European quarrel that we should have kept out of. He was never a Pacifist. That is another thing, is it not? A Pacifist is a different type. He has always said that he would fight for England. [...] He has always said that no war should be fought except in defence of one's country, and the war when it broke out was not in defence of this country. It is now, of course.

Q. May that have been more a matter of political objection than of conscientious objection?

A. Probably.

(TNA HO 283/63)

Mosley in the first year of the war.

Throughout the period from September 1939 to May 1940, Mosley himself kept up a barrage of public abuse in relation to the 'Jews' War'. At mass meetings in Dalston on 8 October 1939 and at the Stoll Picture Theatre on 15 October (at the latter the Horst Wessel Song was sung, together with a parody of 'Onward Christian Soldiers' that contained the lines: 'Die for Jewish freedom / As a Briton always dies' (TNA KV 2/886)) the main theme of his speeches and those of the other speakers was, according to Special Branch, 'the condemnation of Jewish capitalists for starting a war in which Britons had no real interest' (TNA HO 144/21382). The same themes dominated his public and private utterances throughout the 'phoney war'. On 1 March, for example, at a large publicity lunch at the Criterion Restaurant, we find him asserting that:

> the real reason why the British Government had declared war on Germany and now refused to fight Russia [over Finland] was because Britain was controlled by Jews and they desired to see the end of the present German Government so that they could resume their exploitation of the German people.
>
> (TNA HO 45/24895)

BU's public policy was summed up by a prominent official, Brian Donovan, at a meeting of the BU District Officials on 30 January 1940:

It could be summed up in two short phrases, he declared, namely: 'Mosley and Peace', 'Jewry and War'. It was the movement's duty to see to it that whenever people thought of peace they connected it with Mosley, and that they always associated the Jews with war and suffering.

(TNA HO 45/24895)

After the Nazi invasion of Western Europe began on 10 May 1940, one might have expected, if Mosley's policy had been a sincere one, for him to have called all members of BU to arms, now that the position had changed. The 'phoney war' was over, and Britain was in fact in danger. Despite Mosley's later protestations (based on another misinterpreted contemporary document of his), no change in fact took place in BU policy.

May 1940: another misdated and misinterpreted quotation

Mosley had in fact, just before the invasion of the Low Countries, produced a message in *Action* on 8 May which he was later to quote as proof of his having made a call to arms, claiming that it had been written 'after the collapse of the Low Countries and on the eve of the invasion of France'. The passage he later quoted ran as follows:

According to the Press, stories concerning the invasion of Britain are being circulated. […] In such an event every member of British Union would be at the disposal of the nation. Every one of us would resist the foreign invader with all that is in us. However rotten the existing government, and however much we detest its policies, we would throw ourselves into the effort of a united nation until the foreigner was driven from our soil. In such a situation no doubt exists concerning the attitude of British Union.

(Mosley, 1968: 401)

Once more the gloss put upon such a statement, in Mosley's memoirs, was disingenuous because other elements in the article were left out, but above all because he misdated the statement. The statement had been made *before* the German invasion of the Low Countries, and not at the height of it. The extensive use of the conditional tense shows that, in relation to what he believed to be unfounded rumours as to a possible invasion ('stories […] are being circulated'), he was essentially restating the policy that had been formulated eight months before. His later suggestion that it related to the invasion of France (and that he had therefore been calling on BU members to resist the Germans at that point in time) is belied by the facts. No such call was made. In fact, the article from which this passage was taken, entitled 'Invasion Stories and Mediterranean Dangers', suggested that the 'unfounded' rumour of invasion had been fabricated by Italy in order to distract attention from possible events in the Mediterranean if Italy joined the war. The article was almost entirely aimed at making two points: (a) that Britain should have no interest in the Mediterranean, having no business to 'fight for Balkan influences, for Jewish settlers, or superfluous oilfields'; and (b) to *discount* any likelihood of invasion, because 'it is extremely unlikely that any such attack will be delivered', as 'the advantages of the defensive are overwhelming'. So, in fact, the article was produced, not for the reasons Mosley later attributed to it by selective quotation and by wrong dating, but in order to encourage members to *continue* their policy of non-involvement.

What happened after the actual attack on the Low Countries and France? There was no change in BU attitude, and the policy of non-involvement continued. This is puzzling, given the original statement of BU policy in the event of Britain being threatened. As Norman Birkett said at the Advisory Committee which interviewed Diana Mosley in October 1940: 'I have never really quite understood why your husband did not issue a manifesto to his people after the Low Countries were invaded, and say the whole policy of the Union must be reversed?' Lady Mosley replied very much in the spirit of Mosley's own post facto and misleading apologia: 'He did in a sense. In the statement he made at the beginning of the week he told them to obey the law and fight to defend our country.

But Birkett persisted. Throughout the attack on the Low Countries, and throughout the Battle of France, Mosley had maintained the policy of non-collaboration with the war effort:

The myth of Mosley's patriotism 27

> But when the Low Countries were invaded he did not say to his people 'The moment I told you about when we should stand in defence of the country has arrived'. That would have been the finest thing for him to prove his sincerity that I can imagine. I could never imagine why he did not do that.

Lady Mosley's reply was the epitome of airy insouciance:

> I think he was always expecting – I am certain he did – that France would give in, because France was so riddled with Communism, she never had her heart in the war. I think that was what he more or less expected.

She was then specifically asked what attitude she and Mosley had taken 'when the British Army was in that rather dreadful situation'. The response avoided the issue, taking the old line of 'I wouldn't have started from here': 'My husband thought, and it turned out afterwards that he was justified in saying we should not have sent an Army on to the Continent.' She commented that 'it was a wonderful thing when they got away, but they only got away with their bare skins'. No suggestion that British Union should have changed its attitude at this stage.

A repeated question from Birkett, as to why Mosley had not told his followers the time had come to fight, finally produced the telling admission: 'I think he thought we could have a very fair peace.' In other words, the fall of France was only significant to the extent that it might have produced the conditions whereby Britain would have to sue for peace (TNA HO 144/21995).

Mosley's policy of non-cooperation with the war effort had continued, therefore, throughout the German advance. In *Action* on 16 May he had insisted that the Low Countries were no longer strategically important to Britain. In the same issue another article, by Jorian Jenks, continued to attack the 'Jewish War', proclaiming that Britain could 'achieve only poverty and further enslavement by fighting for Fake Freedom and Finance-ridden Democracy'; and an editorial article claimed that 'we are entitled to ask whether what some people call "fighting for Democracy" is not really "fighting for Jewry"'. The German breakthrough at Sedan had taken place two days earlier, on

14 May. Mosley's only reaction, as the crisis became clear over the next week, was to put himself and BU forward, in *Action* on the 23 May, as the man and the movement most capable of negotiating peace:

> The question has been put to me, why I do not cease all political activity in an hour of danger to the country. The answer is that I intend to do my best to provide the people with an alternative to the present Government if, and when, they desire to make Peace 'with the British Empire intact and our people safe'. […] I can conceive no greater tragedy than the British people desiring to make such a British Peace and having no means to express their will.

In other words, he was appealing over the head of the legitimate Government, which in his view would, by continuing the war, be refusing the people the 'means to express their will'; and, at a grave hour in which British forces were engaged with the enemy, he was taking what amounts to a subversive and defeatist position, and making (however unrealistically) a bid for power in the event of a defeat. Added to this, he had now once more revised his statement about when he was prepared to fight and to call his people to action. In September 1939 it had read 'if the life of Britain were threatened'; now, on 23 May 1940, when Britain was in actual fact being threatened, this had been narrowed down to the specific case of Britain actually being invaded:

> I shall continue my political activities unless or until Britain is invaded – if that happens I shall fight for my country. […] Until Britain is invaded I offer the people an alternative to the present Government. If Britain is invaded I fight for Britain.

It was at this moment, at the height of the Battle of France, that Mosley and many of his most prominent followers were interned, on 23–24 May. In the preceding fortnight (as Birkett was to point out to Lady Mosley), instead of urging his people to fight, Mosley had been taking steps 'to see that the organisation was carried on after he was interned'.

The movement, and the newspaper *Action*, continued for a short while. Lady Mosley, who was entitled to visit her husband in prison, 'did what [she] could' to see that the movement was carried on. 'The thing was left in a most appalling mess, as you can imagine, because all the chief men had been taken' (TNA HO 144/21995). The contingency plans for the continuation of the movement had specified people to take the place of all the leading officials (Simpson, 1992: 181–3), but the *rafle* had been too extensive, and such plans failed because of the detention even of those who might have taken over. Only two further numbers of *Action* came out, the last one on 6 June. Mosley continued, however, to work for the continuation of his movement, even from within prison. Lady Mosley told Lady Alexandra Metcalfe, in a telephone call as late as 22 June, that the time she saw Mosley each week was far too short, because of all the many things to do with British Union they had to discuss, and which she had to write down (TNA KV 2/884).

Diana Mosley herself was detained on 29 June, and the British Union was finally banned on 10 July.

Further prevarication, and another questionable document

When Mosley appeared before the Advisory Committee on 2 July 1940, six weeks after his last message in *Action*, he clearly felt it important to try to redefine the meaning of that message. He now appeared to be once more replacing 'invasion' of Britain (the one situation in which he had said on 23 May that he would fight) with the earlier (September 1939) concept of 'danger of invasion'. Selectively quoting from the 23 May message, he said to Birkett:

> Well, at the present time, six weeks later, it is perfectly obvious that situation is upon us and therefore, if I had been free, I should now, before now, have ceased all political activity and advised my people in various ways to concentrate on the defence of the country.
>
> (TNA KV 2/884)

It is worth noting that this statement appeared to suggest that in prison he had not been 'free' to communicate with his people (which as we have seen was untrue).

Mythmaking, and the reinterpretation of quotations from the past (to be a constant in later Mosley accounts of events), already seemed to have begun. We know that Mosley had spent much of the time, when preparing for his appearance at the Advisory Committee, looking through his former published statements. He now produced a new statement addressed to members of British Union, which he had dictated the day before, on 1 July. This statement had been drawn up in collaboration with his solicitor, Oswald Hickson, and called on all members of British Union to 'do everything they can to assist our nation in its struggle'.

The fact that this statement, so markedly different from the statements produced in May, was not produced until the day before the hearing is in itself significant. It is clear, from the events in the six weeks between his own detention and that of Lady Mosley (a mere two days before this Message was composed), that there had been no sign of an intention to do anything of the kind during that period. As an officer of MI5 commented in a letter to Birkett:

> There are a few points brought up by Mosley at the two hearings of his case before the Advisory Committee on which I should like briefly to comment in the light of information in the possession of our office.
>
> <u>Mosley's appeal to members of the British Union to cease all political activity and place their services unreservedly at the disposal of their country</u>. I find it difficult to believe in the sincerity of this declaration. We have been closely watching the activities of Lady Mosley since Mosley's internment. Until the time of her own arrest she was in touch with other Fascists still at liberty with a view to keeping the movement alive. New headquarters premises had been acquired. These activities were being carried on long after the 'danger of invasion' had arisen, and it is impossible to believe that they were being carried on against the wishes of Sir Oswald Mosley himself.
>
> (TNA KV 2/885)

An examination of other areas of Mosley's defence shows a clear intention, on almost every issue, to gloss over anything that might stand against him. He denied, for example, any significant contacts after the outbreak of war with other right-wing leaders such as Captain Ramsay (with whom he had had a whole series of meetings); and he prevaricated about British Union's sources of money. Yet MI5 and Special Branch had clear evidence which contradicted his statements. The Report of the Advisory Committee pointed out the lack of candour which Mosley had shown in most of the evidence he gave:

> This would be the proper place to say that, just as Mosley was anxious to conceal the real truth of the finances of British Union from the Committee, so on many other parts of the case the Committee were satisfied that the full truth was withheld. Captain Ramsay, for example, related remarkable conversations with Mosley, [...] but on this, as on so many other matters on which the Committee had knowledge, Mosley was utterly lacking in candour and frankness.
>
> (TNA HO 45/24891)

The question of Mosley's attitude to his movement's involvement in the war effort appears to be another of these areas of lack of candour. Right up to Lady Mosley's arrest on 29 June, there had been no hint of any instruction for members of the movement to back the war effort; and at the same time an attempt was being made to continue the movement's activities. Only when it was clear that British Union could not carry on, and when Mosley himself was faced with his appearance before the Advisory Committee, was a last-minute statement, contrary to all previous policy, rushed out.

This has been an examination of merely one aspect of the myth-making that was undertaken by Mosley from that point on, and which was to reach its apogee in his post-war apologiae. That myth-making was to be unbelievably influential on most later accounts of his pre-war and wartime activities. As Norman Birkett pointed out in his 1940 Memorandum on the Home Office files relevant to Mosley, those files contained abundant evidence of the movement acting 'for purposes prejudicial to the public safety, the maintenance of public order, and the efficient prosecution of the war' (TNA HO 283/1/6).

Bibliography

Books

Beckett, Francis (1999), *The Rebel Who Lost his Cause: The Tragedy of John Beckett MP* (London: London House).
Dalley, Jan (1999), *Diana Mosley: A Life* (London: Faber & Faber).
Mosley, Sir Oswald (1968), *My Life* (London: Nelson).
Simpson, A.W. Brian (1992), *In the Highest Degree Odious: Detention without Trial in Wartime Britain* (Oxford: Oxford University Press).
Skidelsky, Robert (1975), *Oswald Mosley* (London: Macmillan).

Documents

National Archives (TNA)

CAB 65/7
HO 45/24891, HO 45/24895, HO 144/21382, HO 144/21429, HO 144/21995, HO 283/1, HO 283/63
KV 2/884–886

Newspapers and journals

Action
Daily Despatch (DD)

2
THE RECEPTION OF BRYANT'S *UNFINISHED VICTORY*

The myth of public unanimity against Nazi Germany in early 1940

Surprisingly to our modern eyes, in the Britain of early 1940, during the 'phoney war', a clearly pro-Nazi and anti-Semitic book aroused little adverse comment from the majority of its readers and reviewers, and the positive enthusiasm of a good number of them. This will cause us to revise some of the usual presumptions about public opinion in that period, and to reinforce others.

In January 1940 the historian Arthur Bryant produced a book entitled *Unfinished Victory*. To the modern reader this is a startling book, in the context of the time in which it appeared. It purported to be an explanation of the background to the Nazi rise to power, in order to give the British public a balanced view of the issues; but Andrew Roberts has rightly described it as 'as pure an apologia for Nazism as it is possible to imagine being published at such a time' (Roberts, 1994: 311). The introduction, admittedly, declared that as Britain was at war, 'we shall fight with absolute national unity', while making the case for peace by declaring that such a war 'will be a barren and profitless one' (Bryant, 1940: xxxiii). But the rest of the book went far beyond this comparatively innocuous attitude, as it dealt with Germany's internal regime. Though the introduction seemed to promise impartiality and moderation, claiming that its aim was to educate the British people, who, 'knowing nothing of what the Germans had suffered since the war, failed to realise the causes and social implications of the Nazi revolution' (xvii), the main text of the book rarely seemed to find fault with Nazi aims and ideals; it depicted the British public's concern about some aspects, but merely in order to reassure that public by 'explaining' and 'giving the background to' the German situation. For example, British trade unionists were described as being blinded, because of the persecution of some trade unionists in Germany, to 'the revolutionary reforms that the National Socialist Party was achieving for German freedom' (xix). The final page of the book sums up its tone, as it describes the coming to power of the Nazis in 1933:

> All the bells of Berlin, and beyond that of all Germany, were ringing and everyone seemed to be singing and shouting. 'The new Reich has risen sanctified with blood. Fourteen years of work have been crowned with victory. We have reached our goal. The German Revolution has begun!'
>
> (Bryant, 1940: 263)

Much of this apologia was specifically anti-Semitic. The abortive communist revolution in post-war Germany, for example, was ascribed to the Jews. Hitler was described as seeing the revolutionaries, 'mostly Jews', swarming out of their lorries; most of the responsibility for the revolt was ascribed to the 'Jew, Kurt Eisner' and to the Russian ambassador, 'the Hebrew Joffe'; and 'many of the leaders of the Communist Revolution in both countries [Germany and Russia] were Jews', because 'the children of an exiled but invincible race tended naturally to identify themselves with the forces that wished to overthrow the social order of eastern and central Europe' (102–7).

One of the reasons given for the development of German anti-Semitism was the power and financial domination that the Germans had achieved in the inter-war period. They had profited in the post-First World War property market:

> It was the Jews with their international affiliations and their hereditary flair for finance who were best able to seize such

> opportunities. [...] They made hay as fast as they could. They did so with such effect that, even in November 1938, after five years of anti-Semitic legislation and persecution, they still owned [...] something like a third of the real property in the Reich.
>
> (Bryant, 1940: 137)

But their power over the nation had been even greater than that:

> During the years that immediately followed the inflation, [...] the Jews obtained a wonderful ascendancy in politics, business and the learned professions. Though there were little more than half a million of them living in the midst of a people of 62 millions – less, that is, than one per cent of the population – their control of the national wealth and power soon lost all relation to their numbers. In the 1924 Reichstag nearly a quarter of the Social Democratic representatives were Jews. Every post-war ministry had its quota of them. [...] The banks were practically controlled by them. So were the publishing trade, the cinema, the theatres and a large part of the Press – all the normal means, in fact, by which public opinion in a civilised society is formed.
>
> (Bryant, 1940: 139–40)

Note the obsession with Jewish control of the media, which was so typical of British and German anti-Semitism in this period. Note also Bryant's unquestioning reliance on the arguments and statistics of Nazi propaganda. His attitude was often betrayed by his vocabulary, with phrases such as 'Authorship in Germany almost seemed to have become a kind of Hebrew monopoly', and:

> Every year it became harder for a Gentile to gain or keep a foothold in any privileged occupation. At this time it was not the Aryans who exercised racial discrimination. [...] By the third decade of the century it was the native Germans who were now confronted with a problem – that of rescuing their indigenous culture from an alien hand and restoring it to their own race.

> In the 1920s, said Bryant, the 'Asiatic hordes' of the Jews 'seemed, with all the invincible vitality of their race, to be making of a broken nation their washpot'.
>
> (Bryant, 1940: 140–3)

To understand why Bryant should have produced such a book at such a time, an examination is needed of his attitudes, and his political position, in the inter-war period and in these first months of the war.

Sir Arthur Bryant (knighted in 1954) is now known mainly as a writer of popular history, not particularly valued by professional historians, but influential upon the general public, many of whom have been brought to a real interest in the events of the past by his stirring accounts of British patriotic history in books such as *English Saga* (1940), *The Years of Endurance, 1793–1802* (1942) and *The Years of Victory, 1802–1812* (1942). In the Thirties, however, he had made for himself a reputation as a serious yet readable historian, mainly through his *King Charles II* (1931), and his highly successful life of Samuel Pepys in three volumes (1933, 1935 and 1938).

The book on Charles II was marked by a Conservative vision of that king as a protector of traditional British interests. Bryant's own politics were strongly Conservative. In 1929 he had become educational adviser to the Bonar Law Conservative College at Ashridge, and produced his first book, *The Spirit of Conservatism*, imbued with nostalgic Baldwinite traditionalism. Shortly thereafter he became the editor of the *Ashridge Journal*. In 1937 he became General Editor of the National Book Association, a Tory counterblast to the Left Book Club. (See Berthezène, 2011: 223–39; Green, 2002: 135–6; Griffiths, 2012 *passim*).

Like many people on the Right, Bryant was affected from 1933 onwards by a naive pro-Nazism. As early as 1934 he was describing Hitler as a 'mystic' who had enabled Germany to 'find her soul' (Bryant, 1934: 143–4). By the late Thirties he was producing, in his books, in the *Ashridge Journal* and in a regular column in *The Illustrated London News*, frequent railings against the calumnies with regard to Germany that he believed 'warmongers' to be spreading.

In the build-up to war, he strongly backed Chamberlain's appeasement policy, and appears to have been well thought of by

Chamberlain's circle. In 1939, for example, Horace Wilson asked him, on behalf of Chamberlain, to write an article for the German press on 'the British point of view' (which, though not published, was approved by Chamberlain, and was eventually to form the basis for much of the introduction to *Unfinished Victory*) (LHCMA Bryant C/66). In July 1939 he undertook a visit to Germany to speak to various Nazi leaders. This visit had been approved, 'entirely unofficially', by Number Ten, and Chamberlain afterwards offered to pay Bryant's expenses from Secret Service funds (Roberts, 1994: 304).

Bryant's pre-war attitudes to Nazi Germany, which went beyond Chamberlainite 'appeasement' into the realm of pro-Nazi 'fellow-travelling', were fairly typical of many at the time. After the outbreak of war, however, many who held such views had recanted, and those who had not tended (with the exception of political mavericks such as Sir Oswald Mosley or the Marquess of Tavistock) to express such opinions privately. Bryant's publication of *Unfinished Victory*, therefore, comes as something of a surprise, even though he had been propounding the need for peace initiatives in this period.

All our presumptions about public opinion in the first year of the Second World War would have led us to believe that the public would have reacted with horror to Bryant's pro-Nazism, if not necessarily to his anti-Semitism, and that Bryant had misjudged the mood of the moment, failing to notice that times had changed. And post-facto accounts have sometimes given this picture. A.L. Rowse, for example, has been quoted as saying that '[Bryant's] popularity temporarily slumped'. Andrew Roberts has perfectly correctly stated that after the internment of many of the Nazi sympathisers in Britain in May 1940, Bryant 'quickly appreciated the seriousness of his mistake and embarked on a buying spree of *Unfinished Victory*, which as a result is now a collector's item' (Roberts, 1994: 314–5). This refers, however, specifically to the period after May, a month which was a watershed for many. An examination of the reviews of the book in the intervening period, January–May 1940, shows that reactions were on the whole far more favourable than has been believed; and Bryant's responses to the few adverse reviews, and his correspondence, show clearly that he himself did not at that stage seem to have been at all worried about any effect the book might have (indeed, to have been confident that those in authority would approve of it).

The favourable reviews show us that a section of the public, while in many cases accepting that Britain was at war and that Nazi aggression had to be countered, did not hold strong views as to the nature of the internal Nazi regime. The concept of the war as a crusade to change an appalling regime appears either to have been a later 'war aim', created after the event, or to have been the aim of part of society rather than the whole. The effort to 'understand' Germany appears to have still been uppermost in many minds, as was the appeasement belief in the Allies' guilt for the German post-war situation that had produced Nazism. The continuation of these widely held views into the wartime period shows a continued sympathy for Germany which is, from our later viewpoint, surprising.

When it comes to anti-Semitism, however, the almost complete lack of interest in this question on the part of the reviewers, whether favourable or unfavourable, bears out much of what has been written about British attitudes in this period. This has been the subject of a number of major studies (e.g. Holmes, 1979; Goldman, 1984; Griffiths, 1998; Kushner, 1989, 1994; Kushner and Lunn 1989, 1990; Sharf 1964; Stone 2003). From them, despite differences of emphasis, the following consensus appears to emerge. On the one hand, there was a small minority of rabid anti-Semites in Britain, some of whom continued to produce expressions of their hatred after the outbreak of war. On the other hand, there was widespread 'social anti-Semitism' in Britain, which manifested itself in a number of ways: exclusion of Jews from various social groups; a jokiness about things Jewish based on Jewish stereotypes ranging from love of money to unawareness of 'British' social conventions; depictions, in popular literature, of the Jew as leader of international subversive activity; and, in war situations, a vision of the Jew as coward and profiteer. Though, in contrast to rabid anti-Semitism, social anti-Semitism may have appeared comparatively innocuous, its depiction of the Jew as 'other' could lead to apathy and lack of concern when faced with examples of racial intolerance and persecution. On the one hand, as Dan Stone has pointed out, the British public could manifest a 'casual anti-Semitism' which fell into the trap of accepting the 'reasons' for the Germans' dislike of the Jews (Stone, 2003: 92–8); on the other hand, while Nazi measures could shock people of all views, many people found it possible to ignore the problem altogether, while speaking only of the matters, in relation to Germany, that they believed to be 'important'.

Let us now look at the reviews of *Unfinished Victory*, and at the attitudes of Bryant himself and his publishers, in relation to this background. While the reviewers can be considered as part of an intellectual elite, that elite's views are in themselves significant, and its influence via the printed word is of importance. The preoccupations not only of the admirers of Bryant's book, but also of its relatively few detractors, will, too, be fairly illuminating in relation to the question of the reaction, or lack of it, to the Jewish question in this period.

By far the greatest number of the reviews of *Unfinished Victory* in January–April 1940 were favourable ones. The *Times Literary Supplement* was one of the first in the field, with what in relation to many others was reasonably moderate praise:

> There is a felicity of style and depth of sympathy in his description of German sufferings after Versailles. […] He describes the horrid details of famine in central Europe, the scramble of the Jews for real property during the inflation. […] Having thus won the humane reader to his side […].
>
> (*TLS*, 27/1/40)

Lord Elton, in a favourable review in the *Sunday Times*, felt that Bryant's book would be 'fully opportune' when peace had to be negotiated (*ST*, 4/2/40). *Public Opinion*, with remarkable even-handedness, considered the book to be 'an important commentary on the ideals that actuate both sides in the present war' and 'worthy of the consideration of all thinking people' (*PO*, 26/1/40).

Many stressed Bryant's balance and judgement, and his careful and scholarly use of 'compelling' evidence. Robert Sencourt, in the *Catholic Herald*, for example, spoke of his 'sane judgment, conspicuous insight, and telling expression' (*CH*, 1/3/40). Charles Byles, in the *Illustrated London News*, went even further:

> In contrast to the prejudice and sensationalism common in current war literature, we have here the well-balanced views and narrative of an established and impartial historian, based on a thorough study of trustworthy evidence and written in an attractive and readable style (*ILN*, 17/2/40).

And an anonymous review in the *New English Weekly* took up the same theme:

> Perhaps there is no other living writer, with an historian's knowledge and a poet's love of England, more able and self-controlled than the author of this grave and sombre book. It is a mercy in these days of unbridled prejudice and unmeasured scoffing that so brave and just a document should have been compiled by the cool hands of so English a writer. Because of this fact the book will be read by thousands of truth-loving people in this country, and the generous and kindly core of the real and untrammelled England will glow with the shame of it all.
>
> (*NEW*, 21/3/40)

There were similar views expressed in the *Fortnightly Review*, *Truth*, *St Martin's Review*, the *Church of England Newspaper* and many other newspapers and journals of all kinds (*CEN*, 26/1/40; *FR*, 3/40; *IL*, 19/3/40; *SMR*, 5/40; *TIP*, 6/2/40; *Truth*, 9/2/40, etc.) The greatest accolades for Bryant's work came, however, from the provincial press. H.S. Woodham, in the *Sheffield Star*, for example, wrote:

> I think that this book performs a tremendous public service. [...] It should be in the hands of every leader and politician on the Allied side. It is factual, objective, documented, clear, and is written with sustained power.
>
> (*SS*, 31/1/40)

The *Perthshire Constitutional* thought that 'it is to the author's credit that he has not been influenced by his private opinions and prejudices, but that he has relied on documented evidence' (*PC*, 15/3/40). The *Aberdeen Press and Journal* found the book 'brilliantly and persuasively written', and praised the 'highly informative digressions', such as that upon 'the malpractices of the lower kind of Jew', and 'the rottenness of Communism' (*APJ*, 22/2/40). The *East Anglian Daily Times* described the book as 'powerful and persuasive', and 'without prejudice' (*EADT*, 29/1/40). The provincial press seems to have almost unanimously taken this line (one rare exception was Cardiff's *Western Mail*, which though it found the book 'very able', also found it 'naïvely pro-German' (*WM*, 8/2/40).

In March, *Peace Focus*, which had produced yet another strongly favourable review, noted how little criticism there had been of *Unfinished Victory* in the many reviews it had been given:

> Any book published at the moment which tries to show Germany's point of view is liable to be greeted with the curled lip and the suspiciously-elevated eyebrow, and it is a tribute to Mr Bryant's character and irreproachable integrity that *Unfinished Victory* has not met this fate.
>
> (*PF*, 3/40)

Not that there were no unfavourable reviews, but though often violent, they were also very few and mostly from expected journals (the *Jewish Chronicle*, *Spectator*, *New Statesman*, *Manchester Guardian*, etc.) and from people who had been strongly in the anti-appeasement camp before the war began.

Emily Lorimer, author of the Penguin Special *What Hitler Wants* (1939), wrote in *Time and Tide*: 'All the best and biggest Nazi lies are here, presented with a garnish of scholarship and erudition. […] Please God, your clever book has come too late to take any readers in' (*TT*, 10/2/40). Rebecca West, also in *Time and Tide*, described the book as 'a paean to Hitler so glowing, so infatuate, that it might better have been entitled "Kiss me, Corporal"' (*TT*, 16/3/40). A.J.P. Taylor, in the *Manchester Guardian*, headed his review 'A Nazi Apologist', and drew attention to Hitler's speeches as the main source for Bryant's book, adding that 'Mr Bryant is himself a historian and it is the duty of a historian to weigh evidence, and not to write emotional political tracts' (*MG*, 9/2/40). Richard Crossman, in the *New Statesman and Nation*, at first took a deceptively moderate line: he called 'Mr

Bryant's appeal [...] wholly admirable', but felt that Bryant's heart was 'stronger than his head', which had led to the book sounding like Nazi propaganda. Then Crossman came in for the kill, drawing attention to Bryant's 'close connection with the Conservative Party', and his close involvement with the government's appeasement policy. He concluded: 'If therefore *Unfinished Victory* represents in broad outline the views of the Premier since the outbreak of war, its sincerity, its confusions and its credulity assume a disturbing importance' (*NSN*, 9/3/40).

Bryant's reactions to two of these adverse reviews, in *The Spectator* and in the *Jewish Chronicle*, show his self-confidence in his own case at this time, and, buoyed up by the other generally favourable reviews he had been receiving, his conviction that these particular reviews were malicious and without substance.

In *The Spectator* (which had been prominent in the anti-appeasement camp before the war) on 16 February Christopher Hobhouse (a Conservative anti-appeaser) wrote:

> In the mind of Mr Arthur Bryant [...] the seeds of German propaganda have found a fertile soil. His book is a word-perfect recital of the official list of Germany's wrongs. [...] He attains his climax in a vibrant passage worthy of Lord Haw-Haw. [...] This stuff does not emanate from some obscure member of The Link intoxicated by a week at Nuremberg [...] It is published in the midst of war by a prominent admirer of Mr Chamberlain, a functionary of the Tory Party, and a writer who has done justice to a glorious period in the history of his own free country. One may expect the noise of bands and the waving of flags to turn the head of a debutante, but it is a sorry thing that Mr Bryant should write a hundred pages on the subject of Nazism without showing the smallest appreciation of its true meaning.

Two weeks later, on 1 March, a letter appeared in *The Spectator* from Gerald Brenan, the prominent anti-Fascist writer. In it, he likened Bryant to Dr Goebbels, drew attention to Bryant's close connections to the Conservative Party, and asked what the Conservative Party was going to do about this.

At this point, Bryant decided to reply to both men. In a letter to *The Spectator* on 8 March, he started by making one or two pedantic points about Hobhouse's review, and then added: 'There is not a sentence of Mr Hobhouse's curious review which I could not cap by some contradictory sentence or paragraph from my book.' This is an example of Bryant's technique (later described by the *Jewish Chronicle* reviewer) of producing every so often mild reproofs of Nazi cruelty as a token of his fairmindedness, but immediately following them with explanations or a defence. Under attack, he could then point to these favourable comments in isolation. Bryant did not go into further detail, however. Having dismissed Hobhouse's review as something so 'curious' that it was unworthy of reply, he then denied ever having held any Conservative Party post such as had been ascribed to him. In this, as Hobhouse was to point out, he was being disingenuous. What were his posts as governor of Ashridge Conservative College, and editor of the *Ashridge Journal*, but those of a 'functionary of the Tory Party'?

Bryant then turned to personalities, saying: 'Probably Mr Brenan – I cannot speak for Mr Hobhouse, who has honoured me by staying as a guest in my house – does not believe me.' After all these preliminaries, he finally came to the nub of his argument, namely that he had expected attacks from the Left, but not from a Conservative such as Hobhouse; that he had been writing from the point of view of an ex-Serviceman (which occasioned a jibe against Hobhouse for not yet being in the Services); and that his postbag had been full of letters almost unanimously praising his book:

> What more can I say? This is still a free country. My views represent or commit no one but myself. I expected them to be misunderstood, and in some quarters to be misrepresented, though not, I confess, by Mr Hobhouse. I wrote them as a survivor of the last war, as Mr Hobhouse, if he later serves in His Majesty's armed forces, will, I hope, be of this. It is from ex-Servicemen that most of the letters I have received about the book – all but two expressing approval – have come. It was solely in the hope that the sacrifices of brave men would not be subsequently wasted a second time by the folly of others that it was written.

A week later, on 15 March, Hobhouse wrote defending his 'curious review' and deploring Bryant's *ad hominem* remarks. Yes, he had been a guest of Bryant's, but that was when he had thought Bryant had been a Conservative like himself. His description of Bryant as a 'functionary of the Tory Party' was correct. There had been no misrepresentation. As for the 'white feather' implication, it was beneath contempt; ill health had prevented Hobhouse from undertaking military service.

Some issues arise from this dispute, apart from Bryant's overwhelming confidence in his case. One is that a perusal of his correspondence in this period *does* show an overwhelming preponderance of favourable letters (LHCMA Bryant E/10, E/18, E/60, F/3a, C111). Unlike many other people, he is unlikely to have 'weeded out' any adverse ones. Indeed, he seems to have kept everything sent to him over the years, including letters on other matters that reflect very unfavourably upon him. A good example of this is his retention of the Duchess of Atholl's letters to him in late 1937 and early 1938 (LHCMA Bryant C/63). Secondly, in this 'phoney war' period he did in fact see the book as being a blow for peace, even at this stage. Throughout the period from September 1939 to May 1940 Bryant had been involved in various groups and initiatives to further the idea of a negotiated peace with Germany (Griffiths, 1998: 210–13; Roberts, 1994: 307–11). Thirdly, Bryant had indeed been closely involved in that section of the Tory Party (as opposed to Hobhouse's) that had been strongly pro-appeasement, and, as we have seen, had been encouraged by Chamberlain (unofficially) when he undertook a visit to Germany to consult with Nazi leaders in July 1939. He had used the *Ashridge Journal* in 1938–9 as a vehicle to produce pro-Munich (and indeed often pro-Nazi) views (Roberts, 1994: 298–9).

What is interesting in the reviews of Bryant's book is that its supporters sometimes mentioned (favourably) Bryant's views on the Jews, but that its opponents almost invariably ignored that question. They were far more concerned with Bryant's clear approval of Nazi policy at a time when Britain was at war with Germany. What appears to us a major component of Bryant's book – its blatant anti-Semitism – appeared to them merely one detail hardly worth taking up as a major issue. (This reinforces our earlier discussion about British attitudes to anti-Semitism in this period.) The review in the *Jewish Chronicle* did of course take up this issue more centrally. Bryant's reactions to this review provide us with the second of the controversies we will be examining.

In the *Jewish Chronicle* on 23 February, G. Warburg wrote, among other things:

> *Unfinished Victory* is, from first to last, nothing but a defence of Nazi Germany's policy. [...] In his endeavour to explain and excuse Nazi misdeeds, Mr Bryant accepts almost every anti-Jewish allegation of the Nazi propaganda machine.

Bryant did not reply to this review immediately. His correspondence with *The Spectator* in March, however, seems to have sparked off a desire to respond to other 'curious' reviews of his book, and on 15 March a letter of his appeared in the *Jewish Chronicle*. In it, by using selective quotations, he attempted to point out the reasonableness of his position:

> As the introductory chapter explains, the book sets out to show how the present astonishing and disastrous despotism in Germany came into existence and to explain why it is supported – as it apparently is – by the German people. But it certainly does not defend that policy, as your reviewer states.

He went on to say that he himself was in no way anti-Semitic. In reply, the *Jewish Chronicle* reviewer, while clearly not believing this, and while maintaining his attack upon Bryant's treatment of the Jewish question, clearly felt it necessary on 15 March – in a sentence which sums up the whole world of British pre-war attitudes to the Jews – to proclaim Bryant's right to be anti-Semitic if he so wished:

> Mr Bryant denies that he is an anti-Semite. In my review there was not a single word implying that Mr Bryant is anti-Semitic. If he is, he is, of course, entitled to his views. If he is not, he ought to have explained why he carefully collects all the Nazi allegations against the Jews, why he refrains from saying that they are Nazi allegations and instead retails them as undisputed facts.

> The effect of Mr Bryant's methods must be to impress upon the average reader that the Nazi case against the Jews is a strong one; and the faint praise found now and then for 'Hebrew genius' and 'decent Jews' resembles very much the 'good Jewish friends' of everyone who has brought false charges against the Jews and is faced with the hopeless problem of proving them.

Furthermore, Warburg also produced the best description of Bryant's methods of obfuscating the issues that we have:

> Mr Bryant denies that his book is nothing but a defence of Nazi Germany's policy, and gives some quotations to show that he disapproves or regrets Nazi methods. Yet every mild reproof of Nazi cruelty is at once followed up by statements to explain and even sometimes to defend these brutalities.

Bryant's confidence in the rightness of his cause is thus evident in the letters he wrote in reply to some of the adverse reviews of his book. In this he was buoyed up by the vast bulk of the favourable reviews his book had been given (and his belief that only political opponents would be likely to have written adverse ones); and by the many letters of praise he had received. It will now be worth looking at his own views, and his publisher's, at the various stages of the creation and reception of *Unfinished Victory*.

Bryant and Macmillan

Unfinished Victory was published by Macmillan and Co., Bryant's personal contact being Harold Macmillan, Conservative MP for Stockton-on-Tees. Macmillan was one of the Conservative group that had been most opposed to the appeasement policy of the Chamberlain government before the war.

At first sight, therefore, it seems extraordinary that Macmillan should have been responsible for the appearance of *Unfinished Victory* at the height of the war. In an attempt to explain this, a comment of Macmillan's is often quoted: to a query from Lovat Dickson, a member of the company, about why Macmillan was prepared to publish 'a book in favour of Munich', Macmillan is said to have replied: 'We are publishers, not policemen; everybody should be free to say what they like.' But this quotation, from its context in Dickson's memoirs, clearly refers to the aftermath of the Munich settlement in 1938, when Bryant was *planning*, but had not yet written, a book on Munich (commissioned by Dickson) which would be entirely opposed to the cause for which Macmillan was campaigning so tirelessly. It has no relevance to Macmillan's attitude to the actual text of *Unfinished Victory* when it was published in the wartime period (Dickson, 1963, 209–10; Letter, Dickson to Bryant 17/12/38, LHCMA Bryant C/96)

The first half of what was to have been the book on Munich eventually became *Unfinished Victory*; but the context in which it was published was completely different. The praise for Nazism which underlay the desire to 'understand' the background to the regime had not been entirely out of place in pre-war Britain, where such pro-Nazi sentiments would scarcely excite comment. When the country was at war, however, such praise for the enemy would seem out of place. It might appear to us, with hindsight, that Bryant, by publishing it in this changed situation, was making a grave mistake. Yet, as we have seen, in early 1940 the opinion of many people seemed to have remained much the same as before the war, with the book being welcomed.

What is surprising is to find Macmillan, the anti-appeaser, actively encouraging Bryant to publish the book, even after the outbreak of war. Bryant had been very slow in producing the manuscript, the last part of which only reached the publishers in August 1939. By 11 September, eight days after the outbreak of war, Dickson wrote to Bryant to inform him that the proofs were ready. On 15 September, Macmillan wrote to Bryant, suggesting that he should:

> transform the book now in type into a study of the mistakes of the last peace and the way of avoiding them in the next [...] which you could publish in the immediate future. I believe that there would be a very good chance of success for this book within a few months' time.

Bryant, though he felt that the book was 'a valuable property in reserve', and that 'it would be better to wait', appreciated Macmillan's position and the losses that would be made if nothing appeared, and wrote on 16 September to say that he would try to take the first part of the book, on the mistakes of the peace and the emergence of Nazism, while leaving the 'Munich' part of the book to be published later 'in another work'. Though he felt that they were thereby truncating what could later have been the equivalent of Keynes's *Economic Consequences of the Peace*, he appreciated that Macmillan might feel, after paying out so much, that he could not wait for 'that problematical return' (LHCMA Bryant C/96).

By the end of October Bryant had prepared the new version. He wrote to Macmillan on 29 October:

> As it now stands it is purely historical and little open to criticism: the story stops at 1933 and there is no attempt to discuss subsequent more familiar and more controversial events.

In this Bryant was clearly deluding himself. Lord Halifax, the Foreign Secretary, to whom Bryant had sent the proofs, wrote to Bryant on 30 October, saying he had read them 'with interest and profit', but warning him 'of the use to which such a publication at this moment would be put by the German Government'. Perhaps, he said, 'before you finally decided you would think it well to let the Prime Minister see them, if you have not already done so, and also allow me to consult our Foreign Office people as to the effect in Germany' (LHCMA Bryant F/3a). Macmillan's reaction on 31 October was far less cautious:

> My dear Bryant, […] I am quite sure that your book can be published early in the new year with success. I have looked again through the proofs, and it seems to me that in the form in which it now stands it will make a completely satisfactory volume […] The more I think of it the more I feel that publication will be very timely. […] I am really very keen about your new book and I believe it will be most timely.

He did, however, suggest that Bryant should write an introduction 'to explain your position clearly to the public':

> You should tell the public the story of the book – how you began it in the months before the war, and although you realised that the views expressed would be unpopular in certain quarters, you hoped that an honest review of the events of the last war and the mistakes made following it, might help English and German public opinion towards a settlement of European problems by peaceful methods. Events have outstripped you, and the decision to plunge Europe into war was taken. You laid aside the book thinking that it was no longer worth while doing any work upon it; and then looking it through a few weeks ago you found that it still remained apposite and necessary to thinking people who perhaps from different angles of view are beginning to consider war aims and the kind of peace that should follow victory.

In other words Macmillan, while realising that the situation had changed, did not seem to be aware of the pro-Nazi stance in the book that was later so obvious to other commentators; and he made no objection whatsoever to the strongly anti-Semitic character of such a large part of what he had been reading. This is a telling commentary on attitudes to anti Semitism, even among 'liberal' thinkers, in this period.

By the end of November Bryant had indeed produced an introduction, but, in a manner typical of his usual work procedures, this was largely a reuse of the text that he had produced in July 1939, at the Prime Minister's and his adviser Sir Horace Wilson's request. This was far from what Macmillan had requested, having originally been composed for a German audience. It listed a lot of the British people's presumptions about Germany, while distancing itself from them, and producing 'explanations' of what the British had misunderstood about the background to Nazism. Macmillan, nevertheless, seems to have been satisfied with this. He wrote to Bryant on 30 November, saying that 'the preface with your corrections has gone to the printers tonight', and stating with satisfaction that there was a possibility that the Book Society would be interested in the book (LHCMA Bryant C/96).

Shortly after the publication of *Unfinished Victory*, Harold Macmillan, as a member of the Amery Committee on aid to Finland, was sent to Finland on 10 February 1940, returning to Britain on 1 March. On his return he appears to have gathered from his anti-appeasement friends their opinion of the book, and consequently to have undergone a sea change in his own views. By 12 March the Duke of Buccleuch was reporting to Bryant that 'Harold Macmillan and his friends' were spreading the idea that *Unfinished Victory* was 'pure and open Nazi propaganda' (LHCMA Bryant C/111).

It is at this point that Macmillan appears to have decided that Bryant should no longer figure on the firm's list of authors. His tactics were, however, circuitous. When Bryant's contracts had been negotiated with Macmillans, he had had a number of outstanding contracts with other publishers. It had clearly been understood that this was the case, and that Macmillans would try to get those contracts transferred to them. The new contracts with Macmillans were signed in the knowledge that such negotiations might not be successful. In a letter on 23 April, however, Macmillan used the problem of the existence of these other contracts to suggest that Bryant's contracts with Macmillans should now be 'put into abeyance'. Though couched in emollient and flattering terms ('I do want you to regard yourself still as our author'), the request was a very firm one.

What is interesting to us, however, is his use of *Unfinished Victory* in this letter (and Bryant's response to this). Macmillan mentioned *Unfinished Victory* purely in the context of its not being a market success (and avoiding any mention of its content):

> As I think you are probably aware, we have not made a profit on the publication of *Unfinished Victory*, but we have done something which I hope is equally valuable, that is shown you our desire to co-operate with you and our willingness to do anything reasonable to assist you in your work.

Macmillan, of course, was completely unaware that Bryant, through Buccleuch, knew what he had been saying about *Unfinished Victory*. One can hardly believe that Bryant, who knew Macmillan's views, was taken in by Macmillan's comments. He certainly took great care over his reply. He produced a lengthy draft on 25 April, but the letter was finally sent off, with alterations, on 3 May. This letter not only declared how sorry he would be if their connection was broken ('I hope it will be a long and prosperous one') and rebutted Macmillan's view of events in relation to the contracts, but also, feigning to believe the emollient words in which Macmillan had clothed his message, suggested that 'if you really want to consider me as ultimately your author – and it is kind and flattering of you to wish it', this could still be arranged. He ended by thanking Macmillan for his 'very kind letter', fully reciprocating 'the kind personal things you say in it', and signed himself (underlining the word 'very'), 'Yours <u>very</u> sincerely.'

Macmillan appears to have been nonplussed by this letter. He nevertheless returned to the attack on 9 May. In the process, he produced a new version of his own role in relation to the publication of *Unfinished Victory*. Where we have seen him, in October 1939, encouraging an uncertain Bryant that the book could be published 'with success', and would be 'very timely', he now claimed that a 'hard-headed' publisher would have tried to persuade Bryant that the book was 'out of joint with the times':

> *Unfinished Victory* was an unprofitable venture. When war broke out and the book had not been completed, a hard-headed publisher, thinking only of the public he was to find for the book, would have attempted, I think, to persuade you that it was plainly out of joint with the times. My attitude was not that, because I knew you held your views sincerely, and because I wanted you to have some reward for the work you had undertaken so valiantly.

Ignoring Bryant's suggestion that Macmillans should negotiate to take over the main outstanding contract with another publisher, he now reiterated his request that the contracts should be annulled.

Bryant's reply, on 14 May, is a very interesting one in that, while being 'puzzled by your letter', he finally accepted the situation, but also took the opportunity of putting Macmillan on the spot over his attitude to *Unfinished Victory* by contradicting his new version of events:

> I fully appreciate your position about *Unfinished Victory* – and no-one regrets it more than I. But you yourself said in the early stages of the war that you felt it might become a very valuable property, like Hankey's *Ordeal by Battle*, and subsequently made valuable suggestions which I followed. That things have turned out as they have is – I am glad to say! – neither of our faults: the blame is Hitler's.

Bryant's continuing confidence in the rightness of his book, combined with what seems to have been a desire to tease Macmillan on the basis of what he already knew about the other's real attitudes, led him to suggest that he should now produce for Macmillans 'a new and updated completion of *Unfinished Victory* telling the fuller story – as G.M. Young keeps urging me to do'. Even his final acceptance of Macmillan's demands contained a further barb of the same kind:

> If on the other hand you would rather cut your losses – though I hope one day *Unfinished Victory* either in its present or, as I hope, a fuller form will more than repay you – I shall fully understand and am quite ready to cancel the contracts.

In his reply on 19 May Macmillan leaped at this agreement, and took the opportunity of saying 'how much I have valued your co-operation'. Without realising what Bryant had been getting at in his references to *Unfinished Victory*, he echoed Bryant's statement: 'I do not at all regret the publication of *Unfinished Victory*. As you say, the disappointment is the fault of Hitler, not of us.' He said he had asked his brother Daniel to write to Bryant an official letter from the firm. This Daniel did on 21 May, cancelling the contracts (LHCMA Bryant C/96).

Bryant never wrote for Macmillans again.

Not only was there an on the whole favourable reception, in early 1940, of Bryant's *Unfinished Victory* among reviewers and among those who wrote letters to him, it is also clear, both from his responses to adverse reviews and his correspondence with Macmillan, that up to May Bryant was still convinced that he had been entirely justified in writing the book. What, then, caused the change which Andrew

Roberts has described, whereby in late May Bryant, appreciating 'the seriousness of his mistake [...] embarked on a buying spree of *Unfinished Victory*' (Roberts, 1994: 315)?

One explanation may be the new situation created by the change of government. As long as Chamberlain was Prime Minister, Bryant could bask in the knowledge that his pre-war writings and activities had had government approval, and in the belief that they still had it. Though Halifax might show some misgivings about the appearance of *Unfinished Victory* in January 1940, the new introduction to that book had been approved by Chamberlain when it had first been written before the war; and Bryant was constantly writing to Halifax and other prominent Tories, in early 1940, about the theories of his group Union and Reconstruction and other matters of the same sort. He also tried to involve Halifax in the secret peace negotiations he and others undertook via the Dane Bengt Berg in February 1940 (LHCMA Bryant C/69). Whatever Chamberlain's and Halifax's actual views at the time (and Halifax's innate courtesy may have made Bryant unaware of any misgivings he may have had), Bryant clearly believed his own views to be in harmony with theirs. His confidence in this is shown by the fact that, after a month of reviews had appeared, he decided in late February to send complimentary signed copies of the book to the Prime Minister, the King, Queen Mary, Sir John Reith and the Imperial War Museum (Letter to Lovat Dickson, 27/11/40, LHCMA Bryant C/96).

The advent to power of Winston Churchill, and the new resolve he brought, must have shown Bryant just how out of touch he was with the new political situation; and the imprisonment of so many fellow travellers of the Right in late May (including a number of people who had worked closely with him) must have shown him the danger of his own attitudes and actions. At the same time as pro-Nazi groups such as Information and Policy were going out of existence, Bryant wound up his Union and Reconstruction movement.

Bryant's realisation of danger was timely. In late May 1940 Lovat Dickson of Macmillans (by now working on behalf of the government) consulted Bryant's fellow historian Hugh Trevor-Roper, to ask whether Bryant ought to be interned under Defence Regulation 18B. Apparently Trevor-Roper advised against this, as Bryant would no doubt 'change with the times' (Roberts, 1994: 315). From that point on Bryant did indeed change, producing his series of highly patriotic books starting with *English Saga* (1940), and articles in the *Ashridge Journal* which spoke of the rise of Hitler as a 'terrible calamity', and referred to 'the vile and evil things we are fighting' (Roberts, 1994: 316).

After May 1940, too, a majority of the British people seems to have woken up to the real situation in relation to Germany. This study of Bryant's published writings and public reactions to them in the period January–May 1940 has, however, shown us just how uncertain that public's attitudes were in that earlier period. In their acceptance of pro-Nazi views the public may have been naive; but in their obliviousness to the implications of Nazi anti-Semitism they were typical of their time.

Bibliography

Books and articles

Berthezène, Clarisse (2011), *Les conservateurs britanniques dans la bataille des idées: Ashridge College, premier think tank conservateur* (Paris: Sciences Po).

Bryant, Arthur (ed.) (1934), *The Man and the Hour: Studies of Six Great Men of our Time* (London: Philip Allan).

Bryant, Arthur (1940), *Unfinished Victory* (London: Macmillan).

Dickson, Lovat (1963), *The House of Words* (London: Macmillan).

Gilbert, Martin (1966), *The Roots of Appeasement* (London: Weidenfeld and Nicolson).

Goldman, A (1984), 'The Resurgence of Anti-Semitism in Britain during World War Two' *Jewish Social Studies*, 46, 1, 37–50.

Green, E.H.H. (2002), *Ideologies of Conservatism* (Oxford: Oxford University Press).

Griffiths, Richard (1980), *Fellow Travellers of the Right: British Enthusiasts for Nazi Germany, 1933–39* (London: Constable).

Griffiths, Richard (1998), *Patriotism Perverted: Captain Ramsay, the Right Club and British Anti-Semitism, 1939–40* (London: Constable).

Griffiths, Richard (2012), 'G.A.W. Tomlinson and H.W.J. Edwards: Two Tory Writers and the "People's Literature" Movement of the Late Thirties', *Llafur*, 11, 1, 83–108.

Holmes, Colin (1979), *Anti-Semitism in British Society 1876–1939* (London: Edward Arnold).

Kushner, Tony (1989), *The Persistence of Prejudice: Anti-Semitism in British Society during the Second World War* (Manchester: Manchester University Press).

Kushner, Tony (1994), *The Holocaust and the Liberal Imagination: A Social and Cultural History* (Oxford: Blackwell).

Kushner, T. and Lunn, K. (eds) (1989), *Traditions of Intolerance: Historical Perspectives on Fascism and Race Discourse in Britain* (Manchester: Manchester University Press).

Kushner, T. and Lunn, K. (eds) (1990) *The Politics of Marginality: Race, the Radical Right and Minorities in Twentieth Century Britain* (Special number of *Immigrants and Minorities*) (London: Frank Cass).

Roberts, Andrew (1994), *Eminent Churchillians* (London: Weidenfeld and Nicolson).

Sharf, Andrew (1964), *The British Press and Jews under Nazi Rule* (Oxford: Oxford University Press).

Stone, Dan (2003), *Responses to Nazism in Britain, 1933–39: Before War and Holocaust* (Basingstoke: Palgrave Macmillan).

Documents

Liddell Hart Centre for Military Archives, King's College London (LHCMA)

Arthur Bryant Papers (Bryant):

C/63 Correspondence, Duchess of Atholl

C/66 Appeasement correspondence, 1938–9

C/69 Correspondence: R.A. Butler, Lord Brocket, Duke of Westminster, Lord Halifax

C/96 Correspondence with Macmillan

C/111 General correspondence

E/10, E/18, E/60 Correspondence with individuals

F/3a Correspondence about *Unfinished Victory*

Newspapers and journals

Aberdeen Press and Journal (APJ)
Ashridge Journal
Catholic Herald (CH)
Church of England Newspaper (CEN)
East Anglian Daily Times (EADT)
Fortnightly Review (FR)
Illustrated London News (ILN)

Irish Independent (II)
The Irish Press (TIP)
Jewish Chronicle (JC)
Manchester Guardian (MG)
New English Weekly (NEW)
New Statesman and Nation (NSN)
Peace Focus (PF)
Peace News (PN)
Perthshire Constitutional (PC)
Public Opinion (PO)
The Spectator
St Martin's Review (SMR)
The Star (Sheffield) (SS)
Sunday Times (ST)
Time and Tide (TT)
Times Literary Supplement (TLS)
Truth
Western Mail (WM)

PART II

Peace and war, high-mindedness and low connections: the Duke of Bedford and the peace movement

PART III

3

EVANGELICAL ANTICAPITALISM

The strange case of the Duke of Bedford

We will find the Duke of Bedford recurring in almost every chapter of this book. For this alone he is worthy of detailed study, including an examination of the various influences – intellectual, spiritual and personal – which contributed to the behaviour of this remarkable figure.

Of all the pre-war admirers of Nazi Germany, Bedford was the one who was to maintain the highest profile in the wartime years. Not for him the subterfuges of so many in the new situation. Admittedly, there was a short period after the first wave of DR 18B arrests of May–June 1940 when he kept a lower profile; but that was a very temporary phase, and he was soon producing many further public statements, in print and eventually in the House of Lords, which were not just anti-war, but also full of pro-Nazi attacks on what he saw as the bad faith of the British Establishment. Amazingly, he escaped detention throughout this time. His high profile made him a rallying point, and he gave considerable support, financial and other, to a number of the extremist movements that began to emerge from 1942 onwards. Behind all his activities lay a profound conviction that he was right in all he did, and a consequent lack of concern for the personal consequences of his actions and words.

Early life

Hastings William Sackville Russell, later to be the 12th Duke of Bedford, was born on 21 December 1888 at Cairnsmore House, Kirkcudbrightshire, the only child of Lord Herbrand Russell and his wife Mary. Five years after his birth his father succeeded as the 11th Duke of Bedford, and Hastings was given the courtesy title of the Marquess of Tavistock (the name by which he was to be known throughout the inter-war period and during the first year of the Second World War). His childhood was lonely, and spent mainly at Woburn Abbey, the family estate in Bedfordshire. His father was 'a selfish and forbidding man, with a highly developed sense of public duty and ducal responsibility, [who] lived a cold, aloof existence, isolated from the outside world by a mass of servants, sycophants and an eleven-mile wall' (Bedford, 1959: 86). His mother (the famous 'Flying Duchess' who was to take up aviation in her sixties), was profoundly deaf, short-tempered and dismissive of anything short of perfection. As her son was later to say:

> Her rather hasty temper and impatience with any form of incompetence, coupled with the fact that she sometimes punished me severely for things I did not even know were wrong, made me afraid of her. [...] It was bad luck both for my parents and for me that I was a sensitive, nervous child, unable to acquire skill in many of those pursuits in which they desired that I should excel and unable to adapt myself to surroundings by which they hoped that I would benefit.
>
> (Bedford, 1949: 58–9)

After a succession of private tutors, Tavistock was sent to Eton for two years. There he was miserable, partly because of the 'unwelcome attention of bullies', partly because 'I was no good at school games and despised them' and partly because this fastidious boy was shocked by the sexual immorality there. For years he was to have terrible nightmares stemming from his experience of Eton (Bedford, 1949: 61–7).

In 1907 he went to Balliol College Oxford for four years, where he obtained a Fourth in History. There, too, he was unhappy. The only ray of light was the chaplain, the Revd Henry Gibbon, with whom he remained in touch in later years. It was Gibbon who inculcated in him the strong evangelical Christian beliefs that were to dominate the rest of his life.

In 1912, acceding to the wishes of his father, Tavistock joined a territorial regiment, the 10th Middlesex. This was an unhappy experience for him, as it soon became clear that he was thoroughly unfitted for the military life. At the outbreak of war in 1914 he refused to rejoin the regiment. At this his father wrote to say that he never wanted to see him again, and that he was taking steps to disinherit him. They were not to meet again for over twenty years. Luckily for Tavistock, he had already had £15,000 a year settled on him, and it was impossible for his father to break that trust.

Through Robert Whitwell, an Oxford don interested in the YMCA, in 1914 Tavistock became a helper at a camp near Portsmouth, where he worked for five years (his bad eyesight saving him from military service). On 21 November 1914 he married Whitwell's daughter Louisa.

From 1919 onwards he immersed himself in Christian and social work. He had by now become a fervent pacifist, and spoke on various platforms. When he preached in a Birmingham church in 1926, he stated that lies had been told during the war, for recruiting purposes. In the same speech it is alleged that he defended the ex-Kaiser's record and attacked England's cause; several ex-servicemen walked out (*BP*, 29/10/26).

It was in 1928 that he discovered the other cause that was to obsess him for the rest of his life – monetary reform. In that year he read Charles Marshall Hattersley's book *This Age of Plenty*, and soon became influenced by the theories of Arthur Kitson and, more fundamentally, those of Major C.H. Douglas and his Social Credit movement. These theories were to colour all his subsequent political ideas. They led him, however, onto dangerous ground. Many of those who in the inter-war period promulgated monetary theories which challenged capitalism, including Kitson and Douglas, saw in the Jews the driving force behind 'International Finance', which they described as the 'Money Power'. Tavistock was no exception, and these ideas were to colour many of his later attitudes towards Nazi Germany and Britain's war effort in the Second World War.

Meanwhile, his private life had become very unhappy. He left the family home in 1934, feeling his position to be impossible, as he believed that his wife was infatuated with their children's former tutor, the Revd Cecil Squire, whom he had sacked in 1930 on the basis that he had introduced Lady Tavistock to Anglo-Catholicism, alcohol and frivolous activities such as golf, all of which had caused her to give up her Christian social work. After Squire's dismissal, he claimed, she had made his (Tavistock's) life unbearable, scarcely speaking to him except 'with a grunt', and behaving 'as though she felt a violent repulsion to his presence in the bedroom'. Meanwhile she had continued to see Squire (and his mother) frequently.

Left without resources, Lady Tavistock brought a lawsuit against her husband for 'restitution of conjugal rights' in 1935. Tavistock, obstinate as ever, declared his intention to defend the case because 'I am now desperate and shall not care how much I hurt myself or how much dirty linen we wash in public'. At the hearing (which caused great public interest), the judge showed considerable sympathy for Lady Tavistock, whose relationship with Squire had almost certainly been an innocent one. He pointed out how single-mindedly Tavistock had been obsessed by his evangelical interests and activities, and unable to see his wife's need for something more in life. 'Lord Tavistock', he said, 'takes a rigid and austere view of life, and dislikes many things, some of which he calls "pagan", but which most men do not actively dislike. He dislikes [...] alcohol, tobacco, playing cards for money and betting. He does not play games, and said he took very little interest in his wife's dress' (*ES*, 13/11/35).

The complete breakdown of the marriage was clear. Lady Tavistock described her husband as 'the most cruel, mean and conceited person she had ever met'. And the rest of his family seems to have held the same view. His son John was later to describe Tavistock as being 'the loneliest man I ever knew, incapable of giving or receiving love, utterly self-centred and opinionated' (Bedford, 1959: 87). This was borne out by Tavistock's treatment of John later on, when he cut him off without a penny in 1939 because of what he considered to be an unsuitable marriage to a divorcee 'of the wrong class'. By the late Thirties Tavistock was more lonely and isolated than ever.

Pre-war political involvement

Meanwhile, Tavistock had been single-mindedly pursuing his interests, which were becoming increasingly political. By the late Thirties his interest in monetary reform had led him to an admiration for the Nazi regime, which he believed to have been challenging the 'Money Power', and to a belief that entrenched Jewish interests were fomenting war against the Reich, in revenge for Hitler's treatment of the Jews and in order to safeguard the financial system on which they thrived. He found much to admire and little to criticise in the policies of Hitler's Germany, which, as he wrote in a letter to the press in 1938 at the time of the *Anschluss*, 'gave German youth faith and hope in the future, restored their self-respect, and did much to reduce unemployment' (*NEW*, 24/3/38). As the danger of war approached, his pacifism became infected with a belief in Germany's desire for peace, and in the 'bad faith' of the British political establishment, which, he believed, was determined to give a dog a bad name.

Soon it was not just a question of ideas, but one of action. He had by 1938 decided to support a number of the extreme right-wing groups which expressed admiration for Nazi Germany. Special Branch had, by early 1939, begun to take an interest in him. In February 1939 they reported that he had been giving 'substantial donations' to Mosley's British Union, and that he had attended a luncheon of the BU London administration held at the Criterion Restaurant on 24 February (TNA HO 144/21281). Meanwhile, he took every opportunity to give vent to his opinions on public platforms throughout the country.

In April 1939 Tavistock co-founded a new political movement, the British People's Party (BPP), in collaboration with two men with whom he was to be closely connected for the rest of his life – Ben Greene and John Beckett, both former members of the Independent Labour Party (ILP). Beckett had been a leading member of the British Union of Fascists, and had left that party with William Joyce in 1937 to found the National Socialist League, the title of which group accurately portrayed its debt to Nazism. Tavistock became president of the BPP, Beckett the general secretary and Greene the treasurer. There were several other known right-wing extremists on the Executive, including Lord Lymington, John Scanlon and H. St John Philby. The membership also included Anthony Ludovici, Robert Gordon-Canning and Hugh Ross Williamson.

In July 1939 the BPP fought the Hythe by-election, with Philby as its candidate. Among their main speakers were Tavistock, Beckett, Greene, Admiral Sir Barry Domvile, Captain Vincent Collier, Lady Pearson and Dr Meyrick Booth. Much of their rhetoric was devoted to praise of Hitler, who had 'restored one of the greatest races in the world to the position of one of the foremost nations in the world as it was at the present time' (*HSA*, 8/7/39), and to criticism of British policies towards Germany. During the campaign the BPP produced a pamphlet, *Alien Money Power in Great Britain*, which attacked the Conservative candidate by suggesting that the City firm for which he worked was run by Jews.

The 'phoney war'

The advent of war did not curb Tavistock's activities. He immediately set up a body to co-ordinate anti-war activity, called the British Council for a Christian Settlement in Europe (BCCSE), with himself as chairman and John Beckett as secretary. Press reports of its first public meeting on 14 October were explicit as to the pro-Nazi nature of the proceedings:

> About 150 Britons met in London yesterday 'to bring peace to the world'. They praised Hitler. They reviled the British Government. They ended by sending a message to Mr Chamberlain calling on him to start peace negotiations.
>
> (*SE*, 15/10/39)

As MI5 later put it, 'Wittingly or unwittingly, wickedly or in child-like innocence, [Tavistock] had become an instrument of Nazi propaganda' (TNA KV 2/793). Tavistock's views became even clearer in an article he published in *Action*, BU's newspaper, on 11 January 1940, in which he accused the government of responsibility for the war, by its encouragement of the Polish government 'to adopt an intransigent attitude'. On 9 February he published another letter, in *Truth*, in which he excused Hitler's 'so-called acts of aggression' and pointed out how much more reprehensible Russia's actions had been 'than anything that Hitler has ever done'.

Meanwhile, between October and December 1939, Tavistock had been taking part in a number of secret meetings with leading figures from the various 'patriotic societies' with a view to collaborative activity. These figures included Mosley, Admiral Domvile, Captain Ramsay, Lord Lymington and General J.F.C. Fuller, together with other members of BU, the Right Club, the Nordic League, the Link, the BPP and Lymington's *New Pioneer* group (TNA HO 45/24895; NMM DOM 56).

His attendance at these meetings was, however, interrupted by a new venture that he undertook in early 1940, which was to bring his name vividly before the public. In January, via an intermediary, he approached the German Legation in Dublin 'to see if the German Government would agree to peace on reasonable terms' (Bedford, 1949: 181). Henning Thomsen, Secretary to the Legation, conveyed certain peace proposals to him, which purported to be official. Tavistock passed on these proposals to Lord Halifax, the Foreign Secretary, whose officials showed considerable scepticism in relation to them (one of them noting that Tavistock's 'particular opinions dispose him to make more excuses for Herr Hitler than would generally be thought reasonable') (TNA FO 800/318/19). Halifax himself expressed doubts as to the authenticity of the proposals. Nevertheless, on 7 February Tavistock published a letter in *Truth* praising Hitler and floating the possibility of a negotiated peace (while not yet revealing the proposals). He also, on 13 February, invited to his house a number of the leading figures from the pro-Nazi Right to discuss the matter. They included John Beckett, Robert Gordon-Canning, Ben Greene, Lord Lymington, Admiral Domvile, General Fuller and the Earl of Mar (a strong Mosleyite). They discussed the peace proposals for about two hours, and how to deal with Chamberlain (seen as an obstinate figure) and with Halifax (NMM DOM 56, 13/2/40).

Tavistock now decided to go to Dublin. He obtained Halifax's permission, though not his support, Halifax writing to him on 17 February: 'While I naturally could not prevent you from going over to Dublin if you wished to do so, you will understand, of course, that there could be no question of your going in any official capacity or of your being entrusted with any mission from myself' (Tavistock, 1940: 22). The visit took place in late February. Then, on 29 February, Tavistock invited another group to his house to discuss the latest developments. This group was a mixture of pro-Nazi enthusiasts and of relatively respectable searchers after peace. Alongside Norman Hay, the Earl of Mar and Admiral Domvile, the group included Lord Darnley, Robert Sencourt and the pro-peace Labour MP Richard Rapier Stokes. Tavistock reported to them on his trip to Ireland, but made it clear that 'this Government don't want peace' (NMM DOM 56, 29/2/40).

It was at this stage that the whole thing became public. The pacifist ILP MP John McGovern, who had been an ally of Tavistock throughout these proceedings, leaked to the *Daily Express* the German terms and Tavistock's response. On 1 March the newspapers contained full details. They were violent in their denunciations of Tavistock, saying that he had 'accused the British Government of responsibility for the war'. They also evoked Beckett's Fascist past, and his association with the man [William Joyce] now known as 'Lord Haw-Haw' (*DT*, 1/3/40). In the House of Commons, on 4 March, it was reported that the German government and the German Legation in Dublin had officially repudiated the proposals.

Tavistock could never learn, however. Convinced that this repudiation had occurred only because of the British government's mishandling of the situation, he now brought out, at his own expense, a pamphlet containing the full correspondence between himself and Halifax, entitled *The Fate of a Peace Effort*. This brought his views even more clearly before the public eye. Meanwhile the BCCSE held further public meetings which, though billed as discussions of the peace proposals, in fact contained diatribes against the 'warmonger' Churchill and paeans of praise for Hitler, with Tavistock insisting that 'changed circumstances render the breaking of pledges perfectly excusable', and that Hitler's breaches of international law had been 'actuated in response to extreme provocation' (TNA TS 27/522/27). At a large 'peace meeting' held at the Kingsway Hall on 3 April 'to address the public on the Tavistock Peace Plan', attended by about 1,500 people, the chairman was John Beckett, and the speakers Tavistock, John McGovern and Hugh Ross Williamson. Tavistock declared that 'there was no doubt about the sincerity of [Hitler's] intentions', and said that he had had 'great provocation immediately after Munich'. Williamson violently attacked Winston Churchill, whom he accused of trying to 'whip up war' against Germany, and praised the chivalry of the German Navy, 'wildly cheered by a section of the audience'. McGovern, usually perceived as a straightforward ILP pacifist, nevertheless spoke here in a pro-Nazi vein, praising Hitler for what he had done for the working class, while also speaking movingly of the sufferings brought by war to German and English mothers. Hecklers were violently thrown out by fascist-style stewards (*FP*, 4/40). Special Branch noted, however, that 'it appears that a good number of middle-class people are already caught by this Nazi propaganda'. The audience appeared mainly to consist of 'members of the Peace Pledge Union, the British Union, the Imperial Fascist League, and some Socialists from the ILP and other Left organisations' (TNA HO 262/6).

Tavistock was by now aware that he was not *persona grata* with the authorities and that there was a danger that he might be imprisoned. But, as he wrote in a private letter on 1 April, 'the Government may think twice before they put a marquis in prison' (TNA HO 45/25729).

After May 1940

The May arrests under Defence Regulation 18B, however, gave Tavistock some cause for concern. Given the arrests of Ramsay, Mosley, Beckett and Greene, he no longer appears to have thought that the government would think twice before putting a marquis in prison. He had been expected to speak at a meeting at Holborn Hall on 16 May, but was 'unable to attend owing to illness' (TNA TS 27/522). Sending some of his pamphlet literature on 9 June to a political acquaintance, Frederick Bowman, he advised that it should be given only to individual contacts known to be sympathetic, as this was the time for quiet, personal work among people already against the war. In the same letter he stressed that there was a grave danger that he might be imprisoned like Mosley and Beckett, and asked Bowman to destroy the letter (TNA HO 45/25729).

On the death of his father in August 1940, Tavistock succeeded to the dukedom. He was not to take up his seat in the House of Lords, however, until December 1941. And, though he now had three major residences – Woburn in Bedfordshire, Endsleigh in Devon and Cairnsmore in Scotland – he was for the next year and a half to spend almost all his time at Cairnsmore. A statement made by his associate Frederick Bowman after his arrest (at which time Tavistock's extensive correspondence with him had been found in his possession by the authorities) may throw some light on this situation:

> I understand that following my arrest his Grace has been bluntly told that he must not leave Scotland, and he has moreover been specifically forbidden to take his seat in the House of Lords.
>
> (TNA HO 45/25729)

One cannot be sure, however, that this was the reason for Tavistock's retirement to Cairnsmore. A later report by MI5 throws little further light on the matter:

> With the removal of his Fascist collaborators to prison, [Tavistock] appears for the time being to have ceased his efforts. […] The Duke's actual removal from the scene of his former activities to his Scottish retreat seems to have escaped notice in the Battle of Britain.
>
> (TNA KV 2/793)

By December 1940 the Duke was under active consideration for imprisonment under Defence Regulation 18B – but nothing came of this either then or when the matter was reconsidered in June 1941 and August 1941 (TNA HO 45/25747).

Gradually, Bedford (as we must now call him) began to become more politically active. As MI5 reported, for a while 'it seemed that he would not emerge from his comfortable obscurity'. He did, in fact, eventually emerge, 'but so cautiously that it was not for some months that we were able to identify him definitely as the author of a series of pamphlets which came to light in the autumn of 1940'. Of one of these pamphlets, 'Have Britons Brains', Professor Ernest Barker expressed the view that 'it could only emanate from a German source as no English person whatever his beliefs could have been its author' (TNA KV 2/ 793).

From late 1941 onwards the Duke began writing over his own name about the war situation. He forged an extraordinary alliance with the anarchist Guy Aldred (who saw Bedford as a man of great integrity, who shared his attitude to the war), and published many of his articles from 1941 to 1944 in the magazine *The Word*, published in Glasgow by Aldred's Strickland Press.

Meanwhile, he was coming before the public eye for a number of other reasons, including, as we shall see in a later chapter, critical government statements about him in the House of Commons, and populist press attacks relating to his alleged reluctance to allow the railings from the London squares on the Bedford estate to be taken for the war effort.

MI5 noted that, thanks to all this publicity, the Duke 'attracted considerable public notice during October and November' (TNA HO 45/25747). The government became uneasy about him once more. On 9 November 1941 Lord Swinton, Chairman of the Home Defence (Security) Executive (HDSE), told MI5 that he thought the Duke should be detained under DR 18B (TNA KV 2/793). On 17 November the War Cabinet discussed this question without coming to any conclusion, partly owing to warnings from the Attorney General as to the legal justification for such action (TNA CAB 65/ 20). The most likely cause for the Cabinet's inaction, however, was the view expressed later in a letter by one of MI5's officials: that Bedford's credit was too great in the pacifist community for action to be risked (TNA KV 2/793). On 7 December Bedford was, however, put on the 'Suspect List' (the list of those to be immediately arrested in the event of an invasion).

The events of October/November 1941 seem, paradoxically, to have spurred Bedford into greater activity (no doubt because, having had such publicity, he had nothing to lose). He took up his seat in the House of Lords, finally, on 3 December 1941, and delivered there in the following months a number of provocative speeches attacking Churchill's belligerency and 'the attempt, by the moneylending financiers and big business monopolists, to destroy the relatively sane financial system of the Axis Powers' (Hansard, 2/6/42). He also published his views extensively, not only in pamphlets and in *The Word*, but also in the much more widely circulated *Peace News* (the organ of the Peace Pledge Union), in which, in a number of prominent articles over the next three years, he took his usual strong line on international finance, Churchill the warmonger, Britain's responsibility for the war, the reasonableness of Hitler and the shortcomings of the Jews.

Meanwhile, as we shall see, he was using his great wealth to fund various extremist (though remarkably unsuccessful) movements: the British National Party and the English Nationalist Association, and later the revived British People's Party.

As the war wore on, and it became clear that there was going to be an Allied victory, Bedford became ever gloomier. As he stated in a letter to Arthur Bryant on 5 July 1944, he was convinced that international financiers were already working hard to re-establish the old order throughout Europe, and that the British government was complicit in this (LHCMA Bryant H/1). In May 1945, as the war in Europe ended, he was still publicly proclaiming that the 'glorious victory' had been won solely for 'Soviet tyranny and Big Finance' (TNA KV 2/795). In an obituary of Hitler in Bowman's anti-Semitic journal *Talking Picture News*, he declared that 'Hitler's virtues [had] caused his destruction to be ordained by the financiers of the City and Wall Street, using the politicians as their puppets' (*TPN*, 25/5/45), and at the death of Roosevelt he described him as 'an inveterate and unscrupulous warmonger, and a tool of Big Finance' (*The Word* 5/45). And, though in the immediate post-war period he moderated the anti-Semitic thrust of his public expression of views, there remains little doubt that he in fact remained true to what he had always believed (TNA KV 2/795; Griffiths, 2010: 253).

The attempt to revive his pre-war political activities from early 1945 onwards through a new-style British People's Party formed in collaboration with John Beckett, though there was some initial success, was in fact doomed to failure in the anti-fascist atmosphere of Britain in the immediate aftermath of the war. On 9 October 1953 Bedford died of gunshot wounds on his Endsleigh estate in Devon. Though the coroner's verdict was accidental death, there seems little doubt that (as his son believed) he had committed suicide.

When we try to assess the Duke of Bedford's motives, we are confronted with a very complex picture. He was a lonely, introverted character, unable to forge human relationships, possibly as a result of his strange upbringing. This lack of human contact may have contributed to his conviction that he was right in all he thought and did, and that it was the world that was out of step, and not him. And then there was the succession of obsessions which ruled his life – evangelical Christianity; pacifism; Social Credit; financial reform. These in their turn led to a 'conspiracy' vision of human behaviour (in particular of the behaviour of those in power in Britain and in America), and to a belief in the sinister machinations of capitalists and Jews, who were forcing the West into war.

As Lord Simon, the Lord Chancellor, pointed out in 1941, the Duke was fortunate in being a British subject. 'If he was a German and was in Germany and if he gave expression to the reverse opinions and denounced Hitler and all his works, and found excuses for Hitler's enemies', then he would have been dealt with very differently there (Hansard, 18/11/41). Yet, though Bedford did not face prison, he did receive public opprobrium which would have broken a less single-minded man.

Many of his underlying attitudes were, of themselves, admirable. Many members of the peace movement, who tended to see the best in him, admired these qualities, while failing to see how they had been undermined by his obsessive nature and by the specific hatreds that his obsessions had induced. Many of them, amazingly, seem to have been unaware of his pro-Nazi and anti-Semitic activities (even though these had been plastered across the press). Indeed, even in our own day, when I mentioned to a clergyman friend of mine that I was writing about the Duke of Bedford, he said: 'Oh yes! That admirable peace campaigner.'

One cannot, however, fail to admire the tenacity with which he was prepared to hold to the most unpopular views at great personal cost to himself, and to brave the unpopularity and indeed hatred that he aroused in the British public. He may have been arrogant in his conviction that he was always right; but underneath it all, he was an unworldly, sincere but opinionated man, whose naivety led him to ideas that blended ill with his very real Christian ideals.

Bibliography

Books

Bedford, Hastings, Duke of (1949), *The Years of Transition* (Edinburgh: Dakers).
Bedford, John, Duke of (1959), *A Silver-Plated Spoon* (London: Cassell).
Griffiths, Richard (2010), 'Anti-Fascism and the Post-War British Establishment', in Nigel Copsey and Andrzej Olechnowicz (eds), *Varieties of Anti-Fascism: Britain in the Inter-War Period* (Basingstoke: Palgrave Macmillan).
Tavistock, Marquess of (1940), *The Fate of a Peace Effort* (High Wycombe: Marquess of Tavistock).

Documents

The National Archives (TNA)

CAB 65/20
FO 800/318
HO 45/24895, HO 45/25729, HO 45/25747, HO 144/21281, HO 262/6
KV 2/793, KV 2/795
TS 27/522

National Maritime Museum (NMM)

Admiral Sir Barry Domvile's Diary, DOM 56

Liddell Hart Centre for Military Archives, King's College London (LHCMA)

Arthur Bryant Papers, Bryant H/1

Newspapers and journals

Action
Birmingham Post (BP)
Daily Express
Daily Telegraph (DT)
Evening Standard (ES)
The Free Press (FP)

Hythe and Sandgate Advertiser (HSA)
New English Weekly (NEW)
Sunday Express (SE)
Talking Picture News (TPN)
Truth
The Word

4

'HOW CAN THE GERMANS HONESTLY BE BLAMED?'

The infiltration of the peace movement

Pacifism is an honourable creed. While its understanding of the evils of war is shared by many who nevertheless find themselves forced by events to take sides in a human conflict, its adherents distinguish themselves by a single-minded refusal to countenance war under any circumstances. It has a long history in Britain, from the seventeenth century onwards, with such religious bodies as the Quakers playing a leading role.

The immense loss of life in the First World War, and the conditions in which it had been fought, brought many new adherents to the pacifist cause in the inter-war period; and, as it became probable that Europe was once more sliding into war, the peace movement in Britain started organising itself in a far more coherent way, and was soon well on the way to becoming a mass movement. The turning point in pacifist affairs came in the Thirties, as the threat of war became ever more insistent. In 1934 the Revd Dick Sheppard published a letter in the *Manchester Guardian* inviting men to send him postcards pledging never to support war. So many people responded that the Peace Pledge Union (PPU) was formed, and was to become the driving force behind pacifist activity from then on. In 1936 *Peace News*, which had recently been founded by the Quaker Humphrey Moore, became the official organ of the PPU. By now the peace movement was a force to be reckoned with, as various government responses during the course of the war were to show.

While many pacifists maintained the purity of their ideals, in the late Thirties and early Forties there was nevertheless a significant minority, which included a number of senior members of the movement, whose views became tempered with a desire to see the best in the motives of Nazi Germany, and, in some extreme cases, positively to promote pro-Nazi attitudes. In part this may have been due to naivety; but one must also consider the fact that, from 1939 onwards, the various fascist and pro-Nazi movements were actively encouraging their members to join the PPU.

While examining this phenomenon, we must always bear in mind that the vast majority of pacifists remained untarred by this particular brush. Some of the manifestations of this attitude had, however, such a high profile that they had a certain amount of effect, both on the behaviour of fellow pacifists and on the perception of the peace movement held by the authorities and the general public. This is an area which led, at the time, to a great deal of confusion, both on the part of pacifists and on the part of the authorities; and that confusion has continued, in accounts of the period 1939–1945, to our own day.

The build-up to war

It is hardly surprising that pacifists supported the appeasement policy of the Chamberlain government in 1938. As the Czechoslovakian crisis developed, however, *Peace News* added to this support a tendency to make judgements on the international situation which went beyond even-handedness and excused Nazi policies. Editorials talked of Germany's 'moral case', and articles and letters decried Czechoslovakia as an artificial state which had no reason for its existence, a 'magpie state' gathering other people's possessions into it (e.g. *PN* 9/7/38, 13/8/38, 24/9/38, 22/10/38). The choice of contributors at this time conveys something of the editor Humphrey Moore's attitude. They included such entrenched enemies of the Czechoslovak state as the

Hungarian activist Ivan Nagy and Bertram de Colonna (author of *Czecho-Slovakia Within* and *Poland from the Inside*), as well as the well-known pro-Nazi enthusiast Dr Meyrick Booth. The latter, in a letter published on 27 August, congratulated *Peace News* on its 'capital series of articles on the problems of Central Europe'.

In the immediate aftermath of the Munich crisis the Peace Pledge Union published a pamphlet by Clive Bell, entitled *Warmongers*. Mark Gilbert has summed up the contents of this book as follows:

> In this pamphlet, Bell contended explicitly that Britain should renounce her continental role entirely, permitting Germany to 'absorb' France, Poland, the Low Countries and the Balkans. In a masterpiece of euphemism, he described this policy as 'uniting the Continent under German leadership'. The warmongers of Bell's pamphlet were not Hitler and Mussolini, but British public figures, such as Churchill and Sir Stafford Cripps.
>
> (Gilbert, 1992: 499)

After the Kristallnacht of November 1938, one of the tactics used by writers for *Peace News* was to attempt to excuse Nazi Germany's vicious treatment of the Jews by pointing out that Britain had been guilty of similar things: 'The action taken against the Jews in 1938 was hardly worse', they claimed, 'than that in the East End of London in 1914 when shop windows were repeatedly smashed.' Indeed, arguments were used similar to those of British fascist anti-Semites in the same period, who pointed to British 'atrocities' against the Arabs in Palestine in order to excuse Nazi excesses: 'Some Englishmen might remark, "Why don't the Germans let the Jews live?" But the Germans would retaliate with "Why don't the English leave the Arabs alone?"' Readers were urged not to be 'too unctuous', and to bear in mind that far worse things had happened under British colonial rule (*PN*, 26/11/38, 20/1/39).

The German invasion of Prague on 15 March 1939, which caused so many appeasers to realise that trust in Hitler was futile, and which even gave a number of pro-Nazis pause for thought, does not seem to have done much to affect the attitudes expressed in *Peace News*. Humphrey Moore, in his editorials, referred to 'the evident genuineness of Germany's readiness to discuss just claims'. He deplored the guarantee given to Poland and the 'anti-German hysteria' that appeared to have taken over in Britain. The Germans, he asserted, could not be blamed 'for believing that the new policy is one only of encirclement and that they can expect no more justice from it than they have hitherto experienced'. Hitler, he said, was 'an idealistic dreamer', but even he would be able to perceive the sinister reality behind the policies of his opponents (*PN*, 24/3/39, 7/4/39).

Much of these attitudes can be interpreted as a combination of naivety and of gullibility with regard to so much of the pro-Nazi publicity which was available at the time. A rather more sinister influence was, however, beginning to emerge.

The fascist dimension

The year 1939 saw the beginnings of an overlap between the activities of the PPU and those of the various pro-Nazi groups and individuals who flourished at the time. This was in part because, after March 1939, no major political grouping was left to put forward a peace agenda. As I have said elsewhere, 'apart from pacifists like the Peace Pledge Union, and selective pacifists like the ILP, the only strong peace movement came from the hard core of positive enthusiasts for Germany who remained' (Griffiths, 1980: 363). This included, of course, Mosley's British Union, which further developed its highly successful 'peace campaign' at this time; but it also included lesser groupings such as Lord Tavistock's British People's Party (BPP), Lord Lymington's British Council against European Commitments (BCAEC) and Admiral Domvile's The Link. Members of the PPU were often sucked into such movements, their motives ranging from naivety to complicity. Alongside this, however, there were also conscious efforts made by the fascists themselves to collaborate with the PPU, and indeed in some instances to infiltrate it.

Many pacifists attended Mosley's 1939 anti-war rallies. Far more sinister, however, were the various contacts made between the PPU and dubious pro-Nazi movements such as the BPP and The Link.

Ben Greene had become a member of the PPU in late 1938. In January 1939 he set up a 'Peace and Progressive Information Service'

(PPIS), advertised in *Peace News* on 20 January as having been formed, with PPU sponsorship, to 'expose the falsity of War Propaganda'. Much of his material for this service was initially provided (before his expulsion from Britain later in the spring) by Dr Gottfried Rösel of the Anglo-German Information Bureau (Lewis, 2010: 220). A further source was H.R. Hoffmann of *News from Germany*. MI5's assessment of the PPIS is a very accurate one:

> Throughout these publications no good word is said in favour of any British aim or endeavour; very serious allegations are repeated concerning the treatment of Arabs in Palestine by the British; definite sympathy is shown for the aims of Hitler and Mussolini for territorial readjustment in Europe, and the actions of the Dictators are presented in the most favourable light.
> (TNA KV 2/489)

Greene's description of the PPIS in *Peace News* in January 1939 aroused immediate criticism from Rose Macaulay, who in the next week's edition voiced the suspicions aroused in her by the Service's 'rather questionable title', and by Greene's clearly pro-German statements about its aims. Rose Macaulay was a prominent figure in the body of PPU members who vigorously protested, at intervals, against the 'fascist' tendencies in *Peace News*. On this occasion, suspecting that the facts of the international situation were being 'cooked' by people such as Greene, she remarked that 'some of us have long been rather uneasy about the culinary methods of *Peace News*' (*PN*, 27/1/39).

At the Annual General Meeting of the PPU in April 1939 Ben Greene, deploring the fact that 'pacifists did not seem to be able to rally peace opinion' and that Britain was 'living under a dictatorship of vested interests', called on the PPU to 'get in touch with every other body which opposes war' (*PN*, 21/4/39). Given that the British People's Party, of which he was a prominent founder-member, had just been formed that month, his hidden agenda is clear to us with hindsight, though it was not so to the members of the PPU at the time, and their association with the BPP was to flourish for the next few months, with advertisements appearing regularly in *Peace News* for meetings of the BPP and the related movement, the Campaign against War and Usury.

The infiltration of the peace movement 79

Meanwhile, an even closer relationship was being formed by the PPU, this time with The Link. In a letter to Dr Erich Hetzler (the SS officer in charge of the British section of the Ribbentrop Bureau in Berlin), Cola Ernest Carroll of The Link reported on 25 May:

> I have been fostering our association with the Peace Pledge Union because it is a powerful organisation which is definitely friendly to our aims, anxious to assist them, and willing to listen to us in matters affecting Anglo-German relations.
>
> (TNA KV 2/836)

Clearly negotiations with (unnamed) individuals at the PPU had reached an advanced stage, because Carroll continued as follows:

> There is a possibility that The Link may in due course take over the foreign correspondence of the Peace Pledge Union in this sense: that the many thousands of letters which the PPU receives daily on the subject of foreign affairs would be handed over to us to be dealt with. I think we can very safely co-operate with the PPU for no other reason than that we can rely on having as much standing with it as any other of its elements, and we are quite capable of making our weight felt.
>
> (TNA KV 2/836)

The idea that the PPU should entrust all its correspondence on foreign affairs to The Link is hair-raising! Yet it is significant that in this very month the PPU incorporated details on The Link in its *Peace Service Handbook* as part of the list of societies working for international reconciliation (Ceadel, 1980: 281).

One wonders who the individual PPU members were, who negotiated with Carroll. One pointer may be that Canon Stuart Morris, the chairman of the PPU Council and generally regarded as a man of high principle, actually joined The Link in early June. To some of his fellow members of PPU this was shocking, and precipitated something of a crisis in the movement. This crisis showed that, whatever the pro-German line taken by some of the PPU's leaders, among the rank and file there were a good number who were uncomfortable with these trends (though an equally large number who could see no harm in them — as is witnessed by the number of PPU members who attended local Link events throughout the country in 1939).

It was in the course of June and July that this controversy came to a head. On 9 June, in a letter to *Peace News*, Rose Macaulay questioned whether 'membership of the Nazi society The Link' was 'compatible with real and thought-out pacifism', and deplored the fact that so many pacifists 'should thus seem to abandon the cause of freedom and tolerance and abet their persecutors'. A week later, the *Daily Telegraph* carried a report on a memorandum by the Research Department of the Economic League, which alleged that the PPU was being used as a channel for Nazi propaganda, and cited its connections with The Link through the *Peace Service Handbook*, as well as pointing to the extensive participation by PPU members in local Link meetings. Stuart Morris wrote to the *Telegraph* to rebut the inferences made in these claims (*PN*, 21/7/39).

Meanwhile, the Executive Committee of the PPU was beginning to show concern about the movement's connection with the British People's Party. It noted that 'difficulties had arisen among groups and members owing to the connexion (through Ben Greene) between the British People's Party and the Peace and Progressive Information Service', and that there was a feeling 'that because the PPU had helped Ben Greene, a British People's Party member, to launch the information service, the PPU must have some connexion with the party'. This was repudiated. It was stated that the PPU had no responsibility for the information service, and that the BPP was in no way 'supported by or associated with' the PPU (*PN*, 21/7/39).

The executive committee's attitude did not, however, seem to have any effect on *Peace News*, which, in the same issue in which this decision was reported on 21 July, praised the PPIS's Bulletins Nos 11 and 13, and also published Stuart Morris's defence of The Link. The editor, Humphrey Moore, whose editorials had become progressively more pro-German, was obviously essentially in agreement with Morris. On 4 August he published an article by Ethel Mannin entitled 'Anti-Fascist Propaganda is Dangerous!', which claimed that nothing had contributed more to the war-mentality of the masses than rabid anti-Hitlerism. The main cause of all this, said Mannin, was the Jews:

> The intensity of Jewish racial feeling, and Jewish interests vested in Big Business and the Press, necessarily contribute very heavily to this smash-Hitler brand of anti-Fascist propaganda. […] The racial feeling of the Jew is such that he might perhaps be forgiven a certain blind spot which makes him prepared to plunge the world into mass-slaughter.

A week later, on 11 August, Mannin returned to the fray in an article entitled 'This Atrocity Business', which rubbished claims of Nazi atrocities and at the same time produced the well-worn argument that the British had been just as bad in Palestine:

> The intensity of Jewish racial feeling in partnership with Jewish financial interests makes a formidable alliance. […] Meanwhile, mass emotion is stirred by stories of Nazi brutality, floggings, concentration camps, Jews forced to scrub out lavatories (which is apparently only an 'atrocity' when Jews are forced to do it), and the rest of it. […] Every atrocity that the propagandist imagination can produce is accepted, whereas, when it comes to a matter of the British in India and Africa and Palestine, cruelties and injustices become 'a mass of falsehood'. […] Any alleged atrocity committed by an Arab against a Jew is a 'fact' – because the Jews are working hand in hand with the British whereas the Arab is merely the wicked animal that defends itself when attacked.

The anti-Semitic statements from these two articles were gleefully quoted, on 26 August, in British Union's journal *Action*.

On 6 August, however, Humphrey Moore went on holiday, and the deputy editor, Andrew Stewart, took over. Immediately the tone of *Peace News* changed. In his first editorial, on 11 August, entitled '"The Link" and All That', Stewart declared:

> If The Link were to be proved conclusively to be an agency of Dr Goebbels I think those members of the PPU who continued

to belong to it would be well advised to give some thought to the implications of the Peace Pledge, and the same advice seems to be desirable for those who think that membership of British Union, Sir Oswald Mosley's Fascist organization, is compatible with membership of the PPU.

Meanwhile, in its 11 August edition the *News Chronicle* gave an interview to Morris, alongside an announcement that he was a member of The Link. In this interview he stated: 'I am all for giving a great deal more away [to Hitler]. I don't think that Mr Chamberlain has really started yet on any serious appeasement.' A special meeting of the PPU was held the next day, at which it was agreed that a statement dissociating the PPU from The Link should be sent out. Morris, however, defended The Link in a letter to the *News Chronicle*, and also sent out a letter to PPU Group Leaders, which stated:

> In my judgement the significance of the attack on The Link (and through the Link on the PPU) lies in the fact that it is really part of a general attempt to create prejudice and hatred against Germany, to deny that there is any justice in the German claims, and to prevent any further attempt to meet her legitimate needs. I felt it necessary to stand firm, not so much in defence of The Link as such, but against such warmongering.
>
> (*PN*, 18/8/39)

On 18 August Stewart produced a powerful editorial in *Peace News*, in which he examined the record of The Link, quoting pro-Nazi and anti-Semitic speeches (recorded in the *Anglo-German Review*) made at its meetings by Admiral Domvile, Captain Ramsay, Richard Findlay and others. In an understated way, Stewart said he had enough evidence that 'the leaders of The Link stand for a philosophy vastly different from mine', and advised that the PPU should steer clear of them. He then appealed directly to Morris:

> In all friendship, respect and humility I appeal to Stuart Morris, and to my other comrades who are members of The Link, to read the sentiments I have quoted above and to judge for themselves the mentality they reveal.

As war approached, therefore, the peace movement was in disarray, divided between those who saw no harm in joining with fascist anti-war groups and those who saw this as a betrayal of PPU ideals. After war broke out on 3 September, one might have expected such dissensions to disappear and fascist connections to cease. But it was not to be.

The 'phoney war'

As we have seen, the immediate reaction of many of the pro-Nazi groups at the outbreak of war was to disband. This move was mainly for public consumption, however, and many of their more prominent members continued with activities of various kinds, and sought for other forms in which to survive. One of their main tactics was to encourage their members to join the PPU. In October, for example, Special Branch noted that 'recently, nearly all the members of the Nordic League have joined the Peace Pledge Union'. This was a cynical move, they said, as 'the NL is no more pacifist than Hitler' (TNA HO 144/22454). In November, Liddell of MI5 stated: 'We have conclusive evidence that Nordic League members were advised to join the PPU en masse.' He noted also that there were close links between the PPU and both The Link and British Union. He felt that 'it would be in the interests of the rank-and-file members of the PPU itself that this penetration of the PPU by the Fascists should be brought to public notice' (TNA HO 45/25392). Other sources tell us that 'literature and membership forms' of the PPU had been handed round at recent meetings of British Union (TNA KV 2/494).

The British People's Party, and its offshoot the British Council for a Christian Settlement in Europe, did continue; and the presence of Lord Tavistock and Ben Greene in both of them ensured the adherence of a good number of members of the PPU. Indeed, the stated aim of the British Council for a Christian Settlement in Europe (BCCSE) was, as set out in a message to all members of the BPP, to approach, with a view to collaboration, 'organisations like the Peace Pledge Union, Fellowship of Reconciliation, Social Credit organisations, Co-operative Guilds, religious organisations and any others likely to be sympathetic' (TNA KV 2/494). In October 1939 the BCCSE produced a leaflet entitled *A Statement on the European Situation*. The signatories contained many of the usual suspects – Tavistock, Beckett, Greene, Philby, Gordon-Canning, C.E. Carroll, Dr Meyrick Booth, the Earl of Mar, Sir Alliott Verdon Roe, Hugh Ross Williamson – but also leading members of the PPU, including the Revd Donald Soper, Eric Gill and Laurence Housman. At the first meeting of the BCCSE on 14 October, at which, as we have seen in the last chapter, the movement's true colours became clear, 'the Peace Pledge Union was much in evidence' (*SE*, 15/10/40).

Throughout the 'phoney war' period, members of the PPU continued to dabble with the BCCSE and other questionable peace groups. At the large public meeting held by the BCCSE in April 1940, for example, it was calculated that about 40 per cent of those present were members of the PPU (TNA TS 27/522/27). None of them seem to have realised what the ILP newspaper the *New Leader* (which itself was violently anti-war) pointed out on 18 April 1940: that the only reason the fascists were anti-war was because 'the British Government is engaged in war with Fascist Germany', and because to them 'Hitler is a hero'. The *New Leader* believed that co-operation by its readers with fascists or with 'Hitler-defending pacifists' (by which they presumably meant the PPU) would not assist the cause of peace, and would harm the cause of Socialism. It is nevertheless significant that leading pacifist members of the ILP and the Labour Party, such as the MPs John McGovern and Richard Rapier Stokes, still saw no problem in collaborating with more 'fascist' anti-war campaigners.

The association of the PPU with 'fascist' anti-war groups was by now leading to considerable public disaffection from the movement. At a meeting of the PPU in Morecambe on 1 May, at which Lord Tavistock was the main speaker, there was considerable heckling. Tavistock, declaring that 'the Peace Pledge Union was on the side of God', asserted that 'financiers in this country are out to smash Hitler's trade system, a system with which they cannot compete', and that the Jews had to some extent brought persecution on themselves. This no doubt dumbfounded the audience, which had come to attend what they thought was an ordinary PPU meeting. Amid the heckling, one woman shouted: 'You go and live with Hitler and take your Peace Pledge Union with you' (TNA KV 2/793, and *MHV*, 8/5/40).

In the meantime, some rogue elements within the PPU were paddling in even murkier waters. One example of this is the booklet 'Plan of Campaign', published by the PPU in early 1940. It was the re-publication of a piece produced some years before by the Dutch anarcho-pacifist Bart de Ligt (who had died in 1938) which gave advice as to how to make a war impossible by 'direct individual action':

> Render useless for mobilisation and war the telephone, telegraph, wireless etc [...] Render useless bridges, railways etc [...] by practising the most effective non-co-operation, boycott and sabotage.
>
> (TNA INF 1/139)

When the press drew attention to the existence of this pamphlet, it was withdrawn from sale in London, but could still be bought in Manchester, Birmingham and other provincial cities.

This was a mere aberration, however. Far more serious was the impression given to the popular mind, that the PPU was in cahoots with the fascist movements, and therefore, in this wartime situation, potentially treasonable. The pacifists seem to have reached this position mainly through a single-mindedness in relation to the pursuit of peace that rendered them blinkered to the dangers of their associations. One must nevertheless bear in mind that there were, within and without the PPU, a number of sharks swimming among the minnows.

May 1940 onwards

In July 1940 Humphrey Moore gave up the editorship of *Peace News*, becoming instead deputy editor. He was succeeded in the editor's chair by the Christian Marxist intellectual John Middleton Murry. Anyone who thought that this meant a change of policy would, however, have been mistaken. Soon, Murry was speaking of Nazism as 'the destined instrument' of European unification, and suggesting that 'National Socialism relative to any other form of society is a good thing' (Gilbert, 1992: 504). He was convinced that 'the destruction of Nazism by military victory is an end neither rational nor religious; it is the plausible name we give to our collaboration in international anarchy' (*PN*, 31/1/41). For him, the German 'new order' was 'a serious thing – possibly an enduring contribution to the economic problems of Europe', and 'if we persist in cherishing the notion, sedulously circulated by the minds in control of our propaganda machine, that the German economic "new order" is a grinding tyranny imposed by military duress – then we are preparing for ourselves a most bitter disillusionment' (*PN*, 14/3/41). All this led a commentator like George Orwell to bemoan the decline in British pacifism:

> The most interesting development of the anti-war front has been the interpenetration of the pacifist movement by Fascist ideas, especially anti-Semitism. After Dick Sheppard's death British pacifism seems to have suffered a moral collapse; it has not produced any significant gesture nor even many martyrs, and only about 15 per cent of the membership of the Peace Pledge Union now appear to be active. But many of the surviving pacifists now spin a line of thought indistinguishable from that of the Blackshirts ('Stop this Jewish War' etc), and the actual membership of the PPU and the British Union overlap to some extent.
> (Orwell, 1941)

The authorities, too, were already becoming disquieted by Murry's editorship. A Home Office report on the previous six months, produced in December 1941, read:

> Some concern was felt over the pro-German tone of some articles in *Peace News* (the weekly organ of the Peace Pledge Union), mainly from the pen of Mr Middleton Murry.
> (TNA HO 45/25747)

Peace News continued in the same mode throughout the war, with articles by Murry, Hugh Ross Williamson and others justifying Hitler's invasion of Prague, bad-mouthing the Poles and attacking the 'warmongers' Churchill and Beaverbrook. It also developed some new variants on the theme. With Laval's return to power as Head of Government of France in April 1942, Murry and his contributors appear to have been bowled over by the vision of a former left-wing pacifist governing a European nation. On 17 April Murry's editorial characterised Pétain and Laval as 'loyal Frenchmen trying to save their country according to their lights', and dismissed the idea that Laval was a 'sinister villain'; on 24 April 'A Pacifist Commentary' deplored the 'flood of almost hysterical abuse which has been let loose on Laval', and pointed out that his 'career as a responsible and realistic French politician will bear examination better than his rivals', and that 'another point worth mentioning is that Laval is essentially a pacifist'. This theme continued through the months that followed. Similarly, in 1942 a series of pro-Japanese articles appeared over a number of months, with Ethel Mannin in the vanguard. On 22 May her article 'Why Men Hate' dismissed all stories of Japanese atrocities: 'Does anyone for a moment suppose that if the Japanese were on our side they would be anything but a chivalrous and lovable people?' Mannin was obsessed by what she saw as the fabrication of atrocity stories by the West. In an article on 14 August 1942 she returned to the theme of the Jews:

> Strong feeling, both among intellectuals and the masses, can always be aroused over the Nazi treatment of Jews, even over the most unsubstantiated stories, whereas what the British and the Jews, jointly, did to the Palestine Arabs in recent years left them cold. But some of us interested in the Arab nationalist cause have plenty of fully authenticated stories of atrocities in that connection every bit as hair-raising as anything Mr Brendan Bracken or Cardinal Hinsley can think up about the Poles.

Indeed, she said, an American journalist friend of hers had sat *in London* writing a piece of reportage on the 'Nazi organized "pogroms"' of the Jews in Germany, which was entirely based on material collected in Britain. 'All this atrocity and retribution propaganda', she wrote, 'should be regarded by pacifists as evil and dangerous.'

Meanwhile, by mid-1941 the Duke of Bedford had been welcomed to *Peace News* with open arms, and became one of its leading contributors. On 31 October 1941 he produced the lead article, attacking those ministers of religion who supported the war, entitled 'Why the Churches Have Betrayed their Master'. This article was given almost all the first page of the journal. On 7 November a review of his pamphlet 'What a Game!' appeared, which described it as 'perhaps the most reasonable and reasoned analysis of the actual war-situation today to be obtained anywhere'. Further major articles by Bedford, often lead articles, appeared fairly regularly in the months that followed. They contained his usual material about the faults of the Poles, Britain's responsibility for the war, the 'tyranny of international finance and Big Business', the sins of the Soviet Union, the need for Britain to repent of her past deeds towards Germany, and so on. In them Bedford, like so many other anti-Semites at the time, while deploring the Nazis' treatment of the Jews, pointed out that the Jews were in fact responsible for everything they got:

> I do not overlook the very serious provocation which many Jews have given by their avarice and extravagance when exploiting Germany's financial difficulties; by their association with commercialized vice; and by their monopolization of certain professions. I also do not overlook the part played by certain prominent Jews in that international financial system which has long enslaved the civilized world.
>
> (*PN*, 30/10/42)

Despite (or because of?) these articles, in 1943 Bedford was elected to the Council of the PPU. Meanwhile, members of the PPU were getting involved with the other anti-war groups that grew up in the second half of the war. Special Branch noted in 1943, for example, that though a party like the British National Party attracted many fascists and right-wingers, it also attracted many pacifists who thought that its anti-war stance was pacifist. *Peace News* did not merely print articles by Bedford; it also carried advertisements for his pamphlets and collected speeches, and also for Aldred's journal *The Word*. Murry, moreover, at one point seriously overstepped the mark by attempting to distribute the Duke's publications overseas. In June 1941 MI5 intercepted a letter to Murry from Professor Rudmore-Brown, Professor of French at Trinity College, Dublin. In it, Rudmore-Brown said that Murry need not worry any more about getting the Duke of Bedford's pamphlets to Ireland, as he, Rudmore-Brown, had now received copies of them. MI5, while feeling that the Duke's 'effusions' were not of any great harm in Britain, because people knew him as 'a pacifist and a crank', were nevertheless 'most disquieted' to find that 'attempts [were] being made to pass his propaganda material to Eire and to the USA' (TNA KV 2/793).

As the war continued, MI5 received a number of apparently unconnected bits of information which implicated Murry in activities linked to the extreme pro-Nazi Right. In August 1942, for example, he figured on the MI5 list of prominent members of the British National Party (BNP), along with such luminaries of the Right as Major-General Fuller, Norman Hay, Collin Brooks, Hugh Ross Williamson and Ben Greene (TNA HO 144/21845). He had originally been quoted, at the meeting forming the BNP on 22 May 1942, as a potential major supporter of the movement, and he was already known as a member of the Constitutional Research Association. Later on, in 1944, it was noted that he was present at private lunches involving Admiral Domvile, General Fuller, Major Harry Edmonds, the Earl of Portsmouth (the former Lord Lymington) and others. He was also keeping up his connection with Ben Greene. In May 1944 he arranged for Greene to address a series of PPU meetings on the subject of English liberties, and inserted a statement about these in the issue of *Peace News* for 19 May (TNA KV 2/492).

His choice of company was unfortunate. MI5, summing up his wartime role in 1945, made it clear that he had been under observation by Section F3 (the anti-terrorist section) for some time, and described him as not being 'purely pacifist':

> Middleton Murry, whose great intellectual gifts enabled him to wield a vitriolic pen as editor of 'Peace News', was in 1941 a foundation member of Major Harry Edmonds' Constitutional Research Association and he maintained close contact throughout the war with its leading members – Edmonds, Major-General J.F.C. Fuller, the Earl of Portsmouth, Admiral Sir Barry Domvile and the rest. How far his pacifism was coloured by participation in their Fascist way of thinking is a matter of doubt; but that it was so coloured to some extent was clear from much of what he wrote and said.
>
> (TNA KV 4/58)

The only other leading PPU member to cause concern to the authorities in these years was Stuart Morris, but his 'misdeeds' appear to have been caused more by a lack of understanding of the ways of the world. In August 1942 he got involved in a matter that was treated very seriously by the authorities. He had for some time been interested in Indian affairs, and in particular in the role of Gandhi. He was contacted by Thomas Williams, an employee of the India Office, whose duties included the collection of secret and confidential waste paper for pulping. Williams offered to supply information to Morris from this material which could serve as ammunition in his Indian campaign. Morris accepted the offer. When this was discovered, Morris was charged under the Official Secrets Act, tried *in camera* in December 1942 and condemned to nine months in prison. The Council of the PPU distanced itself from him at this stage. The following resolution was passed for publication at a meeting on 23 January 1943 (though a minority of members of Council were unwilling to accept his resignation as general secretary) (TNA KV 4/58):

> Owing to the fact that the trial was held in secret, the Council is not in possession of the defence offered by Stuart Morris. From the facts before it, when the matter was discussed at its last meeting, it considered that his action had been both improper and indiscreet, and, while not suspecting him of any unworthy motive, wishes it to be known that he acted entirely on his own initiative and without the knowledge or consent of the Council and officers of the Union.
>
> (*PN*, 26/2/43)

In this case, MI5 was more charitable than the PPU. While remarking that this case showed 'how a man to whom it would be natural to attribute high principles may be prompted by an interest in political matters and by strong and unorthodox opinions on them to commit a serious offence', it noted that he had not solicited the information, and that he had not, after receiving it, made any disclosure of it, 'though between August and December 1942 he had had plenty of time to do so had he wished'. Nevertheless, MI5 came to this general conclusion: 'that it is unwise to rely on the honourable conduct, even in wartime, of high-principled persons associated with branches of minority opinion' (TNA KV 4/58).

Morris was indeed highly-principled, but his besetting fault was an inability to perceive the true nature of those he associated with. Even after the war we find him in September 1945 at a meeting with the Duke of Bedford, Cola Ernest Carroll, John Beckett, Robert Gordon-Canning and several others, discussing the setting-up of a new political organisation, of which they intended him to be chairman. Beckett and Bedford were already heavily occupied in reviving the BPP, but this other planned organisation seems, from the names of those discussing it, to have been seen as an overarching body containing members from a number of former right-wing organisations, an adjunct to the BPP something on the model of the old BCCSE. Morris appears to have been wanted as some kind of front-man, because, as MI5 surmised, 'whatever his faults, [he] is not regarded by the general public as a Fascist' (TNA KV 2/1519). In the event, neither the organisation nor the chairmanship materialised, but the occasion does show just how, before, during and after the war, the unsuspecting Morris could be used by specious crypto-fascists who used the peace cause as a cover. Compared with him, Murry was a much more knowledgeable operator.

This study of the peace movement's links with pro-Nazi movements and ideas should not have blinded us to the fact that a very large number of pacifists, and indeed of members of the PPU, had little to do with such causes, and that many did in fact protest strongly at what various prominent individuals had been saying and doing. It is also clear that those pacifist individuals who dabbled in pro-Nazi propaganda had very little real effect upon events. Indeed, all they succeeded in doing was to compromise and weaken the principled anti-war message, which might otherwise have been more effective. To that extent, it may even have been the case that they helped the war effort. What this particular study has shown is, yet again, what a tangle of motives lay at the base of so much of the opposition to the war.

Bibliography

Books and articles

Bell, Clive (1938), *Warmongers* (London: PPU).

Booth, Meyrick (1937), *Peace and Power* (Letchworth: Wardman).

Ceadel, Martin (1980), *Pacifism in Britain 1914–1945* (Oxford: Clarendon).

Gilbert, Mark (1992), 'Pacifist Attitudes to Nazi Germany, 1936–45', *Journal of Contemporary History*, 27, 3, 493–511.

Griffiths, Richard (1980), *Fellow Travellers of the Right: British Enthusiasts for Nazi Germany, 1933–39* (London: Constable).

Lewis, Jeremy (2010), *Shades of Greene: One Generation of an English Family* (London: Jonathan Cape).

Lukowitz, David C. (1974), 'British Pacifists and Appeasement', *Journal of Contemporary History*, 9, 1, 115–27.

Orwell, George (1941), 'London Letter' to *Partisan Review*, 3 January, in *The Collected Essays, Journalism and Letters of George Orwell* (London: Secker and Warburg, 1968).

Documents

The National Archives (TNA)

CRIM 1/1736
HO 45/25392, HO 45/25747, HO 144/21845, HO 144/22454
INF 1/139
KV 2/489, KV 2/492, KV 2/494, KV 2/793, KV 2/836, KV 2/1519, KV 4/58
TS 27/522

Newspapers and journals

Action
Morecambe and Heysham Visitor (MHV)
New Leader (NL)
News Chronicle
Peace News (PN)
Sunday Express (SE)

PART III
Defence Regulation 18b and its after-effects

5

THE WATERSHED

The arrests of May–June 1940 and their aftermath

The wave of arrests which started in May–June 1940 created a defining moment in the lives of a great many people – not only those who were imprisoned, but also the many who remained free, but who thereafter felt the shadow of internment hanging over them. These arrests governed the actions and thoughts of most of the people whose wartime experiences will be described in this book.

The government had, of course, had the power to make such arrests for a long time before this. Defence Regulation 18B, which had been passed on 1 September 1939 and amended on 23 November, stated that the Home Secretary could order the detention of any person suspected to be 'of hostile origin or associations or to have been recently concerned in acts prejudicial to the public safety or to the defence of the realm or in the preparation or instigation of such acts'. Only a handful of British nationals were arrested at the outbreak of the war in September 1939, however, none of them being of great significance. Most of the action taken at this time was against foreign nationals known to have been politically active. Movements like British Union (BU) were allowed to continue very much as before, and the 'phoney war' period saw a great deal of activity by many figures on the pro-Nazi Right, much of it secret (though monitored by such bodies as MI5 and Special Branch), but much, also, in the light of day.

Suddenly, in May 1940, new emergency legislation was passed. On the evening of 22 May the Privy Council passed a new Defence Regulation 18B (1A), which was put into effect the next day, without having been made public or scrutinised by the House of Commons. This new version of the Regulation, significantly, looked not to people's actions in the past, but to their potentiality for action in the future. Political organisations were particularly targeted. The Home Secretary could order the detention of anyone he believed to be a member of an organisation which was either subject to foreign influence or control, or of which the persons in control 'have or have had associations with persons concerned in the government of, or sympathies with the system of government of, any Power with which His Majesty is at war'. This was because of:

> a danger of the utilisation of the organisation for purposes prejudicial to the public safety, the defence of the realm, the maintenance of public order, the efficient prosecution of any war in which His Majesty may be engaged, or the maintenance of supplies or services essential to the life of the community.

Essentially, the changes in the Regulation meant that, in a time of war crisis, preventive detention was deemed necessary, based on people's *potential* for subversive activity rather than on what they might already have done. The main organisation targeted by such legislation was clearly British Union.

Why was there this sudden change of policy? The ostensible trigger for such action had been the arrest of the American Embassy code clerk Tyler Kent, and the revelation that he had been conveying confidential documents to members of the Right Club. It was believed that such information was being passed on to the enemy. MI5 had been infiltrating and monitoring the Right Club's activities for some time, however, and the suspicion is that the raid had been engineered at this specific time because public perceptions of the dangers of Fifth Column activities (sparked by the belief that Holland had been betrayed by such inner subversion) were at their height, and because a scare would provide MI5 (which had been pressing for some time for more stringent action against the 'enemy within') with the opportunity to persuade the government to act. There is no doubt that, in the parlous situation faced by the Allied armies and with fears of what might happen, the British people and the government were in a state of jitters. The Right Club debacle may have tipped the balance; but the clampdown would probably have taken place in any case. It is interesting to note that a week before, on 15 May, Winston Churchill, within five days of coming to power, had asked the War Cabinet, on the basis of a report on the 'Fifth Column Menace', to agree to an extensive round-up of 'enemy aliens and suspect persons' in Britain. The Home Secretary, Sir John Anderson, had opposed premature action (and merely proposed, as politicians tend to do, the setting-up of a committee). Churchill nevertheless saw internment as a national necessity. The Tyler Kent affair proved to be an opportunity for Churchill's wishes to prevail. One of the immediate problems to be faced was that of the difficulty, under then current legislation, of proving previous subversive activities on the part of those to be arrested; this was one reason why the new legislation referring to the potential for such activity was rushed through.

Of those arrested on 23 and 24 May, apart from foreign nationals the vast majority were officials of BU, headed of course by Sir Oswald Mosley. Other prominent right-wingers were also detained, however, including Captain Ramsay of the Right Club, and Ben Greene and John Beckett of the British People's Party (BPP). Over the next few months many others were arrested, including major activists from the various anti-war groups, such as Admiral Domvile of The Link and his associates Captain George Pitt-Rivers and Cola Ernest Carroll. The vast majority of the British detainees were, however, rank-and-file Fascists.

At first the detainees were housed in ordinary prisons – Brixton, Stafford and Walton (Liverpool) for the men, Holloway for the women. Soon, however, it became clear that the number of detentions had far exceeded what had originally been planned for, and a series of camps were organised, often consisting of a number of streets surrounded by security barbed wire and towers, or other suitable sites such as the camp at Ascot, which was housed in the winter quarters of the Bertram

Mills Circus. Eventually it was decided, because of fear at what might happen on the mainland in the event of an invasion, to set up camps on the Isle of Man (though a number of prominent detainees remained in Brixton and Holloway prisons). The most well-known of the Isle of Man camps was Peveril Camp at Peel, which consisted of some large holiday boarding houses and terraces of smaller houses.

The total number of 'fascist' detentions under DR 18B and DR 18B (1A) has been calculated as 753 – small, when compared with the 28,000 enemy aliens detained, but very substantial nevertheless (Simpson, 1992: 190). Though further detention orders were made over the next few years, the majority of rank-and-file BU detainees were released within the first year. By the end of 1941 only 200 BU members were still in detention, and this fell to 130 in Spring 1942. Some of the more prominent figures remained, however, and in early 1942 a policy decision was made to continue detention indefinitely for Sir Oswald Mosley, Lady Mosley, Captain Ramsay, Captain Robert Gordon-Canning, Admiral Domvile, John Beckett and several other leading figures. In March 1943 it was again decided to continue detention in these cases. By late 1943, however, most of these people were released – for example, Domvile in July, Gordon-Canning in August, Beckett in October and Arnold Leese in December. In November Mosley himself was released, for reasons of ill health. Captain Ramsay, however, had to wait till September 1944, and some of the more extreme rank-and-file – including Richard Findlay of the Right Club and A.T.V. Hepburn-Ruston of BU (father of Audrey Hepburn) were not released until April 1945 (Simpson, 1992: 382–96).

DR 18B detainees had the right to appeal to the Home Secretary. These appeals were heard by the Advisory Committee, a body with members who could be described as 'pillars of society', initially presided over by Norman Birkett KC. Soon, when its load (which included aliens) became too great, the Advisory Committee divided into four panels with considerably more members. Much of the information we have on the previous activities of some of these detainees comes from the records of the Advisory Committee, which appear on these individuals' Home Office files. The Committee sometimes found itself at odds with MI5, which deplored what it saw as the Committee's 'liberal' attitude to the detainees, while Birkett and his colleagues were convinced that MI5 was 'illiberal, disorganised and incompetent' (Simpson, 1992: 285). By the end of October 1940 the Advisory Committee had recommended release in 199 cases out of the 317 it had heard. MI5 had, however, disagreed in 111 of these cases, and tended to get its way. It was at this stage that things came to a head, and it was decided that MI5 should no longer have an automatic veto over the Committee's decisions. It was for this reason that so many detainees were released by early 1941 (Simpson, 1992: 294–6).

In rare cases detainees had recourse to the courts, but uncertainty as to the precise legal reasons for detention made judgments difficult. Most such cases were unsuccessful, but there was one which was outstandingly successful – that of Ben Greene. Greene, who had been released mainly because of errors made by the Security Services, is of particular interest to us because of his later activities, as is Aubrey Lees, who was released on the advice of the Advisory Committee. These two men's careers both before and after detention and release show just how arbitrary the judgments could be in such cases.

Aubrey Lees

Aubrey T.O. Lees was a colonial civil servant who had served in Palestine as Assistant District Commissioner for the Jaffa District. There he had come to his superiors' attention as being in strong sympathy with the Palestinian Arabs, and opposed both to the Jews and to British policy in the Mandate. In December 1938 he was granted three months' leave in England, 'because he had been engaging in anti-Semitic and pro-Arab activities' (TNA HO 45/25728/235). In January 1939 the Colonial Office offered him a post in Hadhramaut in the Aden Protectorate, but he refused it, because he wished to return to Palestine.

The Colonial Office does not seem to have known what to do with this awkward customer. During the London Palestine Conference, which took place between 7 February and 17 March, Lees was in close contact with the Arab delegation, and on 24 February he was hauled in to an interview with the Colonial Office's Director of Personnel, and accused of helping the Arab Centre. His leave was extended, with full salary, for two months from 7 March. Month by month thereafter, the leave was further extended. In June he was informed by the Colonial Office that his employment was under consideration. This convinced him, as he wrote to a friend, Mrs Nina Elliott, that 'this Jew-ridden government' would probably sack him (TNA HO 25728/105). However, the extensions to his leave continued. War broke out in September, but made little difference to his situation. In December he was finally offered a post in the Gold Coast, which he accepted. He was appointed, subject to a medical certificate. By late March 1940 he had not yet provided this certificate. When it was finally produced, his departure was arranged for 7 June, and he was told that the Secretary of State would brook no further postponement. In May, however, he requested a further postponement, owing to baggage delays to his possessions from Palestine. This game might have continued ad infinitum, but it was overtaken by events. On 22 June he was arrested and taken to Brixton prison (LHCMA: Lees).

Why was he arrested? And why was he so reluctant to leave Britain? The answer to both questions lies in his activities in London in this period. Like many pro-Arabists at the time, he was not just anti-Zionist but also violently anti-Semitic, and soon after his arrival in London began to frequent the extreme circles around the Nordic League, the Imperial Fascist League, The Link and the BPP. He attended a number of their meetings, becoming close to major figures including Margaret Bothamley, Lord Ronald Graham and Arnold Leese. He handed on to these movements details of alleged British brutality and Jewish atrocities in Palestine. He had developed a great admiration for Nazi Germany, as is shown not only by these activities, but also by some very revealing letters he wrote at the time. Special Branch became aware of these views and activities, noting that he made 'no secret of his great admiration for the Nazi regime and openly criticizes the British Government on account of "its failure to get rid of the Jewish menace"' (TNA HO 45/25728). In mid-1939 Lees joined the Right Club. It is interesting to note that, despite his connections with all these organisations, Lees did not join BU. Indeed, Mosley seems to have regarded him as a potential liability, describing him as 'absolutely certifiable' (TNA HO 283/13).

After the outbreak of war The Link, the Nordic League and the Right Club, as we have seen, ostensibly ceased to operate. Most members faded away. There remained, however, a rump who continued with activities which were by now seditious. In a report on 16 September into the Nordic League, Special Branch reported that most of its members had decided to do nothing to prejudice the country's interests. However, Lees was singled out as being one of a small group who were 'prepared to go further', having been enlisted by Captain Ramsay for various forms of direct action, including the distribution of leaflets justifying Germany's actions and showing that World Jewry were the instigators of the war (TNA HO 144/21382). As a prominent member of the Right Club, Lees took part in negotiations between the RC and other groups with an eye to collaboration (TNA HO 144/22454). Meanwhile, he was also in demand in these circles as a speaker against the Jews and against the British actions in Palestine. On 8 November 1939 Admiral Sir Barry Domvile attended a meeting at Sir Oswald Mosley's house, attended by many luminaries of the Right including Captain Ramsay, Lord Lymington, Norman Hay, H.T. Mills and others, at which Aubrey Lees gave a 'very interesting' talk about 'atrocities in Palestine'. Domvile noted that 'he has been on extended leave for a twelvemonth', because 'he knows too much' (NMM DOM 56, 8/11/39). Lees later attended, as Domvile noted, a couple of the other meetings of representatives of the various 'patriotic societies', on 6 December 1939 and 7 February 1940.

In 1939–40, while Special Branch had been monitoring most of the activities of the right wing groups with which Lees had been associating, his name had occurred, though sporadically, among their reports. At the time of the first DR 18B arrests in May 1940, however, they decided to examine his case in a more systematic way. On 24 May, a report listed his contacts in the right-wing underworld, and commented on his pro-Nazi and anti-Semitic views and activities (TNA HO 45/25728/244). This was followed by a further report on 8 June, which among other things mentioned his membership of the Right Club. On 22 June he was arrested.

Lees appealed against his arrest, and appeared before the Advisory Committee on 19 July and 1 August. On the basis of what we have seen, the case against him would seem to have been far stronger than that against many other DR 18B detainees; but the Security Services had made a basic error in the 'Reasons for Order' they supplied to the committee. The basic ground for his arrest was stated to be membership of British Union, and activity in furtherance of its objects. Yet it was easy enough to prove that, whatever his activities in other extremist organisations, Lees had never been a member of BU. The committee, on this basis, and on the basis of his 'explanation' of his activities, recommended his release. MI5 demurred, insisting that even if he had never been a member, he had been an active supporter; also, that 'the committee had been gullible, and too ready to accept Lees's version of events' (Simpson, 1992: 305). In the event, MI5 was overruled and Lees was released on 1 October 1940, though placed under a Restriction Order, and also placed on the Suspect List of those to be arrested in the event of an invasion. The Home Secretary noted: 'I agree that we must let him out but I shall not be at all surprised if we have to lock him up again very soon.' Within a month Lees appeared to prove the Home Secretary right. On 10 November Lees attended, with one or two others, a meeting at the flat of Molly Stanford of the Right Club (Stanford having been released in September). This meeting's main purpose had been to discuss 'means of organising aid for internees of Fascist or Right-wing persuasion', and to plan a chain letter advocating peace on the lines of a suggestion from the New British Broadcasting Service (NBBS, a German station which broadcasted Nazi propaganda to Britain). At this meeting, however, Lees went further than this, proposing that they should once more start advertising the NBBS, as they had done in the period before the May arrests. Stanford opposed this, saying that there was now the danger of a five-year sentence for such activity. One of those present, however, was an MI5 agent, and Lees's indiscretion was reported back. Within a week the Home Office recommended that Lees should be re-interned, on the basis that his proposal had been 'to assist the enemy by giving currency to the enemy's propaganda' (TNA HO 45/25728). The Home Secretary, however, decided to take no action 'on the very meagre statement from an informant' (Simpson, 1992: 298–307).

So Lees remained free. However, Lord Lloyd, the Colonial Secretary, who on Lees's release in October had informed him that his appointment in the Gold Coast still stood, now changed his mind, and on 10 December Lees was informed that Lloyd had decided that he must retire from the Colonial Service. Moreover, his Restriction Order remained in place, and he remained on the Suspect List for the rest of the war. MI5 continued to keep an eye on him, and he maintained contact with the extreme Right (for example, corresponding extensively with Domvile and others). In the last year of the war he was to play a leading role in the revived British People's Party and in the negotiations for a National Front after Victory. He was one of William Joyce's correspondents during the latter's time in prison in late 1945, prior to his execution.

Ben Greene

Ben Greene is a very good example of the way in which over-eagerness on the part of MI5 could lead to the case against an individual being completely botched, even though in abstract it would seem to have been entirely justified. Greene was heavily involved in questionable activities before his arrest, and continued in the same vein after his release; yet for historians of DR 18B his detention has too often been seen, on the basis of the case made for his release, as an example of a miscarriage of justice pure and simple. As others more closely involved have pointed out, however, Greene escaped detention mainly because the authorities had 'over-egged the cake', not only using an agent provocateur in order to entrap him, but also accusing him of far graver actions than he had in fact committed. The simple case against him, based on properly verifiable evidence, would have sufficed to justify his detention (Hart, 1974).

Ben Greene, a cousin of Graham Greene, shortly after the First World War had become a member both of the Labour Party and of the Society of Friends. Having worked for Clement Attlee in his successful Limehouse election campaign in 1922 (where he worked alongside his future collaborator John Beckett), he joined the Independent Labour Party (ILP) in 1924, and in the same year was appointed by Ramsay Macdonald as a political secretary in the new Labour administration. In 1931, and again in 1935, he stood (unsuccessfully) as Labour candidate for Gravesend. As Ben Pimlott (1977) has shown in his history of the inter-war Labour Party, Greene attained much prominence in the 1930s as the organiser of the 'Home Counties Labour Organisation', whose aim was to 'provide satisfactory representation of local constituency organisations' on the National Executive. Its success was great, and gave thereafter much more power to the local parties, but Greene was given little of the credit for this. 'Most Labour leaders', writes Pimlott, 'continued to regard him with extreme distaste. Greene's pro-German sympathies were partly responsible for this' (Pimlott, 1977: 129).

Greene had indeed gained a reputation for pro-Nazism. Pimlott, for reasons we will see later, eventually removed his original forthright mention of this from his book, merely confining himself to referring to 'his eccentric interest in Nazi Germany'. But there is no doubt that within the Labour Party Greene was considered, as his agent in Gravesend alleged, to have 'pro-Nazi sympathies'. Hugh Dalton taxed him with this, saying that he had 'made it clear on several occasions that your attitude towards the Nazi regime in Germany is not that generally adopted in the Labour Party' (Pimlott, 1977: 129).

We have already seen some of Greene's activities in the period before May 1940. However, it is worth pulling them together here, and filling them out to give a full picture. In late 1938 Greene resigned from the Labour Party because he was 'out of sympathy with the Party and its opposition to Chamberlain's policy'. He joined the Peace Pledge Union (PPU), though he had 'never been very sympathetic with it', mainly because, he said, having left the Labour Party, he felt left 'high and dry' and 'had nowhere to turn' (TNA KV 2/489). Almost immediately, he set up within the PPU his pro-Nazi 'Peace and Progressive Information Service'. In April 1939 he was one of the founder-members of Tavistock's British People's Party, becoming the treasurer. At various BPP meetings, Greene publicly declared that the party had been formed primarily to 'combat the war propaganda', but also to oppose the system of 'Usury' (a code word for 'Jewish Money Power') which underlay capitalism (TNA TS 27/522). He took a major part in the BPP's by-election campaign in Hythe in July 1939.

After the outbreak of war, when Tavistock subsumed the BPP into the wider movement the British Council for a Christian Settlement in Europe (BCCSE), Greene once more took a major part. At its first public meeting on 14 October, the press reported of Ben Greene's contribution:

> He doesn't even think that we shall win the war. Nor does he think that Hitler's invasions of Austria, Czechoslovakia or Poland were acts of aggression. He thinks Hitler was quite right.
>
> (*SE*, 15/10/39)

MI5 reports corroborate this press account, noting that Greene had described British policy as 'one of bluff and treachery', and that he had 'sneered at those who said we could not trust Hitler', declaring that 'Hitler had been justified in all he had done', and using such phrases as 'those of us who admire him [Hitler]'. One of the officers present described Greene's speech as 'certainly the most blatantly pro-Nazi public speech I have ever heard' (TNA TS 27/522).

Greene later claimed to have left the BPP in November 1939, but though there is indeed on file a letter of resignation from his treasurership, in which he cited reasons of pressure of work, this letter is misleading. It transpires that this resignation was actually caused by pressure from his bank manager, who had threatened to refuse credit to him for his firm, Kepston's, if he did not give up political activity (the letter was registered and kept, presumably as proof to the bank). Greene did not in fact leave the BPP or the BCCSE. Though he had a period in hospital in early 1940, he remained active within both bodies, as did his brother Edward and his sister Katherine (TNA KV 2/489). He continued to speak at their meetings, and at other public meetings in London and the provinces, well into 1940 (TNA TS 27/522, HO 144/21382), on a variety of topics, including the 'definite menace from Jewish capitalists' (*NET*, 20/3/40). He also wrote letters to the press advocating BCCSE policy. More importantly, he wrote the BPP's propaganda pamphlet *The Truth about this War*, published in December 1939 with a preface by John Beckett. Clement Attlee, in a letter of 23 December to Greene's wife Leslie (he was godfather to their son), described this pamphlet, which she had sent him, as 'one of the nastiest pieces of pro-Hitler propaganda that I have met for a long time' (Lewis, 2010: 228). A German translation of it, *Die Wahrheit über diesen Krieg*, was published in exactly the same format a month later, and used as propaganda by the Germans (TNA FO 371/25102).

It was hardly surprising, therefore, that Greene was included (as was Beckett) in the first wave of arrests in May 1940, as the BPP, like BU, matched perfectly the definition of a subversive organisation that was contained in Defence Regulation 18B (1A). Greene's statements, publications and activities all contributed to the case against him. (The only surprise was that Lord Tavistock was not included in the *rafle*).

Yet Greene was eventually released after a series of hearings had ended with his order being suspended. Why was this?

The authorities had made a basic error. Instead of arresting Greene because of his membership of the BPP and the activities we have seen, they went much further, his 'Reasons for Order' being erroneously given as 'acts prejudicial'. On the basis of evidence provided by a rogue MI5 agent provocateur, Harald Kurtz, to whom Greene had spoken in March and April, he was accused of 'secret actions and intentions' which included subversive activities, communications with Germany and asking Kurtz 'to tell his friends in Germany that there were men in this country ready to take over the government after a German victory, men trained in and filled with the proper spirit of National Socialism'. In other words, Greene was being accused of being a traitor. The history of Greene's various interviews and appeals, extending over many months, has been examined in detail by Brian Simpson. Suffice it to say that Kurtz was found to be extremely unreliable and the case against Greene to be seriously flawed. On 9 January 1942 he was released. (It is interesting to note that, though the evidence against Beckett had also relied on statements by Kurtz, no move was made to suspend the order against him (Simpson, 1992: 341–75).)

Shortly after his release, in March 1942, Greene brought an action for libel and false imprisonment against the former Home Secretary Sir John Anderson. This was doomed to failure. As Brian Simpson puts it:

> Greene, who was a poor witness, was presented as a blameless pacifist, whom no reasonable person could believe to be 'of hostile associations'. In cross-examination the Attorney-General had no difficulty in showing that his political activities, both before and during the war, could easily be viewed as showing support for Nazi Germany.
>
> (Simpson, 1992: 374)

Greene's counsel withdrew the action, and costs of £1,243 were awarded against Greene.

Imprisonment seems merely to have confirmed Greene in his views. MI5 noted in August 1942 that, while still in Brixton, he had been discussing 'the promotion of a new political party', and that in the months since his release he had already been in touch with 'other well-known persons of extreme Right-wing sympathies'. There was no doubt, they concluded, that he was already 'actively dabbling in politics' (TNA KV 2/491). This involvement, as we shall see, was to remain constant throughout the rest of the war.

The effect of imprisonment upon the detainees

On the whole the detention regime was spartan, but bearable. In 1940 the British Union detainees, though many were at first confused and disheartened, were soon being organised and encouraged along fascist lines by powerful personalities among them, while the authorities made no attempt to deter such activities (no doubt because they helped to create orderly camps). At Ascot, the initial organisation was provided by Tommy Moran, the ex-boxer who had stood as BU candidate at the Silvertown by-election in 1940, and had fleetingly taken over the reins as Acting Leader of BU in May 1940 after Mosley's arrest, only to be arrested himself shortly thereafter. Moran's systems were, however, fairly 'conservative', and were soon overtaken in the camps by the more radical policies of Charlie Watts, former organiser of the BU London Cab Drivers Group, who founded the suitably named 'Hail Mosley and Fuck 'Em All Association', which rallied many of the formerly disheartened into a coherent body dedicated to keeping the 'sacred flame' alive (Macklin, 2007: 14–17). So successful were these activities, and the camaraderie that they inspired, that contrary to the government's expectations BU members became, as MI5 commented, 'more set and hardened in their political convictions than when they were detained' (TNA KV 4/58). This was to have considerable importance after their release.

While the more working-class elements within BU were thus being cemented together by their common experience, leading figures from further up the social scale were likewise finding new friendships, and being strengthened in their convictions. Ben Greene, for example, met Captain Ramsay in Brixton Prison, and was so bowled over, that after the latter's release he saw a great deal of him, believing him to be 'the leader whom this country needed and the political figure who best embodied the principles which the English Nationalist

Association [Greene's new movement] had at heart'. He spent much of his time, in late 1944 and early 1945, acting in Ramsay's interests, having Ramsay to stay at his house for at least half of each week, and visiting Ramsay's constituency to try to safeguard his position with regard to re-election. In a letter addressed to Ramsay's constituents in the *Peeblesshire Advertiser*, written on 23 November 1944, he described, from his observation of Ramsay in prison, 'his courage, his bearing and his upright dignity under all circumstances'. He even, on Ramsay's advice, sent his son to Eton (with Ramsay exerting his influence, from Brixton, to get him accepted)! Ramsay and Robert Gordon-Canning, too, had become firm friends, and were to see a great deal of each other after their release. Admiral Domvile, who had made good new friends in Brixton, felt, on receiving news of his release in July 1943, that he had deserted his comrades (NMM DOM 56, 29/7/43). He spent much of the next few weeks going back to visit them. While in prison he had developed a Jewish conspiracy theory whereby a body he called 'Judmas' was set on world domination (and had of course in the meantime conspired to bring about his, Domvile's, downfall). He declared, 'I have little doubt that Judmas was the real arbiter of one's fate as an 18B' (Domvile, 1947: 105).

Domvile provides a good example of the narrow range of contacts which ex-detainees tended to have in the outside world. Though on his release he did not immediately participate in overt right-wing activity, his social contacts over the next few months were almost exclusively former right-wing activists from a variety of circles. For example, he invited to meals at his house, on various occasions, Norman Hay, Commander Woollard of The Link, Mrs Ramsay, Anne van Lennep (one of the leading figures in the Right Club's subversive activities in early 1940), Quentin Joyce (William Joyce's brother), Mrs Muriel Whinfield (former BU parliamentary candidate and DR 18B detainee), Commandant Mary Allen ('pioneer policewoman of the world' and a BU enthusiast), Sir Ernest Bennett MP (of the Right Club), H.T. ('Bertie') Mills, Major Hammond Foot of the British Democratic Party, and many others. Among those he corresponded with were Aubrey Lees, Arnold Leese and Collin Brooks. He also visited, or lunched in central London with, various other luminaries of the Right. Some of these were new acquaintances, to whom he appears to have been attracted because of their having had similar experiences to his own. On 30 August 1943, for example, he lunched at the Isola Bella restaurant in Frith Street with Gerald Hamilton and Monsignor Barton Brown. Hamilton had been imprisoned under DR 18B 'for attempting to promote peace on terms favourable to the enemy'. Monsignor Barton Brown, a Catholic cleric, had known Hamilton since the early 1920s, and had been involved with him in the activities that had led to his detention. Domvile's conversation over lunch with Hamilton and Barton Brown followed the usual pattern of mutual commiseration and indignation (NMM DOM 56).

Domvile seems at this stage above all to have been aggrieved and seeking the company of fellow spirits. As we shall see, however, he would before long be prepared once more to participate in group activities of a less innocuous kind. His opinions remained as intransigent as ever. In this he was typical of many ex-detainees.

It would be wrong, however, to think of there being two exclusive groups of ex-detainees – the rank-and-file BU members and the middle-class 'nobs'. The parties and dances given for ex-DR 18Bs in 1945 brought together people from both ends of the spectrum, whether detainees or sympathisers – from Lady Pearson, the Earl of Mar, Sir Barry Domvile, Captain Ramsay and Captain Robert Gordon-Canning to East End figures like Alf Flockhart, Arthur Robert Beavan, Robert Dunlop, Charlie Watts and Tommy Moran. The fact is, their common experience brought them all together without reference to class.

The continuing contacts between former detainees of all kinds, together with the stiffening of their resolve caused by the experience of detention and by their continuing sense of injustice, would have seemed fertile ground for further political activity; but as we shall see in the next chapter the future for such activity was to be very mixed.

Bibliography

Books, articles and interviews

Domvile, Admiral Sir Barry (1947), *From Admiral to Cabin Boy* (London: The Boswell Publishing Company).

Hart (1974): Conversation of the author with Sir Herbert Hart (formerly of MI5) and Lady Hart (née Jenifer Fischer Williams, formerly the private secretary to Alexander Maxwell, Permanent Under-Secretary at the Home Office at the time of the Greene affair).

Lewis, Jeremy (2010), *Shades of Greene: One Generation of an English Family* (London: Jonathan Cape).

Macklin, Graham (2007), *Very Deeply Dyed in Black: Sir Oswald Mosley and the Resurrection of British Fascism after 1945* (London and New York: I.B. Tauris).

Pimlott, Ben (1977), *Labour and the Left in the 1930s* (Cambridge: Cambridge University Press).

Simpson, A.W. Brian (1992), *In the Highest Degree Odious: Detention without Trial in Wartime Britain* (Oxford: Oxford University Press).

Documents

The National Archives (TNA)

FO 371/25102
HO 45/25728, HO 144/21382, HO 144/22454, HO 283/13
KV 2/489, KV 2/491, KV 4/58
TS 27/522

Liddell Hart Centre for Military Archives, King's College London (LHCMA)

A.T.O. Lees Papers (Lees)

National Maritime Museum (NMM)

Domvile diary, DOM 56

Newspapers

Northamptonshire Evening Telegraph (NET)
Peeblesshire Advertiser
Sunday Express (SE)

6

THE RE-EMERGENCE OF EXTREME RIGHT-WING MOVEMENTS IN BRITAIN, 1940–5

After the arrests of May–July 1940, the scope for any continuance of organised right-wing activity of the kind undertaken up to this time became extremely limited. One might have presumed that this situation would continue for the duration of the war; but gradually various forms of political activity began once more to emerge (though the activists concerned did remain a beleaguered minority).

By early 1942, as we have seen, the majority of DR 18B detainees had been released. What became of them from then on? Though for most of the British Union (BU) detainees their Fascist beliefs had been enhanced rather than discouraged by their incarceration, hardly surprisingly most of them failed to convert this into any kind of political action once they had been released, particularly given the ever-present prospect of further detention. At this stage, they stuck together mainly because of their shared experiences and views.

The Security Services had some concerns, however, about a grouping of middle-class BU ex-detainees which formed itself in 1941–2 around the influential figure of Derek Stuckey, formerly BU District Leader of the Combined English Universities. When Stuckey was detained in June 1940, his wife Gladys (also a keen BU member) had continued to run their farm at Three Mile Cross, near Reading. There, in March 1941, she was joined by ex-detainee Heather Donovan (TNA KV 2/1221), former Women's District Leader for Westminster (and wife of Brian Donovan, the Assistant Director General of BU, who was not to be released until November 1944). In September 1941 Stuckey was released, and in June 1942 Howard Biggs, a close associate of Stuckey's as former BU Assistant District Leader (Propaganda) Oxford, joined them all at the farm (giving it as his address to the authorities). Gradually, a larger group of ex-detainees tended to gather at the farm, from 1942 until the end of the war. MI5 described them as mostly being young, well educated and strongly imbued with BU ideas. They included Howard Biggs, Heather Donovan, Ralph Temple Cotton (BU Regional Inspector for Devon and one of the eight persons to whom Mosley had arranged to delegate powers in certain contingencies), Eric Whittleton (a prominent member not only of BU, but also of The Link, and a frequent pre-war writer in the press against 'Organised Jewry'), Brian O'Donohue (described as being, though 'well educated', also 'fanatical, aggressive and offensive'), and two local men, Percy Bates (former Chief Organiser for the BU in Reading) and his son Cyril Bates (BU candidate in Reading Municipal elections in 1938) (TNA HO 45/25722).

A close eye was kept on this group. It was noted that though Stuckey clearly retained his Fascist sympathies, he was 'not engaging in any political activities at the present time', and that 'though he still described himself as a hardened supporter of British Union policy, he had lost his faith in the leaders of the movement, who he thought had hoodwinked both Mosley and the rank and file', and was therefore 'determined to take no part in politics during the war'. Stuckey's 'desire for self-aggrandisement' was nevertheless noted, and also the fact that the group was 'enthusiastic, ambitious and desirous of power'. It was felt that they were capable, given their loss of faith in the leaders of the movement, of eventually forming a council, a 'nucleus from which the re-birth of the party could be achieved' under the leadership of Stuckey (TNA HO 45/25722). It is worth noting that Stuckey was one of the comparatively small number of people who figured, from 1942 onwards, on the 'Suspect List' (of those to be immediately arrested in the event of an invasion) (TNA HO 45/25568), which must have meant that the authorities suspected that a German invasion and the possibility of a German victory would nullify the reasons for his inaction. What is clear, however, is that any interest by the authorities in Stuckey's group was based mainly on concern for its future potential after the war, and that any immediate threat was perceived as occurring only if the country was invaded.

Not all groups were to remain so static, however. From 1942 onwards there had emerged, here and there, signs of more serious political activity, though, by the nature of things, this was fragmented and cautious. Initially, the main aim seems, like that of Stuckey's group, to have been to prepare for a fascist resurgence in the future, rather than to undertake subversive activities in the present. Gradually, however, this changed. Though these groups often felt constrained to hide their anti-Semitic, Fascist, or pro-Nazi character behind more bland public pronouncements (because most of the British public by now associated all 'Fascist' movements with the enemy), they continued to pursue such policies behind this facade. They also began to appeal directly to the 'peace' lobby, and at times attracted naive pacifists who failed to grasp the pro-Nazi and/or anti-Semitic presumptions that lay behind their pronouncements.

The beginnings of organised political activity, and the formation of the BNP, followed by the ENA

Whereas most ex-detainees were still keeping a low profile in 1942–3, an active minority, mainly from the working-class elements within British Union, became involved in various attempts at political organisation. The first manifestation of this – on the surface a fairly innocuous one – was the formation in early 1942 of the DR 18B Detainees (British) Aid Fund. The leading lights in this were stalwarts of Mosley's East London contingent. The chairman was Robert George Dunlop, formerly second-in-command of the Limehouse Branch of BU (Linehan, 1996: 63–4). The social secretary was Lawrence W. ('Alf') Flockhart, former BU District Leader for Shoreditch. The ostensible aim of this Fund (which was registered under the 1940 War Charities Act) was to help former detainees financially, legally and medically.

There is no doubt, however, that it also served to foster camaraderie among these people, who proudly wore their DR 18B badges in place of their BU ones. Only gradually was it realised by the authorities that there was more to it than this, as is shown by the changing views of the Home Secretary, Herbert Morrison. Originally he had considered the Fund to be a fairly harmless organisation, but by 1943 he was telling the Cabinet that it was serving 'as a nucleus for a political party until the ban on the BUF is raised'. Contemporary accounts described the Fund as a centre for praise of Hitler, insults to Churchill and rabid anti-Semitism (Macklin, 2007: 31–2).

On 6 December 1942 an adjunct to the Fund was formed, the '18B Publicity Council', ostensibly aimed at publicising the iniquities of the DR 18B system and the sufferings of individual detainees. However, comments at the time of its formation show it to have been seen by participants, such as Francis Yeats-Brown, as a revival of the BU. It was chaired by that prominent anti-Semite Captain Arthur Rogers of the Liberty Restoration League. Neither of these bodies, however, aimed for political activity in the present. Indeed, as Guy Liddell of MI5 noted in his diary on 8 April 1942, the chief use of the DR 18B Fund to the authorities was that it brought to light 'the names and addresses of those who were still active supporters of the movement' (Liddell, 2005: 241).

Further, in early 1942 more active groups of ex-detainees started forming. Often these groups were initially unaware of each other's existence. One group formed itself around the recently released Tommy Moran. Moran, however, was governed by his usual caution, and also by blind obedience to Mosley. He followed the instructions that Mosley had given from his prison cell, advising abstention from all activity which might bring former members of BU into conflict with the law (TNA HO 45/25394). His main declared aim was that his members should meet in social groups so as not to lose touch with each other. Some of his followers were impatient with this policy, and soon Moran was to find himself being carried along into much more active commitments. It is interesting to note that the more hard-line Charlie Watts was by now part of his circle.

Much of the new impetus came, however, from another group formed in early 1942. Those involved met for the first time on Sunday,

5 April, in a pub in Pimlico called 'The Enterprise'. Almost all of the leading figures in this group were BU members (and mostly ex-detainees): Ron Stokes (an extremist member of the Harrow branch of BU, who in 1939 had become a member of the Right Club, and who now, after release from detention, was wanted for evasion of military service); Flo Hayes (former BU Women's District Leader for Bournemouth); Ann Good (former BU Women's Canvass Organiser, 7th London area); Pat Howard; Thomas Maclean; and a number of others (TNA HO 45/25394).

The man who turned out to be the most important figure in the group, however, had very different political affiliations. As Special Branch noted, his sympathies were not so much with the BU as 'rather with the Duke of Bedford'. This was Edward Godfrey, 'an embittered and class-conscious proprietor of a chain of fish and chip shops, [...] who is both bitterly opposed to the war and violently anti-Jewish'. Godfrey also had connections with Admiral Sir Barry Domvile (still in prison under DR 18B), under whom he had served in the Navy (TNA HO 144/21845). He was to be a prime mover in subsequent subversive activities.

At 'The Enterprise' Stokes read out a scheme for reorganisation of the BU into a new movement, pointing out that though Mosley had forbidden such activities at that stage, this was undoubtedly because Mosley, in prison, was in an 'awkward position'. In the discussion which followed, Godfrey advised that no reference should be made to Fascism in the new Movement's manifesto, and that it should state its ostensible object to be anti-Communist. The meeting agreed that it should be called the 'Union of British Patriots' (TNA HO 45/25394).

Shortly thereafter, they discovered that Tommy Moran, too, was active. They accordingly made contact with Moran and his followers on 19 April. Moran was at first dismissive of them, and suggested that they should join him, because he already had a movement in existence – 'a British Union movement'. For the next few weeks there was much discussion among the interested parties. On Wednesday, 20 May, representatives of both groups met at the 'Dover Castle', a pub in Bethnal Green which was a regular meeting place for Fascist ex-detainees. Neither Godfrey nor Moran was present, and it was agreed that it was essential for them, and Watts, to come to a further meeting, arranged for two days later at the same pub. Though it turned out to be impossible to contact Moran and Watts in time, this second meeting nevertheless took place. Stokes came 'as an agent for Godfrey', and made a statement on his behalf, in which he said that the new party was to be called the British National Party (BNP), and that its principles were to be based on the writings of the Duke of Bedford, who would finance the opening of party headquarters in as many districts as possible. Eventually a 'monster meeting' would be held 'in the largest hall available in Central London', at which various prominent figures (who, Stokes claimed, had already agreed to the main policy of the party) would be elected as the leading officers of the BNP. These included General J.F.C. Fuller, Viscount Lymington, Major Harry Edmonds, Captain Bernard Acworth, John Middleton Murry, the Duke of Bedford, Collin Brooks, Lord Sempill, Captain Russell Grenfell, Rex Tremlett (past editor of *The Blackshirt*), Edward Greene (brother of Ben Greene) and S. Glasgow. When given this list of names, MI5 noted that 'all the people included on the list are of interest to F.3' – F.3 being the section of MI5 concerned with 'Terrorism, excluding Irish Terrorism' (TNA KV 2/872). The plan, said Stokes, was to nominate candidates in all by-elections:

> The whole process will be done in a legal manner and no illegalities will be permitted. All mention of Fascism, National Socialism, British Union, or some such names will be very strictly barred. The party will fight on an anti-Communist policy. […] The party, although anti-Jewish, will not come out as such and no mention of this policy will be made until the party is strong enough to fight that opposition that the Jews would give.

The whole scheme, said Stokes, 'had been carefully planned to hoodwink the Security departments of the present Government in order to eventually gain power for British Union'. Godfrey would be the only person among the 'top men' to know the extent to which BU would control the new party, and he would as far as possible place BU members in responsible positions in the districts, so that, 'when the occasion arises when it is suggested that BU can take over open control', it would, having picked men in all the positions of power, 'have no difficulty in coercing the controlling body of the new Party to support British Union' (TNA KV 2/872).

These proposals appear to have been an attempt to create a compromise between Godfrey, Moran and Watts. Much now depended on a meeting between these three. That meeting, held a week later, was not a success. Godfrey was determined that the new party should not be openly associated with BU. Moran, the Mosley loyalist, would not give any allegiance to the new party 'unless he could be satisfied that the new organisation gave its entire allegiance to Mosley, and would allow Mosley and his supporters to take over openly at the appropriate time'. He was afraid that 'other persons running the British National Party might steal Mosley's thunder, and when Mosley was released he might find these others in a much stronger position'. He demanded acceptance of Mosley as Leader (TNA HO 45/25394).

Godfrey apparently at this stage felt that the group might need to accept Moran's terms. However, he soon, together with Stokes, decided to break with Moran and the irreconcilable BU supporters, who from now on, though they continued to meet (joined by other East End stalwarts such as Arthur Beavan), very much took a back seat. Godfrey would not, the Security Services reported, accept Mosley as Leader and 'was angling for the support of Right-wing people hostile to Mosley'. They also noted that by now the British National Party was 'regarded with some hostility by the group of Fascists led by Moran' (TNA HO 144/21845).

The British National Party, in its eventual incarnation, was very different from anything that Moran had envisaged. It was in no way a continuation of the BU (Stokes being the last active link to that party), and it no longer 'associated with the main groups of released 18Bs'. It had attracted a number of prominent figures, including General Fuller, Norman Hay, Major Hammond Foot (formerly of the British Democratic Party and the Nationalist Association), Sir Alliott Verdon Roe, H. St John Philby, Collin Brooks, John Middleton Murry and Dr Margaret Vivian, and had set up offices in a small room in Trafalgar Square. MI5 noted that the BNP's policies were unlikely to appeal to anyone apart from those who followed the views of the Duke of Bedford – and it is significant that Bedford had by now set about funding the new body, and that Bedford's associate Ben Greene (who had been released from detention in January) had by October 1942 started acting in an advisory capacity to Godfrey, and indeed carried around with him visiting cards in the name of the British National Party (TNA KV 2/491).

The BNP's views and attitudes were strongly influenced not just by the policies of the Duke of Bedford but also by those of the 'back-to-the-land' school: international finance was to be abolished, peace was to be negotiated (the root cause of the war having been the machinations of international finance against Germany), and the land was to become the basis for the nation's material and spiritual welfare. To these policies were added the setting-up of an authoritarian government, the abolition of political parties and government by referendum. Anti-Semitism figured obliquely in the movement's policy statements, particularly in their references to international finance and to the dangers of 'Alien Influence and Infiltration' (TNA HO 144/21845). As Special Branch put it, the movement had developed 'a specious programme calculated to appeal to the advocates of a negotiated peace, anti-Semitism, and monetary and agricultural reform' (TNA HO 45/25398). They assessed about fifty per cent of the membership as being former 'members of some Fascist party or in some way connected with Fascism'. The rest were 'mostly cranks interested in Social Credit or some kind of monetary reform, or people who thought that the anti-war policy of the party was pacifist'. One of Godfrey's main concerns, they noted, was 'to conclude the war'; he had 'looked with disappointment at our successes in Africa as being likely to postpone the day of a compromise peace with Germany', and 'the successes of our Russian allies are causing him anxiety' (TNA HO 144/21845).

The movement's activities were mainly in the form of publications. It started a newspaper called *British National News* and published several pamphlets, including two by the Duke of Bedford producing his usual arguments about the causes of the war, two by the Scottish anti-Semite Alexander Ratcliffe (author of *The Truth about the Jews*) and the reprint of an article by Collin Brooks, originally published in *Truth* on 5 June 1942. This last publication was strongly anti-Semitic, and had caused something of a stir when first published (TNA HO 144/21845).

Public activities were few. A BNP march to the Cenotaph was planned shortly after Remembrance Day to lay a wreath inscribed 'You Have

Been Betrayed'. This was banned by the police (*The Times*, 22/10/42). On 21 February 1943 a meeting was planned at the Stoll Theatre, to be addressed by the Duke of Bedford, but the party 'lost its booking when the Stoll management realised the strength and volume of the public indignation against such a body being permitted at this time to hold a meeting in the heart of London' (*The Week*, 18/2/43). Though the movement's membership was relatively tiny, it does appear to have aroused considerable public opposition. As Tony Kushner has noted: 'The BNP created an enormous reaction, with protest marches and petitions for its banning involving thousands of people' (Kushner, 1989: 33).

Despite the Duke's financial support, the BNP did not flourish. In early April 1943 the decision was taken to dissolve it and to create a new movement, which under a different name would continue the same policies (though with different tactics). The new name was the English Nationalist Association (ENA). Godfrey saw himself continuing as leader (TNA HO 144/21845). The Duke of Bedford, however, dissatisfied with Godfrey's performance, clearly thought otherwise. He seems to have realised that the blatant nature of some of the BNP's racist publications and policies was bleeding 'respectable' support from it. On 20 April he summoned Godfrey to his Bedfordshire seat at Woburn, together with Ben Greene (TNA HO 45/25398). We have no record of what was said on this occasion, but from then on Greene became the dominant figure in the ENA (becoming 'Vice Governor' – there was no Governor) with Godfrey taking a more background role. The inaugural luncheon of the new Association (which targeted the middle classes far more assiduously than the BNP had) was held on 15 June 1943. Official invitations were sent to a great many public figures (though not many seem to have responded.). The card sent to Sir Basil Liddell Hart gives us some insight into the movement's new care to appear moderate, while still containing sly references for the initiated. It bears the heading 'Magna Carta Day – 15th June 1943', with below it a picture of St George slaying a dragon. The 'Declaration' accompanying it is at first sight fairly innocuous, though it makes an oblique reference to politicians being 'the instruments of powerful financial and corrupt capitalist interests', and another to the 'financial imperialism' which was attacking 'the integrity and independence of the English nation' (LHCMA LH 2G/123/1).

The Association also hoped to obtain support from former BNP members, and 'although feeling a great spirit of rivalry with Mosley and the BU, [was] ready and willing to accept old BU members into its ranks'. The ostensible object of the ENA, MI5 noted, was the restoration of English liberties (in which it was similar to the Liberty Restoration League), and like the LRL, the ENA hid behind this facade a well of anti-Semitism. Greene was cautious about revealing this publicly, however: 'In his words in private he is violently anti-Semitic, although the ENA in its public utterances plays down this fundamental part of their policy so as to avoid a Fascist imputation.' For similar reasons, though the movement was generously funded by the Duke of Bedford (who was possibly the 'Governor' for whom Greene was 'Vice-Governor'), his name did not appear openly as a supporter because of the controversy around his name at this stage of the war. By September 1943 Greene was also receiving considerable financial support from a further source, Percy Lovely, a wealthy former funder of BU (TNA KV 2/492).

In December 1943 Godfrey stood at the Acton by-election as an 'English Nationalist' and obtained 258 votes (Kushner, 1989: 32). By early 1944, however, Greene had finally broken with Godfrey owing to a fundamental disagreement about strategy. Godfrey had wanted the ENA to have a policy of open anti-Semitism; Greene, supported by many of the new members he had attracted, had 'insisted on working secretly and underground'. A series of meetings between the two men had no effect, and in March 1944 Godfrey 'withdrew in frustration and bitterness to a farm in Somerset' (TNA KV 2/492). (He was later to start an abortive movement of his own, which he called 'The English Legion'.)

Greene had meanwhile been having talks with a number of leading members of other right-wing groups (devoted to monetary reform or agricultural reform or anti-Semitism or peace agitation or all these things), such as the Jewish conspiracy theorist Lt-Col. John Creagh Scott of the Service for Economic Action, Ronald McEwan Huggard of the Honest Money Association, Major Harry Edmonds of the Constitutional Research Association (CRA) and Norman Hay. His aim was to arrange some kind of effective co-ordination of effort. These talks, however, came to nothing, and by late 1944 Greene appears to have been distracted from the ENA's business by a number of extraneous circumstances. First, he found more and more of his time taken up as manager of his family engineering firm, Kepston's in Berkhamsted, which had been going through difficulties. Secondly, he was fully occupied at this time with his support for Captain Ramsay, in Ramsay's constituency and elsewhere. In these circumstances, the ENA gradually lost momentum. By the end of 1944 the Duke of Bedford was turning once more to John Beckett with a view to the revival of the pre-war British People's Party.

The British League of Ex-Servicemen and Women

It was in 1944 that another contender appeared among these resurgent movements of the Right. The British League of Ex-Servicemen and Women had been in existence since 1937. It was originally very similar to the British Legion, one of its main policies being the question of adequate pensions for ex-servicemen. It had been a highly respectable body; but by 1944 it had been hijacked by a number of former BU members. The movement's title and origins provided suitable initial cover for their activities. The main figure in this takeover was Jeffrey Hamm. Among the other members were two men who had been closely involved in BU agricultural policy: Victor Burgess, who had joined BU during its involvement in the East Anglian tithe wars, and Robert Saunders, former BU District Officer for West Dorset. The movement was strongly anti-Semitic, and involved itself in street violence in those areas of London that had a significant Jewish population. Like all such movements, it had fissiparous tendencies, and Burgess soon left to form his own 'Union of British Freedom'. The British League of Ex-Servicemen is mainly of interest for the fact that it was later to be a strong element in Mosley's Union Movement, founded in 1947. In the 1944–5 period there were movements, however, which initially appeared far more worthy of consideration, of which one of the most important was the revived British People's Party.

The British People's Party

John Beckett had been released from detention in October 1943. In early 1944 the Duke of Bedford provided Beckett and his wife with a cottage on his estate at Chenies in Buckinghamshire. Beckett and the Duke kept closely in touch, and by the beginning of 1945, MI5 noted, they had decided to revive the party they had formed in 1939, the British People's Party, which 'had been defunct since Beckett's detention in 1940'. They also planned to publish a new periodical in support of the Party. This, the *Bedford Newsletter*, appeared in January 1945, its name soon being changed to the *People's Post*. The first issue of the *Bedford Newsletter* sold over a thousand copies (TNA KV 2/795, KV 2/492).

The attitudes of Beckett and Bedford at this time epitomise the uncertainties felt by former anti-Semites and fascists in the new situation of widespread anti-fascism created by the war (Griffiths, 2010). Both were ambivalent, but in different ways. An article in the issue of the *People's Post* for 20 April 1945 illustrates Beckett's new attitude. He had on the one hand already expressed a desire that the expressions 'anti-Semitic' and 'Social Credit' should be banned from the revived BPP and from the Newsletter (TNA KV 2/492). On the other hand, it appears that his anti-Semitic impulses were too strong to keep up this attitude. His April article, called 'Justice for the Jew: The British People's Party Policy', was ostensibly pro-Jewish, claiming that 'No Christian can accept a policy of discrimination owing to race and creed. [...] Our test must be that of the action of the individual and it must not be applied *en masse* to any section of the population'. Soon, however, his true colours began to emerge. First, the alien nature of the Jews was stressed: 'It is undoubtedly true, and it should not be offensive to say so, that the presence of this large number of people of Eastern origin with an outlook very different from our own creates a grave problem.' Thereafter, the link between the Jews and Usury (which 'must go!') was pointed out. The final sentences of the article trod an unconvincing path between tolerance and racial abuse:

> We cannot indulge in racial abuse which can only end, if successful, in stimulating lawless treatment of the Jewish people, nor can we shut our eyes to much of the evidence of unhelpful Jewish activities we see around us. If there are good Jews, we wish them

peace and happiness; those who abuse our hospitality have no right to expect to continue doing so, and it is difficult to understand why Jews who claim they are good citizens insist on spoiling their own cause by shouting 'Jew-baiter' whenever the less desirable sections of their community are exposed.

(*PP*, 20/4/45)

This was far less immediate than Beckett's pre-war fulminations against the Jews. The need to pay lip-service to tolerance, and to appear to be defending the Jews, was something new. Beneath it, however, the old animosities still lurked. Moreover, the fundamentally unchanged nature of the new BPP was shown by the appointment of the veteran anti-Semite Aubrey Lees to the post of treasurer (TNA KV 2/1520). Lees was to play a considerable part in the affairs of the Party. Other people from pre-war extremist groups also homed in on the BPP. Its office for the *People's Post* at 33 Maiden Lane, manned initially by Beckett and Katherine Greene, also eventually had on its staff two anti-Semitic stalwarts of the Imperial Fascist League: Elizabeth Berger and H.H. Lockwood (TNA KV 2/1519; NMM DOM 58, 10/1/46, 28/1/46).

In late 1944 the veteran right-winger A.K. Chesterton, who had served in the British Army in East Africa, had returned to Britain owing to ill health. He soon set about forming a new group, entitled 'National Front after Victory' (NFaV), which he hoped would bring together the disparate right-wing groups then in existence. Talks took place with the BPP, the BPP's principal negotiators being Beckett, Aubrey Lees and H.H. Lockwood (Thurlow, 1987: 243). Beckett, however, mistrusted Chesterton, who had not, like him and so many others, gone to prison for his beliefs. Little came of these negotiations, and even though the NFaV gathered in some groups such as the remnants of Ben Greene's ENA, and other prominent figures such as H.T. Mills, Ben Greene and the Earl of Portsmouth (the former Lord Lymington), it was short-lived.

The BPP was to continue after the war, at first fairly successfully, as we shall be seeing in a later chapter; but it, too, found it difficult to maintain any momentum, particularly in the changed post-war situation.

The Constitutional Research Association

The CRA was a body of a very different order. Many of its most prominent members were examples of what could ironically be called 'the great and the good', and its meetings tended to take the form of lunches and dinners at some of London's smartest and most respectable venues (such as the discreet Brown's Hotel in Dover Street – an old-fashioned hotel frequented by the respectable upper-middle classes and the higher clergy – and the less discreet Café Royal in Regent Street). Yet behind its apparently innocuous title, and its acceptable meeting places, there lay disguised a movement as anti-Semitic and pro-Nazi as the other bodies we have been considering. Like so many movements of this type, the CRA held strong views on monetary reform. This in turn led to admiration for Germany, which had successfully opposed international finance, and to support for Germany's cause. As with Major C.H. Douglas's Social Credit party (which the CRA greatly admired, Douglas being invited to speak at a CRA meeting), it also led almost inevitably to anti-Semitism.

The CRA was considered by MI5 to be one of the most important pro-Nazi groups operating in Britain in the later part of the war (Macklin, 2007: 126). Though a body with this name had been in existence since late 1941 (TNA KV 4/58), its activities had not initially been particularly effective. In 1943, however, it began to take the form just described. At this stage Major Harry Edmonds set about organising regular lunches and also attempting to make of it a far more coherent and active body. MI5 began to note the larger scale of operations (TNA KV 2/873). At first, these meetings appeared fairly harmless. It was only when, in late 1943, MI5 managed to infiltrate an agent into this body, that 'all (or almost all) became clear' (TNA KV 4/58), and a more sinister picture began to emerge.

Edmonds, the moving force behind the CRA, had 'form' as a pro-Nazi. Indeed, as late as 9 May 1940, eight months into the war, he had written an article for Norman Hay's *Information and Policy* justifying Germany's policies because of the iniquitous peace terms and the subsequent encirclement of Germany 'under the direction of France', which had led to the 'national despair and degeneracy' of the Weimar period, from which Germany 'was only rescued by Hitler and National

Socialism'. A great power had now arisen, he wrote, which 'under the leadership of a genius' had found a new 'national pride and solidarity' and 'freed itself from the restriction of weak encircling powers'. Meanwhile, France and Britain had continued to pursue the heinous policy of 'International Finance', from which Germany was saving the world (Edmonds, 1940).

Edmonds had been a Staff Officer in the Naval Intelligence Division (of which Admiral Sir Barry Domvile had been Director until 1930), and after Domvile's release from prison on 29 July 1943 he paid the first of many visits to him on 7 October (NMM DOM 56, 7/10/43). Meanwhile, in late 1943 he organised a lunch at the Savoy, which MI5 declared to have been attended by 'many persons under investigation by F.3' (TNA KV 2/873). Domvile and a number of other senior military and naval men had by now became central to Edmonds's plans to reorganise the CRA. For this purpose he held a number of small meetings, bringing together, for example at lunch at the Charing Cross Hotel on 27 January 1944, Admiral Domvile, General Fuller, Commander Russell Grenfell (the naval officer whose post-war revisionist book *Unconditional Hatred* was to deplore the 'victimisation' of Germany by those who had brought about the war, while excusing Hitler's acts of aggression), Rex Tremlett and an architect called Smith (NMM DOM 57, 27/1/44). Smith may have been the MI5 operative who reported back to MI5. At all events, it was reported, on the 27 January meeting, that 'all those present were said to show hatred of the Jews and the Americans, and admiration for the Germans. They were convinced the present war was entirely due to the influence of International Finance' (TNA KV 2/836). Further such intimate lunches took place at the Charing Cross Hotel later in 1944, in which Edmonds, Grenfell, Domvile, Fuller and Smith were joined by the Earl of Portsmouth (Lord Lymington) and John Middleton Murry.

Larger-scale lunches were organised in the course of 1944, such as one at the Café Royal on 11 May. By now various other big fish were getting involved, including Lord Sempill. Sempill in turn introduced Edmonds to Lord Bennett (the former Canadian Prime Minister who in the Thirties had notoriously allied his Conservative Party with the Canadian fascist and anti-Semite Adrien Arcand's Christian National Party) (Lester, 2002: 227–32). Lord Hankey (the former Cabinet

Secretary who had later become a Minister under Churchill from 1940 to 1942) also became a member. In August MI5 reported that Edmonds had been planning an Advisory Council chaired by Hankey, and consisting also of Bennett, Portsmouth, Sempill, Domvile and Fuller, with Edmonds as honorary secretary. (Later, Major-General Sir John Kennedy was added.) Edmonds saw the Council as a kind of 'Fire Curtain' behind which 'those who appreciate the whole racket would press for the breaking of the money power'. These more obscure figures were described by Edmonds as 'our gang', consisting of various lesser right-wing activists: the ubiquitous Ben Greene, together with the equally ubiquitous Norman Hay, Russell Grenfell, Harold Vezey Strong, Rex Tremlett, Ronald Huggard and H.T. Mills. It was believed the Duke of Bedford would also give his support (presumably financial) (TNA KV 874).

The account of a meeting on 8 November 1944 (present: Edmonds, Tremlett, Huggard, Mills, Ben Greene and a number of others) gives us something of the tenor of the more informal conversations of 'our gang'. Lord Moyne had just been assassinated in Cairo by the Stern Gang, and Edmonds hailed this as a 'bloody good thing', in that it would draw people's attention to 'Jewish terrorists'. The question was then raised as to whether Lord Hankey (who was not present) might be a Jew:

> Edmonds said that Fuller had once told him that Lord Hankey had complained to him, Fuller: 'You know, people think that I am a Jew and of course I am not.' One of those present suggested that it was not uncommon for Jews to say that sort of thing, but all agreed that Lord Hankey certainly did not look like a Jew.
>
> (TNA KV 2/874)

During the more formal part of the meeting, Edmonds deplored the likelihood that Germany would be defeated, because 'that means the old financial gang, which is behind the whole of this show, will be back in power' (TNA KV 2/874).

Throughout early 1945 well-attended monthly lunches of the movement were held, usually at the Café Royal. Anti-Semitism continued to be one of the major themes. Tying this in to the 'constitutional' remit of the movement, Edmonds and Ben Greene began to extol the virtues of Magna Carta: 'According to them, Magna Carta contained a clause protecting the English from the Jews who, in those days, were regarded as aliens and infidels and as persons with whom His Majesty was at perpetual war' (TNA KV 2/492).

After the war (as we shall see in a later chapter) the CRA, like the BPP, despite considerable initial activity, found it hard to find a suitable role for itself, and finally faded away.

Conclusion

Those anti-Semitic and/or pro-Nazi groups that were formed during the course of the war from 1942 onwards were tentative, and often secretive about their true nature. But, as Tony Kushner has pointed out, though these movements were on the whole 'feeble enterprises', they 'filled a function of keeping a fascist and anti-Semitic tradition in Britain alive' (Kushner, 1989: 36). The widespread anti-fascism of the time naturally hindered any attempt to publicly revive pre-war fascist attitudes. The fact that a number of individuals and groups did make such an attempt bears witness to the resilience of such attitudes in these circles. During the war itself the desire for peace had meant that there was some support for movements such as these, provided they managed to conceal some of their more extreme characteristics. With the end of the war, the two main groups of this kind that still remained (the BPP and the CRA) lost the anti-war justification (which had attracted a number of naive pacifists) and tried in vain to find a new role for themselves.

Bibliography

Books and articles

Beckett, Francis (1999), *The Rebel Who Lost His Cause: The Tragedy of John Beckett MP* (London: London House).

Edmonds, Major H. (1940), 'Behind Democracy', *Information and Policy*, 9 May.

Grenfell, Captain Russell, RN (1945), *Unconditional Hatred: German War Guilt and the Future of Europe* (New York: Devin-Adair).

Griffiths, Richard (1998), *Patriotism Perverted: Captain Ramsay, the Right Club and British Anti-Semitism, 1939–40* (London: Constable).

Griffiths, Richard (2010), 'Anti-Fascism and the Post-War British Establishment', in Nigel Copsey and Andrzej Olechnowicz (eds), *Varieties of Anti-Fascism: Britain in the Inter-War Period* (Basingstoke: Palgrave Macmillan), pp. 247–64.

Kushner, Tony (1989), *The Persistence of Prejudice: Antisemitism in British Society during the Second World War* (Manchester: Manchester University Press).

Lester, Normand (2002), *The Black Book of English Canada* (Toronto: McClelland & Stewart).

Liddell, Guy (2005), *The Guy Liddell Diaries, Vol. I: 1939–1942* (ed. Nigel West) (London: Routledge).

Linehan, Thomas P. (1996), *East London for Mosley: The British Union of Fascists in East London and South-West Essex 1933–40* (London: Frank Cass).

Macklin, Graham (2007), *Very Deeply Dyed in Black: Sir Oswald Mosley and the Resurrection of British Fascism after 1945* (London and New York: I.B. Tauris).

Pitchford, Mark (2011), *The Conservative Party and the Extreme Right, 1945–75* (Manchester: Manchester University Press).

Thurlow, Richard (1987), *Fascism in Britain: A History, 1918–1985* (Oxford: Blackwell).

Documents

The National Archives (TNA)

HO 45/25394, HO 45/25398, HO 45/25568, HO 45/25722, HO 144/21845
KV 2/491, KV 2/492, KV 2/795, KV 2/836, KV 2/872, KV 2/873, KV 2/874, KV 2/1221, KV 2/1519, KV 2/1520, KV 4/58

Liddell Hart Centre for Military Archives, King's College London (LHCMA)

Liddell Hart Papers, LH2G/123

National Maritime Museum (NMM)

Admiral Domvile's diary, DOM 56, DOM 57, DOM 58

Newspapers and journals

Information and Policy (IP)
People's Post (PP)
The Times
The Week

1. Sir Oswald Mosley
Source: Getty Images

2. Sir Arthur Bryant (with Sir John Glubb Pasha)
Source: Getty Images

3. Captain and Mrs Ramsay at a society wedding
Source: Getty Images

4. Harry St John Philby
Source: Getty Images

5. Peveril Internment Camp, Isle of Man
Source: Getty Images

6. William Joyce
Source: Getty Images

7. Mrs Dorothy Eckersley
Source: Getty Images

8. General J.F.C. Fuller
Source: Getty Images

9. The 2nd Duke of Westminster, with Coco Chanel at the races
Source: Getty Images

10. Lord Redesdale giving away his daughter Deborah at her wartime wedding
Source: Getty Images

11. Captain George Lane-Fox Pitt-Rivers (Churchill Archives Centre, The Papers of George Henry Lane-Fox Pitt-Rivers)

12. Lord Sempill and Ernst Udet, the German flying ace
Source: Getty Images

PART IV
Renegades

7

'LONG BEFORE 1939 I HAD BECOME AN ADMIRER OF THE NAZI SYSTEM'

Five British broadcasters for Nazi Germany

Wartime broadcasting by the Nazis to Britain has been associated, in the popular mind, above all with William Joyce ('Lord Haw-Haw'). Yet there were a great many other British people who undertook such activities. Their motives were extremely varied. On the one hand, there was Joyce and a number of other people whose pre-war political views had led them to espouse Germany's cause (some claiming that, by opposing the Jewish and Communist threat in this way, they were in fact being loyal to Britain). At the other extreme, there were people who ended up in Nazi employment almost by accident – either because they had been unable to get out of Germany at the outbreak of war and needed money, or because they saw it as a way of getting out of being sent to a prisoner of war camp or internment camp (or, in Pearl Vardon's case, because she had fallen in love with a German soldier in occupied Jersey, and had followed him back to Germany) (TNA KV 2/256, HO 45/25811, CRIM 1/1781). There were many gradations between these two extremes.

The case of William Joyce has been very well documented. He had been one of the most remarkable figures in British Union (BU) in the early Thirties, an extraordinary mixture of the intellectual and the thug. He left BU, together with John Beckett, in 1937 and founded the National Socialist League. In August 1939, with the approach of war, he and his wife Margaret left for Germany, convinced that their future lay there. Eventually they both became leading broadcasters to Britain, 'Lord and Lady Haw-Haw'. Joyce's contributions were violently pro-German, often sardonic and effective both because of the accuracy of much of the reporting and by the manner of its presentation. His main aim was to undermine the morale of the British people. After the war he was condemned to death for treason.

Joyce and a number of other 'renegades', including John Amery, who not only broadcasted but also recruited volunteers for the 'British Legion of St George' to fight alongside the Germans, and who like Joyce was executed at the end of the war, are of interest because of the virulence and unshakeability of their beliefs; but their motives and actions were remarkably clear-cut. There is more uncertainty about certain other broadcasters, who present a much more complex picture and are for that reason in some senses more interesting. It will be worth looking at three of these, Margaret Bothamley, Dorothy Eckersley and Henry William Wicks, who moved in the same pro-Nazi circles as each other in London before the war, and who started from a strongly pro-Nazi position, unlike many of their fellow broadcasters. Their cases are complicated by their changing attitudes as the war went on, by their subsequent 'rewriting' of history, and by the consequent difficulty, for us, of disentangling their motives at every point, even when we have objective documentation to place against their accounts. Two of them were accompanied by children in their late teens (Eckersley's son James Clark and Wicks's daughter Margaret), who also took up careers with the *Reichsrundfunk* (the German Broadcasting Corporation), careers which were in fact more successful than those of their parents. One of the more interesting aspects of the histories of these five people is the surprising discrepancy between the ways in which they were treated by the British authorities after the war (a discrepancy which illustrates in microcosm the disarray of the British authorities and the courts in relation to the treatment of the vast array of renegades).

For these reasons, these people, who before the war were fairly typical examples of the more extreme British enthusiasts for Nazi Germany, give us some insight into a complex series of issues relating to British collaboration with the Nazis on their home ground.

Miss Margaret Bothamley

Margaret Bothamley (1879–1948) was one of the central figures in the pro-Nazi society of pre-war London. The daughter of a wealthy London solicitor, at the age of 17 she went to Germany to study music in Weimar. According to her later account, she had at that time a short-lived marriage with a German called Adolf Bleibtreu, with whom she lived for only two or three days before returning to her studies in Weimar. She never saw him thereafter, and a few years later heard that he had died (TNA CRIM 1/1763). Whatever the truth of this story, she lived the rest of her life as an unmarried woman. In the mid-Twenties she spent much time in Austria, Czechoslovakia and Hungary, and there developed some of the opinions which were to dominate her life thereafter:

> I learned that the Treaty of Versailles was not restoring order in Europe, but was creating economic and social chaos. I also found that the plans for the Red Revolution, organised from Russia, were underground and going on just as much despite the Red Revolution having been defeated in Hungary.
>
> (TNA CRIM 1/1763)

In 1931 she made a four-month visit to Germany, and was 'horrified' at the social disintegration of the Weimar Republic. Once the Nazis came into power in 1933, she felt that this new regime was 'developing hope and courage' in the nation. From 1933 to 1939 she spent several months of each year in Germany as 'an admirer of the Nazi system', which was 'taking a positive attitude towards the elimination of social evils'.

On 22 October 1936 she gave a talk on the radio from Berlin, entitled 'A Statement by an Englishwoman about National Socialist Germany', which, she later said, had been given 'at [her] own urgent request'. This was later published in pamphlet form in Britain. In it she described how pre-Nazi Germany had been poisoned by an 'alien penetration' and by 'the concentration of her land, industry and wealth in the hands of speculative international finance'. This was all part of 'the Jewish world problem' which the Nazis had come in to solve (Bothamley, 1937).

In Britain, Bothamley wrote prolifically about this issue. An article written for *The Patriot* at the time of the *Anschluss* in 1938 is typical. 'The Jewish question', she asserted, 'was behind the determination to assert the "independence" of Austria.' Austria had not in fact been independent, because of the power of the Jews there. 'Vienna had been made to obey, if not to love and honour, the power from which Germany had freed herself.' Germany's takeover of Austria was therefore to be welcomed (Bothamley, 1938).

In the meantime, she had built up a considerable reputation in London pro-Nazi and anti-Semitic circles. At his death in 1933 her father had left her enough money to guarantee her an independent existence, and she went to live in a spacious flat at 67 Cromwell Road. There she gave many smart cocktail parties which were attended by a cross-section of well-heeled Nazi enthusiasts – including Lord Ronald Graham, Aubrey Lees, Robert Gordon-Canning, and a number of Germans including the political publicist H.R. Hoffmann, who edited the English-language propaganda journal *News from Germany*. From these parties, festive groups would go on to political meetings such as those of the Imperial Fascist League and the Nordic League. Margaret also played a major part in the Anglo-German Fellowship, The Link and the Right Club.

Among Bothamley's close friends were Mary ('Mollie') Stanford and Anne van Lennep (both of them members of the Right Club). An MI5 Report described Stanford, van Lennep and Bothamley as all three being of 'strongly pro-Nazi views' (TNA KV 2/832).

As war approached, on 30 July 1939 Admiral Domvile took a 'Link' party (including Margaret Bothamley and Anne van Lennep) on a 'friendship visit' to Munich (NMM DOM 56). When the party returned to London on 6 August, Margaret Bothamley stayed in Germany for her usual annual visit. Her account, at her post-war interrogation, of what then happened is incomplete and at times unreliable. It runs as follows. She ended up in wartime Germany almost by accident. 'I was taken by surprise, and had I known what was going to happen, I would have taken steps to return home to England.' When war broke out on 3 September, she immediately went to Berlin. On her arrival she reported to the authorities and asked permission to return to England, but was told this would not be possible until at least December. She was, however, given preferential treatment. She was not interned, and apart from having to report once a month, was otherwise entirely free. She ascribed this 'to my being known in Berlin as having given lectures in England in favour of Anglo-German fellowship to save Europe from Red Revolution.' Furthermore, as she was short of money the Deutsche Bank made a special arrangement for a large sum to be transferred to her from her local bank in England. In June 1940 she was finally informed that her application to return to England had been refused. A month later, she received the telephone call which started her broadcasting career (TNA CRIM 1/1763).

Other evidence, however, suggests that some of this account is untrustworthy. First, as opposed to trying to get to England (and being prevented from doing so), it is probable that she made a conscious decision to stay in Germany. A post-war statement by a close colleague of hers (Dr Friedrich Schoeberth, deputy head of the English Language Broadcasting Section) points to this: 'I myself thought that she had accepted bad advice in staying in Germany thinking that the war would only be a short war' (TNA KV 2/430). Secondly, despite the lack of information she gave about the period from September 1939 to June 1940, we have evidence that she was probably fairly active in this period. On 12 December 1939, in London, Mary Stanford (who had been corresponding with Bothamley) wrote to another Nazi sympathiser, Mrs Muriel Whinfield: 'Do you know Margaret Bothamley by name? She is not very far from Lisa – in Brussels – Lisa being in Antwerp' (TNA KV 2/832). ('Lisa' was almost certainly Lisa Kruger, a German spy who was a friend of Mrs Whinfield.) MI5, which intercepted the letter, presumed that Bothamley was now working for the Germans, and had been sent by them to Belgium. And on the face of it this does seem likely, because, if the German government had been as adamant as she claimed in refusing to let her leave Germany, it is odd that they should have let her travel on a visit from Germany to neutral

Belgium (from which she would have been able, if she so wished, to return to England).

If she did indeed go to Belgium, she clearly returned thereafter to Germany. By early 1940 frequent letters were passing between Stanford in London (who with van Lennep was now heavily involved in the anti-government activities of the rump of the Right Club) and Bothamley in Germany. These letters, written in a fairly puerile code, were sent via intermediaries in neutral Holland and Belgium (and intercepted by MI5), and showed 'strong pro-Nazi sympathies'. Stanford was to continue her correspondence with Bothamley right up to early 1943, and possibly beyond (TNA KV 2/833).

In February 1940 MI5 declared its conviction that Bothamley was 'assisting the enemy'. In March Special Branch (which had just made raids on Stanford's flat and on Anne van Lennep's house) concurred with this view, on the basis of Stanford's and van Lennep's correspondence with her (TNA KV 2/832).

Whatever the actual facts may have been, Bothamley did begin to broadcast for Nazi Germany some time in the course of 1940. Johannes Schmidt-Hansen, Head of the English Service of the *Reichsrundfunk*, told her that 'he had heard of [her] talks in England and [her] contributions to the English newspapers', and asked her to do some talks on the same lines, and to broadcast them in English to England. She readily agreed, 'with the condition', she later said, 'that I should not speak against England, but that I should show the way in which I considered the English people were being deceived about Germany in the interests of European Red Revolution'. It was agreed that she should write and broadcast two talks a week. Within a few days she began work, and continued this regular routine right through until March 1945. After the war she explained her actions thus:

> The reason I worked at the Rundfunk was that it was my only opportunity to warn English people of the danger England was incurring in being influenced by propaganda against Germany and in favour of Soviet Russia [...] I was troubled at doing these broadcasts but felt like a mother who saw her children in danger and could only call to them from a house which was not on

speaking terms with mine. That would not deter me from warning England how she would suffer if she took this attitude to the one country in a position to withstand Soviet imperialism.

(TNA CRIM 1/1763)

Bothamley thus still saw her actions as those of a patriot. This, of course, explains why she had a photograph of the king on her desk at the *Rundfunk* (a fact of which much was to be made at her trial – though nothing was made there of her parallel pre-war display of many portraits of Hitler in her London flat). As in the case of a number of other 'perverted patriots' of her type, her pro-Nazism had, in the pre-war situation, been entirely compatible with her patriotism. But she failed to realise that now, in wartime, the two attitudes were incompatible, and that the broadcasts she made were treasonable by the fact that they actively aided the German war effort. Her fellow broadcasters noted the extreme nature of her commitment, and that she was 'very firm in her Nazi ideals' and 'an ardent Nazi to the end' (TNA CRIM 1/1736). Indeed (though in early 1945 she became quite nervous about the way things were going) (TNA KV 2/430), she was one of the few British broadcasters to continue right to the end of the war, going first from Berlin to Apen on 13 February 1945 because of the Russian advance, and then to Hamburg in early April. At the beginning of May, just before the capitulation, she changed her name to Maria Bleibtreu to avoid detection, and went to live at a private address in Hamburg, where she stayed for the next eight months. In late January 1946 she was discovered and put in prison, where on 2 February she was interrogated by Major Reginald Spooner of British Military Intelligence.

Much of the justification she gave Spooner for her activities consisted of her usual evocation of the Jewish and Communist threats (from which England could only have been saved by making peace with Germany), and her usual praise for Nazism and vilification of the Jews. Why, she asked, had the British public been fed such anti-German propaganda before and during the war? It had been, of course, a result of 'the Jewish influence behind much of the British Press, the cinemas and other avenues to public opinion', which had been 'working up public opinion against Germany'. She stressed that she believed that everything she had done had been in the interests of England (TNA CRIM 1/1763).

Bothamley returned to England on 6 March, and was committed for trial at Bow Street on a charge of 'with intent to assist the enemy, having entered the service of the German broadcasting system'. Her trial took place later in the month. Her counsel had wisely decided (despite her initial protests at this) not to allow her to give evidence – such evidence might well, as in her interview with Major Spooner, have given vent to all her pro-Nazi and anti-Semitic prejudices (predictably, Admiral Domvile was disappointed not to hear her in this mode) (NMM DOM 58, 26/3/46). Instead, with her mouth shut, it was possible for the defence successfully to depict her as a very muddled and completely innocuous old lady. Rebecca West was clearly taken in by this in her account of the trial. Describing the various broadcasters on trial, West said, solely on the basis of what had been said *about* Bothamley: 'The most sympathetic among them was an elderly lady called Miss Margaret Frances Bothamley […] She was in a state of complete confusion' (West, 1949: 118). This description has coloured most subsequent accounts. As Adrian Weale has rightly said:

> *The Meaning of Treason* is characterized by the author's attempt to draw conclusions about its subjects from the statements read out in their defence and, importantly, by their physical appearance and demeanour as she observed them in the dock. This is certainly an acceptable practice in journalism but not in history. Whatever West's intentions were, the book is seriously flawed as a basis of our view of the British traitors in the Second World War. Unfortunately, that is what it has become.
>
> (Weale, 1994: 3)

Despite the fact that Bothamley's interrogator, Major Spooner, had specifically noted that he found her 'intelligent, astute and wily', and that she was 'anything but a frail and silly old woman' (TNA CRIM 1/1763), the defence's ruse worked. On 27 March Bothamley was given a very mild sentence: twelve months' imprisonment 'in the first division', the most lenient of regimes.

Mrs (Frances) Dorothy Eckersley and James Clark

Mrs Eckersley (d. 1971) was a close friend of Margaret Bothamley, whom she had known 'on and off' since the 1920s, and whose cocktail parties she attended at Cromwell Road in the late Thirties. She later described Bothamley as having been the person who had 'most interested [her] in the Nazi ideals' (TNA CRIM 1/1736).

The daughter of a colonel and a relative of Virginia Woolf, Dorothy was born in 1893 in Aldershot. She has been described as having, like Bothamley, an exaggeratedly 'upper-class voice'. In 1921 she married Edward Clark, who worked in the BBC's music department. They had one son, James. By 1928 she was separated from Clark and had started an affair with Peter Eckersley, the famous BBC engineer. She married Eckersley, after he had divorced his wife, in 1930 (the situation being part of the cause of Eckersley losing his job with the BBC) (Eckersley, 1998: 269–308).

Dorothy had been a member of the Independent Labour Party and a strong admirer of Soviet Russia, but in the mid-Thirties, as her son James recalled, 'she slipped right over to the other side, to National Socialism [...] You see, having been very Left, a dictatorship was not abhorrent to us' (Muir, 1991). In 1935, after a visit to Germany, she and her husband Peter had become enamoured of the Nazi regime. Peter (who, as a member of the British Union of Fascists, acted as Mosley's main adviser on radio matters) was from now on uncompromising in his pro-Nazi views, as was illustrated by a dispute at a dinner party given by Kenneth Clark (the famous art historian), recounted in their memoirs both by Clark and by another guest, Maurice Bowra. Clark described him as an 'indoctrinated Nazi', and Bowra as 'an avowed and uncompromising Fascist'. Eventually, Clark turned him out of his house. (Clark, 1974: 273–4; Bowra, 1966: 346–7).

Peter and Dorothy visited Germany for their summer holidays each year up to 1939. In 1937 they were both invited by Unity Mitford to a Munich restaurant where she knew Hitler was going to be; 'and there' said Dorothy ecstatically, 'I gazed on him' (TNA CRIM 1/1736). In 1937 and 1938 they both attended the Nuremberg Rallies. In Britain Dorothy was meanwhile getting involved with a variety of pro-Nazi and anti-Semitic groups. She joined the Anglo-German Fellowship, the Imperial Fascist League and The Link, and attended meetings of William Joyce's National Socialist League and Carlyle Club. (On at least one occasion she stood bail for Joyce from police custody: Bergmeier and Lotz, 1997: 96.) In 1939 Dorothy and Peter both joined the Right Club.

On 19 July 1939 Dorothy sent her son James (aged 16) to pursue his studies in Germany. She herself went to the Salzburg Festival and to visit friends in Hungary, and on her way back called in to Berlin to see James. They were both there when war broke out. A few days earlier Peter Eckersley had phoned from London, expressing the opinion that it would be all right for them to stay. When war broke out, Dorothy decided: 'instead of returning to England, [...] to remain in Berlin with the many German friends I had. I was persuaded that things would soon be alright and that it was "only the Polish business".' The question of internment did not even enter her head. 'Everything was going on normally and I was able to attend suppers, cocktail parties, etc.' She did register with the police, and had to report once a week (TNA CRIM 1/1736).

Soon, however, their circumstances changed. Peter had promised to send money through Spain, but none arrived. The authorities did nothing to help. (What a difference from the treatment given to Margaret Bothamley by the Deutsche Bank!) By November Dorothy began to look desperately for work. She turned to influential friends for help, and they came up with the idea that Eckersley and Clark 'should assist in the German Wireless Propaganda Service'.

On 15 December Dorothy was contacted by Schmidt-Hansen of the *Rundfunk*, and asked to come in for tests as an announcer. She was then offered 20 marks a day for the job: 'I was delighted, as I was desperate for marks.' She broadcast every day, her role being merely to announce the daily programmes:

> The greater part of the programmes I announced were musical items, news in English, talks in English etc. All were propaganda directed against England, and some of the commentaries were ghastly and frightful in their subject matters.
>
> (TNA CRIM 1/1736)

Though her pre-war pro-Nazism had been as strong as Bothamley's, her motivation in broadcasting seems to have been more mercenary than political; yet, dislike the broadcasts as she may have (and we only have her later word for it), she apparently had no compunction in announcing them.

Her son James Clark meanwhile had, a few days after his mother, been called in for interview, and was put on the air as a newsreader. Though he was taken off for a while, he was reinstated in February 1940. He became the English section's number two speaker (after William Joyce), earning 400 marks a month (Bergmeier and Lotz, 1997: 96). He was later to explain his attitude thus: 'I appreciated that my broadcasts were entirely anti-British, but I had at that time no objection to this as I was still in the hysterical state of mind which had been fostered by the Nazis' (TNA CRIM 1/1736).

We have little contemporary evidence to help us assess Eckersley and Clark's post-war statements about their activities from 1939 to 1945, and for the most part we can only place their two independent accounts recorded in CRIM 1/1736 (each given without knowledge of what the other was saying) against each other, and against infrequent other sources. From here onwards I will mainly be quoting from these two interviews, making it clear when necessary who is speaking.

Clark stated that as early as August 1940 he had come to his senses and begun to react against the Germans as a British patriot, and that he repeatedly discussed things with his mother, who agreed that they must try to find a way to get out of their situation. They nevertheless continued broadcasting, in his case right up until July 1942. He said that his mother and he had 'more or less drifted through 1941, both of us continuing our work and too intimidated to take any active steps'.

Yet Dorothy's reactions when in October 1941 she was taken off the air do not seem to match this version of events. We know that her dismissal had not been of her own volition. There had been complaints about her 'plaintive' voice (her 'upper-class' tones being obviously less effective than Joyce's less authentic 'haw-haw' accent) (Bergmeier and Lotz, 1997: 96). She was not (as we would expect from the later accounts) relieved by losing this job, but complained that she had been 'demoted'. She was not at first given very much to do. 'They all said that if I wanted to work there I could sit there and see what they could give me.' So sit there she did. Eventually, in February 1942 she was put in a lesser job trawling the archives for information to be used in anti-British broadcasts. This 'very pleasant' job lasted till January 1943.

Clark fell seriously ill in mid-1942 and had to have four months' sick leave, his last broadcast being on 19 July 1942 (BAK R55/230, in Bergmeier and Lotz, 1997). He claims that his mother and he had decided to exaggerate this illness as a basis for an attempt to sever their connections with the German broadcasting system. Clark was sent to stay with friends near Vienna, the Count and Countess von Zeppelin, while Dorothy Eckersley continued in her employment at the *Rundfunk* archives, 'our only means of support'.

Clark returned to Berlin in November 1942, still unfit for work. In January Dorothy had an accident at work (falling, and suffering concussion), as a result of which she had to give up her job. According to Clark, she used this illness in order to break away from her employers, but Dorothy said merely that she had been seriously ill, and an invalid for the next two years, 'never fit for work again'. Clark spent the period January–March 1943 nursing her through her illness. German archives describe how, in April, it was agreed to give the Eckersleys financial support, given 'the political importance of the work of Mrs Eckersley and her son, and the political consequences which a passive response of the RRG [*Reichsrundfunk*] would engender. Considering the political and military situation it is almost essential to support Mrs Eckersley with a one-off payment of 1,000 marks' (BAK R55/230, in Bergmeier and Lotz, 1997).

Meanwhile, Eckersley and Clark tried to get exit permits to go to friends in Hungary, but these were refused. The 1,000 marks had soon gone; they were now without any income. Dorothy resorted to selling articles of personal property. She also turned to an old friend from pre-war London, Idabelle von Bülow, the American wife of a German officer. In July 1943 Idabelle left to join her husband in Poland, after making arrangements to help Dorothy, who from September 1943 to November 1944 received 500 marks a month from the Propaganda Ministry. Dorothy declared that she took this money 'to protect me from working'. Clark's version of this is quite different. According to him, though 'certain well-meaning friends' had arranged for these payments to be made, he and his mother 'continually refused this'.

It was in late 1944 that Eckersley and Clark finally broke with the broadcasting authorities. In October 1944 the Germans wrote saying it was essential for Clark to return to work at the *Rundfunk*. Dorothy replied, saying her son was too ill. In November she received a visit from an official of the Propaganda Ministry, who reminded her that Goebbels had authorised the payment of her monthly subsidy without requesting anything specific in return, and 'enquiring what she and her son proposed to do now that the war had entered a critical phase' (Bergmeier and Lotz, 1997: 97). Alarmed by this, Dorothy decided to return to the Propaganda Ministry all the money that had been paid to her, which she did on 16 December (it is not clear how she was able to do so). In a letter to Schmidt-Hansen she said: 'I cannot tell you how thankful I am for allowing me to repay the 8,000 marks. It is a great load off my mind. I ought never to have accepted it.' It is worth noting that she carefully kept copies of the banker's draft, and of her letter to Schmidt-Hansen, for eventual use in evidence (the letter was read out at her trial in December 1945, and the draft produced at the same time). On 24 December she and her son were both arrested, and after a short period in prison sent to separate internment camps, where they remained until the Liberation. Clark, now aged 22, was eventually interrogated at the Internment Camp at Terni, in Italy, on 18 June 1945, and Eckersley by Captain (later Major) Reginald Spooner, at Libenau Internment Camp on 2 July.

On 29 October they were both repatriated to face charges of aiding the enemy. At her interrogation on 2 July 1945, Mrs Eckersley had stated:

> The reason I worked for the Germans was money. When I began I no more thought I was working for the Germans than anything. I was only doing it to get money to support myself.

When the warrant was read to her at Croydon airport, she exclaimed, 'I am bowled over by the wording. I never did anything with intent to help the enemy. I only did it to get our bread and butter. What I did did not help the enemy one ha'p'orth' (*The Times*, 2/11/45). (Yet it is worth noting that this claim appears to be contradicted by the *Rundfunk*'s 1943 statement about the 'political importance' of her work.)

Eckersley's insouciance – her failure to recognise the treasonous nature of her activities – is even more disquieting than Bothamley's firm commitment to the Nazi cause. The judge was clearly not impressed by her defence. Sentencing her to twelve months' imprisonment on 10 December 1945, he said: 'You gave yourself wholeheartedly to the Germans. You were perfectly willing to, and did, assist in the propaganda which you yourself describe as propaganda against England.'

James Clark's defence was more effective. He and his mother had clearly, like so many other people in their position, begun to repent of their activities when, by 1943–4, it became more likely that the Germans would lose the war, and at that stage they started trying to break free from the *Rundfunk* and the Nazis. Clark claimed, however, that their change of heart had dated from as early as 1940:

> Approximately August 1940, I was somewhat shocked by the air raids on London and other towns in England. It was this news that brought me to my senses and I began to feel that I had a certain pride as an Englishman with a corresponding hate of the Germans. [My mother and I] had many discussions as to how we could get out of the position in which our foolishness had landed us. […] This was at the end of 1940.

As if to counteract any suspicion that it was Germany's changed circumstances in the later stages of the war that had prompted their eventual break with the *Rundfunk*, he stressed to his interrogator that 'it will be appreciated that I was trying to break from the Germans whilst they were still all victorious'. It is worth noting, however, that Clark's successful broadcasting career did go on until July 1942, and his mother's less spectacular work in the archives until January 1943. Major Spooner, who was not entirely convinced that he had heard everything he should have from Mrs Eckersley ('Mrs Eckersley said she would tell me all I wanted to know. I would not say she is a vague person. I don't think she told me all that she was able to'), expressed his doubts, in relation to her correspondence with the authorities in 1944 protecting her son against returning to work, as to whether there had been any such efforts before that date to prevent her son from broadcasting.

Clark's other defence, and a far more convincing one, was based on his youth, and on his initial gullibility and enthusiastic reception of Nazi lies. His interrogator, Detective Inspector Donald Fish, giving evidence at the trial, declared that he was convinced that Clark had been 'entirely frank' with him, and 'that he had repented long since of anything he had done in the past'. The judge concurred with this, and was far more impressed by Clark's evidence than by his mother's. He merely bound him over for two years, saying: 'I do not believe you have ever been a traitor. I think you were caught up with many others in that abominable and most insidious propaganda which was imbued with the so-called tenets of the Nazi youth organisation.'

Henry William Wicks and Margaret Wicks

H.W. Wicks (1893–1979) was a very different figure from those we have been studying. He is an extreme example of the way in which ideologies such as Nazism and anti-Semitism could affect people who were already emotionally vulnerable. In his case, this vulnerability consisted of a form of persecution mania that left him open to any influences that could help to explain the nature of the dark forces that lay behind his frustrations. Margaret (b. 1922), who became far more heavily involved than him in the Nazi machine, was his adopted daughter, the daughter of his brother-in-law John Arthur Dowsett. (There was another adopted child, Derek Malcolm, b. 1926.)

When Wicks later wanted to justify his actions, he was capable of weaving an even more complicated web of lies and obfuscation than most of those in the same position as him. If we had to rely on this evidence alone, we would be on shaky ground. Luckily, however, there are a great many contemporary documents (some of them used by MI5 to puncture his claims), on which our account will mainly be based.

Wicks was a compulsive litigant and a conspiracy theorist on the grand scale. An insurance agent, in the early Thirties he had a serious dispute with the Sun Life Assurance Company of Canada on the basis of his widespread allegations as to the company's financial viability. The company, after confessions by two of Wicks's associates that they and Wicks had been furthering their own business by predicting Sun Life of Canada's imminent collapse, wrote to all its branch offices about the matter. This coincided with the collapse of Wicks's own business. He issued a writ for libel. In the course of a trial in April–May 1934 his action was dismissed with costs, as were three further defamation cases he then brought against individual Sun Life employees. By now he was bankrupt. Meanwhile, he was also harassing his own solicitor Leslie Burgin, whom he believed to be part of Sun Life of Canada's conspiracy against him.

When Wicks found that Gurney, the company's representative who had investigated his affairs, was now prosecuting a former employee called Chapman for fraud and forgery, he sent Chapman a letter of support which contained defamatory statements about Gurney. But Chapman pleaded guilty, and gave Gurney the letter. Sun Life of Canada now saw a way to deal once and for all with Wicks, and gave financial support to Gurney to prosecute him. In January 1936 Wicks was condemned to twelve months in prison for criminal libel (Spencer, 1979: *passim*).

This was to change Wicks's life completely. One of his fellow prisoners in Wormwood Scrubs was Arnold Leese, leader of the Imperial Fascist League. Leese's teachings were a revelation to Wicks. At last, he felt, he had found the nature of that mysterious power that lay behind the sinister conspiracy against him. As he later wrote in a letter to H.R. Hoffmann: 'When I met Arnold Leese in prison I became enlightened as to the part played by the Jews, and from then on worked with our Fascist friends for peace and understanding with Germany' (TNA KV 2/421).

After his release in December 1936 Wicks called at the German Embassy to establish a continuing contact. He also began moving in German circles in London, and was in contact with various members of the British extreme Right, such as John Beckett, Captain George Pitt-Rivers, Admiral Sir Barry Domvile and Commander Cole of the Nordic League, as well, of course, as his mentor Arnold Leese. His case was taken up by the Nordic League, and by a number of other rightwing movements. This enabled him to produce a pamphlet setting out his grievances, printed by the British Union printer Arthur E. Baker (TNA KV 2/420). He was also frequenting Margaret Bothamley's salon at 67 Cromwell Road, where among others he met Mary Stanford,

Robert Gordon-Canning, Aubrey Lees and the German propagandist H.R. Hoffmann.

In the late Thirties Wicks's obsession with Burgin (whom he still saw as central to the conspiracy against him) took a new turn. Burgin, a Liberal National MP, had become Minister of Transport in 1937. His prominence, and his appointment as Minister of Supply in 1939, gave Wicks free rein with regard to conspiracy theory. By now, believing erroneously that Burgin was Jewish, he proceeded to weave a web of accusations around him, to do with complicity in international arms deals. These accusations he later outlined in the unpublished manuscript of a book entitled 'A Non Pareil Case' (SCC, Wicks).

In April 1938 Wicks paid a short visit to Germany, at the expense of the German government (TNA FO371/21782). There he made contact with Dr Karl Schmidt, an official in the *Sicherheitsdienst* (secret service). In the spring of 1939 he returned to Berlin, shortly followed by his wife Caroline and their two children Margaret and Derek, now aged 17 and 13. This was to be an extended stay. To the British Embassy, Wicks gave as his address as that of Dr Schmidt (TNA FO 371/23091).

On 26 May 1939 Wicks wrote to H.R. Hoffmann (who lived near Munich), reminding him that they had met at Miss Bothamley's, and declaring that he and his family had come to live in Germany 'as political refugees from Jew controlled England'. From this letter we learn that he had already been preparing 'highly appreciated' broadcast propaganda for the German government. In a number of further letters to Hoffmann in June-August, we gather that he had been trying (armed with a letter of introduction from Arnold Leese) to contact Julius Streicher (the violently anti-Jewish editor of *Der Stürmer*), and that he believed that the story he and his family could tell 'would shock and stagger the whole civilised world' (TNA CRIM 1/1767).

He then told this 'story', on 17 July, in a press interview for the newspaper *Der Angriff*, under the headline 'An English Refugee: the Jews are Terrorising the English People' ('Ein englischer Flüchtling: Die Juden terrorisieren das englische Volk'), in which he said he had given himself and his family over to the protection of the Reich because there was a Jewish terror power in London that made it no longer possible for British people to speak freely. The influence of the Jews in England was responsible for the criminal war fever that reigned there. The Jewish power was, he said, strengthened by the presence in the Cabinet of people like the criminals Burgin and Hore-Belisha (the Secretary of State for War, and a target for anti-Semitic attacks throughout this period).

This caused a storm in Britain. Several newspapers published articles quoting this interview (e.g. *DT* 18/7/39, *DS* 18/7/39) and questions were asked in the House of Commons on 20 July. In an interview over the telephone to the *Daily Sketch* Wicks reiterated his accusations of a 'Jewish reign of terror' and of 'Government corruption', and declared that only in Germany did he feel safe. His son, he said, was already in a Hitler Youth camp, and his daughter was doing social work for the German government (*DS* 19/7/39).

Wicks was later to claim that the *Angriff* article had been published without his knowledge, and that he had had no hand in its writing. Its similarity to statements in his contemporary correspondence and to his interviews with the British press shows, however, the falseness of this claim.

After further questions were asked in the House of Commons on 3 August, Margaret Wicks's natural father, John Arthur Dowsett, wrote to her, begging her to return to England. Her reply was a refusal to do so, on the grounds that 'in Germany we have found perfect peace and happiness'. She wanted to remain there, she said, until all the 'talk of war and preparation for war in England' was over. She added that she would shortly be returning to her studies at Wannsee (a Hitler Youth school) (TNA KV 2/419).

On 2 September Wicks wrote to Hoffmann, saying that war was now inevitable, and that he felt it his duty to form a 'peace front' to enlighten his fellow countrymen as to how they were being exploited 'for Alien finance and for the joint enemies of Britain and Germany'. He asked Hoffmann's advice as to which would be his best path: to bring his family down to Bavaria and work with Hoffmann to this end, or to work from a neutral country like Denmark where it would be easier to keep in touch with 'those in England who are of our way of thinking' (TNA CRIM 1/1767). Wicks was later to claim that his attempts to get to Denmark in the days immediately preceding the outbreak of war were patriotic, in order to escape Nazi Germany. Given the plans outlined here, this was patently untrue.

After the outbreak of war on 3 September, Wicks, as a guest of Dr Schmidt, was exempt from being registered as an enemy alien. In mid-September he was summoned to the *Rundfunk*, and told that the Nazis wished to use him for their propaganda service. He was set to write scripts for broadcasting. MI5 suggests that he was fairly useless to the Germans: 'They paid him, but his writings were so full of his personal (and now outdated) history that they were useless' (TNA KV 2/419). Nevertheless, in July 1940 he did write 'a short, topical and therefore useful article' about the DR 18B detention in Britain, that month, of Admiral Domvile and Captain Pitt-Rivers. It appeared in Hoffmann's *British News and Views*, and in it Wicks gave vent to his usual accusations about the state of Britain:

> The Underworld of Jewish Plutocracy in its headlong retreat has taken – as prisoners of war – a considerable number of the very cream of the British race and immured them in prisons under conditions of some secrecy [...] Admiral Domvile is a prisoner of Jewish Plutocracy. Captain Pitt-Rivers [...] resented the Jewish occupation and domination of England by the satellites of International Jewry, Churchill, Eden, Burgin, Duff Cooper and their clique.
>
> (Wicks, 1940)

By late July 1940, however, the Germans were beginning to tire of Wicks. Not only were his scripts on the whole fairly useless, he was also 'making an intolerable nuisance of himself in Berlin', in a series of public and vituperative exchanges with people he believed to have wronged him, at times having recourse to his usual tactics of distributing libellous pamphlets. His disruptive behaviour, 'from an enemy-alien who had proved himself of negligible value as a propagandist, was more than the German authorities could stand' (TNA KV 2/419). He was arrested and interned in late July in an internment camp at Wülzburg, in Bavaria.

At Wülzburg, the other detainees were extremely wary of him. From their later evidence we learn that he arrived in the camp 'with a bad reputation, thanks to his pre-war ("Angriff") publicity', and that he compounded this by joining 'the small "pro-German" group [...]

openly pandering to the Germans'. Fellow detainees viewed him as 'one of the worst and most unsatisfactory characters in the camp' and an 'out-and-out pro-German', who assisted the Germans in the office and administrative work. They were 'generally warned to beware of him as he was suspected of being an informer'. One more charitable detainee, while admitting that Wicks 'had a bad name in the camp', did comment that he was 'not so much pro-German as a crank' (TNA KV 2/419). In September 1941 the Wülzburg internees were transported to Ilag (Internierungslager) VIII, in a town further east called Tost. By February 1942, however, we learn from a doctor's certificate that Wicks had developed heart trouble serious enough for him to be excused work in the camp (SCC, Wicks).

Meanwhile, his adopted daughter Margaret had for the previous couple of years been working for Interradio (the German Foreign Broadcasting Company). Surprisingly (for she was clearly a highly valued employee), we do not have much information about her activities, apart from what exists in her father's files. (It appears that there *was* an MI5 file specifically on her, to which various documents from Wicks's file were transferred; but there is no trace of that file in the National Archives.) In early 1942, now aged 20, she was transferred to Interradio's new branch, Radio Metropol. Later that year she approached Dr Harald Diettrich, the head of Radio Metropol, asking him to help her to get her father released, as his health was too poor to withstand life in an internment camp. Diettrich decided to help: 'I said I would do what I could, and a letter was written by my company to the Propaganda Ministry in Berlin. As it was necessary to put forward some reason for asking for his release, the letter said that he might perhaps be of use to Interradio' (TNA KV 2/421). In October 1942 Margaret visited her father, and was allowed to have a private conversation with him. As MI5 later put it, 'What passed at that meeting is a matter for guesswork' (TNA KV 2/419). A month later Wicks, very aware that his daughter was 'of value' to the Germans (SCC, Wicks), was able to return to Berlin a free man, and to rejoin his family.

In April 1943 Wicks started work with Radio Metropol as a freelance writer who was paid fees for the work he did (TNA KV 2/421). Diettrich stated post-war that a month later Wicks, knowing that Diettrich was short of British announcers, drew to his attention (TNA

HO 45/25626) one of the 'small pro-German group' of internees who had been with him at Wülzburg and Tost, John Alexander Ward, who joined Radio Metropol in June, and was to become one of the station's most successful broadcasters, his programmes consisting mainly of 'defeatist, anti-Semitic and anti-Russian propaganda' (TNA HO 45/25826).

By late 1943 Wicks, realising that Germany was losing the war, was already thinking of ways to avoid being caught and tried as a traitor. Typically, his schemes were highly unreal. He tried to persuade the German authorities to let him go on a diplomatic mission to neutral Spain, 'and from there by propaganda provoke mutiny in the British armed forces'. He wrote to the Pope, saying that as the Catholic Church was the only defence against International Finance Power supported by Freemasonry, he wished to live in a Catholic country (i.e. Spain). He also wrote to the International Red Cross, asking them to help him to expose his case personally to Sir Samuel Hoare, the British Ambassador in Spain (TNA KV 2/420–421). In a letter of 11 October 1943 to Willi Wodrich, his daughter Margaret's boyfriend (a government official and an active member of the Nazi Party, who had 'powerful friends in German governmental circles' (SCC, Wicks)), Wicks laid out the reasons for his manoeuvres:

> As I think you know, there are very pressing practical and important problems facing both Margaret and me at the moment. For instance, our going to Spain. This [...] may be a matter of life and death for Margaret and me should the war situation develop so as to throw us into the hands of our enemies who would certainly act without mercy for what we have done, and can do, to help Germany in the struggle for her national existence.
>
> (SCC, Wicks)

The appeal to the Red Cross turned out to be a mistake. They consulted the German authorities about him, and the reaction from German officials, who must already have been tiring of Wicks's gambits, was immediate. As the Red Cross later put it, 'The German authorities, [...] after we had explained your difficult situation to them, decided that the best way of helping you was to intern you in a camp with British civilians'

(SCC, Wicks). On 12 February 1944 Wicks, and his wife and son, were arrested. A couple of weeks later they were sent to an internment camp at Vittel, in northern France.

Margaret did not accompany them. In Wicks's (admittedly unreliable) post-war memoirs, he states that they had expected her to join the family, but that she remained with her lover Willi Wodrich, refusing, over the telephone, even to come to the station to see them off. She continued working with the Nazis, and shortly after this she married Willi Wodrich.

The rest of the Wicks family remained at the Vittel camp until the Allied forces arrived on 12 September 1944. Despite Wicks's pleas to be repatriated to Britain, he was kept in Paris. Gradually the Allied authorities began to realise the activities that this apparently innocuous internee had been engaged in during his time in Germany. By April 1945 he was being investigated by the legendary MI5 interrogator Captain W.J. Skardon (SCC, Wicks). By 18 March 1946 MI5 had prepared a summary of the case against Wicks (TNA KV 2/422), and in May he appeared at the Old Bailey. On 28 May he was sentenced to four years' penal servitude.

And what of Margaret? Now Margaret Wodrich, she wrote from Berlin on 3 June 1946 to refuse to appear at Wicks's appeal (scheduled for November) either for her father or for the prosecution (TNA KV 2/421). She was not pursued by the authorities for her wartime activities, even though she appears to have been not only more successful in her career than her father, but also much more dedicated to the Nazi cause. A nephew of hers, on the Dowsett side of the family, has described her as having, in later life, remained 'a Nazi sympathiser and a holocaust denier' (Muggins, 2009). At all events, she got off scot free (and unless or until a file on her surfaces, we will know no more).

As for Wicks, his November 1946 appeal failed, and he served four years in prison, convinced yet again that there was a dark conspiracy against him.

The sentences

The discrepancy between the sentence meted out to Wicks and those handed down to Bothamley, Eckersley and Clark (not to mention the lack of any proceedings against Margaret Wicks) is striking. All four were tried on the lesser charge of having acted 'with intent to assist the enemy', as opposed to Joyce and Amery (who were tried for the greater crime of 'treason'). Yet Wicks had in many respects seemed to have greater extenuating circumstances than either Bothamley or Eckersley. His pro-German activities had been sporadic and unsuccessful, and his commitment seemed to have been more to himself and to his obsessions than to the Nazi cause. The comparative harshness of his treatment seems even more mysterious when one realises that MI5, in its case for the prosecution, had done much to excuse him, stating that he had been 'less pro-German than pro-Wicks, and less anti-British than anti-Burgin', that he was 'not […] a pro-German or a pro-Nazi, who committed deliberate treason in order to assist the German victory', and that he was 'obsessed with grievances and probably, to some extent at least, mentally unbalanced' (TNA KV 2/419, KV 2/420, KV 2/422).

One possibility is, of course, that as in his pre-war libel trials he may have upset the court by his perpetual interruptions and irrelevancies. Also, so many of his post-war accounts of what had happened were so blatantly false (and could be proved so by documents which he did not realise were in the possession of the authorities), that he probably aroused even more suspicion than he would otherwise have done.

Yet this variation in judicial attitudes is highlighted even more by the decision not to pursue Margaret Wodrich. It is true that James Clark, who was much of an age with her, was merely bound over for two years; but he *had* been brought to trial. It was naturally important, as the judge did, to take into account Clark's youth, and it was also important to bear in mind that he was the son of a powerful and politically opinionated mother who could be considered to have 'brainwashed' him, and whose attitude about the overriding need to earn money at whatever moral cost may have affected him. But in the case of Margaret, Wicks was hardly a powerful father; indeed, he was a failure in almost everything he did, including parenting. And all the evidence seems to show that in 1942, when she was in her early twenties, it was Margaret who had taken the dominant role, having carved out on her own initiative a career for herself, and that it was she who obtained the release of her father and organised a place for him in Radio Metropol. Where he was an inadequate failure, she was clearly a success.

Her German marriage and consequent German citizenship may, of course, have affected things; but the fact remains that she was a British citizen at the time of her wartime activities. One is reminded of the treatment of Margaret Joyce. Yet in the latter case, the authorities had clearly decided, after William Joyce's death sentence, that it was best, 'on compassionate grounds', not to prosecute his wife. While there was 'no lack of evidence implicating her in the treasonous activities of her late husband', they 'did not think that she need be punished further' (TNA KV 2/436).

While there were no such compassionate grounds for Margaret Wodrich (née Wicks), there is little doubt that the authorities were by now getting into quite a tangle as regards sentencing, and as Margaret Wodrich was living happily in Germany as a German citizen, they may have decided to let sleeping dogs lie. Also, one must bear in mind that their sentencing of women was noticeably more lenient than that of men.

Among the men, too, the discrepancies were great. At the trial of Leonard Banning, a former BU member who appears to have entered broadcasting by chance, the judge, while accepting that he 'did not desire to betray [his] country', and that he had acted because he was 'so weak and so strongly determined to look after [him]self', sentenced him to ten years' penal servitude (Doherty, 2000: 21). Walter Purdy of the Royal Navy, who broadcast from 1943 onwards in order to get out of his POW Camp, was tried for treason and sentenced to death (commuted to life imprisonment). Raymond Davies Hughes, an airman who among other things broadcast seditious propaganda in Welsh to the Welsh troops in Italy, and wrote anti-Jewish propaganda for the service, was given five years' penal servitude, reduced to two years on appeal.

These discrepancies, however, fade into insignificance beside the cases of those renegades who were not even brought before the courts. No action was taken, for example, against John Alexander Ward, whom we have seen as a highly-prized broadcaster, regularly producing 'defeatist, anti-Semitic and anti-Russian propaganda' aimed at the

British Army; his activities far outshone those of his fellow internee Wicks, who had first brought him to the attention of the German authorities. No charges either were brought against Kenneth Lander, another broadcaster who had in the course of his broadcasting applied to become a naturalised German and to join the German army (both refused by the Germans). There are innumerable other discrepancies, and one gets the impression that the British authorities, and the courts, were completely out of their depth. In this situation, the difference between the treatments of Bothamley, Eckersley, Clark, Henry Wicks and Margaret Wicks is minimal.

These five characters are of particular interest to students of interwar British fascism. The three adults were typical, in their various ways, of the metropolitan fascist fringe, and their wartime activities in Germany stemmed, unlike those of so many servicemen and others who acted on grounds purely of self-interest or self-protection, in large part from their ingrained beliefs about the Communist threat, the Jewish threat and the virtues of Nazism. Unlike so many of their companions who remained in Britain, they had, with varying degrees of competence or commitment, found a way to put those beliefs into practice.

Bibliography

Books and articles

Bergmeier, Horst, and Lotz, Rainer (1997), *Hitler's Airwaves: The Inside Story of Nazi Radio Broadcasting and Propaganda Swing* (New Haven and London: Yale University Press).

Bothamley, Margaret (1937), *A Statement by an Englishwoman about National Socialist Germany (as broadcast from Berlin October 22nd, 1936)* (Reprinted by Steven Books, London, March 2010).

Bothamley, Margaret (1938), 'The Austrian Plebiscite', *The Patriot*, 21 April.

Bowra, C.M. (1966), *Memories 1898–1939* (London: Weidenfeld and Nicolson).

Clark, Kenneth (1974), *Another Part of the Wood: A Self-Portrait* (London: John Murray).

Cole, J.A. (1964), *Lord Haw-Haw – and William Joyce: The Full Story* (London: Faber and Faber).

Doherty, M.A. (2000), *Nazi Wireless Propaganda: Lord Haw-Haw and Public Opinion in the Second World War* (Edinburgh: Edinburgh University Press).

Eckersley, Myles (1998), *Prospero's Wireless: A Biography of P.P. Eckersley* (Romsey: Myles Books).

Farndale, Nigel (2005), *Haw-Haw: The Tragedy of William and Margaret Joyce* (London: Macmillan).

Griffiths, Richard (2014), 'Antisemitic Obsessions: The Case of H.W. Wicks', *Patterns of Prejudice* 48, 1, 94–113.

Holmes, Colin (2016), *Searching for Lord Haw-Haw: The Political Lives of William Joyce* (Abingdon: Routledge).

Kenny, Mary (2003), *Germany Calling: A Personal Biography of William Joyce/Lord Haw-Haw* (Dublin: New Island).

Muggins (2009), 'Muggins from Sussex', blog: www.genealogistsforum.co.uk/forum/archive/index.php?t-2556.html, 27 December.

Muir, Kate (1991), 'The Englishman who Felt Nazi Germany Calling', *The Times*, 3 May.

Roberts, C.E. Bechofer (1946), *The Trial of William Joyce* (London: Jarrolds).

Spencer, John (1979), 'Criminal Libel in Action – The Snuffing of Mr Wicks', *Cambridge Law Journal*, 38, 1, 60–78.

Stone, Dan (2003), *Responses to Nazism in Britain, 1933–1939: Before War and Holocaust* (Basingstoke: Palgrave Macmillan).

Weale, Adrian (1994), *Renegades: Hitler's Englishmen* (London, Weidenfeld and Nicolson).

West, Rebecca (1949), *The Meaning of Treason* (London: Macmillan).

Wicks, Henry William (1940), 'The Distinguished British Patriots Sir Barry Domvile and Captain G.E. Pitt-Rivers', *British News and Views*, September.

Documents

National Archives (TNA)

CRIM 1/1736, CRIM 1/1763, CRIM 1/1767, CRIM 1/1781
FO 371/21782, FO 371/23091
HO 45/25626, HO 45/25811, HO 45/25826
KV 2/256, KV 2/346, KV 2/419, KV 2/420, KV 2/421, KV 2/422, KV 2/430, KV 2/832, KV 2/833

National Maritime Museum (NMM)

Admiral Domvile's Diary, DOM 56, DOM 58

Bundesarchiv, Koblenz (BAK)

R55/230

Selwyn College, Cambridge Library (SCC)

Papers of H.W. Wicks (Wicks)

Newspapers and journals

Der Angriff (DA)
Daily Sketch (DS)
Daily Telegraph (DT)
The Times

PART V

Pro-Nazism, patriotism, hatred, fear, remorse: the extraordinary variety of motives among former 'fellow travellers'

8

'HAVE YOU FOUND MANY LAVALS AMONG YOUR GALLOWAY FRIENDS?'

Wartime and post-war disputes between three former 'fellow travellers of the Right'

After the crackdown of May–June 1940, the pressures on those pre-war Nazi sympathisers who had not been detained was intense. Some had, of course, taken a straightforward patriotic line once war had been declared in 1939, with those of an age volunteering for military service; and at the opposite extreme there were others who were to continue their pre-war agenda even after June 1940 (at times to the extent of undertaking subversive activities); but there were many intermediary positions between these two extremes, as people tried to adjust to the new situation. One of these was the attempt, made by a number of people, to cover their tracks by publicly drawing attention to their repugnance for pro-Nazism and by denouncing their former colleagues. An outstanding example of this is the relationship between three former 'fellow travellers of the Right', who had for years been friends and neighbours. This situation was to change radically now, owing to their differing reactions to their previous activities, reactions which give us some inkling of the problems of such people, and of how history became rewritten in the process.

Dramatis personae

These three men were major landowners in Western Scotland: the 12th Earl of Galloway, John McKie MP and our old friend the Marquess of

Tavistock (later 12th Duke of Bedford). Their estates lay in close proximity to each other in the county of Galloway, and they knew each other well. In the period just before the Second World War they each, to a greater or lesser extent, became involved in pro-Nazi activities. Then, after 1940, there were a number of occasions when they seriously fell out with one another – McKie and Tavistock/Bedford during the war, Galloway and McKie in its aftermath.

Two of them, the Earl of Galloway and John McKie MP, had much in common. Randolph Algernon Stewart, 12th Earl of Galloway (1892–1978), lived at his estate at Cumloden, just north-east of Newton Stewart. He had served in the Scots Guards in the First World War, been seriously wounded and become a German prisoner of war. After the war, he settled down into his traditional family duties in western Scotland, and in 1932 became Lord Lieutenant of Kirkcudbrightshire, a post which he held till 1975. He also became chairman of the Galloway Unionist Association, and played a leading role in Scottish freemasonry.

Galloway was a stern and unbending man, heavily conscious of family tradition. Ever since the creation of the title in the early seventeenth century, the Stewarts of Galloway had served the state as politicians, as Lord Lieutenants, but above all as military men, counting several generals and at least one admiral among their number (one ancestor, General Sir William Stewart, had co-founded the Rifle Brigade during the Napoleonic Wars). The 12th Earl was inordinately proud of this history, and expected his family to live up to it and to their public duties (Carpenter, 2004: *passim*). Among the family traditions which he valued, alongside the military virtues, was education at Harrow School, which had been attended by members of the family for at least the previous four generations (Galloway, 1854).

John Hamilton McKie (1898–1958), though a commoner, was the current head of a similarly prestigious family, the McKies of Bargaly. In the fourteenth century King Robert Bruce had given them lands in Galloway in reward for their gallantry at Bannockburn. John Hamilton McKie still owned the lands at Bargaly (just east of Newton Stewart, and very close to Cumloden), and though his main abode was now Auchencairn House, near Castle Douglas, he still kept his Bargaly interests. Generation after generation, since the Union with England, the McKies had represented this area in Parliament, and John Hamilton

McKie, whose grandfather and great-grandfather had both held the seat, was no exception. He was elected Unionist (Conservative) MP for Galloway in the 1931 election, and was returned unopposed in 1935. His neighbour Lord Galloway was his constituency chairman. They had other things in common, moreover. The McKie family had equally strong ties with Harrow, which John had attended (though arriving there just as Galloway was leaving); and McKie and Galloway were fellow members of three gentlemen's clubs (*Who's Who*, 1942). While it was hardly surprising that they should both belong to the New Club, Edinburgh (the club of the Scottish elite) and the Carlton Club, London (the leading Conservative club), it is worthy of note that they both also belonged to another London club called the Bachelors' Club (which has been described as the original for P.G. Wodehouse's 'Drones Club', and was clearly a very lively place) (Lejeune, 1984: 242). It does therefore appear that their paths crossed regularly in London as well as in Scotland.

The Marquess of Tavistock was to succeed his father as 12th Duke of Bedford in August 1940. The main Bedford estates were in Bedfordshire, in Buckinghamshire, in Devon and in central London, but the family had, since the mid-nineteenth century, held Cairnsmore House near Newton Stewart (adjoining the Earl of Galloway's estate) on a long-term tenancy from the McKie family. Since 1887 the Bedford family had also rented from the McKies the nearby Bargaly grouse moor and deer forest on a series of shorter tenancies. This grouse moor will be of central interest in relation to the wartime disputes between McKie and Tavistock.

Tavistock, who had been born at Cairnsmore, had a great affection for the place, and despite his estrangement from his father, in the early 1930s he rented a house nearby from the Earl of Galloway. Then, when his father decided to give up the tenancy of Cairnsmore in 1937, Tavistock took it on from McKie, returning to his 'old and much-loved birthplace', where from now on he was to spend much of his time (Bedford, 1949: 127, 176). He was at Cairnsmore when war broke out, and, though during the 'phoney war' he occasionally came south for political activities, and later (after becoming Duke of Bedford) came down to attend the House of Lords, he was there for most of the war.

As we have already seen, Tavistock was a very different kettle of fish from his neighbours. In contrast with the military Galloway and the traditionally political McKie, he was a lifelong pacifist who had been the despair of his father, and something of an anti-social outsider. All the more strange, therefore, that he too should have been a member of the Bachelors' Club (*Kelly*, 1934). Its convivial atmosphere can hardly have appealed to this introverted character. Perhaps, when looking for a London club, he had asked the advice of his Scottish neighbours!

The build-up to war

Where the pro-Nazi activities of Tavistock, as we have seen, were open and blatant in the lead-up to the war, Galloway and McKie were involved in less public activities that were fully revealed only when in 1990 both men were discovered to have figured on the secret Membership List of Captain Ramsay's Right Club.

Do we have information about the views which led McKie and Galloway to join the Right Club? In the case of McKie, we have plenty. The many political speeches which he gave in his constituency show him to have been not merely a keen follower of the appeasement policy of the British government, but also someone who failed ever to find anything wrong with the German regime, which he strongly admired. He welcomed both the result of the Saar plebiscite in 1935 (*GN*, 19/1/35) and the march into the Rhineland in 1936, remarking favourably on the German proposals that had accompanied it (*GN*, 18/4/36), and in 1938 pointed out the economic and financial benefits that would accrue to Austria as a result of the *Anschluss* (*GN*, 13/3/38). On Czechoslovakia, he spoke of the British public's ignorance of the true facts, which were that this artificial state had held the seeds of friction from the start, and that the German minority had been appallingly treated (*GN*, 5/11/38). He also denied any interference by the Nazi regime in the affairs of the Christian churches in Germany (*GN*, 11/2/39).

A recurrent theme in reports of McKie's speeches was that of his admiration for the German miracle:

One must look back on the past five years and stand in wonder at what Herr Hitler had been able to accomplish. When they thought of that great country reduced as it was after the Great War, paralysed financially and in a most deplorable political condition, it was indeed amazing what Hitler had been able to accomplish.

(*GN*, 26/2/38)

The history of Germany in the last five years was one of the phenomena of history [...] Since the advent of Hitler to power in January 1933, Germany has been raised from well nigh the depths of chaos to the position of a first class power once more.

(*GN*, 13/3/38)

Amid all this admiration for Germany, he was forced to take account of the British public's concern at Germany's treatment of the Jews. He circumvented this by using the techniques I have described elsewhere as being typical of British pro-Nazis who wished to downplay Nazi anti-Semitism:

The mechanisms for excusing Nazi Germany and for placing its 'good' qualities above the drawbacks of its Jewish policy were amazingly stereotyped. They tended to start with a ritual statement of distaste for Hitler's treatment of the Jews, usually followed by a qualification of some kind [...] One ploy was to stress the problems Germany had faced from the Jews, who had taken over much of public life. The particular nature of the middle-European Jew was stressed, and the fact that much of their treatment had been their own fault.

(Griffiths, 1998: 14–15)

McKie's arguments follow this pattern closely, repeating almost parrot-fashion the kind of statements made by the Nazi propaganda machine:

While they [McKie's audience] deplored that [Jewish persecution] should be the case, they must remember that during the years of the great depression in Germany the Jews being the only people with any semblance of prosperity had exhibited the worst characteristics of their race, and although there was no justification for the kind of retaliation that had been indulged in, it was easy to understand how sore many millions of people must have been. In Central and Eastern Europe be it remembered the Jewish population had never shown the consciousness of citizenship.

(*GN*, 13/3/38)

McKie repeated these arguments almost word-for-word on a number of occasions. Amazingly, he even used them when commenting in November 1938 on the Kristallnacht pogrom, an event which had silenced (temporarily) most British anti-Semites. After the ritual deploring of the violence, he went on in this vein: 'There was against the Jewish people in Germany a fierce and deep-set hatred. After the war, when Germany was down…' [Here followed arguments similar to those quoted above] (*GN*, 20/11/38). It is interesting to note that one of the arguments McKie produced to contradict those who opposed giving Germany's colonies back to her because of potential German mistreatment of native Africans, was that the Germans had had some cause for their persecution of the Jews, but had no such cause in relation to Africans (*GN*, 11/2/39).

So McKie's presence on the Right Club list is not particularly surprising, despite the fact that after the war he on several occasions denied having had any significant relationship with Ramsay (whose name, because of his wartime activities, had by now become synonymous with treason). A typical example of this was McKie's post-war statement that in March or April 1939 he had met Captain Ramsay in the inner lobby of the House of Commons, and that Ramsay had asked him if he would like to come to a meeting in the house of a fellow member to hear about Jewish propaganda in this country. McKie claimed to have replied that 'such a thing did not interest him, because he had always, if anything, been pro-Jew, in fact, one of his best friends was a Jew' (*GN*, 30/6/45). McKie's post-war public protestations (of which we shall see more) were clearly replies to accusations about his pre-war relationship with Ramsay.

While we have a lot of information about McKie's views, we do not have quite so much for Lord Galloway. He did not tend to be a public speaker (though at one meeting of the Galloway Unionist Association, which McKie had been unable to attend because of a family bereavement, Galloway as chairman read out McKie's speech on international affairs and specifically on Germany's role, and does not seem to have demurred at it) (*GN*, 18/4/36). What we do know is that Galloway was, like McKie, a member of the Anglo-German Fellowship. He was also a prominent member of that more extreme body, the Right Club (and we shall see that, according to McKie, he privately expressed solidarity with Captain Ramsay at the time of the latter's arrest in 1940).

Galloway, like many on the pro-German Right, was a patriotic militarist who, while opposing the need for war with Germany, nevertheless believed that if it came to war, Britain needed to be properly prepared and properly armed. To that end, on 17 June 1939 he raised and commanded the 7th (Galloway) Battalion of the King's Own Scottish Borderers.

On the Right Club list, Galloway was listed as one of the fourteen 'Wardens', the most senior category of members of the Club. The other Wardens included some of the most prominent figures of the pro-Nazi Right: William Joyce, the 5th Duke of Wellington, Lord Sempill, Lord Redesdale and E.H. Cole (the leading figure of the Nordic League, and in close contact with the Nazi government through the German Embassy in London). Most of these figures were, like Galloway, members of the Anglo-German Fellowship.

The 'phoney war' (September 1939 to May 1940)

After the outbreak of the Second World War, we have no evidence of public pro-Nazi statements or activities by either McKie or Galloway. It is possible that, like many on the Right Club list and like many others who had espoused pro-Nazi policies in the inter-war period, they now found, once war had been declared, that their patriotism took precedence over any other opinions they may have had; or it may have been, as with other members, that they found discretion to be the better part of valour. Whatever the reasons, like many others McKie and

Galloway do not appear to have continued as members of the Right Club, which was hereafter a mere rump of its former self. However, if we are to trust the post-war statements of McKie (who, while attempting to exculpate himself, also pointed the finger at his former friend, with whom he was now in dispute), Galloway continued privately to express anti-war opinions during this period, deploring in September 1939 Britain's entry into the war, saying 'it was madness to enter the war on the Polish issue', and then, on 17 March 1940, sending McKie a message saying that he hoped he would as his MP give support to any move to call off the war. In this account, McKie (possibly for fear of an action for slander) referred cryptically to Galloway as 'a prominent member of the Galloway Unionist Executive'. It is clear, however, from other statements made at about the same time producing the same kind of charges, which we will be considering later, that his target was Galloway, whom he also described, at the time of Captain Ramsay's arrest in May 1940, as having said that 'it was a terrible thing, nay a dreadful thing that a patriot like Captain Ramsay should be detained by a Socialist Home Secretary' (*GN*, 23/6/45 and 30/6/45). Such attitudes were typical of a number of Scottish aristocrats, including Galloway's close friend Lord Carnegie, later Earl of Southesk (at whose marriage Galloway had been best man), who, when questioned in 1990 about his own membership of the Right Club, said of Ramsay: 'He was a very loyal, patriotic man. Churchill was only down on him because he was anti-Semitic' (*ES*, 16/5/90).

On 28 March 1940 Galloway had announced his resignation from the post of Commanding Officer of the 7th Battalion of the King's Own Scottish Borderers, owing to ill health.

McKie, meanwhile, was keeping a low profile. But he was already beginning his denials of his pre-war attitudes. In June 1940 Captain Ramsay's solicitors contacted him, when Ramsay's case was about to be put to an Advisory Committee. The solicitors, who were writing with the same request to a number of other prominent figures whose names Ramsay must have given to them, asked if McKie 'would see his way to put in a good word for Captain Ramsay'. McKie claimed after the war that he 'was exceedingly annoyed, and wrote back in very strong terms to the legal firm informing them […] he for one felt Captain Ramsay had behaved very badly indeed, to put it mildly' (*GN*, 30/6/45). This denial fits very well with McKie's changed attitudes in June 1940, and so this later story is no doubt fairly accurate. It is interesting to note that a number of the other prominent people who were approached at the same time, wrote unlike him, in Ramsay's favour. They included some others who were secretly members of the Right Club, among them Francis Yeats-Brown, Sir Ernest Bennett MP, Dr J.H. Mellotte and Lord Sempill. They stated that 'they were all of the opinion that it was inconceivable that Captain Ramsay could be guilty of any subversive acts or indeed of anything which was contrary to the true interests of this country' (TNA HO 45/25696).

In contrast with Galloway and McKie, during this 'phoney war' period the Marquess of Tavistock did undertake a number of questionable activities, some public and some private. Nothing was going to deter him from his firmly held views, which he did not feel to be in any way unpatriotic. His formation of the British Council for a Christian Settlement in Europe (BCCSE), and the publicity given to the pro-Nazi sentiments produced at its meetings, alerted the general public to his stance, and by Spring 1940 his 'peace proposals', and the press coverage given to them, made him an even better known figure. As even the extreme right-wing and anti-Semitic *Free Press* commented, 'There was no doubt about the sincerity of his intentions, but one was left wondering how an Englishman of the standing of Lord Tavistock could be the victim of such delusions' (*FP*, 4/40). From now on Tavistock became a by-word in wartime Britain for a potential quisling in the event of invasion.

The effect of the DR 18B imprisonments in May–June 1940

John McKie had been keeping a fairly low profile, as far as public statements were concerned, in the first eight months of the war. Suddenly, however, in mid-1940 he sprang into action on the national stage. From now on, he was going to do everything possible to prove to the public and to the government that he was a loyal, patriotic servant of the State, and implacably opposed to pro-Nazism and to subversion of every kind. In this, he appears to have conformed to the pattern of behaviour among some of those who had before the war espoused the pro-Nazi cause, which has been described by Ronald Stent:

> No doubt they suffered from acute embarrassment, if not from a bad conscience. They must have been anxious to obliterate in the public mind their own immediate political past; hoping that if they were '*plus royaliste que le roi*' people would forget their pre-war pro-Nazi propaganda.
>
> (Stent, 1980: 260)

The first manifestation of this, on the part of McKie, was a couple of public attacks he made upon Tavistock in June-July 1940. Why did he choose this time to act? In May 1940 the first wave of arrests under Defence Regulation 18B had taken place, and may have concentrated his mind. Among the first to be arrested was Captain Ramsay. Also, in the raid on Tyler Kent's flat, the 'Red Book', the ledger containing the list of Right Club members, had been discovered and impounded by the authorities (though its existence was not made public at this stage).

Ramsay's arrest must have made it important for McKie, who was also no doubt disconcerted by the solicitors' request in June for support for the gallant captain, to dissociate himself publicly from Ramsay (who was now not merely someone of extremist views, but also under suspicion of acting as a traitor), by producing evidence of his own disapproval of subversive activities. And how better to do this than by pointing the finger at the public's new scapegoat, the Marquess of Tavistock – particularly as McKie had a personal connection with him, and therefore an apparent justification for speaking out? After a speech in his constituency on 15 June, stressing his own patriotism and declaring that 'Germany is the main enemy now' (*GG*, 15/6/40), he moved his artillery onto the national stage on 18 June, attacking Tavistock in the House of Commons. This attack was widely reported:

> Mr McKie (Galloway, U.) said it was desirable that those responsible for administering the Home Department should be fully aware of the activities of certain individuals in lonely parts of Scotland. They were not too friendly disposed towards the present policy of the Government. He knew of certain persons

living in his constituency. One was the Marquess of Tavistock, who was a tenant of his. Questions had been asked about him in the House of Commons, and not very satisfactory answers were given. In view of the fact that we were engaged in a life and death conflict and of the Prime Minister's words of warning to-day, the Home Department in Scotland should take this matter into very serious reckoning. He had received some seven or eight letters from this individual during the eight months we had been at war.

(*The Times*, 19/6/40)

On 17 July he returned to the attack, asking in another debate why John Beckett had been arrested under DR 18B, and not Tavistock.

As we have seen, Tavistock himself was, for a short time, deterred as a result of the DR 18B arrests from continuing his anti-war activities. This turned out to be, however, merely a temporary cessation.

More attacks and complications in 1941

McKie made a new and even more virulent series of attacks on Tavistock (now the Duke of Bedford) in October 1941, at a time when Bedford was once more in the public eye for a variety of reasons. Also, as in 1940, there had been other recent events which had serious bearing on McKie himself.

In late July Captain Ramsay had, from Brixton prison, instituted a major libel case against the *New York Times*, which had accused him of treason. In law, Ramsay had a case, as the newspaper had not researched its facts accurately. But the judge, declaring that he 'was convinced that Hitler would call Captain Ramsay "friend"', and that Ramsay 'was disloyal in heart and soul to his King, his Government, and his people' (*The Times*, 1/8/41), awarded Ramsay merely a farthing in damages, and Ramsay had to pay costs. During the trial the general public heard for the first time of the existence of the 'Red Book', the membership book of the Right Club, and it was made clear that this book was now in the possession of the authorities. This led to a series of requests in the House of Commons for the names on the list to be made public.

Great play was made in these questions, first with the belief that this was a 'list of traitors', and secondly with the fact that a number of MPs' names were on the list. A question by Geoffrey Mander MP on 31 July is typical:

> In view of the fact that it has been stated that a number of distinguished persons, including Members of this House, belong to this rather remarkable organisation, does not the right hon. Gentleman think it would be in the public interest for everyone to know who belongs to it?
>
> (Geoffrey Mander MP, Hansard, 31 July 1941)

The Home Secretary, Herbert Morrison, replied that it would not be in the public interest to reveal the names. The questions continued, however, into mid-September, with the Home Secretary continuing to play a straight bat.

One wonders what the feelings of a number of MPs (including McKie), who had been involved with the Right Club, must have been if they were in the House to hear those questions being asked, uncertain as to whether or when the Home Secretary (a member, after all, of the Labour Party) might eventually accede to those requests. In the public at large, too, interest had once more become inflamed in relation to the former 'Fascist' activities of prominent members of society.

So by the early autumn McKie was again in a position where he must have wanted to stress his patriotic credentials. And as luck would have it, the Duke of Bedford was once more vividly in the public eye in October, because of a statement by the Home Secretary Herbert Morrison and the subsequent furore in the press. Bedford's former associate John McGovern MP had been refused permission to go to Ireland. When that decision was challenged, on 21 October Herbert Morrison made a statement in the House of Commons which pointed the finger at Bedford. He asserted that if an MP was automatically given that right, so could members of the House of Lords. He then referred specifically not only to Bedford, but also to the events of early 1940:

> If my hon. Friend the Member for Shettleston had a right to go, plenty of Noble Lords would insist and would have an equal

right to go. There is one Noble Lord in whom I am interested, who, as long as I am Home Secretary and as long as his opinions and activities are what they are, will not go to Dublin. That is the Duke of Bedford. (An Hon. Member: 'Did he not get permission?'). Not from me.

(Hansard, 21/10/41)

Over the next few days, the press had a field day about this. The *Daily Express*, for example, the next day carried the headline: 'PEACE DUKE WARNED – MORRISON: I AM WATCHING HIM'. From Cairnsmore, the Duke himself gave interviews in which he publicised his views, and said that he would continue to hold them whatever anyone tried to do to him:

Mr Herbert Morrison may shut me up, but it's one of the risks I have to take […] I am prepared to risk imprisonment or internment. Some of my friends have been detained for a long time, and I sometimes wonder why a similar fate has not befallen me. […] I have been against the war from the start.

(*DE*, 23/10/41)

Recapping the whole story of his 'peace effort' in early 1940, he stressed the dire position Britain was now in, from which it could have been saved:

If that opportunity of investigating the chances of a negotiated peace had been taken the position of this country and her Allies would be very much less desperate than it is at present. I think that probably in six months' time I could say that with greater emphasis.

(*GH*, 22/10/41)

Meanwhile, the *Daily Express*, which had fomented much of the criticism of Bedford stemming from Morrison's statement, had found another area in which to attack him. It announced that the Duke of Bedford had resisted the government's attempt to requisition, for the war effort, the railings from the London squares on the Bedford estate

(*DE*, 24/10/41). Having incited the residents of those squares against the Duke, it then reported the residents' anger (*DE*, 25/10/41). These press tactics certainly worked. The next night, members of the incensed public defaced the statue of a former Duke in Russell Square. (The *Daily Express* had targeted this statue, stating that as it was of bronze, it contained a large proportion of copper, 'vital in armament production'.) Part of the face was painted yellow, an empty paint tin was planted upside down on the head, and the words 'Grandfather of a Quisling' and 'Down with the Duke and the Railings' were daubed on the body of the statue (Bedford, 1959: 162).

The press's populist tub-thumping had in this case been based on entirely invented evidence. As Bedford wrote a couple of weeks later to his local newspaper, the *Galloway News*:

> Until the Press started asking questions about them, I had never heard anything about these railings, nor had I been informed of the Government's desire to make use of them.
>
> (*GN*, 8/11/41)

The press, he said, had asked him what he would do *if asked* for the railings for the war effort. To this he had replied that 'as I take up the Christian Pacifist position with regard to war, I naturally would not take the initiative in offering the railings to the Government for conversion into tanks, etc.' However, he had added, if the government decided to requisition the railings, he did not intend to make any resistance to the demand.

So, by reporting a situation which did not in fact exist, and then by leaving out the fact that the Duke *did not* intend to resist the government's request (which had not in fact been made), the *Daily Express* had created a furore of anger against the Duke, who commented:

> It is obvious that the railings question was only raised by the London Daily Press with the object of creating prejudice against me for holding opinions which, at the present time, are not popular.
>
> (*GN*, 8/11/41)

It was at this time, when the Duke of Bedford was so much in the public eye both because of Morrison's comments and because of the railings issue, that McKie took his opportunity of once more presenting himself as a bulwark against sedition. Very publicly, he announced that because of Bedford's subversive activities, he had decided to terminate the latter's tenancy of the Bargaly grouse moor and deer forest as soon as the short-term lease ended. The text of his telegram to Bedford was given in full in the English and Scottish press (e.g. *GH*, 24/11/41).

McKie later tried to explain the publicity given to his decision by claiming that the information had been 'inadvertently' given to the press through a lobby journalist (*GN*, 6/12/41). Inadvertent or not, the story was milked by him greatly during the next few weeks. He stressed at various times his 'sorrow' at having to act in this way:

> He takes this step with great reluctance as far as personal considerations are concerned, but a political difference of the first magnitude had arisen between the Duke of Bedford and himself. […] 'On sentimental grounds', added Mr McKie, 'I feel the ending of the long association very much. For some 54 years the Bedford family have enjoyed the sporting rights of Bargaly, and for a long time the tenancy of the Mansion House as well. Nobody could have wished for better tenants, but at this grave juncture in our national history […] I have come to the conclusion that the irreconcilable nature of our respective views renders no other alternative possible.'

(*GN*, 1/11/41)

Despite this 'reluctance', McKie continued to stoke the fires of the dispute in various ways. He gave the press the text of a letter he had sent to the Prime Minister, enclosing a missive he had received from Bedford in response to the notice to quit, and stating that he had 'received several letters in the same strain from Bedford in the last two years'. The full text of Bedford's letter, which contained his usual arguments against the war and against the 'warmongering' that had led to it, was released to the national press.

Over the next few weeks, controversy raged in the pages of the local Galloway newspaper. McKie kept up his criticisms of the Duke, including suggestions as to the latter's use of Cairnsmore as a refuge from those realities of the war that were being faced by people such as McKie down in London:

> As one who has experienced most of the blitzes over London in the autumn of 1940, and who has seen at all events a little of the conditions in some of the provincial cities as well (possibly more than the Duke of Bedford in the comfortable seclusion of Cairnsmore) […]
>
> (GN, 15/11/41)

Gradually, the local furore died down. In London, however, the authorities continued to be concerned about the Duke of Bedford – and, as we have seen, his activities, both public and private, moved from strength to strength.

John McKie's deselection in 1945

Just as John McKie had wished, in 1940–1, to dissociate himself from both Captain Ramsay and the Duke of Bedford, the Earl of Galloway appears to have decided, later, to turn on his former associate John McKie. In March 1945, with the end of the war in sight, and with a general election impending, the Galloway Unionist Association, at a meeting presided over by Lord Galloway, decided not to adopt McKie as its parliamentary candidate, 'because of the feeling, rightly or wrongly, that he had lost a considerable amount of ground among his supporters'. It was reported that 'they could not go round the constituency anywhere without hearing that Mr McKie was "no good"', and it was strongly felt that he 'would not receive the support of any of the returning service men' (GN, 17/3/45).

The Earl of Galloway, as chairman, had taken a large part in instituting these proceedings, and McKie held a strong grudge against him for it. He described how he had first heard of the matter from the Scottish whip in the House of Commons, who informed him that Galloway had sent a letter of complaint about McKie's discharge of his parliamentary duties. McKie had thereupon been to see Lord Galloway (this was before the March meeting of the Association), without any effect (*GN*, 2/6/45). After he was deselected by the March meeting, McKie declared his intention of standing as an Independent Unionist. This further exacerbated the situation between the two men, with Galloway publicly laying at the door of McKie the blame for a split in the Party which would probably lead to the taking of the seat by a Liberal or Labour candidate (*GN*, 7/4/45).

The *Galloway News*, which was to take McKie's side throughout the controversy, heavily criticised the committee's tactics, and pointed out that nobody seemed prepared to give clear reasons for McKie's rejection. (Sadly, the records of the Galloway Unionist Association for this period cannot be found, and probably no longer exist.) A letter to the paper said that the case was based on 'nothing but gossip' (*GN*, 24/3/45, 26/4/45). A number of possible reasons that emerged obliquely (that he did not answer letters, had a bad attendance record, etc.) were shown to have no foundation. Another cited reason, that the constituency required someone who had been on active service in the Forces, was met by the newspaper with the point that such complaints would have disenfranchised a very large number of MPs. It was felt that there must be something more behind it.

We can get a strong hint of what did lie behind it from some of the questions and the heckling at the public meetings held by McKie once he had decided to stand, and from McKie's own statements which were obviously responses to other criticisms, most of which have not been recorded. Many of the interventions at his meetings were to do with his pre-war public stance in favour of appeasement. At a meeting at the beginning of June, for example, he was questioned closely about this. Did he still think he had been right (*GN*, 2/6/45)?

Criticism of McKie appears, however, not to have restricted itself to his pro-appeasement stance, but also to have extended to his pre-war association with the pro-Nazi faction. One outward sign of this was the way in which his Conservative opponent, Colonel Fergusson, while promising 'not to indulge in personalities', was twisting the knife in relation to those of McKie's (and, incidentally, Galloway's) beliefs which had gone beyond mere appeasement:

> With regard to the Anglo-German Fellowship, he believed many members had been sincere and genuine in their beliefs that a new spirit was afoot in Germany. They had, however, been deluded.
>
> (*GN*, 16/6/45)

Though the criticisms of McKie's pre-war dabbling in pro-Nazism were not recorded, we can gauge their nature by McKie's responses to them. For example, McKie's protests about the tenuousness of his connection with Captain Ramsay can only have been sparked off by suggestions as to his close relationship with Ramsay (even though the public cannot have known, at this time, about McKie's membership of the Right Club).

McKie's other response was to go on the attack against the local Conservatives by ascribing to them the very views that he himself had held, and by claiming that he himself had always been on the side of the angels. The members of the Executive, he claimed, 'belonged to the extreme Right', and were 'the diehard element [...] that constantly opposed Mr Churchill before the war, and that was not very willing to take him on in the first months of his Premiership', while he himself 'belonged to that vast section of far more generous and liberally-minded Conservatism to which the Prime Minister belonged'. He pronounced that 'the insidious doctrine of neo-Fascism must be crushed'. It is interesting to note that one of the questions he was then asked from the floor at this same meeting directly challenged this rewriting of history, by once more stressing McKie's appeasement history, and by asking why he had backed Chamberlain in the crucial debate of May 1940 (*GN*, 2/6/45).

McKie's accusations against the Galloway Conservatives became ever more extreme, with the Earl of Galloway's pre-war and 'phoney war' attitudes being continually, though usually obliquely, targeted. A typical example was McKie's suggestion that the 'clique' in the local Association were against him because of his actions against the Duke of Bedford in 1941:

> *Mr McKie:* Were there any in Galloway who held the Duke's views that Hitler wanted to be the best friend Britain ever had, and that we ought to make friends with him as soon as possible? Surely this

was not the case, although he knew there were some members of the community in Galloway, who were very doubtful about our entry into the war in 1939, and who thought during the 'phoney' period of the war we ought to make the best possible terms with Germany.

Mrs Lawrence: Who are the muddle-heads who made such a grievous mistake?

Mr McKie: Lord Galloway is the president.

(*GN*, 23/6/45)

McKie truly felt, he said, that Galloway had 'stabbed him in the back', though his dagger had been 'neither sharp enough nor long enough to do the foul fell deed' (*GN*, 16/2/45); and when a questioner charged him, at a meeting reported on 30 June, with having said at the time of the Hoare–Laval Pact that Laval was his friend, he hinted at more modern 'treachery':

Questioner: Do you agree now that he [Laval] is a 'twister'?

Mr McKie: Laval's subsequent career has certainly left me in no doubt whatever regarding his 'twisting' propensities.

Questioner: At the same time you had some personal friends in Galloway.

Mr McKie: But Laval was never in Galloway.

Questioner: What I want to know is, have you found many Lavals among your Galloway friends?

Mr McKie: I leave that to the audience to decide.

(*GN*, 30/6/45)

McKie repeated at this meeting his assertion that he had been targeted by the local Conservatives because of his actions against the Duke of Bedford in 1941, and asked whether some of the Association were opposed to him (McKie) because they thought Bedford had been in the right. This, McKie had said on another occasion, was now 'a People's Election, and no attempt to come between them and their choice must be permitted' (*GN*, 2/6/45). He hinted once more at the Earl of Galloway's record, including his support for Captain Ramsay in May 1940, and produced further excuses in relation to his own pre-war attitude to Ramsay. Finally, striking out wildly against his Conservative opponent Colonel Fergusson, he accused him too of pro-Nazi connections, pointing out that he was a nephew of the Earl of Glasgow, 'who went to Germany in 1938, and on his return extolled the Nazi regime in a series of public speeches' (*GN*, 30/6/45).

As the election approached, McKie, who now claimed always to have been a supporter of Churchill against the forces of reaction, and who appears to have believed that Churchill for this reason must be on his side in this dispute, was dumbfounded when Churchill sent a telegram to his opponent Colonel Fergusson saying: 'I do not look upon your opponent, Mr McKie, as in any sense a supporter of mine. I have no desire to see him returned at this election' (*GH*, 28/6/45). This statement of Churchill's seemed to go beyond mere support for the official candidate, and fundamentally to question McKie's suitability. This may, of course, have been because of McKie's pre-war record of support for 'appeasement' policies; but Churchill, aware as he was of the names on the Right Club list, may also have been influenced by the knowledge that McKie had gone beyond appeasement, to downright pro-Nazism.

Those in the constituency who were 'in the know' or had political interests, like the Executive of the Association and the hecklers at the meetings, may well have questioned McKie's past; but the vast majority of the electorate, as the *Galloway News* pointed out, were in complete ignorance as to what the issues were which had caused McKie's deselection, and the newspaper's call for loyalty to him obviously had some effect. Added to that, the Liberals did not field a candidate, and many of their voters appear to have considered voting for McKie to be the best way to defeat the Conservative candidate. At the election on 5 July, McKie won the seat with 13,647 votes to the Labour candidate's 11,822 and the Conservative's 8,032. He sat in Parliament as an 'Independent Unionist' until the Conservative whip was restored to him in 1948. He remained the Member for Galloway, as a backbencher, until his death in 1958. (It is interesting to note how many of those Conservatives on the Right Club list who had, before the war, been 'up and coming men', e.g. Peter Agnew and Harold Mitchell, both of whom had held posts as Parliamentary Private Secretaries to Ministers, failed to live up to that promise in the post-war party.)

Conclusion

The story of these three neighbours shows us something of the complexity of the reactions of pre-war 'fellow travellers of the Right' to the unfolding wartime situation. Galloway, privately taking a pro-peace attitude during the 'phoney war', thereafter deplored the DR 18B treatment of fellow aristocrats and right-wingers at the hands of their social inferiors, while in fact avoiding any open involvement in political matters or open opposition to the war. McKie, while quite probably taking an entirely patriotic line from now on, was so haunted by his past that he felt it necessary to point the finger, both during and after the war, against the kind of people who had shared his views; he also appeared, by the end of the war, to have convinced himself that he had always been a keen supporter of Churchill's attitudes to Germany. Galloway's post-war attitude to McKie may have had similar underlying causes. And then there was the Duke of Bedford, only temporarily deterred by the arrests in May–June 1940, who thereafter sailed on without any qualms, publicly pronouncing the same views however unpopular they may have been. It must be said that, however unreal and unattractive the Duke's views may have been, he nevertheless kept an unswerving adherence to what he felt to be right, whatever the consequences to himself. In this sense, he falls into a completely different category from his ambivalent neighbours.

Bibliography

Books and articles

Bedford, Hastings, Duke of (1949), *The Years of Transition* (Edinburgh: Dakers).
Bedford, John, Duke of (1959), *A Silver-Plated Spoon* (London: Cassell).
Carpenter, Louise (2004), *An Unlikely Countess: Lily Budge and the 13th Earl of Galloway* (London: Harpercollins).
Galloway, 9th Earl of (1854), *Observations on the Abuse and Reform of the Monitorial System of Harrow School, with Letters and Remarks by the Earl of Galloway* (London: Hatchard).
Griffiths, Richard (1998), *Patriotism Perverted: Captain Ramsay, the Right Club and British Anti-Semitism, 1939–40* (London: Constable).
Kelly (1934), *Kelly's Handbook to the Titled, Landed and Official Classes*, 1934.

Lejeune, Anthony (1984), *The Gentlemen's Clubs of London* (London: Bracken Books).

Stent, Ronald (1980), *A Bespattered Page? The Internment of 'His Majesty's Most Loyal Enemy Aliens'* (London: André Deutsch).

Who's Who, 1942.

Documents

The National Archives (TNA)

HO 45/25696

Newspapers and journals

Daily Express (DE)
Evening Standard (ES)
The Free Press (FP)
Galloway Gazette (GG)
Galloway News (GN)
Glasgow Herald (GH)
The Times

9

'I WROTE A VERY FULL AND STRONG LETTER TO THE KING'

Two would-be negotiators

Lord Brocket and the Duke of Buccleuch have often been bracketed together as the most insistent of the aristocratic admirers of the Nazi regime and proponents of peace with Germany. They were very different from most of the people we have been dealing with, however. In no way were they political activists. Both were convinced that their actions were in the best interests of Britain, and both would have been, and were, horrified to be accused of any kind of subversion. They did not join any right-wing movements, apart from the comparatively respectable Anglo-German Fellowship. (While Brocket did agree to speak to the Nordic League on 27 March 1939, he reneged on this at the last moment, and was replaced by General Fuller (TNA HO 144/21379).) Their actions were on the whole open and above board, and they maintained contact throughout with prominent representatives of the British government. Their words and actions did, however, have a considerable adverse effect on Britain's interests, both because of the Germans' perceptions of their importance as peers and associates of royalty (and the resultant belief that their views were influential and shared by many), and because of their own conviction of their importance as unofficial negotiators. Though they seemed so similar in outlook, their reactions after the 'phoney war' interlude were to be totally different from each other.

Walter John Montagu-Douglas-Scott, 8th Duke of Buccleuch (1894–1973), had as Earl of Dalkeith been Unionist MP for Roxburgh and Selkirk from 1923 to 1935, at which point he succeeded his father in the Dukedom. He was the most extensive landowner in the United Kingdom, owning over 280,000 acres. He was also closely connected with the Royal Family, as his sister Lady Alice Montagu-Douglas-Scott was married to the Duke of Gloucester, brother of King George VI. In 1937, at the accession of George VI, Buccleuch became Lord Steward of His Majesty's Household, a post appointed by the king himself. His main addresses were Drumlanrig Castle in Scotland and 2 Grosvenor Place, London SW1.

Arthur Ronald Nall Nall-Cain, 2nd Baron Brocket (1904–1967), came from a family that had made its money in brewing. His father had been created a baronet by Lloyd George in 1921, and a baron by the national government in 1933. He succeeded his father in 1934, having been Unionist MP for Wavertree since 1931. He, too, was an extensive landowner, owning, as he proudly announced in *Who's Who*, 13,000 acres in England and 62,000 acres in Scotland. His main addresses were Bramshill Park, Brocket Hall, Knoydart House (Inverness-shire), and 5 Wilton Crescent, London SW1.

Brocket was at times used as a kind of unofficial envoy to Germany on behalf of Chamberlain in the period up to March 1939, even though occasional doubts were raised by members of Chamberlain's circle as to his reliability, and his preparedness to create the impression that Britain was prepared to give in on a number of crucial issues, in particular on Czechoslovakia (see, e.g., TNA PREM 1/249). However, after the German invasion of Czechoslovakia on 15 March 1939 and the subsequent British guarantee to Poland, both Brocket and Buccleuch began to be seriously at odds with government policies, and ignored the need to conform to the government's new line. They were among those who assailed Halifax, the Foreign Minister, with letters pleading the German cause, and for a return to appeasement (Halifax replying courteously but non-committally). At the same time they undertook private talks with German officials which undermined official policy.

Buccleuch had always felt strongly that Britain could trust the Germans. As he was later to say, he had found since 1933 that everything they said to him was full of 'truth and frankness' (LHCMA Bryant, C111). He was also convinced, as he told Halifax in a letter of 29 March 1939, that Britain would be much aided by his [Buccleuch's] friendly association with leading Germans, who in the aftermath of Prague and the British guarantee to Poland were asking him to come out and discuss matters. He had told them that he would be coming over in late April (TNA FO 800/315/80).

The visit by Brocket and Buccleuch to Germany in April 1939 was in many ways typical of their insouciance, in that it was undertaken in order to attend (together with General Fuller) as honoured guests at the grand celebrations of Hitler's fiftieth birthday on 20 April in Berlin. In the event, having been informed by the British Chargé d'Affaires in Berlin that 'as a high official of the King's Court he would have to consider whether his presence, which of course would be advertised and made much of, might be regarded as not being all square with the present feeling of the King's Government' (TNA FO 800/315/94), Buccleuch decided, after consultation with Buckingham Palace, to leave Berlin before the celebrations. Brocket and Fuller remained and took a full part in the festivities. Buccleuch had made good use of his few days in Berlin, however, meeting Ribbentrop, various Foreign Office officials and other leading Nazis (who were presumably the 'leading Germans' who had been asking him to come over to discuss matters). On his return to Britain he assailed representatives of the government with his views on the international situation. Believing that 'the Nazi leaders did not want war', he stressed to R.A. Butler of the Foreign Office the 'moderation' of the German demands in relation to Danzig and the 'intransigence' of the Poles, mainly because of Britain's guarantee to Poland (TNA FO 371/22970). He later, on 24 April, sent a written memorandum to Butler, which explicitly backed German claims not just to German-speaking territories (Austria, Sudetenland, Memel and Danzig) but also to Bohemia and Moravia:

> It does not seem unnatural that a very strong and powerful Germany should wish and endeavour to recover or to incorporate Austria, Sudetenland, Bohemia, Moravia, Memel and Danzig.

> Our chief quarrel seems to be with their method, but there is perhaps some justice in their argument that no results have ever come from asking or from conferences or from other methods. It seems inconsistent to admit many errors in the Versailles Peace Treaty and to put the *whole* blame now on Germany for what has occurred.
>
> (TCC, Butler, G10/3–12)

Butler thanked him for his 'full and interesting letter', declaring himself to be 'much relieved to know of your work and attitude' (TCC, Butler, G10/3–12).

Meanwhile, Brocket and Buccleuch were holding private conversations with various Germans. This came to a head when Sir Alexander Cadogan, Permanent Under-Secretary of the Foreign Office was informed, on 26 June, via a foreign informant, that they had had a meeting with Baron Geyr of the Ribbentrop Bureau, at which they 'had made it quite clear to him that this country would not interfere if Germany took Danzig', leaving Geyr with the impression that 'there was no doubt at all […] that the British public was not behind the Government either in regard to the Russian question or in most of their other plans'. The informant had pointed out to Geyr that 'neither of these gentlemen represented any political party'; but Geyr had responded that 'they may not represent a party, but the Duke of Buccleuch is the Duchess of Gloucester's brother, holds a post in the King's Household and is a Privy Councillor, so he must obviously know', and that Brocket 'as a member of the House of Lords must speak with some authority' (TNA FO 800/315/244). (An earlier meeting of the two men with Geyr, in early May, had been commented on by Claud Cockburn at the time, with warnings as to the danger of giving the German propaganda machine the opportunity to claim that the German government had 'the British aristocracy in its pocket' (*The Week*, 10/5/39).)

As soon as he had heard about the June meeting, Halifax wrote to the two men to ask them to explain themselves. Both denied that they had said anything of the kind; but Buccleuch's response on 29 June, in which he took the opportunity to make the case to Halifax at length for letting Germany have Danzig, elicited the following marginal note from Cadogan: 'All this makes me think that the upshot of the Duke's talk very likely produced the effect that we are told it did' (TNA FO 800/315/267).

In July, further accounts were reaching Halifax about Brocket's activities. Writing to Brocket on 13 July, he taxed Brocket with having produced statements that were 'being misused by those near to the German Chancellor to discredit the warnings which the PM and I have tried to give'. Nevertheless, Brocket continued to make contact with influential Nazis. As Halifax commented to one of his correspondents, Philip Conwell-Evans, in a letter of 14 July, he had heard stories of 'the extent to which Brocket's attitude was now being exploited in circles near to Hitler to induce disbelief in our determination to resist further aggression' (TNA FO 800/316/67).

The outbreak of war brought little change in behaviour. Buccleuch was one of a number of peers who met on 12 September, with the Duke of Westminster in the Chair, to promote the need for a negotiated peace (TNA FO 800/317/7). By the end of October Lord Gort had reported to Halifax conversations which it was reported Brocket and Buccleuch had been having with the Italian ambassador. Halifax commented:

> I would not put it past either Brocket or Buccleuch to have said something pretty stupid to the Italian ambassador. […] I have heard something of their activities with others and they would certainly be anxious to get the war stopped by way of some peace discussions, without satisfying themselves, as we should feel it necessary to do, as to the security on which these peace discussions might proceed.
>
> (TNA FO 800/328)

Both men also continued to write letters to the Foreign Office, advocating the need to negotiate peace; these letters were no longer addressed to Halifax (whom Buccleuch accused, in a letter of 20 February, of 'throw[ing] difficulties and creat[ing] complications in the way of any sensible suggestion' (TNA FO 800/321)), but to Butler (though they must have been disappointed that Butler's responses were by now much more non-committal). Buccleuch also made one direct approach to

Cadogan (Colville, 1985: 83). By now Buccleuch was convinced that the war would do nothing but play into the hands of Soviet Russia, Jews and Americans (Newton, 1996: 153; LHCMA Bryant C111).

Buccleuch decided in December to write what he described to Arthur Bryant as 'a very full and strong letter' to the king, laying out his views on the international situation. He did not receive a reply, and on 19 January told Bryant he was wondering how to follow his letter up, presuming that 'people there have told him I am pro-Nazi which is all rot' (LHCMA Bryant C111).

Meanwhile, Brocket had been caught up in a scheme for 'direct action' in relation to a completely unrealistic proposed venture, via a Dane called Bengt Berg, to contact Goering, who was believed to be a channel for peace. As Andrew Roberts has shown us (Roberts, 1994), Arthur Bryant was the person deputed to bring these negotiations to the attention of Halifax and the Foreign Office. The British negotiators were among other things prepared to sign away Polish and Czech independence. Halifax sent Bryant one of those letters of rebuff at which he was by now becoming quite practised; nothing came of the scheme.

All these activities, by both Brocket and Buccleuch, were overtaken by a time of crisis for them, when Churchill came to power on 10 May 1940. On 12 May Buccleuch finally received the long-awaited response from the king to his letter of December 1939. In it the king ignored the points Buccleuch had been making as to national policy, and confined himself to asking him to resign the Lord Stewardship. This decision to dismiss Buccleuch was not, as some commentators have presumed, taken at the request of Churchill. It was the king's own decision, as is witnessed by a note from Buckingham Palace to Churchill dated 14 May, informing him of the king's decision to change the Lord Steward 'for reasons which are probably known to you but which I could, if required, explain' (TNA PREM 5/209). As Martin Pugh suggests, the king must have judged it 'politic to distance himself from someone who was regarded as pro-Nazi' at this time of national crisis (Pugh, 2005: 307). On 1 June the Duke of Hamilton was appointed Lord Steward in Buccleuch's place.

The British newspapers did not make anything of this dismissal (either from ignorance or from loyalty to the Crown), but two months later, on 21 August, the *New York Times* featured it prominently, saying that the news had 'just leaked out'. The article raised some interesting questions. While many of its statements are quite possibly inaccurate, it nevertheless gives us a good picture of the kind of rumours and opinions that were prevalent in London at the time. The king had removed Buccleuch, it said, 'in the widespread drive against Fifth Columnists'. There were rumours that 'the Duke had been confined to his estates in Scotland', but these had been denied, and he had been seen in London recently, though at present was staying at Drumlanrig Castle. It was reported that 'some high authorities [had] wanted to go further than merely dropping the Duke of Buccleuch from his post, and make an "example" of him' (*NYT*, 21/8/39).

Be that as it may, the Duke does not seem to have been deterred by all this from continuing to promote a negotiated peace. On 22 July, for example, he was one of the co-signatories of a memorandum sent to Churchill by a peace group including several peers, in which the example set by the newly-formed Vichy Government in France was quoted as an example of what Britain should be considering, because overcoming Hitler by force might well bring about a Communist revolution (Bod., Stokes, Box 22).

Nevertheless, Buccleuch did take a lower profile from then on, and was far more concerned at the impression he might be giving to the authorities; though, as we shall see, this did not prevent him from getting involved once more when the opportunity arose.

Brocket was a very different matter, however. Buccleuch's demotion, and the arrests in May 1940 of so many of their acquaintances, appear to have affected him deeply, and he suffered a severe nervous breakdown, 'brought about by the aspersions thrown at him from all quarters'. When James Lees-Milne visited him on 20 June 1942 he had still not recovered, being unable to walk any distance and suffering from a weak heart. This had led to him being rejected for military service. He spent the rest of the war on his estates (Lees-Milne, 2006: 39).

In late 1940 Buccleuch remained, however, still cautiously open to ideas of 'peace moves' with Germany, and now found himself embroiled in a rather dubious scheme put forward by an old acquaintance of his called James Lonsdale Bryans. Bryans was an adventurer of precarious means, who sported a monocle, an Old Etonian tie and visiting cards giving as his place of residence Brooks's

Club (he was in fact a member of that club until he was asked to leave because of his attitude to the club servants). In early 1940, during the 'phoney war', having claimed close contact with a leading German diplomat, Ulrich von Hassell, Bryans had managed to persuade the British government of his bona fides, and had gone to neutral Italy and Switzerland 'with the connivance if not the approval of the Foreign Office' to contact von Hassell and conduct negotiations. During this period Bryans had had frequent contact with Buccleuch and Brocket. The FO had soon realised, however, that he was 'completely unreliable, [having] completely exceeded his brief', and had had nothing further to do with him. Now, in late 1940, he re-emerged on the scene. He was by now living in Madeira, but was planning further attempts for 'peace moves', for which he needed to go to Switzerland to see von Hassell. He wrote on a couple of occasions to Brocket, asking for funds for this purpose. His first letter, written in August, received no reply. The second, written in October, was intercepted by MI6 later that month, together with a letter to a Leipzig publisher who was going to publish a book for Bryans. By December 1940 Bryans was in Lisbon, hoping to renew negotiations with von Hassell in Switzerland, and possibly to travel to Germany to see Hitler or Ribbentrop. But all this was made difficult, he said, by the non-cooperation of the Portuguese government and by shortage of money. In February 1940 he wrote once more to Brocket (again no reply), and also sent an urgent telegram to Buccleuch on 22 February asking for money, as delay would be disastrous if he was 'forced home abandoning work'. Buccleuch lurched into action. The same day he wrote to Brocket, asking his views on Bryans, and stating that Nevile Henderson, the former ambassador to Berlin, when asked about Bryans, had written '*very* highly of him'. There appears to have been no reply from Brocket (TNA KV 2/2839).

The same day, too, Buccleuch wrote to Butler, asking to see him and suggesting Bryans as a suitable intermediary with the Germans, citing Henderson as someone who could vouch for him. Meanwhile, MI5 had warned the Foreign Office of the probability of an approach from Buccleuch. Butler was by now far more wary of the Duke's initiatives, and handed on the letter to Cadogan with the following terse comments:

'A full and strong letter to the King' **201**

You should see.

I'm afraid I've so far insulted the Duke as not to answer.

He then telephoned and said should he go slow?

I replied very slow.

There it stands.

On 24 February Buccleuch wrote again to Butler. The FO's reception of his approach had obviously concerned him. In this letter he apologised for having disturbed Butler, and described Bryans's turning up again as 'inconvenient'. He did not wish, he said, to write 'too favourably or too badly' of Bryans. The latter was 'presumably bankrupt and owing money, […] thus his motives and choice of role may be more suspect and there may be other complications in making use of him'. He then went on implicitly to criticise the FO's role in all this: 'I was mildly surprised that the Foreign Office gave him facilities and encouragement a year ago, thus committing themselves.' All this bears out MI5's later comment that 'the Duke is so cautious and so afraid that his actions may be misinterpreted by the authorities that he has not done anything effective on Lonsdale Bryans' behalf' (TNA FO 371/26542).

Meanwhile the letter which Bryans had sent to his German publisher in October 1940, and which had been intercepted by MI6, had surfaced. In it he had referred to his hatred of democracy and to the Führer's faith and genius, had attacked 'the democratic Jew press' and had bemoaned 'the folly of this war, which has been built up round the false slogans of democracy and machinations of a Jew-led "Front Populaire" backed by international finance'. Clearly he was either a double agent, or at best a negotiator strangely in tune with Nazi ideas.

MI5 feared above all that the German government might have been 'using Bryans for the purpose of obtaining information as to the extent and strength of a pro-German peace group in this country'. And indeed, in his letter to the German publisher, Bryans seemed to be fulfilling such a purpose when he wrote: 'There are many who feel as I do in England and in USA, and some of them are people of supreme influence' (TNA KV 2/2839).

Cadogan noted on the file on 26 February: 'The intercepted letter from Bryans to the German publisher is sufficient condemnation of

Bryans as intermediary.' A few days later, in another note, he described Bryans as 'a wash-out and a crook' (TNA FO 371/26542).

Bryans was brought back to Britain in February and interrogated by MI5 in March, but no action was taken against him under Defence Regulations. This was clearly because of the embarrassment that this would cause the Foreign Office for its earlier encouragement of him. As Stamp of MI5 commented, 'I should like to see Mr Lonsdale Bryans detained but the position is very delicate, and it is, I think, certain that if he were detained he would peach on the Foreign Office and his story would be all over the country.'

The Duke of Buccleuch, strangely enough, kept up his contacts with Bryans after the latter's return to Britain. The doubts he had expressed to Butler do not seem to have deterred him from this. MI5 noted in the succeeding months that Buccleuch and Bryans had been having interminable conversations on the telephone. And over two years later the contacts were continuing. In September 1943 Buccleuch sent a number of letters to Bryans, some with enclosures. Sadly, we do not know the contents of those letters. Though the MI5 file indicates their existence, they have been removed (TNA KV 2/2839).

From 1941 onwards, Buccleuch spent a great deal of his time at his castle in Scotland, keeping on the whole a fairly low profile. He smarted, however, at the treatment he was receiving, including surveillance. As he wrote to Butler on 24 February 1941:

> I regret that, however much some of your colleagues may have considered me a nuisance, they should regard me with suspicion rather than as a friend and ally. Even now some find it desirable to have me watched, as far as I can see more with the intention of causing me trouble than of finding fault (TNA FO 371/26542).

Old habits died hard, however. On his visits to London, Buccleuch continued to speak in the same way as before. Hugh Dalton chronicled one such occasion in his diary on 30 May 1941:

> I hear that the Duke of Buccleuch said the other night at some Club that he thought we ought to make peace, and that

Lord Gort, who was present, leaped to his feet and denounced him in unmeasured terms as a 'decadent Duke' and much else!

(Dalton, 1986: 216)

Such was the Duke's reputation, that when it was heard that Hess had flown to Scotland in May 1941 to meet a 'Scottish personality' (and it was not yet known that this 'personality' was the Duke of Hamilton), many people, including Dalton, presumed that this must be the Duke of Buccleuch (Dalton, 1986: 203), or at least that Buccleuch was one of those with whom Hess had been intending to negotiate (Beaverbrook, in Maisky, 2015: 356).

For the rest of the war there is no evidence of further initiatives by Buccleuch. He still occasionally, privately, bemoaned the war, as in a letter to Bryant on 11 July 1942, claiming that 'the penalty for Europe seems to me far more severe than if other means had been tried'. But, as he philosophically commented, 'that however is rather out of date' (LHCMA Bryant C/111).

The Bryans episode sums up what was wrong with the approach taken by Brocket and Buccleuch before and during the war. Both, while believing themselves to be important negotiators who knew better than the government, were in fact naive and limited. James Lees-Milne described Brocket as a 'fundamentally nice, but stupid' man (Lees-Milne, 2006: 39). Cadogan commented on Buccleuch, 'The Duke appears to be such a simple person that I am afraid it's dangerous for him to dabble in these things, and I wish he wouldn't' (TNA FO 800/315/267). Both Brocket and Buccleuch, however, though meaning well, had been dangerous – far more dangerous, in the effect they had on German pre-war policy, and on German views of the extent of pro-Nazism in Britain, than any of our home-grown fascists.

Bibliography

Books

Colville, John (1985), *The Fringes of Power: Downing Street Diaries 1939–1955* (London: Hodder & Stoughton).

Dalton, Hugh (1986), *The Second World War Diary of Hugh Dalton 1940–45* (ed. Ben Pimlott) (London: Jonathan Cape).

Lees-Milne, James (2006), *Diaries 1942–1954* (London: John Murray).

Maisky, Ivan Mikhaelovich (2015), *The Maisky Diaries: Red Ambassador to the Court of St James's 1932–1943* (ed. Gabriel Gorodetzky) (Newhaven, CT and London: Yale University Press).

Newton, Scott (1996), *Profits of Peace: The Political Economy of Anglo-German Appeasement* (Oxford: Clarendon Press).

Pugh, Martin (2005), *Hurrah for the Blackshirts! Fascists and Fascism in Britain between the Wars* (London: Jonathan Cape).

Roberts, Andrew (1994), *Eminent Churchillians* (London: Weidenfeld and Nicolson).

Documents

The National Archives (TNA)

FO 371/22970, FO 371/26542, FO 800/315, FO 800/316, FO 800/317, FO 800/321, FO 800/328
HO 144/21379
KV 2/2839
PREM 1/249, PREM 5/209

Liddell Hart Centre for Military Archives, King's College London (LHCMA)

Bryant Papers, C/111

Trinity College Cambridge Library (TCC)

R.A. Butler papers TCC, G10/3–12

Bodleian Library (Bod.)

Richard Rapier Stokes papers

Newspapers

New York Times (NYT)
The Week

10

'THE INTERNMENT OF A PERSON OF HER SOCIAL STANDING MIGHT GIVE THE PUBLIC A WRONG IMPRESSION'

The charmed lives of various 'pillars of society'

The activities of many of the socially prominent people who were involved, in various ways, with pro-Nazi or anti-Semitic activities before and/or during the war had been very similar to those of the people from lesser strata of society who were arrested under the DR 18B legislation in mid-1940. Yet very few of them shared that experience of detention. Sir Oswald Mosley, Captain Ramsay and Admiral Domvile were interned, it is true, as were a number of lesser 'gents' such as Captain Robert Gordon-Canning, Captain H.W. Luttman-Johnson and Captain George Lane-Fox Pitt-Rivers; but an extensive array of dukes, barons, earls, viscountesses and assorted aristocrats, together with other 'pillars of society', managed to escape such a fate.

These people present a very varied picture, stretching right across the spectrum of pro-Nazi activity. In the pre-war situation, and in the first year of the war, at one extreme one had those who joined, and often played prominent parts in, the various extremist movements: British Union (BU), the Liberty Restoration League, The Link, the British People's Party, the British Council against European Commitments, the Right Club, etc.; then you had those whose anti-Semitic prejudices led them into racist or pro-German public statements, and those who for other reasons made pronouncements on the virtues of the Nazi system; and finally, at the other end of the spectrum, you had those who, convinced that they might be able to avert war with a nation they believed to be trustworthy and in many ways admirable, used their social position to put pressure on the government to temper its attitudes. Wide-ranging as these attitudes and activities were, they had a number of things in common. All of these people were firmly convinced that Britain should not make war against Germany; and almost all of them seem to have assumed that they had a God-given right to speak as they chose, and to exert an inordinate influence in public affairs. And, in the reactions of the authorities to them, we only too often see that their views as to their importance were deferentially shared by those around them, or that, given their position and their contacts, it was deemed inadvisable to tangle too strongly with them.

Their attitudes, once war was declared, were equally varied. Some renounced their previous views. Others continued with them. Some of the younger ones fought in the Services, but privately retained their views. Some kept a low profile. One eccentric, Lady Downe, actively sought detention, but was denied it.

In this chapter we will be looking at a small cross-section of such people, assessing the possible grounds for detention that their cases may have presented, and looking at their reactions to the arrests of May-June 1940 and at their activities thereafter. They are merely a selection from among many other aristocrats, some of whom have been, or will be, studied in more depth in other chapters.

Lady Pearson and Viscountess Downe

These two ladies, widows in their late fifties and early sixties, were both prominent figures in British Union, dominating the local party in their respective areas. As major BU activists, one would have expected them to be arrested and interned alongside so many of their colleagues in mid-1940; but it was not to be. In part this appears to have been due to their influential connections. They did, however, differ completely from each other both in their political attitudes and in their reactions to these events.

Grace Pearson (b.1880), the widow of Sir Edward Pearson, a highly successful civil engineer who had died in 1925, was very well connected. Her brother was Sir Henry Page Croft, the prominent right-wing Conservative MP (later Lord Croft). Her sister Anne, the dowager Lady Brocket, was the stepmother of the 2nd Lord Brocket. Her brother-in-law was Weedman Pearson, the successful businessman and Liberal politician who had become the 1st Viscount Cowdray. Grace herself appears to have been a powerful woman, who brooked little in the way of opposition. She was also strongly anti-Semitic, as was shown by her language about her niece Diana's prospective marriage in 1936 to a German Jew, Fred Uhlman (Uhlman, 1998: 255–9).

In the Thirties Grace became heavily involved with the British Union of Fascists (BUF) and an array of other right-wing movements. In 1934 she became chairman of the Sandwich Branch of the BUF. In December 1936 she was nominated as the prospective British Union parliamentary candidate for Canterbury. In 1938 she joined The Link, becoming chairman of that movement's Canterbury branch. Admiral Domvile, when he met her in March 1938, was much taken with her, while admiring the strength of her Fascist convictions (NMM DOM 55, 4/3/38). By 1939 we find her actively supporting the British People's Party and speaking for its candidate H. St John Philby at the Hythe by-election in July.

The war did not change her views or activities in any way. Clearly regarded as one of the foremost representatives of British Union, during the 'phoney war' she became a regular attender at the meetings held in London by Mosley, Ramsay, Domvile and others between November 1939 and April 1940 to co-ordinate the various right-wing 'patriotic societies' in their opposition to the war. She was also listed by Special Branch prominently among those who attended Mosley's well-attended propaganda lunch at the Criterion Restaurant on 1 March 1940.

All this contributes to making Lady Pearson one of the people one would most have expected to be detained in mid-1940. She was in fact arrested, and taken to the police headquarters in Maidstone on 4 June. When her brother, now Lord Croft and Under-Secretary of State for War in Churchill's government, heard of this, however, he asked for an immediate interview with Sir John Anderson, the Home Secretary, in the course of which he berated Anderson for what he described as an 'outrageous act', and demanded her release (Gottlieb, 2000: 248). Within days, Lady Pearson was free. Her agent, R.R. Bellamy, and her secretary, Mrs de Grey Whitham, were not so lucky; nor were various other Canterbury and Sandwich fascists. In other words, the big fish swam free, and the minnows were caught in the net (Simpson, 1992: 208–9).

These events did not pass unnoticed. On 4 July a number of MPs began to ask questions in the House of Commons as to why Lady Pearson had been arrested and then released, and 'what representations were made on her behalf and by whom.' Sir John Anderson, the Home Secretary, replied at length about the procedures for arrest, ending with these somewhat misleading words:

> The lady was detained on 4th June. A report was sent to me by the police, and after consideration of this report I decided on 8th June that the case was not one for an order under Regulation 18B. My decision was based on the facts and circumstances reported to me by the police.
>
> (Hansard, 4 July 1940)

The questioners were not satisfied, however. On 11 July they returned to the attack, asking what restrictions had been placed on Lady Pearson. Anderson replied that she was 'precluded from being in any area which is a protected area […] and also required to notify the police of any change of address'. He was then asked whether he could assure the House that no modification of these restrictions would take place 'because of the fact that this lady is related to a Member of the Government'. Anderson once more protested his impartiality:

> Perhaps I ought to tell the House that the decision taken in this matter was taken by me personally after consideration of the facts reported by the local police and that no extraneous consideration or argument whatsoever was taken into account.
>
> (Hansard, 11 July 1940)

Despite these assurances, many people believed that Lady Pearson had escaped detention because of her connections. This does not seem to have bothered her very much, though she kept her head low for most of the rest of the war.

Dorothy, Dowager Viscountess Downe (b.1876) came from a different strand of the British upper classes from that of Lady Pearson. Her background was rural, agricultural and landowning. She was born Dorothy ffolkes, the only child of Sir William ffolkes, 3rd Baronet, a considerable Norfolk landowner and, like his father and grandfather before him, a Conservative MP for the area. In 1902 she married John Dawnay, who in 1924 became the 9th Viscount Downe. The Downe family owned vast estates in Yorkshire. John died in 1931, and was succeeded as Viscount Downe by his and Dorothy's son Richard. Dorothy, as Dowager Viscountess, returned to her family estate at Hillington in Norfolk, which had been left to her by her father. She was very 'hands-on' in the running of this estate. In 1934 she became Deputy Lieutenant for Norfolk. She was a close friend of, and a former lady-in-waiting to, Queen Mary. Other members of her family, too, moved in Court circles: her uncle, the Rector of Hillington (later the 5th Baronet ffolkes), was Chaplain to King George V, and her son Richard had been a Page of Honour to the king.

Her interest in politics of the Right had started in the 1920s, when she was living on the Downe estates in Yorkshire. She was one of the many titled and landed people who joined Rotha Lintorn-Orman's 'British Fascists', becoming the Commander of the North Riding Yorkshire County Command. The British Fascists (BF) were basically an anti-Communist movement, concerned with support for law and order in the event of a Communist revolution. Dorothy chaired and addressed a number of BF meetings in Yorkshire, but appears to have found no contradiction in also being president of the Conservative Women's Association of Scarborough.

On her return to Norfolk in 1931 she became chairman of the Conservative Women's Association of King's Lynn. In 1933 she heard Mosley speaking at a meeting in King's Lynn, was bowled over and joined the British Union of Fascists. Four years later, in 1937, she resigned her membership of the Conservative Party and became British Union prospective parliamentary candidate for North Norfolk.

She announced on 12 July 1937, in the pages of *Action*, that she had 'left the Conservative Party with disgust, and joined the British Union, in which movement she saw hope for the future of Britain, which she could not see in any other Party'. We have no evidence of anti-Semitic views or activities on her part, though she showed considerable admiration for Hitler, of whom she had several portraits in her house. It was the agricultural policies of BU (which was at this time targeting the farming communities of East Anglia) that appear to have particularly attracted her, and on several occasions she invited Jorian Jenks, BU's agricultural expert, to come and speak locally. Mosley was a frequent visitor. Dorothy also proselytised widely among the local farming community. It was she who first introduced Henry Williamson (who was farming at Stiffkey) to Mosley and to Jenks, and it was under her influence that he joined British Union.

Unlike Lady Pearson, she does not seem either to have joined other movements of the Right before the war, or to have undertaken any serious activity in the 'phoney war' period. Indeed, while maintaining her Fascist ideals, nevertheless, once war had begun, she showed some opposition to the Nazi cause. The Norfolk police reported that she had expressed considerable disgust at the German invasion of Norway, Holland and Belgium, and had taken down the portraits of Hitler that she had in her house. Her correspondence had been monitored, and MI5 noted that she 'was not concerned in the spreading of pro-Nazi propaganda' (TNA HO 45/23686). Her attitude appears to have been what she outlined in an interview with the *Daily Express* on 23 July 1940: that she believed that Britain should continue the war, but that she remained a Fascist. When the wave of arrests occurred in mid-1940, however, she was still, as MI5 admitted, an important official of British Union, and therefore clearly liable for arrest.

The fact that she was not arrested gave rise to a certain amount of comment. In mid-September Richard Rapier Stokes MP asked a question in the House of Commons as to why she had not been detained, when a number of King's Lynn working-class BU supporters had been. Sir Alexander Maxwell of the Home Office made enquiries about the case, and MI5, in a letter dated 22 September, gave him their reasons for inaction. They agreed that Lady Downe was 'undoubtedly an official of British Union at the time the arrests of British Union officials took place'. They asserted, however, that 'she was playing no very active part in the organisation of the movement', and also cited her apparent change of mind on the war. Their most revealing comment was, however, the following:

> We also considered that the internment of a person of Lady Downe's social standing might give the public a wrong impression of the importance of British Union.
>
> (TNA HO 45/23686)

They also noted, in passing, that 'there were indications that she was anxious to become a martyr', and that 'we did not think this wish should be gratified' (TNA HO 45/23686).

Lady Downe did indeed have a sense that she had been unfairly spared. In a letter to Lady Redesdale she said that she had expected to be imprisoned with the others, and that now, when things felt fairly safe again, 'I really feel so ashamed of being free!' (Gottlieb, 2000: 248).

The queries continued. On 14 November Oswald Hickson, the solicitor who had acted on behalf of so many of those imprisoned under DR 18B, published a letter in *The Times* which alleged that favouritism had been accorded to Lady Downe. Lord Swinton, chairman of the Home Defence (Security) Executive, asked for a report on the matter. This report, dated 24 November, for the first time made it clear that Stokes's question in the House, and Hickson's letter in *The Times*, had been instigated by Lady Downe herself. It cited in evidence a letter from Hickson to Lady Downe (undated), which ran:

> I saw Mr Stokes yesterday. He is ready to put the questions to the Home Secretary, on the whole matter, but I should like to know if you have any objection to a question being put to the Home Secretary as to why you have not been detained, while certain working class members in your constituency have. Please don't hesitate to stop me having this question asked, because I will not have it put if you don't like it. At the same time it would be rather a strong position to take up.
>
> (TNA HO 45/23686)

The report continued: 'Lady Downe would obviously like to put herself in the position of a martyr, but we regard her as a rather stupid old woman, and we have been unwilling to gratify her desires in this respect.' Swinton, writing to the Home Secretary Herbert Morrison on 26 November, while not dissenting from this view, did point out: 'When all officials were being interned, I should have thought that Lady Downe might have been included in the omnibus; indeed, more so than some of the small fry.' It was now too late, however. 'As things are, it would be foolish to intern Lady Downe now as a past Fascist. If she makes any mischief in the future, that will be a different matter.' He suggested that if Morrison got a further question in the House, he 'might take the line of discounting her as a foolish old lady, old enough to know better, but not entitled to the trouble and cost of internment' (TNA HO 45/23686).

During the rest of the war, Lady Downe spent much of her time working on behalf of the DR 18B Detainees (British) Aid Fund. She retained her commitment to Mosley and British Union, and after the war joined Mosley's Union Movement. There were a number of other aristocrats who were heavily involved in British Union activities (including notably the Earl of Mar); none of them seem to have shared the fate of so many of their fellow members.

Further prominent figures

There were a number of other prominent people who, having been involved in pro-Nazi views and activities, might well have been considered for arrest – but who escaped. As we look at a small number of examples, we will see that their cases vary considerably.

The Duke of Wellington and the Duke of Westminster, for example, had held known anti-Semitic and pro-Nazi views, while encouraging several of the extremist movements devoted to those causes. Arthur Wellesley, 5th Duke of Wellington, succeeded to the dukedom in 1934. He had served in the Grenadier Guards in the Boer War and the First World War. In the late Thirties he played a prominent role in three major extremist movements, being president of the Liberty Restoration League, chairman of the Co-ordinating Committee, which co-ordinated the work of the 'patriotic societies', and a Warden of the Right Club, whose meetings he chaired (his name being one of the two that Captain Ramsay was prepared to reveal publicly).

Hugh Richard Arthur Grosvenor, 2nd Duke of Westminster (nicknamed 'Bendor'), was 'fervently anti-Semitic' and had a reputation for 'anti-Semitic rages' (Vaughan, 2011: 54, 114). He was also implacably opposed to war with Germany. In the weeks before the war, at a time when The Link was under considerable public attack, he decided publicly to support the movement by joining it – as Domvile said, this was splendid and a great advertisement for the movement (NMM DOM 56, 21/8/39). An altercation the Duke had with Duff Cooper, two days before war broke out, was typical of his style and views. Lady Diana Cooper describes him as beginning by 'abusing the Jewish race', praising the Germans and 'rejoicing that we were not yet at war':

> When he added that Hitler knew after all that we were his best friends, he set off the powder-magazine. 'I hope', Duff spat, 'that by to-morrow he will know that we are his most implacable and remorseless enemies'. Next day 'Bendor', telephoning to a friend, said that if there was a war it would be entirely due to the Jews and Duff Cooper.
>
> (Cooper, 1953)

One week after the outbreak of war, on 11 September, Westminster convened a meeting at his house, attended by eight other people: the Duke of Buccleuch, Lord Rushcliffe, Lord Arnold, Lord Mottistone, Henry Drummond Wolff MP, Sir Philip Gibbs, the Vicar of St Alban's Church and one other. At this meeting a Memorandum was produced, which all (with the exception of two – Lord Mottistone and the Vicar of St Alban's Church) approved. This Memorandum blamed the war on the Jews and international finance:

> The newspapers – especially those controlled by the Left and the Jews – take the line that no peace is possible until Nazism has been destroyed root and branch. […] With the succession of Hitler to power, there began at once a world-wide and incessant barrage of propaganda against Germany, because of its regime. International propaganda left no lie untold to exacerbate feeling

against the Reich. The motives of those who conducted this propaganda were many and various. Chief of them was the anger of international finance against the country which had flung down the gage to the system by which the international financier – who is an exploiter, never a producer – had accumulated his wealth and power.

(TNA FO 800/317/7)

The government was fully aware of such activities on the part of Westminster. However, after Churchill had warned him off, he took a lower profile thereafter. (The suggestion that, through his former mistress Coco Chanel and her lover the German agent Hans Gunther von Dincklage, he had been involved in a proposed 'peace move' with the Germans during the course of the war (Vaughan, 2011), appears merely to have been a product of Chanel's ability to use 'names' in the pursuit of her own ends.)

Unlike Westminster and so many others, Lord Redesdale (David Bertram Ogilvy Freeman-Mitford, 2nd Baron Redesdale) changed his attitude to Germany completely once war had been declared. The father of Unity Mitford and Diana Mosley, he had in the pre-war period come to share their views, and became a constant spokesman for friendship and understanding with Germany, objecting to 'Britain's persistently un-English treatment of Germany', and describing Hitler as 'a right-thinking man of irreproachable sincerity and honesty', who was 'in the life he leads and in all that he does, an example they [the Germans] can be proud to follow' (*The Times*, 14/3/36). He was a member of the Anglo-German Fellowship. In 1938 he became a member of the Council of The Link, and in 1939 a Warden of the Right Club. When war broke out, however, Redesdale's innate patriotism took over, and he rejected Nazism and accepted Germany as the enemy – all the easier because this essentially simple man's acute xenophobia had always made him see 'the Huns' as enemies, a view only tempered for a while by his obsession with Hitler. The reversal was painful, however. Something of his new mood (in part, of course, caused by his daughter Unity's situation after her botched suicide attempt) is to be seen in a photograph of him giving away his daughter Deborah at her marriage in 1941 to Lord Andrew Cavendish (later Duke of Devonshire).

Patriotically, and modestly, this old soldier is wearing his simple Home Guard uniform for the occasion. His face is drawn, and it is hard to recognise the lively pre-war Redesdale in this gloomy figure. On the other hand Redesdale's wife Sidney, who had always been a far more profound believer in Hitler and his policies, did not follow his example. She remained a staunch pro-Nazi. They lived mainly apart from 1943 onwards.

Of the Redesdale children, Unity, who had been so obsessed with Hitler, had attempted suicide in Munich at the outbreak of war, succeeding only in inflicting serious brain damage to herself. She was repatriated, and thereafter cared for by her mother until her death in 1948. Diana, unrepentant as always, was imprisoned under DR 18B, eventually being housed with her husband Sir Oswald Mosley in Holloway prison. Two others, however, were in their different ways illustrative of the situation whereby young men of a fascist disposition, fighting for their country (often with distinction), could still retain their pre-war views on Hitler and Nazism. Tom Mitford, the Redesdales' only son, who was to die in action at the head of his troops in Burma in March 1945, had confided to James Lees-Milne only eight months earlier, on 27 August 1944, his continuing beliefs:

> I asked him point-blank if he still sympathised with the Nazis. He emphatically said Yes. That all the best Germans were Nazis. That if he were a German he would be one. That he was an imperialist. He considered that life without power and without might with which to strike fear into every other nation would not be worth living for an Englishman.
>
> (Lees-Milne, 2006: 167)

Similarly, Derek Jackson, Lord Redesdale's son-in-law, had on 27 June 1942 shocked Lees-Milne by his expression of his views:

> Derek is positively pro-Nazi. What a catching disease Mitfordism is! There is Derek, a gallant man older than me, a rear-gunner in airforce blue, awarded a DFC, in private life a brilliant scientist, saying that we can't win the war, that he loathes the British lower classes who have forced him into this unnecessary war (absolute

tosh!), and that the Germans know the best way of treating them, which is to crush them under heel.

(Lees-Milne, 2006: 40)

Lord Ronald Graham and his elder brother, James, the Marquess of Graham (sons of the 6th Duke of Montrose) present a rather more complicated picture, including active participation in fascist activities. Lord Ronald had been one of the best-known figures in the anti-Semitic and pro-Nazi circles of pre-war London, frequenting Margaret Bothamley's salon and attending meetings of most of the extremist societies, including the Nordic League and The Link. In 1939 he joined the Right Club, of which he became a Steward, and he was one of the small band of hard-line members who kept the Right Club going during the period of the 'phoney war', right up to May 1940. There was no sign of him changing his views at any time. His brother, the Marquess of Graham (the future 7th Duke of Montrose), who had lived in Southern Rhodesia since 1930, was in London at the outbreak of war, and immediately signed up as a Lieutenant in the Royal Naval Volunteer Reserve, and was assigned to HMS Kandahar. While on leave in early 1940, however, he joined his brother in a number of his activities, including a meeting between representatives of the Pro-British Association and members of the Right Club on 29 February, and also Mosley's Criterion lunch on 1 March, which was attended by an array of right-wing anti-war enthusiasts. He also joined the Right Club at this stage (as his name's late position on the membership list shows). His views, and his larger-than-life personality, seem to have impressed the activists he met at this time, to the extent that one of them, Aubrey Lees, proposed in the presence of Lord Ronald and Richard Findlay 'that Mosley would be got rid of, and a brother of Lord Ronald Graham, who is in the Royal Navy, would take his place' (TNA HO 45/25728/1181). The Marquess, whose short and peripheral involvement in these circles certainly did not warrant any action by the authorities, returned to his ship, and continued to serve with distinction in the Navy throughout the war. It is surprising, however, that Lord Ronald, whose multifarious activities in the period up to May 1940 had been so carefully monitored by MI5, never faced detention, even though his close associates Richard

Findlay, Jock Houston, Aubrey Lees, Anna Wolkoff and, of course, Captain Ramsay, did.

Among the prominent people who escaped detention was Major-General J.F.C. ('Boney') Fuller, whom we have seen as an inveterate participant in a number of right-wing activities inspired by his dogged anti-Semitism, his admiration for Nazi Germany and his opposition to war with Germany. It had, apparently, been decided by Army Security that he had no 'unpatriotic intentions'. He continued, however, to be monitored by MI5. Mosley was puzzled by Fuller's non-internment, wondering whether the intention was to 'use' him. Fuller's wife's view was that 'They'll never arrest Boney; he knows too much' (Dorril, 2007: 511–12). Another reason may have been powerful 'protectors' within the upper ranks of the army. Whatever the reason, Fuller remained at large.

Another such figure, who however appears to have had rather less lenient treatment from the government, was Captain George Drummond, chairman of Drummond's Bank, who had often entertained, among other distinguished members of society, the Prince of Wales and the Duke of York (the future George VI) at his house Pitsford Hall, near Northampton. Drummond was described by Admiral Domvile as 'madly pro-German and anti-Jew' (NMM DOM 56, 5/5/39). Earlier in the Thirties he had tried to form his own association – the 'British Movement' – and in 1938 he became president of the Northampton branch of The Link, and in 1939 a member of the Right Club. He was at the same time a strong enthusiast for Mosley. Before the war he was a close associate of Domvile, Fuller, Carroll, etc., and during the 'phoney war' took a prominent part in discussions between representatives of The Link and the British People's Party.

Suddenly, in May 1940, Drummond 'announced that, as he was unable to "fit himself in any longer with life as it is lived in the average English community", he was moving to the Isle of Man'. His departure may, however, have been less voluntary than this statement suggests. A fellow member of The Link was later to describe how he had called at Pitsford Hall and found Drummond being interrogated by 'detectives'. Drummond, he said, had taken him on one side and given him a thousand pounds in cash, instructing him to look after his family 'if I go inside' (Coupland, 2000: 81–2). Clearly Drummond was expecting to be arrested. As Coupland suggests, 'possibly, Drummond's self-exile may have been pressed on him as an alternative to internment'. If so, it is interesting that he was exiled to the Isle of Man, where so many of his less fortunate companions were in internment camps, and that his place of exile should have been a magnificent private mansion owned by him, Mount Rule. Popular tradition in the Northampton area (which may of course be an exaggeration) has it that Drummond was 'placed under house arrest by MI5 and banished from England' (*NCE*, 2014). Drummond remained at Mount Rule after the war.

There was considerable reluctance, on the part of the authorities, to imprison prominent, usually titled, people under Defence Regulation 18B (1A). The regulation had been introduced as a preventive measure to detain people who, it was believed, might be a threat to wartime Britain. There was therefore no need for detailed evidence such as would be required for ordinary arrest. A very large number of people were in fact detained on the basis of previous associations, or recorded statements and opinions, or suspicion of subversive activity. Most of the prominent people we have been looking at, here and in other chapters, were on this basis ripe for arrest, as had been their less prominent – and less fortunate – associates. Governmental reluctance to detain such people had, in individual cases, specific causes, such as concern for pacifist opinion, in the case of the Duke of Bedford, or the need to keep secret the fact that Japanese codes had been broken at Bletchley, in the case of Lord Sempill. But the wide-ranging nature of this phenomenon, and actual statements made by the authorities in some of the cases we have seen, are bound to lead us to believe that undue attention was being paid to their position in society. In part this may have been due to natural deference in the class-based society of the Thirties and Forties; in part, as other statements have made clear, it was because of the detrimental effect on international opinion (and particularly American opinion) that might have been caused by the revelation of the extent of anti-war feeling among the British aristocracy. The Duke of Bedford may have been near to the mark when he pondered why he had not been arrested:

> I have heard on good authority that the Home Secretary actually ordered my arrest […] but I also have reason to believe that Mr Churchill vetoed this amiable project. I should like to think he was inspired by motives of humanity and justice but some feel that the imprisonment of peers would have created in America so deep an impression of the strength of the anti-war movement in Britain that the task of dragging the USA into the war would have been made much less easy!
>
> (Bedford, 1949: 188)

Be that as it may, most of these people appear to have lived charmed lives, compared with the great number of more unfortunate foot-soldiers, who had far less power or influence (or, indeed, capacity for mischief).

Bibliography

Books and articles

Bedford, Hastings, Duke of (1949), *The Years of Transition* (Edinburgh: Dakers).

Cooper, Lady Diana (1953), *The Light of Common Day* (London: Hart-Davis).

Coupland, Philip (2000), 'The Blackshirts in Northampton, 1933–1940', *Northamptonshire Past and Present* No. 53.

Dorril, Stephen (2007), *Blackshirt: Sir Oswald Mosley and British Fascism* (London: Penguin Books).

Gottlieb, Julie (2000), *Feminine Fascism: Women in Britain's Fascist Movement 1923–1945* (London and New York: I.B. Tauris).

Lees-Milne, James (2006), *Diaries 1942–1954* (London: John Murray).

Roberts, Andrew (1994), *Eminent Churchillians* (London: Weidenfeld and Nicolson).

Simpson, A. W. Brian (1992), *In the Highest Degree Odious: Detention without Trial in Wartime Britain* (Oxford: Oxford University Press).

Uhlman, Fred (1998), *The Making of an Englishman: Erinnerungen eines deutschen Juden* (Zurich: Diogenes).

Vaughan, Hal (2011), *Sleeping with the Enemy: Coco Chanel's Secret War* (New York: Vintage Books).

Documents

The National Archives (TNA)

FO 800/317
HO 45/23686, HO 45/25728

National Maritime Museum (NMM)

Admiral Domvile's Diary, DOM 55, DOM56

Newspapers and journals

Action
Northampton Chronicle and Echo (NCE)
The Times

11

'HIS IMPETUOUS NATURE, OBSTINACY AND FLAWED JUDGEMENT'

A bull in a china shop

Lord Sempill presents us with the extreme case of someone who, under grave suspicion of subversive activity, and at the same time clearly espousing and expressing pro-German and pro-Japanese views, while having previously played a leading role in various extremist pro-Nazi groups, managed to escape detention.

Colonel William Francis Forbes-Sempill, 19th Baron Sempill, was a Scottish peer who in his youth, as Master of Sempill (eldest son of the 18th Baron Sempill), had been a brilliant air pioneer. In the First World War he had a distinguished career, serving in the Royal Flying Corps and the Royal Naval Air Service, ending as a colonel in the Royal Air Force. He retired from military service in 1919. Between 1920 and 1923 he led a British delegation of former naval airmen to Japan, to assist the Japanese in setting up a naval air force (Sempill, 1924). His interest in the air continued throughout this time, and by the early Thirties he was breaking a number of records for long-distance non-stop flight. He was something of a glamorous figure. In 1934 he succeeded his father as Baron Sempill, living at Craigievar Castle, Aberdeenshire and at 120 Pall Mall, London. He took his seat in the House of Lords as a Conservative peer.

Already, in the 1920s, he was beginning to show signs of that lack of judgement and unconcern for the national interest that were to dog his later career. After the Anglo-Japanese alliance had come to an end in 1921, suspicion had been aroused by Sempill's close relationship with the Japanese authorities, and he was kept under surveillance from his return to Britain in 1923 onwards, with his phone being tapped and his mail intercepted. By September 1925 it had become clear, from his correspondence with Captain Toyoda, the Japanese Naval Attaché in London, that Sempill had been passing on classified information about aircraft that were being developed. This information was clearly being paid for. It was decided to 'keep a close look-out' on the situation (TNA KV 2/871). By 1926 further indiscretions by Sempill, in relation to plans for a top-secret new flying boat, led to him being interviewed by MI5, but at a subsequent meeting, chaired by the Foreign Secretary Sir Austen Chamberlain, it was surprisingly decided not to prosecute him under the provisions of the Official Secrets Act. This was possibly because of his position in society, but possibly also because any publicity would have led to the revelation that MI5 had had access to Japanese communications. Sempill merely received a reprimand – and from then on was denied access to any classified information. In 1926 the Greek government offered him an appointment as aeronautical adviser to their government – but 'the relevant authorities' in Britain decided 'that Sempill should not go to Greece with the blessing of the Air Ministry and, should he go there, he would go strictly as a private individual' (TNA KV 2/872). In the early 1930s he took on a commercial job as a representative of the Japanese aeronautical firm Mitsubishi.

By the Thirties he had begun to show more extreme political leanings in the European sphere, joining an array of dubious right-wing movements. In January 1934 he had joined the English Mistery (discussed in Chapter 12) (HRO, Wallop 15M84/F379). He soon began, like many inter-war aviators, and like many who like himself were concerned with monetary reform, to show an interest in Nazi Germany. At first this merely took the form of membership of the Anglo-German Fellowship. As war approached, however, he became entangled in a variety of pro-Nazi and anti-Semitic groups, often playing a prominent role within them. In July 1938 he became a member of the ruling council of The Link. In 1939 he became a member of Captain Ramsay's newly formed Right Club. Though the names of members of this group were, as we have seen, on the whole kept secret at the time, MI5 had become aware of Sempill's membership of it as early as October 1939 (Mrs Ramsay having boasted of his membership in the presence of an MI5 operative). MI5 was also aware that Sempill had agreed to chair a meeting of the Nordic League on 7 October 1939 (though the cessation of public activity on the part of the NL at the outbreak of war led to the cancellation of that meeting) (TNA KV 2/872).

Three of the constants in Sempill's life, before, during and after the war, appear to have been a chronic shortage of money (MI5 established that he had very considerable debts), an indulgence in far-fetched schemes at home and abroad to generate revenue (for which he often made use of the names of prominent contacts of his) and a disregard for any advice from officialdom. One example will suffice. In February 1939 Sempill wrote to the Foreign Secretary asking for letters of introduction to King Carol of Romania and to the British Minister in Bucharest, as he intended to go to Romania to explore 'trading potentialities' between the two countries. He was informed that such a mission was already under consideration and that 'for the time being the despatch of any unofficial representatives such as he was then contemplating would be unfortunate'. He nevertheless decided to go, arriving in Bucharest with a letter of introduction from Lord Lloyd (the former High Commissioner in Egypt, out of office since 1929). The Foreign Office wrote to their man in Romania: 'His activities are not ones which we consider should be encouraged as we have some doubt as to whether he has the financial backing which he claims.' A guarded warning was conveyed to the Romanians to this effect, saying that His Majesty's Government was unable to vouch for him. Nothing further seems to have come of this scheme (TNA FO 371/23851).

At the outbreak of war Sempill rejoined the Royal Naval Air Service, and was given a post in the Department of Air Material at the Admiralty, where he served under his old friend Winston Churchill, First Lord of the Admiralty. This would, on the face of it, appear to make his case a very simple one: like many other people who had dabbled in pro-Nazi activity in the pre-war period, it would appear from this that his patriotism must have made him choose loyalty to his country now it was at war. The situation was not so simple, however, and his activities in several spheres, during the course of the war, would seem to show that the leopard had not changed his spots.

Above all, there were his continuing activities in relation to the Japanese. Britain was not at war with Japan, of course, until December 1941; but Japan was definitely seen, well before this, as a dangerous and possibly belligerent power. Given Sempill's previous activities in relation to Japan, it is amazing that he was taken on by the Admiralty in 1939, and particularly in such a sensitive position, in a department dealing with the provision of planes and other equipment. Soon he began to return to his old form. MI5, who had continued to take an interest in him, in June 1940 intercepted Mitsubishi correspondence which discussed the continuance of his regular fee for information in view of 'the use both direct and indirect of Lord Sempill by our Military and Naval Attachés in London'. The Admiralty wrote to him about this, and he 'gave a solemn undertaking that he would have no communication with Japanese or British subjects regarding matters connected with the Naval service'. In August 1940 the Director of Naval Intelligence drew the government's attention to the 'apparently undesirable contacts of Lord Sempill's'. Yet still nothing was done about him (TNA KV 2/872).

It was not until the autumn of 1941, as war with Japan became ever more likely, that things finally came to a crisis. Churchill was shocked to read a telegram (decoded at Bletchley Park) from the Japanese Chargé d'Affaires in London to Tokyo, dated 13 September, which contained detailed information on Churchill's own most recent and most secret activities. He asked the Foreign Secretary Anthony Eden to check the Chargé d'Affaires's British contacts. Eden came up with five Englishmen who acted as informants for the Japanese Embassy: prominent among them were Sir Edward Grigg MP, who had been 'warned', and Lord Sempill, 'suspected of receiving a subvention from Japanese funds', together with another close associate of Churchill's also employed at the Admiralty, Commander McGrath of the Royal Naval Air Service. Churchill was appalled that these men had such a close relationship with the Japanese. He wrote to Eden, instructing him immediately to close down 'the activities of this English nebula':

At any moment we may be at war with Japan, and here are all these Englishmen, many of them respectable, two of whom I know personally, moving around collecting information and sending it to the Japanese Embassy. I cannot believe that the Master of Sempill and Commander McGrath have any idea of what their position would be on the moment of a Japanese declaration of war. Immediate internment would be the least of their troubles.

On 3 October Eden sent Churchill further information about Sempill's activities, in the form of a tapped telephone conversation between Sempill and Captain Kondo at the Japanese Embassy, warning that on no account must the Japanese ring him when he was at the Admiralty (Aldrich, 2000: 47).

Churchill's immediate response was that Sempill must be cleared out 'while time remains', whereupon Sempill was informed by the Admiralty that he must choose between resigning his commission and being fired. However, Churchill, who appears to have had second thoughts, declared that he had only meant that Sempill should leave his job at the Admiralty, not that he should resign his commission. It was decided that one suitable course of action might be for Sempill to be posted to Northern Scotland, with MI5 being duly informed so that they could take any necessary precautions. As a first step, Sempill agreed to resign from the Admiralty at the end of November (TNA KV 2/872).

On 7 December Japan attacked Pearl Harbour, and the next day Britain declared war on Japan.

One possible reason for all this uncertainty as to how to deal with Sempill was that Churchill feared the adverse publicity that might arise, if the public realised that, despite fears as to Sempill's reliability, it had been decided to employ him in such a sensitive role at the Admiralty. Churchill's own judgement could be called into question, because it was he as First Sea Lord in 1939 who had taken that decision. Another possible reason was that any action taken against Sempill might also have revealed the extent to which the British codebreakers had mastered the Japanese codes.

What are we to make of Sempill's activities in relation to Japan? One is tempted to think that he was surprisingly unaware of the implications of what he was doing. He had always got on with the Japanese, and was convinced that war with Japan must at all costs be avoided. He was also convinced of his own importance. During the course of 1941 he had tried, with others, 'to work out a settlement for the Far Eastern situation through the means of a four-power pact between Britain, America, China and Japan', approaching Ernest Bevin for support, and speaking on the matter in the House of Lords (TNA KV 2/872). His relations with the Japanese Embassy may well at this stage of the war have been merely on this level. It is perhaps significant that, when it came to finding out who had conveyed private information to the Japanese in 1941, his was merely one among five names given of people who had contacts with the Embassy, as someone who *might* be the guilty party. And when his flat and office were searched on 11 and 12 December 1941, 'nothing of an incriminating nature was found' (though he had kept some files from his Department, which he should not of course have done). So the jury remains out, and one is tempted to share the view expressed by the National Archives that 'on the evidence of these [MI5] files, Sempill's activities on behalf of the Japanese [...] were motivated less by any desire to help the enemy or make money than by his own impetuous nature, obstinacy and flawed judgement' (TNA, Notes on files KV 2/871–875). MI5's description of him is even more telling. In September 1943 they noted that he was 'the kind of man who likes to make contact with foreigners, whether in an official position or not, and is completely without any kind of discretion'. On another occasion three months later, it was noted: 'Sempill is an adventurer and I doubt whether he has any very convinced opinions upon politics' (TNA KV 2/872–873).

Nothing seems to have ruffled Sempill, even after he left the Admiralty at the end of 1941. His activities, and his conviction as to his own rightness, continued to give problems to the authorities. In early 1942 he asked permission to visit Eire; permission was refused on 2 April, whereupon he decided to make a visit to Northern Ireland instead, from 4 to 9 April. In October 1942 he hit the headlines for supporting a speech by Lady Snowden which had called for a negotiated peace with Germany. He continued to express such views publicly in the succeeding months (e.g. *NR*, 5/11/42; *Truth*, 11/42) and was also in contact, like so many previous would-be negotiators, with Björn Prytz of the Swedish Legation (TNA KV 2/872).

He was also adept at using his contacts to help him to positions where he could both voice publicly his political opinions, and also possibly pick up some financial advantage. A good example of this was his visit to Canada in 1943–4. He had started, on 7 September 1943, by sounding out his old friend Air-Commodore Archie Boyle, now Director of Intelligence at the Air Ministry, as to the possibility of a trip to Canada ('on an official matter') being approved. Boyle, clearly embarrassed at this contact, passed the letter on to MI5, asking what he should say: MI5's view was that 'it would be very undesirable to grant an Exit Permit to Lord Sempill having regard to the grave suspicions held about him as a result of his connection with the Japanese, especially an Exit Permit to the American continent where they are very Japanese-conscious'. Sempill was very indiscreet, they said: 'In this country we are able to keep some kind of check on him but if he were allowed to go abroad, there is no knowing what he might do.' A later note reiterated that danger, particularly as 'the case might at any time again become active'. Boyle was informed that 'we should actively oppose the granting of any Exit Permit to Sempill unless it were very strongly supported' (TNA KV 2/872).

In December 1943, however, Sempill applied directly for a permit to travel to Canada. He was told that such a permit could not be granted until the authorities knew which government department was supporting the request, and the reasons for that support. Sempill, clearly taken aback, said that he was not yet in a position to let them know. Three days later he had found his support: Canadian Army Headquarters was backing him, on behalf of the Knights of Columbus, a Canadian Catholic Welfare Association. MI5 had to give in, even though they were aware that it would have been 'child's play for him to get some well-meaning and high-ranking officer to sign a paper to say that the visit was necessary', and despite concern as to the dangers:

> By reason of his social position he can easily obtain information of a confidential kind. If he can turn this information to his own pecuniary advantage, he will not be over-scrupulous about

imparting it to others, even though there may be a considerable risk of its getting into dangerous hands.

(TNA KV 2/873)

Sempill left for Canada in late December. It did not take long for troubles to emerge. First, the Knights of Columbus found that he 'cold-shouldered them' from the start. They were 'disgusted with his lack of interest in their organisation', and considered him to be 'devoting his time and attention to his own interests, "whatever they may be"'. This alerted MI5 to the question of what those interests actually were, though it was difficult to find out, because he had 'many irons in the fire' (TNA KV 2/873).

Even more problematic, however, were Sempill's excursions into the Canadian political scene. As MI5 later reported:

> On arrival in Canada he did what we all expected, namely, he made indiscreet political speeches. For instance, he talked about his pet theories on economic reform, theories which, because of their relation to Social Credit, are regarded as very controversial in Canada. He crowned his indiscretions by writing a letter to the Speaker of the Alberta Legislative Assembly – he had been invited to occupy a seat on the floor of the House at the opening of that Assembly – thanking him for the honour and repeating his theories about Social Credit.

Disturbed by all this, the High Commissioner for Canada decided in February 1944 that Sempill had 'overstayed his welcome', and that 'critical, if not sinister, interpretations are being put on his continued presence', a major concern being the 'security aspect'. It was also clear that 'he was never really sponsored by the Canadian Army and [had] taken advantage of the trip to engage in personal business negotiations in which neither the British Government nor the Canadian Army are interested in any way'. The High Commissioner decided 'that Sempill ought to go home as soon as possible', and sent a signal to the Dominions Office in London to ask them to try to arrange for him 'to be recalled forthwith'. Such tactics do not seem to have worked, however, because Sempill, resilient as always, remained in Canada for a further considerable period. Messages to prominent Canadians appear to have had no effect whatsoever, as, dazzled by having a British Lord among them, affected by his undoubted charm, and believing his own account of his accomplishments, they refused to hear anything against him (TNA KV 2/873).

One other result of Sempill's time in Canada was that in June 1944 MI5 was seriously embarrassed by a query from the American Embassy, asking 'for information about Lord Sempill and in particular about his anti-American and pro-Japanese views' (TNA KV 2/874).

One of the reasons for MI5's concerns about letting Sempill visit Canada had been that he was 'in touch with well-known Fascists and anti-Americans' in Britain. And indeed, Sempill's wartime activities did not confine themselves to public pronouncements and foreign trips. He had kept up his former right-wing interests and activities, and had begun involving himself, in Britain, with the secretive right-wing movements that were emerging. The first evidence of this was when he was listed, at the meeting forming the British National Party in May 1942, as one of the notables who had agreed to accept office in the party. Later he became involved with the British National Party's successor, the English Nationalist Association. In late 1942 and early 1943 he had begun corresponding with a number of right-wing anti-war activists including Norman Hay and the Duke of Bedford. He had a particularly prolific correspondence with Major Harry Edmonds, who drew him into his Constitutional Research Association, of which Sempill became a leading member after his return from Canada. MI5 had been keeping tabs on him, of course, throughout this period (TNA KV 2/872–874).

Sempill's wartime activities were of a piece with what he had been doing pre-war. He was like a rogue elephant, trampling down any criticism of his views or actions, and proceeding on his way without any self-questioning. His pre-war involvement in pro-Nazi and anti-Semitic movements had shown him to be a visceral member of the extreme Right, and a strong proponent of peace with Germany. His return to similar movements after his resignation from the Admiralty showed a complete disregard for the changed situation brought about by the war. Similarly, his uncritical and public support for Japan, whether or not he actually undertook subversive activities in this area, showed an inability to understand Britain's situation. It was almost as though he had been isolated from any understanding of how to behave.

The question of why he was never interned is an interesting one. His activities in relation to the Japanese embassy would seem to have amply justified such an action, as would his previous involvement in so many anti-war and pro-Nazi organisations. While concern about revealing that Britain had accessed Japanese codes may have prevented him from being publicly accused of treasonous activities, the reasons for detention did not need to be made public; and at any rate, his other varied activities would have provided ample cause for detention. One is left to presume, as was suggested in the last chapter, that the imprisonment of such a prominent figure could be deemed to be detrimental to perceptions of how strong pro-German or pro-Japanese feeling was in Britain; or else that it was Sempill's social position and his many powerful contacts that deterred the authorities. Nevertheless, MI5 kept him under close observation throughout this period (as is shown by the five fat files in the National Archives), and he was also kept on the Suspect List of those to be arrested in the event of an invasion. Apart from that, he seems to have been left alone.

Bibliography

Books and articles

Aldrich, Richard J. (2000), *Intelligence and the War against Japan: Britain, America and the Politics of Secret Service* (Cambridge: Cambridge University Press).

Sempill, Colonel the Master of (1924), 'The British Aviation Mission to the Imperial Japanese Navy', *Journal of the Royal Aeronautical Society*, XXVIII, 553–84.

Documents

The National Archives (TNA)

FO 371/23851
KV 2/871, KV 2/872, KV 2/873, KV 2/874, KV 2/875

Hampshire Record Office (HRO)

Papers of the 8th Earl of Portsmouth (Wallop)

Newspapers and journals

News Review (NR)
Truth

12

'YOU KNOW THE JEWISH RACKET AS WELL AS I DO'

The vagaries of the 'back-to-the-land' school

A prominent feature of the pre-war Right was what is often called the 'back-to-the-land' school. Through many of their ideas, these people were the direct antecedents of today's ecological movement; but while there were clearly many among them whose concerns were solely with agricultural reform and with a return to our roots in the soil, there was also a significant number whose outlook has been described as 'organo-fascism'. While calling for a revival of rural values, and a return to the rootedness of the English people in the land, this school also spoke of the danger from foreigners, particularly the Jews, who were not merely rootless and un-English, but also responsible, through their dominance of international finance, for most of the ills of the modern world. Some, moreover, such as George Pitt-Rivers, agreed with Anthony Ludovici's view of the need for a eugenic solution to Britain's ills (Stone, 2002). In other words, they shared many of the preconceptions of the anti-Semitic extremists of the period. As Dan Stone, in his study of this movement, has pointed out:

> The problem is explaining how a group of people who could put forward such visionary ideas about farming, food and care

for the environment could at the same time – and not as a random corollary to these ideas but as fundamental to their articulation – argue for a holistic philosophy of nature which embraced concepts of race, culture and gender that are immediately recognisable today as fascistic.

(Stone, 2003:151)

Some of the more extreme among these people became obsessively convinced that Nazi Germany was an example to be followed; and, as the Thirties progressed, they campaigned more and more for peace with Germany. Prominent at this end of the spectrum was Lord Lymington, whom Dan Stone has characterised as one of the most extreme of the group. He was surrounded by many like-minded figures such as Anthony Ludovici, George Pitt-Rivers, Norman Hay and John Coast. Another group of agrarian specialists, within the British Union of Fascists (BUF), contained people such as Jorian Jenks and Robert Saunders. A number of other figures, such as Rolf Gardiner and Henry Williamson, while not being so involved as these in actual political activities, nevertheless conformed strongly to the pattern just described, and were just as strongly attracted to Nazi Germany, writing extensively in that cause and maintaining close contact with Lymington and his group.

There was, therefore, a wide variety of 'back-to-the land' enthusiasts for Nazi Germany, and it is hardly surprising that their wartime activities should have been equally varied. Let us look at some individual cases.

Lord Lymington and Norman Hay

Two close friends and associates exemplify this variety. Lord Lymington and Norman Hay shared many views on race, tradition, Nazi Germany and anti-democracy, and had worked together for at least ten years up to and after the outbreak of war. Then in May 1940 Lymington sought to dissociate himself from Hay's activities (much to Hay's disgust). Later in the war they both once more, to greater or lesser extent, became involved with various extreme right-wing movements; but by then their attitudes to Nazi Germany appear to have differed considerably.

Gerard Vernon Wallop (1898–1984), Viscount Lymington, was the heir to the 8th Earl of Portsmouth (he was to succeed to his father's title in 1943). After serving in the First World War, he settled down as a landowner in Hampshire. He was deeply concerned with problems relating to the land, and came under the influence of such organic thinkers as Rolf Gardiner and Professor George Stapledon. From 1929 to 1934 he was Conservative MP for the Basingstoke constituency, but resigned, causing a by-election, because of his frustration with the democratic process (Portsmouth, 1965: 118–25).

We know little of Norman Hay's early life, except that he was some years younger than Lymington, and a graduate of Imperial College who in the Thirties held a number of scientific and management posts, including a spell with Courtaulds. He described himself as 'a lifelong student of politics and industrial developments' (*IP*, 1/3/39).

These two men first came into contact in 1930 through their involvement in the English Mistery, a quasi-masonic movement founded by a man called William Sanderson, whose book *Statecraft* (1927) had laid down mystical rules for government based on race, tradition, service, property (the ideal being a return to feudalism) and an economic system no longer dominated by the 'moneyed interests', the 'controllers of finance'. The movement was particularly obsessed with the danger of aliens polluting the English stock. Terms suitable for stockbreeding were used, and the influence of the eugenics theorist Anthony Ludovici ensured that eugenics was strongly on the agenda (Sanderson himself declaring that the movement owed a great deal to the inspiration of Ludovici). This aspect of the movement is highlighted by a letter from Lord Iddesleigh to Norman Hay on 21 January 1931, declaring his firm opposition to the Mistery because of its belief in the sterilisation of the unfit (HRO Wallop 15M84/F379).

The inaugural meeting of the Mistery on 28 May 1930 was addressed by Ludovici and Sanderson; Norman Hay was one of three people who joined the movement at this meeting. On 10 September a declaration undertaking lifelong support for the Mistery was signed by Hay, Sanderson and two others, Hay being given the post of 'Chief Syndic' (HRO Wallop 15M84/F382). Lymington did not join the movement until shortly after this, but he soon became one of its leading figures; he took over the post of 'Chief Syndic', and Hay was demoted to 'Deputy

Chief Syndic'. Hay was responsible for bringing several prominent figures into the Mistery in the mid-Thirties, including John Boyd-Carpenter, R.A. Butler, Derek Walker-Smith and Lord Sempill (HRO Wallop 15M84/F379).

Sanderson often confided to Hay and to Lymington his views (often acerbic) on the other members. His comments to Lymington on Norman Hay are particularly interesting:

> Hay will never be a popular personality. But he is sound all through. The youthful exuberance that made him chatter too much has been kept severely in check. [...] He is absolutely devoted to the Mistery.
>
> (HRO Wallop 15M84/F382)

Hay continued to work alongside Lymington for the rest of the Thirties. Lymington had now become the dominant figure in the movement. When, in December 1936, Lymington removed Sanderson from the chancellorship of the Mistery, this caused a split, with the majority of members, including Hay, following Lymington into his new movement, the English Array, founded in August 1937. One of Lymington's first acts, as 'Marshal of the Array', was to appoint Norman Hay as 'Marshal for Staffordshire' (*QGEA*, 7/37).

Lymington had, in his time as MP, shown his firm objection to 'Jewish aliens' entering Britain (Kushner and Knox, 1999: 148). His book *Famine in England*, published in early 1938, shows some of the reasoning behind this attitude. While on the one hand it expressed, in straightforwardly back-to-the-land terms, his heartfelt conviction of the need for a new policy with regard to agriculture, particularly in relation to the danger of famine if war were to break out, on the other it expressed racial concerns about 'our northern stock', which was being adulterated by 'the people of the ghettoes and the bazaar' (Lymington, 1938: 21–2, 43, 84, 203). In these views Lymington was typical of a number of the rural revivalists. As Philip Conford has pointed out:

> The argument runs as follows: agriculture had been sacrificed for the sake of industry and free trade, and Jewish interests, through their involvement in industry, shipping, import–export

and finance, had benefited from this policy. The concept of wealth had been corrupted, so that it was now identified with the abstract figures of an accountant's ledger rather than the natural resources and human skills on which all societies depend. There were cultural factors, too: the Jews, it was argued, had no commitment to the countries they lived in, and particularly not to any national soil. In the frequently-used and transparent code of the time, they were 'rootless cosmopolitans', perceived as a threat to the traditional rural culture which men such as Wallop and Gardiner wished to revitalise.

(Conford, 2005: 80–1)

In the view of Kushner and Knox, Lymington injected into this xenophobic tradition 'a heavy dose of völkisch romanticism and frequent pro-Hitlerism' (Kushner and Knox, 1999: 148). In 1937–8 Lymington became convinced that Nazi Germany presented a solution to the problems he had been pinpointing. His publicly expressed views became ever more pro-Nazi and anti-war. In *Famine in England* he had contrasted the 'spiritual awakening' of Nazi Germany with the present state of Britain. Later in 1938, he decided to take political action. Believing that war with Germany 'would benefit no one but the Jews and the international communists' (*QGEA*, 10/38), in September he founded the British Council against European Commitments (BCAEC), in which he, as president, was joined not only by a large number of the English Array (including Hay), but also by a number of leading fascists from more extreme groups, such as his vice-president William Joyce and his secretary John Beckett, both of the National Socialist League. The Imperial Fascist League was represented by Arnold Leese and P.J. Ridout (inventor of the motto 'PJ' – 'Perish Judah!'); and other members included such right-wing luminaries as A.K. Chesterton, Major-General Fuller, Admiral Domvile, Captain George Pitt-Rivers and Lord Tavistock.

In December 1938 Lymington went one stage further, with the founding of *New Pioneer*, a monthly magazine, major contributors to which were a roll-call of the extreme Right: Beckett, Ludovici, A.K. Chesterton, Fuller, John Scanlon, and H.T. Mills. Typical of the tone of this journal was an article entitled 'The War of the Jews'

Vagaries of the 'back-to-the-land' school 237

Revenge', which described the European dictatorships as having risen in revolt against the 'chains of usury', in a 'liberation of the national soul against an alien stranglehold and intrusion'. For this reason, it said, the Jews were pushing England into a war of revenge. Lymington believed that 'war with Germany would mean the end of white civilisation as we know it'. *New Pioneer* also objected to Britain receiving Jewish refugees from Nazi Germany, on the basis that 'cross breeding between utterly alien types is physically wrong and psychologically dangerous' (*NP*, 5/39, 7/39 and 8/39).

Throughout this period Lymington had been corresponding regularly with Hay. On 23 March 1939, for example, he wrote to him to say that Hitler's Prague coup was a 'damn nuisance':

> He [Hitler] has done the only logical thing in the stupidest and worse [*sic*] possible way, weakening Chamberlain and throwing everyone back in the arms of the Jews and the Wall Street racketeers. […] I sometimes wonder whether one of his lieutenants is not either in the service of the Jesuits or the Jews.
>
> (HRO Wallop 15M84/F189)

In August 1939 Hay (who had by now become a member of Ramsay's Right Club) founded his own journal, *Information and Policy*, in collaboration with his fellow Right Club member Lancelot Lawton, a journalist formerly of the School of Slavonic and East European Studies. Lawton had pro-Nazi and anti-Semitic form. In 1939 he had spoken on a number of occasions to the Nordic League, arguing on 17 April that Germany 'must have the Ukraine', which was 'necessary for the economic existence of the Greater Reich' (TNA HO 144/21379/285) and on 28 August, saying that if Hitler's lead in welcoming the Communists could result in 'the enemy' (the Jews) being broken, 'then he for one would welcome the Communists' (TNA HS 9/892/12).

Hay and Lymington were to continue some of their activities, though less openly, in the 'phoney war' period, September 1939– May 1940. As the various 'patriotic' movements tried to hammer out a common anti-war policy in October 1939, Hay had a 'productive' private meeting with Sir Oswald Mosley and Admiral Domvile on the 13th. On 26 October they met again: this time they were joined by Captain Ramsay, Neil Francis-Hawkins (BU), Lancelot Lawton, Lord Tavistock and Hay's old companion Lord Lymington. Over the next few months there were to be several secret meetings of the same kind, at most of which Lymington and Hay were present, together with a number of Hay's fellow Right Club members. In February 1940, too, they were both among those invited to come privately, though on different occasions, to hear Lord Tavistock give a preview of his famous 'Peace Proposal' (NMM DOM 56).

Hay's and Lymington's public profiles were, however, very different from each other in this period. Lymington's newspaper *New Pioneer*, while still indulging in attacks on Jewish refugees, racketeers and war profiteers, had now become silent as far as anti-war and pro-Nazi propaganda was concerned. It ceased publication in January 1940. Meanwhile, Lymington joined the Local Defence Volunteers (the Home Guard) in the area around his estate at Farleigh Wallop, near Basingstoke, as a platoon commander.

Hay's public persona was, however, very different from this, as he continued with his overt pro-Nazi activities. From January 1940 onwards, Hay and Lawton had been organising weekly meetings of Information and Policy, the movement based on the journal of the same name, which were attended by a cross-section of the pro-Nazi Right, including Domvile, Ramsay and Fuller. Speakers included General Fuller and Philip Spranklin, formerly of Goebbels's Munich Foreign Press Office, who just before the war had given to branches of The Link a number of talks about Jewish domination of the British press. One speaker was described as advocating 'Nazi doctrines' of purity of breed, eugenic controls and a master race, and as having stated that though the Germans were 'technically' our enemies, the people of Britain were not at war with Germany (*DT*, 25/5/40).

It was Information and Policy that was to be the cause of the major rift between Hay and Lymington in May 1940. On 23 and 24 May the first wave of arrests under Defence Regulation 18B had taken place. As it happened, there was a meeting of Information and Policy scheduled for the afternoon of 23 May. This was infiltrated by the press, which described the alarm of those present at news of the arrests. Several members immediately went home, including 'a very well-known

Vagaries of the 'back-to-the-land' school 239

major-general' (*DT*, 25/5/40). This was General Fuller, who had left after a short talk with Norman Hay. The content of the meeting was described as positively pro-Nazi. Special Branch noted that, among others, a prominent peer spoke against the Jews who had caused the war (TNA HO 262/6). Chased up by the press after the meeting, Fuller claimed little knowledge of Hay (with whom he had in fact regularly consorted in the previous months) or of Information and Policy (of which he had attended numerous meetings, and had indeed given, according to Domvile, a 'capital address' at one on 25 April). He said that he had believed he had been coming to attend 'a lecture on egg farming' (*ES*, 25/5/40).

This publicity given to Hay's activities proved too much for Lymington, who had received complaints from other members of the Array, saying that it was not fair to 'anyone loyally trying to serve England' to keep Hay's name on the list of members (HRO Wallop 15M84/F187). A few days later he wrote to Hay in the following extremely formal terms:

> Sir,
>
> In view of the reports appearing recently in the press and last night upon the wireless concerning Information and Policy it is necessary that I excommunicate you from the Array forthwith. I was reluctant to do this on press reports, which are notoriously inaccurate, but the news on the wireless and your interview with Bryant Irvine leave me in no doubt that you have jeopardised the good name of the Array, and your friends, however good and loyal your motives may have been. In a time of peril to the country I have no other choice.
>
> In the service of England
>
> Lymington
>
> (HRO Wallop 15M84/F189; Griffiths, 2010: 249)

This expression of disapproval of Hay's overt pro-Nazism exemplifies Lymington's new patriotic stance, now that Britain was at war.

Hay was to write to Lymington later, in far more personal terms (on 5 October 1941, after his release from internment), that he had been dumbfounded at the time by Lymington's attitude:

Dear Gerard, [...] You know the Jew racket as well as I do and I think it very poor support I have had from you just at the moment that mass-hysteria began. I did not expect people on our side to lose their heads as well. I was very shocked that after ten years of political collaboration you should have taken the line you did.

(HRO Wallop 15M84/F189; Griffiths, 2010: 249)

Hay claimed that his internment in May 1940 had been due to the machinations of the Jews.

Lymington had not been arrested. He continued to live peaceably on his Hampshire estate. He was later to be made vice-chairman of the Hampshire War Agricultural Committee, on which he did sterling work to help the war effort, based on the agricultural theories he had expounded before the war. He also wrote extensively on agricultural matters. And, though he was a founder member in 1941 with Rolf Gardiner of the 'Kinship in Husbandry', which has sometimes, because of the past activities of certain of its members, been seen as being what the French would call 'fascisant', there is little evidence, as we shall see when studying Rolf Gardiner, of there having been any dangerous attitudes to Germany within it; its concerns were primarily, as its title suggests, agricultural, with a tinge of anti-capitalism.

Though Lymington's patriotism had led him to a rejection of Nazism, this did not mean that he had given up the other fundamental views that had originally led to his pro-Nazism. In a book entitled *Alternative to Death: The Relationship between Soil, Family and Community*, published in 1943, which was mainly about the importance of the land and of heritage, he at times gave evidence of these continuing views (though the claim, made by some, that this book was primarily anti-Semitic in its nature is an exaggerated one, in that the main thrust of the book is concerned with Lymington's agricultural ideas). There were, however, at times some elements of his former racism lurking in the background in a disguised form in talk about 'the dangers of losing our own character from alien influence and blood' and the depiction of the kind of aliens who were a danger to 'British stock': 'the marketeer, the unscrupulous trader, the slick higgler, the seditious natural underdog and agitator', a type of immigrant 'which was too often

Vagaries of the 'back-to-the-land' school 241

conditioned to the mental slum and the bazaar'. The book as a whole dealt with a number of Lymington's most important themes, including a distaste for international finance and (with more than a whiff of eugenics) the importance of blood and soil, and racial purity. The main change was that Nazism, when mentioned at all, received disapproval. The 'important theme of racial purity' had, Portsmouth opined, been 'often distorted by the catch-cries of fascism and Nazism'; and when he returned to the theme of the destructive force of 'international finance', he now blamed it for the rise of Nazism:

> It would not be unjust to ascribe the *victims* of this war to the policy of international finance, for it is doubtful if Germany would have felt the impetus to install a Hitler or answer the appeal for *Lebensraum*, if it had not been for the system of cosmopolitan lending from Lombard and Wall Streets.
>
> (Portsmouth, 1943: 21, 23–4, 35)

His continuing views on race and international finance (rather than any on Germany) appear to have been what led him, from 1942 onwards, to get involved with some of the secretive right-wing bodies which we have seen emerging at that time. MI5 reported in early 1942, for example, that he had been listed as one of those who had agreed to be sponsors of Godfrey's British National Party (BNP) (of which Hay was a leading member, having come to the attention of Special Branch as a regular visitor to the BNP's headquarters in Trafalgar Square). By 1943 (having meantime succeeded as the 9th Earl of Portsmouth) Lymington was taking part in the regular private meetings with Domvile, Fuller, Edmonds and others (monitored by MI5) which led to the revival of the Constitutional Research Association. In the CRA Portsmouth and Hay were prominent members, amid a welter of other well-established right-wingers including Domvile, Sempill, Fuller, Ben Greene and H.T. Mills. Then, in 1945, Portsmouth became an adherent of A.K. Chesterton's 'National Front after Victory', alongside H.T. Mills, Ben Greene and other former associates (TNA HO 144/21845, KV 2/492, KV 2/872).

Meanwhile, when Ben Greene formed the English Nationalist Association (ENA) in succession to the BNP, Hay was among those with whom Greene met frequently for close consultations. Then, in the first half of 1945, Hay was in close contact with the Duke of Bedford in his attempt to revive the British People's Party. (TNA KV 2/795). Unlike Portsmouth, he remained obsessed with the virtues of Nazism. As we shall see in Chapter 13, in the last weeks of the war he was agreeing with Domvile and Ramsay that they should, whatever the outcome, continue their fight for National Socialism, which had been temporarily eclipsed by Jewish power.

Portsmouth and Hay continued to attend meetings of the CRA after Germany's defeat, though as noted elsewhere, something of the purpose had gone out of the movement. What happened to Hay thereafter we do not know. Portsmouth's post-war activities will be examined in Chapter 13.

Rolf Gardiner

Though he was at various times closely connected with Lord Lymington, Rolf Gardiner (1902–71) was a pro-Nazi of a very different kind. His pro-Germanism had preceded the Nazi accession and was central to his philosophy; and while he gave full vent to his pro-Nazi views in print and in speech before the war, he was 'semi-detached' from the political activities of men such as Lymington, even though he remained closely in contact with them; and during the war he underwent a gradual change of heart that was very different from the more superficial camouflage erected by so many others.

Gardiner is rightly regarded as one of the foremost pioneers of organic farming; he was also a considerable enthusiast, from his undergraduate days in Cambridge onwards, for the return to traditional values and to healthy living, as expressed by folk dance and folk music, by nudism, and by the youth movements of both Britain and Germany (see Boyes, 2011; Fowler, 2011; Jefferies, 2011; Moore-Colyer, 2011).

Gardiner's obsession with Germany was central to all these ideas, and thus preceded the advent of the Nazis by at least a decade. Yet already by the late Twenties and early Thirties we find in his thinking a number of characteristics that were to make the Nazis particularly attractive to him: a tendency to authoritarianism and an admiration of leadership, a concern at the 'impoverishment of national types', and a desire for national regeneration (Gardiner, 1932).

He welcomed the advent of the Nazis, writing an ecstatic article about them in 1933 entitled 'Die deutsche Revolution von England gesehen' ('the German Revolution seen from England'), in which he spoke of the German Revolution as 'the spring storm of a new Renaissance', whose 'manly goals' should be imitated by Britain, which needed to find the same 'discipline of togetherness'. In the same article we find explanations, based on typical Nazi propaganda, for the treatment of the Jews, particularly foreign Jews from the East who had 'added to German Jewry a very unpleasant element' and had misused German hospitality. Most of Gardiner's activities in the mid-Thirties were, however, concerned with his plans for rural regeneration, though he also ran a series of summer camps for international – above all Anglo-German – understanding. The German contingents at these camps were often made up of young SS and SA (*Sturmabteilung*) men, as Otto Bene, Landesgruppenleiter of the Nazi Party in Britain, reported back approvingly to Germany in 1934 (TNA KV 2/2245).

It was during this period that Gardiner began his acquaintance and friendship with Lord Lymington, whose views were so much in accord with his own (including a desire for monetary reform, and an attack on 'usury', which had been part of Gardiner's philosophy ever since he had taken up Social Credit in his undergraduate days). In early 1938, in his very favourable review (for the English Array's *Gazette*) of Lymingon's *Famine in England*, Gardiner praised its fearless treatment of 'the perilous condition to which commercialism, usury and the neglect of traditional wisdom have reduced our country'. He also praised the change of heart brought to Central Europe by Nazism, and stated that while Germany was championing 'the values of earth and breed', England was 'cleaving to the advantages of commerce and usury', and was governed by 'alien, neo-Phoenician ways'.

Though, as was his wont, Gardiner at first remained aloof from joining a political movement, by 1938 he was becoming more and more involved with the English Array. In October 1938, just after the Munich crisis, he addressed them on the virtues of Nazism and the 'regeneration of Hitler's Germany' (*QGEA*, 10/38), and by November he was announcing that he was joining the Array, which he said had 'grasped the nettle of English apathy'. Britain's official policy, he said, was 'dictated by the interests of World Commerce, of financial manipulation'. Hitler was to be trusted. He was 'an idealist and unswerving in his declared purpose' (*SRNS*, 11/38).

By January 1939 Gardiner was writing regularly for Lymington's *New Pioneer*. Some of his articles dealt with his non-contentious interests: National Service Camps, for which he had been campaigning since 1937, and the German Labour Service. But he also wrote about the Jews and the dangers posed by them in the East Baltic, where they had gained unprecedented dominance. He claimed that Britain should not try to resist any German attempts to expand in this area: 'What is at stake is civilisation and the preservation of the world from the roving sand-dunes of the East' (Gardiner, 1939: 147–8).

Meanwhile MI5 and MI6 were beginning to show an interest in his activities. In July 1939 it was reported that Gardiner had given 'a most pernicious lecture in Berlin' which was 'most damaging to this country'. Also, it was reported that at Gardiner's gatherings, even at the Summer Schools of singing, no opportunity was lost of 'putting over Nazi propaganda'. As war approached, authorisation was given on 30 August 1939 for all post addressed to him to be intercepted (TNA KV 2/2245).

Up to the outbreak of war, Gardiner thus presents us with the picture of a fairly typical Nazi enthusiast of a certain kind. His monetarism, his cult of youth, his desire for national regeneration, his mistrust of aliens and of usury – all these things, when taken together with his overwhelming love of Germany, created what verges on a caricature of the 'blood-and-soil' fanatics of the time. Yet even in those last pre-war months his main efforts (as witnessed in the overwhelming majority of his correspondence, such as his letters to Arthur Bryant of 27 January and 6 August 1939) were directed towards the formation of National Service Camps, a project he had nurtured since at least 1937 (LHCMA Bryant E/19).

There is no evidence of Gardiner undertaking such activities as those of Lymington or Hay in the 'phoney war' period, though he did subscribe to the journal *Information and Policy* (TNA HO 262/6). Like many pro-Germanists, he did of course long for a negotiated peace to emerge, but in his case this did not lead to subversive action. It is

Vagaries of the 'back-to-the-land' school   245

only in his private correspondence that we find such ideas being put forward, and the attitude he expressed was shared with many people who did not hold views favourable to the German internal regime. For example, in a letter to Prime Minister Neville Chamberlain on 24 September 1939 he produced the argument which weighed so heavily with those who remembered the First World War: 'The war if waged now will be a war of attrition which will give victory to neither side.' He suggested that Chamberlain should offer to negotiate with a German government that excluded Hitler, with whom it was now 'obviously impossible to negotiate' (TNA KV 2/2245).

That such views were not solely written for government consumption is shown by a private letter to Arthur Bryant on 8 October 1939, in which he not only reiterated his idea of negotiating with leaders other than Hitler, but also expressed a considerable change of attitude towards the Nazi Party. Admittedly, he felt that 'the attempt to destroy the Nazi regime, upon which our bellicose idealists are so furiously bent' was not worth 'the destruction of Christendom and the setting of an impossible burden upon the shoulders of the blameless youth of the future'; but in his assessment of the relationship between inter-war Germany and the Nazi Party he was now showing an awareness of the 'darker aspects' of Nazism:

> One must never forget that the German renaissance of 1933 was essentially twofold: the blending of a long-term reconstructive movement (which had been operative under the blanket of the Weimar Republic) with Hitler's own political and aggressive movement. So long as the Nazi regime gave scope to the reconstructive forces and avoided open war the people could give their loyalty to it, despite any loathing for the darker aspects of the Party. Now that Hitler has gambled with the Reich their loyalty must be badly shaken.
>
> (LHCMA Bryant E/19)

During the course of the war, Gardiner's views on these matters developed still further, as his correspondence with Bryant illustrates admirably. In a letter of 2 January 1940 he was assessing the dual nature of Nazism, 'the fatal mixture of idealism and opportunism' at its core. If

Britain had responded to the idealism, the other side of Nazism might not have come to the fore. Admittedly, he still felt, on 17 October 1941, that Britain could have avoided war by accommodating Hitler's 'reasonable' demands (though also referring to 'Nazi crimes'):

> Does it strike you [...] that Germany had to justify aggression in the West because we denied her an organic Lebensraum in the interests of Europe as a whole in the East? Despite all her crimes, we must remember this.
>
> (LHCMA Bryant E/19)

By 1941 he was mourning the 'uncorrupted Prussia which mistakenly hitched its wagon to the meretricious comet of Hitlerism'. The final stage in his change of heart was reached in 1943, when we find him subscribing completely to the case for war, writing in the Kinship in Husbandry Casebook on 10 June that 'after all it is to convince Germany that her moral attitude is warped and that her fanatical impatience is evil that we have opposed her' (LHCMA Bryant E/60).

So Gardiner's wartime attitudes towards Nazism gradually changed from his pre-war stance; and as most of these ideas were expressed in private correspondence, we have little cause to doubt them. By far the greater part of his wartime correspondence, however, was taken up with the problem of post-war reconstruction. In this his old concerns about the 'need for leadership' and the importance of the soil as opposed to the city, came out once more. The 'Kinship in Husbandry', set up in 1941, while mainly concerned with countering the 'inorganic methods of production' produced by the reactions to wartime emergencies (Gardiner, 1972: 197), nevertheless had echoes of his pre-war concerns (in discussion, the members expressed fears that after the war 'there is a danger that finance may recover its power, with its headquarters in America' (LHCMA Bryant E/51); but there is little evidence of favourable attitudes to Nazi Germany within it. Admittedly, by the end of 1943 Gardiner was using Kinship circulars to deplore Allied bombing of German cities; but that attitude was shared by a number of contemporaries who had strong anti-Nazi credentials (including Bishop Bell of Chichester), and Gardiner was in fact deploring the bombing of civilians by both sides (LHCMA Bryant E/60).

Vagaries of the 'back-to-the-land' school

Gardiner remained politically inactive throughout the war. As a patriot, he requested in June 1940 (just after the main DR 18B arrests) to join the Local Defence Volunteers, but was disturbed to find that his request was refused. In an interview at the Headquarters of the Dorsetshire Constabulary, he declared that he:

> was most anxious to do all he could in this country's interest […] He admitted that he had been keenly interested in the development of English and German friendship, and he had been responsible for classes of German students visiting this country for that purpose, but as soon as the Nazi aggression commenced, he had had nothing further to do with the scheme.
>
> (TNA KV 2/2245)

He was never, it seems, in danger of arrest; but his pre-war opinions made him suspect both to the local population and to the local police. The most incredible reports were compiled by the police throughout the war. In one, it was reported that 'disgusting practices under the influence of hypnotism' had taken place at his property, that 'the shadow of the evil of Gardiner' was very real, and that 'human sacrifices take place under Black Magic decrees'. In another, 'strange rituals' were referred to. In another, Springhead (his property) was described as a 'nudist colony', and it was reported that the Chief Constable of Dorset suspected that Gardiner might be 'a pervert' (TNA KV 2/2245).

Even stranger were the local rumours of treasonable pro-Nazi activity on Gardiner's part. It was suggested that he had his own aeroplane, which he piloted himself; that there was a hut in the woods containing firearms; and that he had planted trees in the shape of a swastika, to guide enemy aircraft. These rumours were investigated by the police, and found to be 'utterly baseless'. Nevertheless, even though there appear to have been no signs of subversive behaviour on his part, he was placed on the Suspect List of those to be imprisoned in the event of a German invasion (TNA KV 2/2245).

After the war, while there is little doubt that Gardiner retained most of his pre-war views on leadership, kinship and the war between the land and finance, there is no evidence whatsoever that he continued to admire the Nazi movement, which in his view had betrayed those 'ideals' by its aggressive foreign policy.

Gardiner is someone who was on the fringe of a great many activities which we tend to regard as potentially 'fascistic': monetarism, anti-capitalism, anti-Semitism, authoritarianism, 'blood and soil' agriculturalism, anti-democracy, admiration of leaders, and so on. The obverse of this is that his back-to-the-land principles, his concern for youth and the future, and his belief in folk tradition could all be shared by many who were not spurred by them into the same political direction as him.

Henry Williamson

Henry Williamson (1895–1977) came to pro-Nazism by a different route from that of most of the other 'back-to-the-landers'. Central to his thought was his experience of the First World War – and in particular the 'Christmas Truce', which he had described vividly in a letter to his mother in December 1914, a letter which was reprinted in *The Times*. In it he described the humanity of the German soldiers, and his realisation that they too thought that their war was a just one. This concept of the 'brotherhood of arms' was to remain constant in Williamson's thought (as in that of many other ex-servicemen), as did the conviction that Europe must never again go to war.

Williamson's approach to the land was in its origin literary, and though he farmed, he saw himself above all as a writer. A major influence upon him, from adolescence onwards, had been the writings of Richard Jefferies. Unlike the other characters we have been considering, Williamson's initial interest was not so much in agriculture (though that came later) as in wildlife. He made his name as a writer with *Tarka the Otter* (1927), and later *Salar the Salmon* (1935), both of which went into innumerable editions; and the titles of other books of his betray the same interest: *The Lone Swallows* (1922), *The Peregrine's Saga* (1923), *The Old Stag* (1926), *The Wild Red Deer of Exmoor* (1931). By the Thirties, however, he had become convinced that farming was 'the backbone of British life and economy', and from 1935 onwards ran, on ecological lines (and not very effectively), a farm near Stiffkey, in North Norfolk, an experience described in his book *The Story of a Norfolk Farm* (1941).

In studying Williamson's spiritual itinerary, we are helped by the fact that, in his later novels, not only are the writings of his autobiographical hero Philip Maddison closely based on Williamson's own ideas from the 1930s, but also Maddison's diary quotations are based on Williamson's own contemporary diaries. This information complements for us the actual contemporary documentation from the 1930s.

It was in about 1935 that Williamson's enthusiasm for Nazi Germany first began. In part, this was based on the sense of comradeship he felt for the German ex-soldiers and in particular for Hitler, whom he saw as 'the only true pacifist in Europe'. It was also based, however, on the great social experiment he had observed on a visit to Germany in that year, in which the German people had been 'shocked into a new way of thought, […] fighting the forces of gold and disintegration', with Hitler destroying the old civilisation and wanting to base a new one on 'the century-old virtues which were maintained in what was old Europe'. This was contrasted with Great Britain, where 'we are gummed up by a financial idea out of date since the beginning of the war in 1914' (Williamson, 1965: 172–97). Hitler was 'a man who had served in the ranks of the infantry, been wounded and blinded by mustard gas, a man who loved Beethoven and lived only for the resurrection of his country's happiness' (Williamson, 1937: 107).

Throughout his life Williamson hero-worshipped a number of figures, including Richard Jefferies, T.E. Lawrence and now Adolf Hitler; to these he soon added Oswald Mosley, because he saw in Mosley the saviour, the epitome of the post-war ex-service generation, who would do for Britain what Hitler had done for Germany. In October 1937 his Norfolk neighbour Viscountess Downe had persuaded him to join British Union (BU), and invited him to come and hear Jorian Jenks, the BU expert on organic agriculture. Then, in December at Lady Downe's house, he met Mosley for the first time, and was bowled over. His enthusiasm for Mosley was never to wane.

As war approached, he became more and more frantic. He was convinced that the guarantee to Poland had been undertaken solely because of the interests of international finance in that country. In late August 1939 he proposed to Mosley that the two of them should 'fly to Germany to see Hitler and get him to put over a speech defining clearly for the ordinary man the fundamental causes of the present crisis'. Mosley said 'I'm afraid it is too late – the curtain is down' (Anne Williamson, 1995: 228).

Even after the outbreak of war, Williamson remained convinced that Hitler, a true friend of England, would never attack in the West. The nine months of 'phoney war' seemed to be proving him right. The attack on neutral Belgium and Holland in May 1940 thus came as a shock. He wrote in his diary on 10 May: 'The (to me) unexpected and scoffed at BLITZKRIEG in France started today against Holland and Belgium. Parachute troops drop in clouds. I feel I was wrong, entirely, about "the only true pacifist in Europe"' (Anne Williamson, 1995: 232).

Yet he was still convinced that Hitler did not wish to attack Britain. As when he had thought of flying to Germany in August 1939, he believed himself to be someone to whom people might listen, he also still believed in Hitler's mission to cleanse Europe from 'international financial interests', a mission which had been sidelined by the war. On 22 May 1940, as the Germans overran France, he wrote: 'I must do something: the war should be stopped. Hitler does not want to destroy Britain, only the international financial interests in Europe.' As the French defeat became more and more certain, he was already thinking in terms of Britain suing for peace, writing in his diary on 24 May:

> I KNOW there will be a chance to save Britain and the Empire intact, even if the BEF is captured. Hitler does not want to destroy the British Empire. […] The war with Germany should never have been, it was an economic war and Britain's destiny is in its Empire and not in Europe.
>
> (Williamson, 1967: 322–3)

Meanwhile, Williamson was having a hard time locally in Norfolk. His views on Nazi Germany had been widely publicised by his pre-war writings, and he had never hidden his membership of British Union (indeed, he had recently painted the BU badge – a lightning flash within a circle – on the wall of his cottage). As with Gardiner, some of the local beliefs were very far-fetched. The villagers believed he had created concrete roads on the farm in preparation for the German invasion, and that a fanlight he had installed to give light on his staircase was a device for signalling to the Luftwaffe. He was subjected to a whole lot of unpleasant incidents, including someone painting white swastikas on his car. At a meeting of the local British Legion, he was accused of 'repeatedly blaspheming against King, Country, and the poor lads out in France'. When he protested to the chairman that this was a lie, he received the reply: 'I don't care a damn if it's a lie or not. I believe it' (Anne Williamson, 1995: 232).

On 14 June he was taken in by the local police, and imprisoned at Wells over the weekend while his farm buildings were searched. On the following Monday he was taken to Norwich, where the Chief Constable said he was to be released, because no evidence had been found against him. The Chief Constable apologised, saying that the police had had to act on the complaints they had received.

Williamson continued to run his farm throughout the war. His biography by Anne Williamson rarely mentions his experience of the war after 1940, but we know that he mainly kept out of things, though at the end of the war he did join A.K. Chesterton's 'National Front After Victory', alongside such figures as Portsmouth, Ben Greene and General Fuller (Kushner, 1989: 35). And he clearly kept to the same views that he had always held. After the war, his series of autobiographical novels, *A Chronicle of Ancient Sunlight* (1951–1969), continued to show the pro-Mosley and pro-Hitler views of its hero Philip Maddison. Williamson's hero-worship was lasting. During the war, it was clear that he had always believed, like so many others, that his ideas were completely compatible with patriotism. He had been distressed by the accusations levelled against him by his Norfolk neighbours, because, as he put it in his diary at the time, 'I have never been pro-Hitler in the sense of being anti-British' (Williamson, 1967: 322).

If one had to sum up Williamson's ideas and actions in one word, it would be: naivety. He always saw everything in black and white, and he was also convinced that his words and actions would carry weight with the great (as when he proposed flying to Germany with Mosley to persuade Hitler, or when in 1935 he proposed to hold, with T.E. Lawrence, a large gathering of ex-servicemen at the Albert Hall in favour of peace and friendship with Germany). But the fact that he lived in something of an unreal world does not mean that he was not important. He was in contact with many people of the Right, and influential on a number of them, such as Francis Yeats-Brown, who wrote to him on 20 August 1943: 'You have amazing energy, Henry. Give us a lead, out of your enthusiasm and experience' (Wrench, 1948: 260). To those who saw agriculture and the natural life as the basis for national regeneration, he stood as a kind of standard-bearer. The back-to-the-land school knew him as one of their own.

Francis Yeats-Brown

Francis Yeats-Brown (1886–1944) was not strictly part of the back-to-the-land school, but his connections with it through Henry Williamson, Rolf Gardiner, Lord Lymington and others, and his eventual conviction as to the importance of agriculture in the future of Britain, make him a kind of adjunct to it. However, his pro-Fascism and pro-Nazism had different sources, and had preceded this enthusiasm.

Without actually being involved in any overt extremist activities prior to the war, Yeats-Brown had nevertheless been a strong apologist for Nazi Germany and other fascist regimes, and an anti-Semite who, while not being in favour of Nazi excesses, reacted strongly against what he saw as the Jewish threat. However, he was also a fervent patriot, and a strong proponent of British rearmament in face of the uncertainties of modern Europe. With the advent of war, his patriotic concerns came to the fore; but, beneath the surface, many of the old beliefs remained, even if Germany had now become an enemy.

He was born in Italy, where his grandfather and father had successively been the British Consul in Genoa. One of his family's properties in particular, the Castello Brown, on the promontory overlooking Portofino, was to remain very close to his heart throughout his life. (It and its history bear an uncanny resemblance to the Castello owned by the Crouchback family in Evelyn Waugh's *Men at Arms* (1952), as does the village in which Castello Crouchback is situated resemble Portofino. It is possible that Waugh had read about it in Evelyn Wrench's biography of Yeats-Brown, published in 1948).

Yeats-Brown was educated at Harrow and Sandhurst, and in 1906 he was posted to India, where he was to serve until 1914 mainly in the cavalry on the North-West Frontier. In the First World War he served in Belgium and France in late 1914, and then joined the Royal Flying

Corps and saw action in Mesopotamia, gaining a DFC. In November 1915 he was captured by the Turks, and was to remain in captivity, under horrific conditions, for two and a half years.

After the war he returned to his regiment on the North-West Frontier, but in 1922 left India and the Army. He spent some time in the United States and Canada before returning to London, where his cousin Evelyn Wrench had offered him an editorial post at *The Spectator*. While there he wrote his memoirs of the Indian Army, *Bengal Lancer* (1930). This was such an outstanding success that he became one of the most famous writers of his time. He decided, in 1931, to retire from *The Spectator* to become a full-time writer.

During the late Twenties Yeats-Brown had become more and more interested in current affairs. Because of his experience of modern Italy he had become an enthusiast for Mussolini and Italian corporatism – so much so that he believed that Britain should follow the Italian example. In August 1933 an opportunity occurred which enabled him to give full vent to his views in print. He was offered the editorship of *Everyman*, an established weekly paper, whose respectable readers must have been bemused by the change that immediately took place in it as he and his collaborators attacked parliamentary government and called for a dictatorship and a corporate state. Yeats-Brown's own editorials, and articles such as Douglas Jerrold's 'The Corporate State in England' (13 October 1933), and J.B. Morton's 'Sleeping England' (3 November 1933), set the tone. This policy aroused considerable enthusiasm in certain quarters, but the directors of *Everyman* strongly disapproved of the line that was being taken, and Yeats-Brown was sacked in November, after only three months.

In early 1934 he became a leading figure in the January Club, purportedly a 'discussion forum' for contemporary politics, but in fact a front organisation for Mosley's British Union of Fascists, designed to attract members of the Establishment. His involvement in this body shows, however, some of the contradictions in his attitudes. Despite the similarity of their beliefs, he was not convinced by Mosley when he saw him in action at a public meeting in November 1934, saying on 1 November 1934 in a letter to Rosalind Constable that 'he should be left alone, and that I'm sick of him. [...] Mosley is too vain to ever be any good, and not human enough' (Wrench, 1948: 183–4). In the same month Special Branch noted that he was severing all connections with the BUF, 'due to his forming a poor opinion of Mosley' (TNA HO 144/20144). As with Rolf Gardiner and several others on the Right, however, rejection of Mosley did not necessarily indicate any change in pro-Fascist or pro-Nazi ideas.

It was in 1934 that Yeats-Brown produced his book *Dogs of War!*, a counterblast to Beverley Nichols's pacifist book *Cry Havoc* (1933). In this book, and in various newspaper articles, he expressed his ardent patriotism, and his conviction that war was a necessary evil in certain circumstances. Indeed, in the present European situation there was every danger of war, and Britain needed to rearm:

> In a world of latent conflicts, mounting armaments, and broken treaties, who can deny that force seems the most probable solution of present difficulties? [...] Patriotism is a very real thing, and an ideal higher than is commonly supposed. The flower of patriotism has been watered by the blood of heroic men and women, whereas the weedy hothouse plant of Geneva has been nourished chiefly on talk and self-interest.
>
> (Yeats-Brown, 1932)

Throughout the Thirties, Yeats-Brown was to hold the view that 'unless the Government wakes up to the tremendous importance of reorganising our defence, the chief Ministers will deserve nothing less than impeachment' (Yeats-Brown, 1934: 179).

Like many on the Right, however, as the Thirties progressed, he succeeded in combining his innate patriotism with an admiration and enthusiasm for Nazi Germany and for other fascist governments. He spent a lot of his time, from 1935 onwards, travelling in Europe as a special correspondent for *The Observer*. He was a strong supporter of the Nationalist side in the Spanish Civil War (speaking in his 1939 book *European Jungle* of Nationalist Spain's 'lofty enthusiasm, self-sacrifice and sanctity'), and supported Mussolini's aspirations in Africa. He considered that the future of France and Belgium lay in being taken over by their domestic fascist movements, the Croix de Feu and Rexism (Wrench, 1948: 222). Above all, he was bowled over by the achievements of Nazi Germany. Convinced that democratic government was a thing of the past, he saw in the Nazi movement a healthy and vigorous antidote to the former state of Germany. The Nazi regime, he felt, was showing the best way to provide a flourishing State and a happy, healthy citizenry (*The Observer*, 10/4/38, 24/4/38). Hitler had impressed him personally:

> I have met many of the notable figures of the world, but only Gandhi and T.E. Lawrence gave me the sense which Hitler does of inner strength and Franciscan simplicity. […] In the personalities of Gandhi and Hitler one saw shining a strange inner light. The same is true of Hitler. […] He sways the individual and the multitude by a power seemingly outside himself. In his lifetime Hitler has received more fervent and more genuine admiration from the masses than any man in history.
>
> (Yeats-Brown, 1939a: 121)

Unlike many of his fellow enthusiasts for Nazi Germany, however, Yeats-Brown did not try to excuse the Nazis' treatment of the Jews. 'It is horrible', he wrote, 'and haunts my conscience whenever I praise the other achievements of the National Socialists, some of which are great and good. The way the Germans have treated their Jews is disgusting' (Yeats-Brown, 1939a: 186); this, despite the fact that this man of contradictions was himself a considerable anti-Semite. To some extent his anti-Semitism had stemmed from his sympathy with Islam (felt since his time on the North-West Frontier) and from his concern with the situation in Palestine, as expressed in a number of outlets such as his article 'Listen, Tommy!', in Lymington's *New Pioneer* in 1939, and the chapter 'The Children of Israel' in his *European Jungle*. Yet, as with so many on the Right who took up the Palestine question in this period, anti-Zionism could also mask anti-Semitic concerns nearer home. Yeats-Brown was convinced, as he later said in a letter to Henry Williamson on 24 November 1942, that many of the ills of modern society stemmed from the Jews, whose aim was to 'rule the world'. And he was also convinced that no more Jews should be allowed to enter England (Yeats-Brown, 1939a: 201–2). Amid all these conflicting attitudes towards the Jews, it is worth noting that in 1939 Yeats-Brown became a member of Captain Ramsay's Right Club.

Yeats-Brown's concerns had been mainly with Hitler's domestic policies, rather than the foreign policy area. Hitler's invasion of Czechoslovakia in March 1939 came as something of a shock to him. He had believed until then in Hitler's good faith. Much of his book *European Jungle*, which came out in April 1939, had been written some time before, and he kept in it, without change, all his usual praise for the Nazi regime. However, he now added on the first few pages his feelings at recent events:

> His [Hitler's] fault is writ large across a startled Europe. None of his neighbours trust him. The law of the jungle prevails. With the breaking of his pledge at Munich our recent hopes of disarmament and reconciliation lie shattered beyond the possibility of quick repair.

He was, he said, nevertheless convinced that he had been right to support Nazi Germany:

> In my view, from 1919 up to September 1938, through twenty years of crises, each more hectic than the last, Germany had reason on her side. She was justified in slithering out of reparations, whose total was never fixed; she was wise to elect Adolf Hitler, who gave back her self-respect; she was entitled to reoccupy the Rhineland, which was German soil; and to take Austria, which had repeatedly voted for reunion; and to rescue the Sudeten Germans. Her methods were rash and her words bitter; but I was prepared to justify the indignation of a great people against the Treaty of Versailles. That is the past. Germany had many cards in her hands, but she has overplayed them, as so often before in her history, and has lost the ace of hearts, which is the confidence of Europe.
>
> (Yeats-Brown, 1939a: 11–12)

These views were shared, that March, by a number of other prominent pro-Nazis; but as time went by, they tended to become less certain in their ideas. Yeats-Brown was no exception. While wanting the government to be firm in relation to German aggression, he was nevertheless convinced that there must not be war. On 3 April, writing to Arthur Bryant to congratulate him on a letter Bryant had written to *The Times*, he said:

> You have said very clearly what I have tried to say in 100,000 words: that we will not tolerate the problems of Eastern and South-Eastern Europe being solved by the German Army; but that a solution to certain problems there must be. The Germans and Italians do not want war any more than we do.
>
> (LHCMA Bryant E/39)

Gradually, he became convinced that war must be avoided at all costs. By 17 July 1939, in a letter to Lord Elton, he was declaring that 'we must not be involved in a war to make the world safe for Stalin or international Jewry' (Skidelsky, 1975: 440–1). In that month he attended Mosley's Earls Court Rally against the war. Typically, he came away still unconvinced of Mosley's capabilities, and repelled by the feeling that Mosley was using the opportunity 'for political ends', yet he 'agreed with three quarters' of what Mosley had said (Mosley's main theme having been that 'A million Britons shall never die in your Jews' quarrel') (Skidelsky, 1975: 440).

Yeats-Brown was torn between patriotic pride in British readiness for war, and his conviction that war would be of advantage only to the Jews and the communists. On 29 July, shortly after making the above statements, he was describing to Arthur Bryant his delight in British preparedness, and in the shock experienced by a Nazi official as he became aware of it:

> Schlottmann of the Deutsch-Englische Gesellschaft came down and spent the day here: it amused me to see his expression as he saw Territorials and Militia entraining, and the ARP offices. He had no idea we were taking soldiering seriously again, and being of the post-war generation who only knows pacifist England, I think his day in Sussex did him good.

As war came nearer, even though he hoped against hope that it could be avoided, he exulted nevertheless in Britain's new-found self-respect. In August he wrote to Bryant:

> We are no longer arrogant bleating pacifists, but English again, and getting down to our own affairs, including the protection of our homes. You should have seen the ARP exercises here yesterday.
>
> (LHCMA Bryant E/39)

Once war had broken out, he set about trying to get war work; but he sensed a certain coolness in the authorities, who had clearly classified him as a Fascist sympathiser, and his requests got him nowhere (Wrench, 1948: 238). He turned once more to journalism, and in November 1939 became military correspondent of the *Daily Sketch*, where he was to remain for a couple of years. By January 1940 he was preparing to write a book and some articles for the British Council about the war effort.

During the 'phoney war' (September 1939–May 1940), however, still obsessed by the need for peace, Yeats-Brown showed some lack of judgement in his activities and his acquaintances. For example, as his letters to Bryant bear witness, he supported the 'Union and Reconstruction' movement, set up by Bryant and the Fascist sympathiser Henry Drummond-Wolff. This movement has been described by Andrew Roberts as 'ostensibly a think-tank for post-war issues, but [...] in fact an anti-war lobbying organization and propagator for national socialist economic ideas' (Roberts, 1994: 307). Yeats-Brown also expressed considerable enthusiasm for Bryant's book *Unfinished Victory* – in this, however, his views coincided with those of a wide spectrum of British opinion in early 1940.

More dangerously, he still continued to frequent right-wing antiwar circles. On 1 March 1940, for example, he was one of the large number of the pro-Nazi and anti-war Right who attended Mosley's grand luncheon at the Criterion Restaurant, at which Mosley proclaimed that 'the real reason why the British Government had declared war on Germany [...] was because Britain was controlled by Jews and they desired to see the end of the present German Government so that they could resume their exploitation of the German people' (TNA HO 45/24895). He had also attended a 'gathering of the clans' on 6 December 1939, aimed at furthering collaboration between the various anti-war groups, to which he was accompanied by his fellow Right Club members Captain Ramsay, H.T. Mills, Norman Hay, Lancelot Lawton, Aubrey Lees and C. Featherstone-Hammond, together with other right-wing figures such as Sir Oswald Mosley, General J.F.C. Fuller, Lord Lymington, Lord Tavistock, Admiral Sir Barry Domvile and Captain George Pitt-Rivers (NMM DOM 56, 6/12/39). Though Yeats-Brown does not appear to have undertaken much in the way of actual activity, his presence at such events was monitored by Special Branch, and can hardly have helped his search for useful wartime employment.

From his letters, it becomes clear that by now, under the influence of Williamson, Yeats-Brown had become an enthusiast for organic farming, and even planned, in 1941, to become a farmer himself, because, as he said in a letter on 13 January, he wanted 'to dig my teeth into realities'; he felt he had found with Williamson 'the very place and atmosphere to save my soul' (Wrench, 1948: 248).

That project, however, had foundered by 1942. For the early part of the war, Yeats-Brown's sole contribution to the war effort was in the Home Guard. Despite his journalistic work as a military correspondent, he was bored. Things became worse when he was bombed out of his London flat in September 1940. He went to live in the countryside, and got more and more depressed. Occasional good pieces of news, such as the defeat of the *Admiral Graf Spee* and its scuttling in Montevideo in December 1940, momentarily cheered him up (he described it as 'the first really cheering news, quite the Nelson touch'); but on the whole he was pessimistic about the war prospects and life in general, as he stated in a letter to Henry Williamson on 8 September 1941:

> I can't see ahead at all – when the war will end, or what I ought to do. [...] There is nothing to write about now: no schemes, plans, ideals seem worth discussing in the present darkness; and to write about things on which we agree – the Jews, for instance – is platitudinous.
>
> (Wrench, 1948: 247)

A further letter to Williamson on 16 February 1942 conveys even more graphically the depths to which he had descended:

> I don't like myself, or my surroundings, or Mr Winston Churchill. Maybe liver? Or a deep-seated sickness of heart. [...] This not being friends with oneself is frightful. After 55 years of myself, I oughtn't to hate this body and brain, whatever their obvious faults. And I'm beginning to. Anyway, bless you. It is good to have a friend who understands, when all the world is so intent on making one do ugly, boring, useless things, and calls one lazy, stupid, selfish, perverted, if one can't, or won't.
>
> (Wrench, 1948: 248–9)

In late 1942, however, he was cheered by the news of victory at El Alamein, and began to feel that the war was winnable after all; though, as he told Williamson in a letter on 24 November, he was uncertain what the world might be like afterwards, and hoped that 'what was good in Nazism' might survive, and the Jews would not take over:

> What of the news? It is good I think, because we can see the end. I don't think Bolshevism will conquer Europe. [...] The frontal attack at El Alamein must have been a feat of high courage, carried out of course by British troops. [...] Am I an optimist to believe that what was good in Nazism will survive, and that the Jews will not rule the world, as they confidently expect, and that this country will be regenerated? On the last point I'm doubtful. It's up to people like you and me – but especially you, with your deep knowledge of the land – to help.
>
> (Wrench, 1948: 258)

Interestingly, in late 1942 he was also fired with a new enthusiasm for British Union, at the time of the formation of the DR 18B Publicity Council. As he exclaimed in a letter to Henry Williamson on 1 December, 'So we aren't all sheep, and we still want to hear of British Union!' (Wrench, 1948: 258).

By mid-1943 Yeats-Brown was hoping that, with their knowledge of Italy, he and his pre-war pro-Fascist friends Harold Goad and Muriel Currey might be called on to help in that country. But, as he lamented to Goad in a letter of 2 July:

You and I and Muriel are suspected of being Fascists. Or do you think that wiser counsels will prevail? They must need people badly who know the people and the language. […] As soon as Sicily is clear I expect we'll attack Taranto, and then get troops into the Adriatic.

(Wrench, 1948: 255–6)

These concerns were, however, overtaken by events. Suddenly, and amazingly, he was provided with a job to help the war effort. Thanks to his cousin Evelyn Wrench (who had a public relations job with the Government of India), he was invited to go out to be attached to Wrench's department, with the rank of Lieutenant-Colonel, to write about the country's war effort. Though this produced a book, *Martial India*, it became clear that Yeats-Brown's health was now very precarious. He died in London on 19 December 1944, at the age of 58.

Yeats-Brown was typical in many respects of those members of the British extreme Right who, while in the inter-war period espousing the cause of Nazism and of European Fascism, retained their basic patriotism. Many of them wanted to help with the war effort once war had been declared and, like him, found it hard to understand why they were viewed with such suspicion, and given so little outlet for their patriotism. Indeed, many were suspected of, and reported to the authorities for, subversive activities which had little basis in fact. Rolf Gardiner summed up their problem, in the letter he wrote to Arthur Bryant about Yeats-Brown in 1944 on the occasion of the latter's death:

Like me, he wanted England to make an entirely different choice of friends in the period between the wars, and to reject the cynical and defensive spirit beloved of the Foreign Office. And so the renewed war filled him with despair and misery from which only his innate patriotism and sense of duty saved him.

(LHCMA Bryant E/19)

Captain George Lane-Fox Pitt-Rivers

George Pitt-Rivers is, compared with most of the other 'back-to-the-landers', a remarkably uncomplicated case, as his opinions and actions were unveering and always predictable. He was the grandson of the famous Victorian archaeologist General Augustus Pitt-Rivers, and (like Diana Mosley) a cousin of Winston Churchill's wife Clementine. He inherited great wealth, and owned a large estate at Hinton St Mary in Dorset. He was a single-minded obsessive, whose concerns centred on eugenics and purity of race. In his *Who's Who* entry he described himself as having 'established the methodology of the science of ethnogenics, interaction of race, population and culture'. He was also a conspiracy theorist, and his book *The World Significance of the Russian Revolution* (1920) alleged that the Jews had been 'the principal agents of economic and political misery in the world, through their dealings in international finance and their actions in promoting democracy and revolution'. His ideas and actions often seem to us completely irrational and unreal; but he did wield some influence in the far-right circles he inhabited.

As a landowner, he strongly approved of the agricultural policies of the BUF, and in 1935, though not a member of the party, he contested the general election under the auspices of the BUF as an anti-tithe candidate, an 'Independent Agriculturalist'. Mosley and William Joyce both came down to support his candidature (TNA KV 2/831).

He was by now strongly in favour of Nazi policies in Eastern Europe, and convinced of the pernicious influence of the state of Czechoslovakia, which he saw as a base for Jewish subversion and for freemasonry. A supporter of the rights of the Sudeten Germans, he visited Czechoslovakia in 1936, and was arrested by the Czech police for his political activities. On his return he boasted that he had been in Czechoslovakia 'working for Hitler'. His interest in Czechoslovakia was to continue throughout this period, culminating in his books (linking that country with the world plot as described in the *Protocols of the Elders of Zion*), *The Czech Conspiracy: A Phase in the World-War Plot* (1938), and *Czecho-Slovakia, the Naked Truth about the World-War Plot* (1939). Convinced that the Spanish Civil War was yet another manifestation of the Jewish world plot, he visited Spain to support Franco. He also went to Belgium to visit the Rexist leader Léon Degrelle.

The abdication crisis led him to be strongly disaffected with the British government, and on Christmas Day 1936 he wrote to the War Office requesting the removal of his name from the Regular Army

Reserve of Officers, 'on the ground that he was not prepared to serve in any capacity a Parliamentary despotism, now styled His Majesty's Government' (TNA HO 45/25725). In a long letter he also expressed 'extreme political views about international Jewry and kindred topics'. By the mid-Thirties he was often in contact with German officials, and in September 1937, as a delegate at the Nuremberg Rally, 'he expounded at great length rabid anti-British views, preferably to German audiences'. On his return, he boasted that Hitler and Goering were his friends; and thereafter he wore a gold swastika badge (TNA KV 2/831). At his London club (Arthur's in St James's Street) he left Nazi propaganda material around, interleaved in the club newspapers (TNA TS 27/514).

As war approached, he became a member of Domvile's The Link and Lymington's British Council against European Commitments. The Security Services noted that frequent visitors to Hinton St Mary included Sir Oswald Mosley, Admiral Domvile, Major-General Fuller and William Joyce.

Pitt-Rivers was a particularly close friend of Admiral Domvile (though Domvile found his incessant talk rather tiring!) and during the 'phoney war' period attended with Domvile a number of the meetings at which representatives of the 'patriotic societies' came together to attempt to create some kind of joint action.

Four days after the start of the May 1940 arrests, Domvile decided to go with his wife to stay with Pitt-Rivers at Hinton St Mary. There they followed from a distance, for some weeks, what was happening to their former colleagues, and spent much time listening to the radio (Haw-Haw and Churchill). Churchill came in for a lot of opprobrium on their part. His 'finest hour' speech on 17 June was described by Domvile as that of a failed drunkard, a traitor to his country whose scheme to forge a new relationship with the French was placing Britain in a relationship with a lot of 'syphilitic Latins' (NMM DOM 56 17/6/40).

Meanwhile Pitt-Rivers's tenants (MI5 described them as disliking and fearing him, and as being likely to lynch him in the event of serious air raids (TNA TS 27/514)) were fomenting trouble. On 27 June the local police came with an order to detain Pitt-Rivers. In face of this, the would-be creator of a master race, despite attempting to put a brave face on things, became just a pathetic, incoherent old man (NMM DOM 56 27/6/40). Just over a week later, after their return to London, the Domviles too were arrested.

When he appeared before the Advisory Committee, Pitt-Rivers proved to be an accomplished rewriter of history. He spoke at great length and with great complexity, and at times thoroughly confused the Committee. In the process he claimed that everything was someone else's fault (as we shall see when we deal with his accusations against John Coast). His various appeals were not acceded to, mainly because the authorities felt that his perpetual voicing of his prejudices was dangerous to public morale. In the event, however, he was released on 21 November 1941 on grounds of ill health (mainly to do with the results of his First World War wounds). He was put on the Suspect List, but kept his head well down for the rest of the war.

Pitt-Rivers was one of the few 'back-to-the-landers' (apart from those closely involved with British Union) to be arrested under DR 18B. In a sense, this was to be expected, given the virulence of his public expression of pro-Nazi views. One cannot help feeling, however, that the crazed ideas of this admittedly unpleasant eccentric were less dangerous than the words and activities of many other far more effective enemies of the state.

John Coast

John Coast appears to have lived two completely different lives – before and after the war – to the extent that one could imagine one was reading the lives of two separate people who had no connection with each other (indeed, few of those who have admired his post-war activities have known anything about his pre-war existence). Before the war, he had been an extreme pro-Nazi and anti-Semitic activist, who mingled in 'back-to-the-land' circles and held a deep admiration for Nazi Germany and the trappings of dictatorship. After the war, he was a liberal supporter of the Indonesian peoples in their search for independence, and the leading European expert in Javanese and Balinese music and dance, as well as having well-attested good relations with many Jews. He provides one of the best illustrations one could have of the folly of trying, *ex post facto*, to force all former fascist sympathisers into a number of precise categories.

Coast was born in 1916, and educated at Cheltenham College. He had become by the late Thirties an employee of Rothschild's Bank, in London. By 1937–8 he had developed a keen enthusiasm for Hitler and Nazi Germany. As his sister Daphne Forde has written in her memoirs:

> He read *Mein Kampf*, and acquired swastikas and various other badges pertaining to the ever growing band of followers of this would-be saviour of the new Germany. John, like many others, was fired by an almost fanatical desire to put the world to rights, mistakenly thinking that Hitler was the man to do so.
>
> (Forde, 1998: 44)

Soon he was associating with leading members of the pro-Nazi and anti-Semitic Right. This began when, during the spring and summer of 1938, he wrote a series of letters to Henry Williamson at his Norfolk farm. Williamson met him in London on 6 July 1938, noting in his diary that Coast had read his series of novels *The Flax of Dream*, and considered him to be 'the prophet of the Idea a new order in Britain & Empire'. Coast declared that he was giving up his job at Rothschild's, which he hated, and was going to come to work on Williamson's farm. He arrived shortly thereafter, having left Rothschild's (Anne Williamson, 1995: 223).

The character Hurst, in Williamson's novel *The Phoenix Generation*, is generally accepted to be closely based on John Coast (Williamson's novels tend to be very close to the facts of his experience, with often only names being changed). Like Coast, Hurst had worked for three years in a 'private bank of the City of London' which had a Jewish name. 'It is like being behind the beak of a great octopus, sucking power after squeezing whole areas of economic death by foreclosing on loans and mortgages.' He had written to Philip Maddison, declaring him to be 'the revolutionary prophet Britain was waiting for'.

> The young man was persistent: Deepwater Farm, he declared, might be the centre of what he had long awaited: 'the protoplasmic dot of an upsurge, a Renaissance'. It was his duty to say so. He was arriving the next day.

When Hurst arrived at the farm, it became clear that he was a fanatical fascist and anti-Semite. He wore a (facsimile) founder-member badge of the NSDAP, the Nazi Party, and declared his support for 'Frolich' (a thinly-disguised William Joyce – 'fröhlich' meaning 'joyous', and a pseudonym that Joyce himself used). He proudly said that he knew 'Captain Bohun-Borsholder' (an equally thinly disguised Captain George Pitt-Rivers). Later in the novel, Hurst invited Maddison to a meeting in London which had been called to oppose the looming war. This meeting was attended by 'Lord Egglesford' (Lord Lymington, whose book *Famine in England* is referred to in the text), an Admiral, described as 'Anglo-German Link' (Admiral Domvile), 'The Duke of Gaultshire' (Lord Tavistock), 'the ex-MP who seized the Mace in the House of Commons' (John Beckett), 'Frolich' (William Joyce) and others. This group, from its membership, is clearly based on Lymington's British Council against European Commitments (Williamson, 1965: 257–9, 362–3).

One may say, 'But this is a novel: Coast may well have been quite different from Hurst, as depicted.' Nevertheless, the facts we have about Coast's activities and contacts at this time support the identification. After leaving Williamson's farm, Coast went to stay with Captain Pitt-Rivers, whose secretary he became. The Chief Constable of Dorset has described a meeting with Coast at Pitt-Rivers's house in Hinton St Mary at this time:

> Captain Pitt-Rivers was out and while I was waiting for him a youth [...] came down to entertain me. He soon started to harangue me and his whole talk was violently pro-Nazi, anti-British, anti-Jewish and anti-Roman Catholic.
>
> (TNA TS 27/514)

While Coast was at Hinton St Mary, Pitt-Rivers was active in fomenting opposition to the billeting of evacuated children on his estate, threatening with eviction any of his tenants who took evacuees. Coast went round the estate, with Pitt-Rivers's younger son, to get people to sign the petition, telling the tenants that 'the evacuated people would be East End Jews, Polish Jews and Czech Communists' (TNA TS 27/514). Pitt-Rivers himself later accompanied Coast to threaten those who had refused to sign. At his later appearance before the Advisory Committee, Pitt-Rivers blamed these activities entirely on Coast, claiming that he himself had had nothing to do with it. In a syndrome we recognise from a number of other cases, he accused Coast of the kind of attitudes he himself had had. In all this, like so many who tried to exculpate themselves before the Advisory Committee and to lay the blame on others, he appeared to 'protest too much':

> This young man was insinuated into my house by [...] Henry Williamson. I used him as a sort of assistant secretary I think for three months and was kind to him. [...] He did a host of harm among my tenants, and was treacherous and disloyal in every possible way. [...] He was – I did not know it at the time – active in what I would call the political underworld, billing himself as a very keen pro-Fascist, Nazi fanatic [...] He was a very pathological young man. He insinuated himself into the confidence of a large number of people; he went to one after another and accused them, he used to frame charges against them to cover what he himself was doing. [...] I did not go myself, but this young man Coast went round and did a lot of damage. He was violently anti-Jew [...] He was going about, as he did with other people, accusing me of what he himself was guilty of.
>
> (TNA TS 27/514)

Pitt-Rivers also said that he had warned Lord Lymington and Rolf Gardiner about Coast (though as we shall see, Lymington's basically favourable attitude to Coast would not seem to back up this claim). While staying with Pitt-Rivers, Coast had come into contact with many figures of the pro-Nazi far Right, including Admiral Domvile (who found him a 'nice young man' when he met him on 6 January 1939), Lord Lymington, Captain Ramsay, William Joyce, Aubrey Lees and Jock Houston. He joined Lord Lymington's English Array (HRO Wallop 15M84/F177). His enthusiasms did, however, lead him into areas that even Lymington found doubtful, as the latter explained in a letter to Rolf Gardiner on 16 January 1939. He had met Coast through Pitt-Rivers, he said, and found him 'a good boy' who 'should be used'. However:

He is, at the moment, very anxious to do a sort of street corner campaign in East London with some very tough and rather doubtful associates. I have warned him as best I can about his associates, but I have not over-discouraged him from burning his fingers, as he is young and enthusiastic enough to want to do it and work it out of his system. It is better that he should scorch his fingers now, while there is plenty of time for them to heal, than later. I told him to get in touch with you.

(HRO Wallop 15M84/F191)

We gather, from Captain Pitt-Rivers's evidence to the Advisory Committee (TNA TS 27/514), that these 'associates' of Coast's were the Nationalist Association, a body founded by 'Jock' Houston in early 1939 as a basis from which to undertake the rumbustious street tactics that were his hallmark. Houston had in 1936 been dismissed from British Union: his NA associate 'Bill' Bailey, like him a former leader of the Shoreditch branch, had left BU at about the same time, because he did not feel it to be anti-Semitic enough. The Nationalist Association held public meetings in the East End several times a week both before the war and during the first nine months of the war, fomenting anti-Semitic emotions in their audiences (Griffiths, 1998: 62–3).

Later in 1939, having been 'befriended by Jock Ramsay' (TNA TS 27/514), Coast joined the Right Club. He continued his Right Club activities in the first months of the war, and was described by Special Branch during this period as being one of 'the most voluble of the clique' around Captain Ramsay, and as being 'definitely pro-German in sentiment' (TNA HO 144/22454). On 3 October 1939 he was one of the six representatives of the Right Club (together with Ramsay himself, John Vaneck, Aubrey Lees, Jock Houston and Mrs Newenham) who attended a meeting to explore anti-war collaboration with the National Citizens' Union, another extremist and anti-Semitic organisation (Griffiths, 1998: 61, 218).

By January 1940 Coast was a private in the Coldstream Guards. He was, however, still involved in Right Club activities. One of the MI5 infiltrators described a discussion that took place at this time between Coast, Anna Wolkoff and other Right Club members (TNA KV 2/677). Coast, like a number of others, does not seem to have found any problem in combining his military duties with a continuation of his fascist activities. His sister describes him as having, despite his 'dislike of the armed forces' volunteered 'almost immediately […] on the outbreak of war' (Forde, 1998: 45). It is likely, from the evidence we have, that he joined the Guards in late 1939; but that later, in 1940–1, finding himself unable to afford a commission in the Guards (for which he had been recommended by Captain Ramsay), he became an officer in the Royal Norfolk Regiment (Noszlopy, 2014: xiv).

Coast, then, went off to fight for his country. His battalion, the 4th of the Royal Norfolk Regiment, arrived in Singapore three weeks before the Japanese invasion in February 1942. After the attack, in which a third of the battalion was lost, Coast and the other survivors were imprisoned, in the first instance at Changi barracks, fourteen miles to the north-east of the island.

In prison it is clear that Coast at first retained certain of his pre-war political attitudes, particularly the negative ones in relation to the Jews. Like many other pre-war fascists, he seems to have been able to reconcile his patriotic service with the retention of his underlying political and racist beliefs. In the camps the prisoners, many of whom were intellectuals or musicians, formed 'universities' for the education of their fellow prisoners (Coast, 2014: 13). Coast became one of the lecturers at these sessions. Part of the content of his lectures was, however, unusual, as his biographer Laura Noszlopy has discovered:

> A historian of the Thai-Burma railway (where John was interned under the Japanese) told me of Coast's […] anti-Semitic lectures given under the auspices of the prison 'universities'.
>
> (Noszlopy, 2009)

Despite these activities at the start of his captivity, he appears, after the experiences of the next three and a half years, to have emerged a completely changed man.

On 31 October 1942 the comparatively bearable life of the camps near Singapore came to an end. Coast and his companions were sent in cattle-trucks to Thailand, where they were to work on the building of the Burma–Thailand railway. As is now well known, the conditions for prisoners working on that railway were horrendous. Coast himself wrote the first full account of this in his book *Railroad of Death*, based on diaries he had surreptitiously kept. This book, which was published in 1946, had an enormous impact, and was to form the basis of many later accounts, including the book and film *Bridge on the River Kwai*, which he and many others felt to contain considerable distortions of the facts. In *Railroad of Death* he records the appalling conditions – the forced labour, inadequate nutrition, callous unconcern for the prisoners' health, and often senseless brutality. He also chronicles the resilience and bravery of so many of the prisoners.

This book reveals to us a considerable change in the moral outlook of its author. No political points are made, and the text is remarkable for its calm and balanced outlook, which shows that while there had been such senseless brutality on the part of the Japanese that at times he could feel nothing but hatred for them, there had also been some who were respected as 'fair and decent' and comparatively 'even-handed and humane'. Later Coast and a number of his fellow prisoners objected strongly to the inaccuracies in the film *Bridge on the River Kwai* (including the depiction of the main character played by Alec Guinness), which they felt had distorted and over-simplified the facts. So much so, that in 1969 Coast produced a television documentary entitled *Return to the River Kwai* to set the record straight. Two of his former fellow captors took part.

The new, moderate and sensitive John Coast who had been created by the prison camps had a further dimension. The racial mix in the camps had led him to think deeply about the relationship between the races. As he put it, 'We English rubbed shoulders and worked alongside every Asiatic race and most European ones.' He noted how the 'Indische Jongens', those of mixed Dutch and Eurasian race, were despised by the Dutch; and how those who were predominantly European in blood 'try to out-Hollandise the Dutch, making themselves loathed by their fellow Indische Jongens whom they affect to despise, and either being laughed at or just used by the full-blooded Dutchmen'. He himself made friends mainly with the less Europeanised Indische Jongens, whom he contrasted favourably with the Dutch:

> Their intelligence is better and acuter than that of the average Dutch soldier – of that I am certain. And they don't laugh at the

Vagaries of the 'back-to-the-land' school 271

elephantine and ponderous jokes of the Hollander with his 'bierbuik' – their sense of humour coincides more exactly with the English. They are musical, artistic and sensitive; and once you get to know them, a very pleasant people.

(Coast, 2014: 216)

All this, and particularly the insensitive nature of Dutch colonialism, led him to predict grave post-war problems in Java:

So what will the ponderous old 'Totok' Dutchman do? He is intensely proud of and often boasts about Java, for it was just before the war a comparatively well-administered, though carefully controlled, colony. But he has created there a problem that is the biggest of its kind in the world and he's got to do something about it. When they have time to divert their eyes from their own affairs, the eyes of Eurasians, Asiatics and Europeans will be focussed on the Java stage.

(Coast, 2014, 216–19)

Coast's friendship with so many of the Eurasian prisoners led, too, to an interest in Javanese and Balinese culture which was to have a strong influence on his post-war career. He had been involved, in a peripheral way, with the amateur dramatics that the prisoners staged. Becoming aware of the outstanding qualities of Javanese music and dance, he soon began to organise performances of it. His 'Anglo-Dutch Theatrical Company' produced 'a Balinese Ballet and an elaborate Javanese-style music and dance show, complete with tin-can gamelan orchestra'. He was later to muse that 'If you'd told me that the war was over and I could go home, I'd have said: not now – let's get this show on first – I'll be ready to go home in a month or so' (Noszlopy, 2014: xxiv). This music and dance was to remain one of his abiding interests – and his post-war involvement in it was to make him famous worldwide.

After his release, Coast returned to London; but he remained obsessed with the Dutch East Indies, their peoples and their culture, and he became determined to return there. In 1945, on a visit to Holland, he set about recruiting Indonesian and Eurasian students from the Dutch universities, and put on a music and dance show at the Embassy Theatre in London, which was a great success.

He joined the Foreign Service, and took up a junior position in the British Embassy at Bangkok, capital of Thailand. He had become a strong supporter of Indonesian independence, and in 1948, giving up his job, went to Indonesia to support the unrecognised Free Indonesian government, often putting himself in danger. He became an international public relations official for President Sukarno. His experiences at this time are described in his book *Recruit to Revolution* (1952 and 2015). Meantime, he had married a Javanese woman.

After four years of fighting, Indonesia finally won its independence from the Dutch in December 1949. Coast now decided to return to his dream of an artistic outlet for Indonesian music and dance. With Sukarno's support, he moved to the island of Bali and opened a guest house there. He sought out a group of musicians and dancers, and took them in 1952 to perform in London's West End, and then on a tour of the USA. It was a resounding success. Balinese dance had not been seen in the West since the Paris Colonial Exhibition of 1931. Even now, 25 years after his death, John Coast is still renowned as a cultural ambassador of the first order.

After this, Coast's career took a very different turn. He returned to London and became a theatrical agent and impresario, specialising particularly in opera, which had been one of his first loves. He made a fortune managing such diverse opera singers as Jon Vickers, Luciano Pavarotti, José Carreras and Montserrat Caballé. He also introduced Ravi Shankar to the West, and presented Bob Dylan in London. Amid all this, in a remarkable return to the past, he put up some money as what is known as an 'angel' (unbeknown at first to Henry Williamson) for the filming of the latter's book *Tarka the Otter*. He died in 1989.

John Coast is a remarkable corrective to all the preconceptions we may have, not only in relation to those we classify as 'fascists', but also with regard to the effects of extensive and brutal captivity upon human beings. He started out as a vicious racial extremist; he ended as a champion of embattled races under colonial rule. He stood for racial and cultural purity on the Aryan model; but eventually he became an enthusiast for alien cultures far from what he would formerly have considered the European norm. Not only this, but his attitudes towards the Jews had completely changed. As Laura Noszlopy, who undertook her research for Coast's biography with the support of his long-term Jewish companion Laura Rosenberg, has pointed out, 'He had very close personal and professional relations with Jewish people throughout his later life' (Noszlopy, 2009).

One only has to look at photographs taken of John Coast before he went out to Singapore, and photographs taken after the war, to see the change from an apparently arrogant, hard and cynical individual to a very much more mature, gentle and reflective human being. His Damascene conversion, moreover, occurred under the most remarkable circumstances. Where the brutality of life on the Thailand–Burma railway physically destroyed many people, psychologically maimed others and so often led to hatred and desire for revenge, Coast (and there were others like him) was able to 'find himself' there, and to reconsider his life and his attitudes.

There were many more 'organo-fascists' than the ones we have considered here, of course. In particular there were those belonging to British Union, including Jorian Jenks, Robert Saunders and Derek Stuckey, all three of whom were imprisoned under DR 18B. Apart from Stuckey (whom we have seen in Chapters 1 and 6), they are, however, mainly interesting for their post-war activities, which we will be looking at in Chapter 13.

The 'back-to-the-landers' were a very varied lot during the war. At the one extreme we have the continuing political activities of Norman Hay; at the other, the complete volte-face of John Coast; and in between, varying mixtures of, and veerings between, patriotism and pro-Nazism in people like Lymington, Gardiner, Williamson and Yeats-Brown. If there is one thing that they have had to teach us, it is that human beings are far more complex than any generalised theories can cover, and that one can rarely, on the basis of previous behaviour, predict the paths that people may tread.

Bibliography

Books and articles

Boyes, Georgina (2011), 'Potencies of the Earth: Rolf Gardiner and the English Folk Dance Revival', in Matthew Jefferies and Mike Tyldesley (eds), *Rolf*

Gardiner: Folk, Nature and Culture in Interwar Britain (Farnham: Ashgate), pp. 65–94.

Coast, John (1946), *Railroad of Death* (London: Hyperion).

Coast, John (2014), *Railroad of Death*, ed. Laura Noszlopy (Newcastle upon Tyne: Myrmidon).

Coast, John (2015), *Recruit to Revolution: Adventure and Politics during the Indonesian Struggle for Independence* (ed. Laura Noszlopy) (Copenhagen: NIAS) (First published 1952, by Christophers, London).

'Cobbett' [Anthony Ludovici] (1938), *Jews, and the Jews in England* (London: Boswell Publishing Company).

Conford, Philip (2005), 'Organic Society: Agriculture and Radical Politics in the Career of Gerard Wallop, Ninth Earl of Portsmouth (1898–1984)', *Agricultural History Review*, 53, 1, 78–96 at 80–1.

Forde, Daphne (1998), *A Stick Called Will* (Henley Beach, South Australia: Seaview Press).

Fowler, David (2011), 'Rolf Gardiner: Pioneer of British Youth Culture, 1920–1939', in Matthew Jefferie and Mike Tyldesley (eds), *Rolf Gardiner: Folk, Nature and Culture in Interwar Britain* (Farnham: Ashgate), pp. 17–46.

Gardiner, Rolf (1932), *World Without End: British Politics and the Younger Generation* (London: Cobden-Sanderson).

Gardiner, Rolf (1933), 'Die deutsche Revolution von England gesehen', in Rolf Gardiner, Arvid Brodersen and Karl Wyser (eds), *Nationalsozialismus vom Ausland gesehen: an die Gebildeten unter seinen Gegnern* (Berlin: Die Runde).

Gardiner, Rolf (1938), Review of Lord Lymington, *Famine in England*, in *Quarterly Gazette of the English Array*, April.

Gardiner, Rolf (1939), 'Germany and the Baltic States', *New Pioneer*, May, 147–8.

Gardiner, Rolf (1972), 'Can Farming save European Civilisation?', reprinted in A. Best (ed.), *Water Springing from the Ground: An Anthology of the Writings of Rolf Gardiner* (Fontell Magna: Springhead Trust).

Griffiths, Richard (1980), *Fellow Travellers of the Right: British Enthusiasts for Nazi Germany, 1933–39* (London: Constable).

Griffiths, Richard (1998), *Patriotism Perverted: Captain Ramsay, the Right Club and British Anti-Semitism, 1939–40* (London: Constable).

Griffiths, Richard (2010), 'Anti-Fascism and the Post-War British Establishment', in Nigel Copsey and Andrzej Olechnowicz (eds), *Varieties of Anti-Fascism: Britain in the Inter-War Period* (Basingstoke: Palgrave Macmillan), pp. 247–64.

Griffiths, Richard (2011), 'The Dangers of Definition: Post-Facto Opinions on Rolf Gardiner's Attitudes towards Nazi Germany', in Matthew Jefferies and Mike Tyldesley (eds), *Rolf Gardiner: Folk, Nature and Culture in Interwar Britain* (Farnham: Ashgate), pp. 137–50.

Hamilton, Alastair (1971), *The Appeal of Fascism* (London: Blond).

Jefferies, Matthew (2011), 'Rolf Gardiner and German Naturism', in Matthew Jefferies and Mike Tyldesley (eds), *Rolf Gardiner: Folk, Nature and Culture in Interwar Britain* (Farnham: Ashgate, 2011), pp. 47–64.

Jerrold, Douglas (1933), 'The Corporate State in England', *Everyman*, 13 October.

Kushner, Tony (1989), *The Persistence of Prejudice: Anti-Semitism in British Society during the Second World War* (Manchester, Manchester University Press).

Kushner, Tony, and Knox, Katharine (1999), *Refugees in an Age of Genocide* (London: Frank Cass).

Lymington, Viscount (1938), *Famine in England* (London: Right Book Club).

Moore-Colyer, Richard (2011), 'Rolf Gardiner, Farming and the English Landscape', in Matthew Jefferies and Mike Tyldesley (eds), *Rolf Gardiner: Folk, Nature and Culture in Interwar Britain* (Farnham: Ashgate, 2011), pp. 95–120.

Morton, J.B. (1933), 'Sleeping England', *Everyman*, 3 November.

Noszlopy, Laura (2009), Letter to Richard Griffiths, 18 January.

Noszlopy, Laura (2014), Introduction to John Coast, *Railroad of Death* (Newcastle upon Tyne: Myrmidon).

Pitt-Rivers, Captain George Lane-Fox (1920), *The World Significance of the Russian Revolution* (Oxford: Blackwell).

Pitt-Rivers, Captain George Lane-Fox (1938), *The Czech Conspiracy: A Phase in the World-War Plot* (London; Boswell Publishing Co.).

Pitt-Rivers, Captain George Lane-Fox (1939), *Czecho-Slovakia: The Naked Truth about the World-War Plot* (London: Boswell Publishing Co.).

Portsmouth, The Earl of (1943), *Alternative to Death: The Relationship between Soil, Family and Community* (London: Faber and Faber).

Portsmouth, The Earl of (1965), *Knot of Roots: An Autobiography* (London: Geoffrey Bles).

The Protocols of the Learned Elders of Zion (n.d.), translated by Victor E. Marsden (London: The Britons Publishing Society).

Pugh, Martin (2005), *Hurrah for the Blackshirts! Fascists and Fascism in Britain between the Wars* (London: Jonathan Cape).

Ramsay, A.H.M. (1952), *The Nameless War* (London: Britons Publishing Society).

Roberts, Andrew (1994), *Eminent Churchillians* (London: Weidenfeld and Nicolson).

Saika, Robin (2010), *The Red Book: The Membership List of the Right Club, 1939* (London: Foxley Books).

Sanderson, William (1927), *Statecraft* (London: Methuen).

Skidelsky, Robert (1975), *Oswald Mosley* (London: Macmillan).

Stone, Dan (2002), *Breeding Superman: Nietzsche, Race and Eugenics in Edwardian and Interwar Britain* (Liverpool: Liverpool University Press).

Stone, Dan (2003), 'The British Far Right and the Back-to-the-land Movement', in Dan Stone, *Responses to Nazism in Britain, 1933–1939* (Basingstoke: Palgrave Macmillan).

Stone, Dan (2011), 'Rolf Gardiner: An Honorary Nazi?', in Matthew Jefferies and Mike Tyldesley (eds), *Rolf Gardiner: Folk, Nature and Culture in Interwar Britain* (Farnham: Ashgate, 2011), pp. 151–68.

Waugh, Evelyn (1952), *Men at Arms* (London: Chapman and Hall).

Williamson, Anne (1995), *Henry Williamson: Tarka and the Last Romantic* (Stroud: Sutton Publishing).

Williamson, Henry (1937), 'Lawrence of Arabia and Germany', *Anglo-German Review*, January, p. 107.

Williiamson, Henry (1941), *The Story of a Norfolk Farm* (London: Faber and Faber).

Williamson, Henry (1965), *The Phoenix Generation* (London: Macdonald).

Williamson, Henry (1967), *A Solitary War* (London: Macdonald).

Wrench, Evelyn (1948), *Francis Yeats-Brown 1886–1944* (London: Eyre and Spottiswoode).

Yeats-Brown, Francis (1932), 'Why I believe in War', *The Spectator*, 30 December.

Yeats-Brown, Francis (1934), *Dogs of War!* (London: P. Davies).

Yeats-Brown, Francis (1939a), *European Jungle* (London: Eyre and Spottiswoode).

Yeats-Brown, Francis (1939b), 'Listen, Tommy!', *New Pioneer*.

Documents

The National Archives (TNA)

HO 45/24895, HO 45/25725, HO 144/20144, HO 144/213729, HO 144/21845, HO 144/22454, HO 262/6
HS 9/892/12
KV 2/492, KV 2/677, KV 2/795, KV 2/831, KV 2/872, KV 2/2245
TS 27/514

National Maritime Museum (NMM)

Admiral Domvile's Diary, DOM 56

Liddell Hart Centre for Military Archives, King's College London (LHCMA)

Arthur Bryant Papers (Bryant):
E/19, E/39, E/51, E/60

Hampshire Record Office (HRO)

Papers of 9th Earl of Portsmouth (Wallop)

Newspapers and journals

Daily Telegraph (DT)
Evening Standard (ES)
Everyman
Information and Policy (IP)
New Pioneer (NP)
The Observer
Quarterly Gazette of the English Array (QGEA)
The Spectator
Springhead Ring News Sheet (SRNS)
The Times

PART VI
Aftermath

13

'CHANGE AND DECAY IN ALL AROUND I SEE'

Further post-war decline

The extremist movements

With the advent of peace, movements such as the British People's Party and the Constitutional Research Association (CRA) lost much of their *raison d'être*. The CRA's lunches continued (now mainly at Brown's Hotel). Lord Sempill became the chairman, and new members were added (including a number already well known to us from other activities of theirs, including John Scanlon, Captain Arthur Rogers, Colonel Creagh Scott and Edward Greene). But with the defeat of Nazi Germany, the impetus for activity had naturally flagged. Edmonds, Domvile and others tried to formulate a new role for the group, and a number of new causes were taken up, including opposition (spearheaded by Domvile), based on the usual presumptions about International Money Power, to the Bretton Woods proposals for an international financial system (NMM DOM 58). In another attempt to find a role (possibly influenced by Mosley's new European initiatives) Edmonds at one stage declared that the future aim of the CRA would be 'to further a western European union on an economic basis which should be Catholic, anti-Communist and opposed to international finance' (TNA KV 2/874). The post-war activity for which CRA is best remembered is, however, its espousal of the cause of the Nazi war criminals being tried at Nuremberg (a cause in which, it must be said, it stood alongside perfectly respectable figures like Bishop Bell of Chichester, Frank Pakenham (the future Lord Longford), Richard Rapier Stokes MP and Reginald Paget KC, MP) (Macklin, 2007: 126–33). After this, the group gradually faded away, and we hear no more of it.

The British People's Party (BPP) followed much the same trajectory, failing to find a role once the war was over. At first, it had some success. In the immediate post-war period Beckett was 'running around for the Duke bringing into the fold everyone he [could] find'. Many of his contacts, as we have seen, were members of other pre-war extremist groups such as Leese's Imperial Fascist League (IFL). For their benefit Beckett came out in his true colours, for example declaring at a meeting between the BPP and the 'Independent Nationalists' in September 1945 that 'no matter what we call ourselves we are really national-socialists'. Everyone present agreed with this statement (TNA KV 2/1519).

The new BPP also attracted at this time a number of other obsessive figures from the right-wing penumbra. These included Waveney Girvan (the 'expert' on flying saucers), Frederick Soddy the eminent radiochemist who had, from the interwar period onwards, been strongly involved with monetary reform, and Air Commodore Gerard Oddie, who became chairman. Beckett, in one of his lighter moments, referred to the BPP as having now become the 'party of the oddies and soddies' (Beckett, 1999: 188). Admiral Domvile was among the party's speakers (KV 2/838).

In March 1946 Air Commodore Oddie stood for the BPP in the by-election for the Combined British Universities seat, and lost his deposit. Various public meetings were held in 1945–6. The party's main activity, however, appears to have been the publication of its views in a variety of outlets. It used the emergence of the Communist threat in the late 1940s to reiterate its long-held anti-Communist credentials, and was among the first to stress the importance of Franco as a bulwark against Communism. At the same time it continued its anti-Semitic insinuations, both in its attacks on 'International Finance' and in its opposition to immigration from Europe, which brought into this country the 'refuse of Europe' (Pitchford, 2011: 15–16). It remained, however, a minority movement, and as time went on, despite the considerable financial support given by Bedford, its fortunes began to wane still further. Beckett and Bedford had miscalculated. In these immediate post-war years, there was little scope for this old-style extremist movement of the Right. In 1953, after the untimely death of the Duke of Bedford, the BPP was wound up.

Not that the extreme Right did not have a future. The British League of Ex-Servicemen's campaign of street violence from late 1944 onwards prefigured the revival of BU activity in Mosley's Union Movement; and though, as Richard Thurlow has pointed out, the 'extremely negative perception of all kinds of fascist activity' in the immediate aftermath of the war meant that Mosley and others were 'very wary and security-conscious' (Thurlow, 1987: 236), an impetus was given to racist activities both by the situation in Palestine and by the influx of immigration from the West Indies. Additionally, Mosley's Union Movement of 1948 and A.K. Chesterton's League of Empire Loyalists (LEL) of 1954 partially succeeded where the earlier movements had not. By addressing new issues (a new vision of Europe and the loss of Empire, respectively), both these movements succeeded in building, though only for a short time, a comparatively more effective power-base. They, in turn, were succeeded by movements of a very different order, which have culminated in the present-day British National Party.

This is not the place to go into the history of the post-war extreme Right, which has been dealt with very effectively by a number of writers (e.g., Macklin, 2007; Pitchford, 2011; Thurlow, 1987). It is enough to say that the old-style fascism of the pre-war period had its last fling with movements like the wartime BNP, ENA, BPP and CRA, and that post-war right-wing extremism, while of course owing a certain amount to it (including the ever-present policy of racism), was on the whole governed by different priorities. Above all, of course, the pro-Nazi crusade no longer had any point.

So what happened to the prominent individuals whose pre-war and wartime activities we have been examining? Apart from Mosley (Macklin, 2007: *passim*), only A.K. Chesterton appears to have adapted fairly successfully to the new situation of the post-war extreme Right, first in 1954 with his League of Empire Loyalists, and then in 1967 with the National Front. Other, lesser figures from the past, including

Jeffrey Hamm, adapted to the new situation for a while, a number of them flourishing within Mosley's new-style Union Movement or within the LEL. Yet many failed to adapt. The fate of most of the prominent figures from the fascist past was dismal. These big fish no longer had a pond to swim in.

Their coping strategies were many and varied. Some of them did attach themselves to the new movements, while never achieving any prominent status within them. Others, while retaining their extreme views, nevertheless stood on the periphery of events. Others cut their losses, and eschewed overt fascist political activity, while some of them pursued their other related interests (whether ecological, or financial, or landowning, or even musical) with even greater single-mindedness. And then there were those who, despairing of post-war Britain, decided to go abroad. The spectrum is very wide, and generalisations are inadequate; but this chapter will, by taking some specific cases, endeavour to convey something of this diversity.

The hard-liners: Gordon-Canning, Ramsay, Domvile, Leese

In April 1945, as the war was drawing to an end, an agent of MI5 managed to attend a meeting between Norman Hay, Admiral Sir Barry Domvile and Captain Ramsay, at which 'each person solemnly undertook to continue the fight for National Socialism whatever the outcome of the war', though 'the Jewish power had been too strong on this occasion' (TNA KV 2/837). Similarly unrepentant was Captain Robert Gordon-Canning, one of the mainstays of the pre-war pro-Nazi Right, who at a sale at the German Embassy in November 1945 bought a large bust of Adolf Hitler for £500, 'to challenge the Jews, to prevent purchase by them, [and] to return it to Germany at a suitable time' (Carlson, 1951: 25). This presumably referred to a time in the future when National Socialism would have returned to power there. John Beckett, writing on 28 November 1945 to congratulate Gordon-Canning on what had been 'a fine thing to do', said he was sure that, if Gordon-Canning had nowhere to keep it, he could find 'people who would take decent and reverent care of it' (TNA KV 2/1519).

Obsessive figures such as these tended to stick together in the immediate post-war months and years. Many had known each other before the war; others had met in prison. Ramsay and Gordon-Canning, as we have seen, had become good friends. Ramsay left his wife in July 1945 and from then on spent much of his time with Gordon-Canning in a house on the latter's family estate in Hartpury, Gloucestershire. A report in the *Sunday Pictorial* in December 1945, while describing them as 'two of the most unpopular men in England', nevertheless painted an almost idyllic picture of their friendship and their life together during the previous five months:

> For the past five months they have been living in the red-bricked Lodge House in Hartpury. They have become inseparable, rarely seen without each other, shooting pheasants together, and leaving together at intervals for London. Of evenings they sit round a large log fire and sometimes talk into the morning about their own peculiar political convictions. 'I have made a staunch friend in Captain Ramsay', Captain Gordon-Canning told me, 'and his presence here has no significance beyond that'.
>
> (*SP*, 16/12/45)

What these two men shared was a virulent hatred of the Jews and an admiration for the achievements of Nazi Germany. For the time being, amid the post-war anti-fascist consensus, there appeared to be little outlet for these views. By 1947, however, the situation in Palestine provided a great opportunity for anti-Semites. In August of that year the murder, in cold blood, of two British sergeants by Jewish Irgun paramilitaries brought things to a head, and violent anti-Jewish riots took place across Britain, particularly in Manchester, Liverpool and Glasgow, but also in Bristol, London and other cities. A part was played in such riots by 'street-wise' movements of the extreme Right such as Hamm's British League of Ex-Servicemen and Women, and Victor Burgess's Union of British Freedom.

Both Gordon-Canning and Ramsay had had considerable pro-Palestinian experience in the pre-war period. Various commentators have pointed out just how much use was made of the Palestinian cause by rabid British anti-Semites from the 1920s onwards

(Cesarani, 1989; Griffiths, 1998: 23–7). In the late 1930s Gordon-Canning was one of the leading British anti-Semitic pro-Arabists (Macklin, 2009). Captain Ramsay, too, as some of his speeches to the Nordic League in 1939 had made clear, mingled pro-Arabism with violent anti-Semitism. Now these two men girded themselves for battle once more.

The investigative journalist Avedis Boghos Derounian, who infiltrated these circles under a pseudonym at this time, drew a distinction between people like Hamm, 'a rabble-rouser, no more', and people who worked 'on much higher levels' like Gordon-Canning and Ramsay. He described a evening he spent at Gordon-Canning's flat, with Gordon-Canning, Captain Ramsay, Admiral Domvile, Enid Riddell (formerly of the Right Club) and Frances Newton. Miss Newton had in 1938 been excluded from Palestine (where she was a resident) because of her 'virulent publications' against the Jews and in favour of the Arabs (TNA CO 733/372/11, CO 733/398/9). She had been secretary of the Palestine Information Centre in London and was now the most prominent member of the Anglo-Arab Friendship Society (other members including known anti-Semites such as the journalist Douglas Reed and Lady Makins of the Right Club, 'whose pro-Arab sympathies were first and foremost motivated by their dislike of the Jews') (Miller, 2008: 156). The conversation over dinner was predictably bloodthirsty, the Jew being their 'diet', whom, as Derounian describes it, they 'minced', 'roasted', 'hanged from Palestinian lamp-posts', 'quartered' and 'massacred'. In his account Derounian picked out certain specific comments made by those present. Gordon-Canning felt that Palestine was 'the only country in the world where the Gentiles can get theirs in against the Jews'. They all agreed that the Arabs would easily win in the coming conflict, and that 'killing off six hundred thousand Jews would be as easy for the Arabs as shooting ducks'. Gordon-Canning said: 'I give the Jew two years after the Arabs win.' Miss Newton told those present of her plans for a quick profit after an Arab victory. She had bought property in Palestine some years before for £3,800 and had recently sold it to Jews for £47,000. When the Jews had been 'disposed of', she would take her property back.

Ramsay declared that 'If we break the back of the Jew in Palestine, we have broken it for a long time to come'. But Gordon-Canning, promising to hold receptions to raise funds for the Palestinian cause, raised a note of caution. He said to Miss Newton:

> We'll help behind the scenes, [but] it wouldn't do for me to appear publicly on your committee. They'll call you Fascist. The Admiral has also been smeared. We'll all work from the sidelines.

It was left for Admiral Domvile to strike a completely unrealistic note. 'We must all help', he said, 'whether with a rifle in our right hand, or with our left hand in our pocket' (Carlson, 1951: 34–6).

This conversation illustrates admirably the dilemma in which people such as this now found themselves. Despite Domvile's silly remark, they were not men of action on the international scene. Nor were they local shock troops like Hamm's men. Nor were they working on a 'higher level', as Derounian suggested. They still aspired to the exercise of influence, just as they had always done. But now they were hamstrung by their own reputations, in an anti-fascist society that had turned against the rhetoric of the pre-war period. They had no influence at all. All they could do was make violent statements, like saloon-bar theorists – statements which verged on the ludicrous, and which led nowhere. Added to this, of course, their assessment of the Middle East situation was seriously deficient, and the eventual outcome made all their predictions worthless. (It is worth noting that Miss Newton had considerable difficulties in relation to her extensive remaining Palestine properties after the creation of the state of Israel) (TNA FO 1022/4).

We hear little of these people after this, apart from the publication by Domvile and Ramsay of memoirs aimed at rehabilitating their reputations (typically, by pointing out the Jewish menace which had brought about their downfall): Domvile's *From Admiral to Cabin Boy* (1947), which blamed everything on 'Judmas', and Ramsay's *The Nameless War* (1952), devoted to justifying the creation of the Right Club and to criticising Ramsay's treatment under the DR 18B legislation. Both these books were published by long-established anti-Semitic publishing companies which had continued after the war – the Boswell Publishing Company and the Britons Publishing Society, respectively. These two books looked back, rather than forward. Ramsay died in 1955. Domvile lived until 1971, but though he joined the League of

Empire Loyalists and the National Front, he played no significant role in post-war right-wing politics.

Gordon-Canning undertook, in the years 1949–50, some activity in the Middle East itself. His self-belief was as usual unrealistic in the extreme, as were the ideas he thought up. In 1949 he visited Cairo, and met the Grand Mufti of Jerusalem and Azzam Pasha, secretary of the Arab League (who, on a visit to London in 1946, had apparently seen any connection with him as something of an embarrassment). On Gordon-Canning's return to Britain he wrote to Azzam Pasha, suggesting that General Fuller should go out to the Middle East to lecture the Arabs on modern warfare to help with future campaigns against Israel – a suggestion which, predictably, was disapproved by the British authorities (Macklin, 2009: 90, 93). Azzam Pasha does not appear to have taken up the suggestion in any way. Thereafter, Gordon-Canning subsided into obscurity. He died in 1967.

Another obsessive figure who continued his activities in this period was Arnold Leese, the leader of the Imperial Fascist League. During the war he had found himself at variance with a number of his members, first because of his condemnation of Hitler's pact with Soviet Russia, and then because of his 'disgust at the German action in Norway'. Now, however, returning to his overriding concern with the Jews, he started praising Hitler once more, and saw Hitler's defeat as having been a victory for the Jewish capitalists. In 1945–53 his journal *Gothic Ripples* contained articles denying 'the fable of the slaughter of six million Jews by Hitler', yet insisting that he *wished* it were true, so long as it were done 'in a humane manner' (*GR*, 1/53). Leese's influence was slight in these years, however, and though his publications were extreme, the readership was limited. Ex-members of the IFL such as Anthony Gittens, Elizabeth Berger, H.H. Lockwood and P.J. Ridout tended now to be more active in movements like the British People's Party and the League of Empire Loyalists. Leese did come to public notice, momentarily, when he conspired to help some escaped Dutch Waffen-SS prisoners of war; but on the whole he faded from the scene. His one 'achievement' in these years was his discovery and mentorship of the young Colin Jordan, who became for a while one of the leading, and most publicly known, figures in the post-war Right, first in the League of

Empire Loyalists and then in a variety of other movements. Leese died in 1956.

The 'back-to-the-landers'

The 'back-to-the-landers' had always, in one sense, lived a double life. Their enthusiasm for fascist-style policies had always been subordinate to their very real concerns about the future of the land. Admittedly, as we have seen, the links between 'blood and soil' could lead them not only to a rejection of various aspects of the modern world, but also to the association of aliens and Jews with those values; and their sense of a need for a revision of the attitudes created by twentieth-century democracy could create in them an enthusiasm for more authoritarian political systems. But the starting point and the end point were always agriculture. It is not surprising, therefore, to find former 'eco-fascists' playing a large part in the ecological movement in the years immediately after the war.

In fact, those agriculturalists who had been prominent in British Union (BU) before the war, and those who had been members of the circle around Lord Lymington, were among the moving forces in the newly formed Soil Association (SA) and in the Rural Reconstruction Association (RRA), a body which had been created in the interwar period, and now, after a period of decline, had been revived in a new ecological form. Jorian Jenks, who had been the main BU spokesman on agriculture before the war, became editor of the SA's journal *Mother Earth*, and Rolf Gardiner, Lord Sempill and the Earl of Portsmouth (the former Lord Lymington) were all on the SA's Council, while Rex Tremlett, Derek Stuckey and Ralph Temple Cotton were also among the founder members of the movement. When we come to the RRA, the Committee included Jorian Jenks, Robert Saunders, Rolf Gardiner, Eric Whittleton, the Earl of Portsmouth and Derek Stuckey. Jenks was the RRA's press secretary and edited its journal *Rural Economy*, while Stuckey was the research secretary (Macklin, 2007: 64–7).

To what extent, however, were their right-wing ideas important in these movements? Was it all some kind of right-wing takeover? Robert Saunders's and Jorian Jenks's comments in their private correspondence do suggest, as Graham Macklin puts it, that the former BU members felt they were able by their manoeuvres to 'inject a central tenet of fascist ideology into an unsuspecting mainstream'. But while Jenks, Saunders and others continued privately to pay lip-service in this way to their fascist ideals, and while they may have privately boasted among themselves about their 'infiltration' of these environmental bodies, there is little evidence of their fascism having any *political* effect in these quarters. Indeed, they appear to have eschewed open declarations of their BU faith, however much they retained it personally. There is far more evidence of the importance, for such men, of the ecological policies they espoused. In other words, for them, however much they may have yearned for their fascist past, ecology was more important than politics. Occasionally, it is true, a fringe monomaniac such as James Wentworth Day, the East Anglian agriculturalist and journalist who had been associated with Mosley in the Thirties, could, in broadcast interviews, unashamedly produce Ludovici-influenced language in relation to the 'mongrelisation' of Britain owing to mixed marriages (Farson, 1958). However, on the whole the former fascist agriculturalists kept quiet about any such views they may have continued to harbour – and the popularity of the Wentworth Day interviews appears to have stemmed mainly from what was now, in the post-war world, perceived as the outlandish nature of his views.

It is interesting to note, among those in the SA and the RRA, members of the group that had formed around Stuckey at his farm during the war: Stuckey himself, Whittleton and Temple Cotton. There is little sign, among these people, of the post-war activities that MI5 had predicted for them. Stuckey had not, as predicted, put himself forward as a leader for ex-BU activists. His concerns now appear to have been predominantly agricultural.

The ecological movement, which has been so influential in the late twentieth and early twenty-first centuries, has embraced, over the years, people of very varied political views. There is no denying that, before 1940, a large number of the people concerned with agricultural issues were, as we have seen, tarred with the 'eco-fascist' brush. It would have been strange if such people had not continued to pursue these interests after the war – and like it or not, they played a very important part in the success of ecological policies. The 'Green' movement tends nowadays to be of a completely different political tinge – but in each case ecological concerns have been more important than political ones. In one sense, one can say that the 'back-to-the-land' fascists succeeded, in the post-war world which was so hostile to their pre-war views, in sublimating their former attitudes into a far wider cause.

Rolf Gardiner was the most eminent, and the most influential, of those 'back-to-the-landers' who continued as active figures after the war. As we have seen, he had become disenchanted with Nazism during the war years; but this did not mean that he did not continue to espouse many of the old views that he had held in the Thirties, particularly in relation to the dangers of plutocracy, democracy and other powers that undermined the return to rural values. He also continued to see Germany as Britain's natural partner in preventing Europe becoming 'engulfed by Slav-Mongolian collectivism and American *en masse* democracy' (Moore-Colyer, 2011: 113). His connections with Germany, therefore, remained strong; and though these connections appear to have been in no way subversive, the British authorities were at first highly suspicious of him. For example, British Intelligence in Germany showed reluctance to 'allow him to enter Germany on any pretext' in August 1946, and in 1949 enquiries were set on foot as to 'the names and security of any young Germans who intend proceeding to Nyasaland under the auspices of Mr Gardiner', who was described as being of 'Fascist sympathies' and 'a crank of the first order, with strong Germanophile sympathies, who flirted with the Nazis before the war' (TNA KV 2/2245). These suspicions were unfounded; Gardiner's main concerns, in these years, were the future of the land, and musical and youth culture.

Gardiner continued on his way undeterred. He was a founding member of the Soil Association, and spearheaded opposition to the governmental encouragement, in the post-war years, of an increase in production through the use of agrochemicals and of factory farming. He pursued these activities in Britain and on the European scene, and also founded a European Working Party for Landscape Husbandry, lecturing at universities throughout Europe and attending UNESCO colloquia. He had meanwhile also been dealing with the colonial officials in Nyasaland (where his family had long-standing interests in the form of a tea-growing estate, the Nchima Tea and Tung Estate) with a view to conserving the land. (He had written about soil erosion in Nyasaland and Uganda as early as the 1930s) (Moore-Colyer, 2001: 209).

By the time of his death in 1971, Gardiner had been showered with honours, culminating with the award, in Strasbourg in 1971, of the Peter Joseph Lenné Gold Medal as part of the Europa Prize for Landscape Husbandry, an award which recognised 'Gardiner's lifelong endeavours for European cultural unity, his work in soil, water and landscape conservation in Dorset and Malawi, and his role as chairman of the European Working Party for Landscape Husbandry' (Moore-Colyer, 2011: 116–17).

Over the last 50 years Gardiner's reputation has grown considerably, not least because of his role as one of the first Cassandras to warn of the ultimate effects of over-consumption. In the final year of his life, as he received the Lenné Gold Medal, he summed this up in the following words:

> Society will have to discipline itself to more selective consumption, to reliance on bare essentials, to thrift. Squandering our resources and reckless consumption lead to ultimate impoverishment and all-pervading illness of soil, plants, beasts and humankind. We cannot afford them. We must adopt a wiser style of living altogether if we are to survive at all.
>
> (Jefferies and Tyldesley, 2011: 1)

These warnings were not heeded at the time, but their message has become ever more urgent over the years.

The African Connection

A number of pre-war 'fellow travellers of the Right' were, predictably, depressed by post-war England to the extent of wishing to escape it. In this these right-wingers were not alone. They were part of a more general exodus. Africa was a particularly popular destination. As Evelyn Waugh put it, after a visit to Southern Rhodesia in 1958, there was a proportion of the white population who were 'English county families who came there in 1946 to escape the Welfare State' and who were 'rapidly becoming middle-class' (Waugh, 1982: 504).

Africa had harboured many adherents of the extreme Right over the years. Before the war, for example, Josslyn Hay, 22nd Earl of Erroll, a leading light in Kenyan society, having joined the British Union of Fascists (BUF) in 1934, became 'Delegate of the British Union of Fascists for Kenya Colony', and was reported as having 'a constructive and energetic plan to convert the Colony to the Blackshirt policy'. He claimed that he had joined the BUF 'because it believes in action, rather than talk. It is obvious', he said, 'that the present system tends to prevent, rather than expedite, action being taken to put to right the affairs of the nation.' Erroll was part of the raffish 'Happy Valley' set, and was murdered in very suspicious circumstances in 1941. His murder may well have been entirely due to personal matters, as was believed at the time; but recent revelations have suggested that there may have been a political cause for it (Trzebinski, 2000: 119 and *passim*).

There is little doubt that many of the other settlers in East Africa had similarly over-simplified reactionary attitudes. Many of them shared the views earlier expressed by the 3rd Baron Delamere, one of the first and most influential Kenyan settlers, who had proclaimed that Kenya was 'a white man's country', and that the African natives were innately inferior, the British race being 'superior to heterogeneous African races only now emerging from centuries of relative barbarism'. By the interwar period, some members of this colonial society were eagerly espousing the eugenic theories of racial superiority and inferiority being promulgated by the European Right, as is witnessed by the formation of the Kenyan Society for the Study of Race Improvement (Campbell, 2007).

In a sense, then, Africa in the immediate post-war period, when decolonisation was merely a cloud on the horizon, seemed an ideal refuge for disgruntled remnants of the pre-war British Right. These included a number of ex-BU members, for example Ian Hope Dundas (Mosley's former Chief of Staff), and also remnants of the pre-war 'back-to-the-landers'. One of these, our old friend the Earl of Portsmouth who went to Kenya, presents us with a very interesting case. He is an example of a leopard who appears to have completely changed his spots. Unlike the Duke of Montrose (the former Marquess of Graham) who in Southern Rhodesia remained a diehard colonialist, maintaining to the end the inferiority of the indigenous African population

(*The Times* obituary, 13/2/92), Portsmouth accepted change, gradually coming to terms with the advent of majority rule, and resolving to work with the new regime in Kenya for the good of the country and its inhabitants.

For a short time in the immediate post-war years Portsmouth had played a prominent role in the new ecological groups in Britain, the Soil Association and the revived Rural Redevelopment Association, but by 1948 he had begun to turn his eyes towards the African continent, where he would be able to farm extensively using his long-standing agricultural expertise. He was not just attracted by the agricultural prospects, however; he also had a romantic vision of the colonial life. After a first visit to Kenya in 1948, on which he bought his first farm, he mused on the 'enchantment of this alien world', and decided that while much of this enchantment lay in the beauty of the surroundings and the picturesque background, 'the first real impact was made by one's fellow Europeans'. He greatly admired 'the old-timers who had made the country, fought for it in two wars, suffered all the slumps and survived, been grudged by mean Home Governments and cheated by currency ramps'. These men, he felt, had 'given their lusty lives to the utmost and found those lives rewarding'. To see them 'was indeed refreshment after the weariness of spirit in drab post-war England, where feeling for life and adventure had for the time been almost totally exhausted'. These were, he declared, 'whole men' (Portsmouth, 1965: 225).

In 1950 Portsmouth moved permanently to Kenya, where he was to remain for the next quarter of a century. As well as farming extensively and successfully, he also took part in Kenyan politics. He became a member of the Executive Committee of the Kenya Electors' Union, of which he was president from 1953 to 1955. He was also chairman of the Forest Advisory Committee for the Kenyan Government from 1955 to 1961, and soon became a member of Kenya's governing body, the Kenya Legislative Council, representing agricultural interests.

Portsmouth learned much in his time in Kenya, and his attitudes underwent a considerable change. Unlike so many of his European contemporaries, he remained in Kenya after independence was declared in 1963, truly believing in co-operation between the races. Indeed, he served the new government as vice-chairman of the East

African Resources Research Council from 1963 onwards. A passage in his autobiography, which appeared in 1965, expresses his new-found philosophy of collaboration and fellowship:

> In the end those of alien origin who stay in Africa, especially in the East Africa I love, may stay less because they contribute to the country's vital economy (that is why East African statesmen ask them to stay), than for what they have to contribute in friendship and love. I know full well that I am producing as much economic welfare as any estate in Kenya. […] But in my heart is the true aristocratic claim to be putting more into African life than I take from it. If I can help the economy well and good; if however humbly I can help the long safari of the mind across a thousand years of bitter experience in a generation, well and better.
>
> (Portsmouth, 1965: 323)

He remained in Kenya until 1977, when a severe stroke necessitated a return to Britain for treatment. He died in 1984.

Lord Brocket and the Knoydart Land Seizures

From colonial and post-colonial Africa we now turn, in a fascinating individual case, to what many Scots believed to be colonial Scotland. In a famous dispute over Scottish land, Lord Brocket (who had clearly recovered well from his wartime nervous breakdown) played a major part. In the 1930s he had bought an extensive estate of 52,000 acres on the west coast of Scotland, the Knoydart Estate. This he had developed as a sporting estate for shooting and fishing. In the process he had dismissed and evicted most of the estate workers, made life difficult for the crofters and made sure that his gamekeepers kept local people off the land. There was considerable local resentment,

Brocket's activities were, in fact, not dissimilar to those of many other English absentee landlords in this period. But what made this a particularly inflammatory case were the extent of the changes made and the personal unpopularity of Lord Brocket, of whom a neighbouring landowner said, 'I am afraid Lord Brocket is very unpopular. He does not seem to understand our people at all' (*NW*, 20/11/48). Locally, people were also aware of Brocket's pro-German activities in 1938–40, and of his lack of war service, in contrast to his ex-service opponents. Knoydart therefore seemed an ideal battleground on which to fight for crofters' rights. The nationalist Hugh MacDiarmid, in an article in the *National Weekly* in 1948 at the height of the dispute, pointed this out:

> Such a fight on a national scale […] is, of course, long overdue, and it seemed likely that it could not be initiated under better auspices. The Knoydart land wastage is a particularly flagrant one. The type of landlord involved made the case a particularly likely one for bringing to a head at last all the subterranean anger at the way in which vast areas of Scotland have been depopulated and turned into private preserves by alien owners. Sooner or later the whole issue must be forced into the area of practical politics. […] Hope centred particularly on the type of landlord concerned. […] Perhaps the trouble is that our people understand Lord Brocket only too well – and have no use for him.
>
> (*NW*, 20/11/48)

During the war the estate had been requisitioned by the Special Operations Executive (SOE) for training of commandos and other special forces. After the war Lord and Lady Brocket had returned – but so had a number of recently demobilised ex-servicemen. Many such men, all over Scotland, having given such service to their country, applied to the Ministry of Agriculture for crofting land, but were informed that none was available. Seeing the amount of such land on private estates which was now unused for crofting, they were seething with resentment. Knoydart became a test case, to see whether direct action might work. On 9 November 1948 seven young ex-servicemen invaded the estate and staked out 65 acres of arable land each, turning them into crofts. In support of their claim, they quoted the Land Settlement Act of the 1920s, which had permitted servicemen returning from the First World War to take over, and farm, land which was under-used. When the news of their actions was reported nationally, there was widespread and enthusiastic support. This was to be a test case, people felt, of great importance.

Brocket, who could be affable, if patronising, with his forelock-tugging English tenants at Bramshill (Lees-Milne, 2006: 38), was at a loss with the more independent-minded Scots, and reacted angrily. He presented them with a Court Order requiring them to get off his land. He hired expensive lawyers, and prepared for a grim fight. But the 'Seven Men of Knoydart' were given bad advice by their own lawyer. Assuring them that they would almost certainly win their case if they abided by the law, he advised them to vacate the land. This they did, and in the process completely weakened their position. Brocket's lawyers pulverised them, and the attempt failed. Their appeal under the Land Settlement Act was dismissed.

Despite winning the case, Brocket appears to have found that the emotions raised locally by it had rendered life at Knoydart uncomfortable. In 1949 he sold the estate and bought a new one in Ireland, the Carton House Estate, the former residence of the Dukes of Leinster. He lives on in Scottish folk memory, however, as is witnessed by some verses of a ballad by the folk poet Hamish Henderson, entitled 'Ballad of the Men of Knoydart' (to be sung to the tune of 'Johnston's Motor Car'):

> 'You bloody Reds!' Lord Brocket cried
> 'Wot's this you're doin' 'ere?
> It doesn't pay as you'll find today,
> To insult an English Peer.
> For you're only Scottish halfwits
> But I'll make you understand
> You Highland swine, these Hills are mine!
> This is all Lord Brocket's Land! […]
>
> Then up spoke the men of Knoydart:
> 'Away and shut your trap,
> For threats from a Saxon brewer's boy
> We just won't give a rap.
> O we are all ex-servicemen,
> We fought against the Hun.
> We can tell our enemies by now,
> And Brocket, you are one!'

> When he heard these words that noble peer
> Turned purple in the face.
> He said, 'These Scottish savages
> Are Britain's black disgrace.
> It may be true that I've let some few
> Thousand acres go to pot,
> But each one I'd give to a London spiv,
> Before any Goddam Scot!'

The ballad ends with an optimistic look to the future:

> You may scream and shout, Lord Brocket –
> You may rave and stamp and shout,
> But the lamp we've lit in Knoydart
> Will never now go out.
> For Scotland's on the march, my boys –
> We think it won't be long.
> Roll on the day when The Knoydart Way
> Is Scotland's battle song.
>
> (Henderson, 2000: 128–30)

Ben Greene and Cambridge University Press

This is another individual case of interest. Ben Greene gave up all political commitments from the Fifties onwards once the CRA and the BPP had folded. From then on he single-mindedly concentrated on developing the industrial firm Kepston, which he had run since the 1930s, but which had suffered from some neglect on his part during the war period. Though his business was 'dogged by financial crises and haunted by creditors', in the 1950s he did in fact invent a new kind of furnace (The Kepston Hydrogen Furnace), which was a great success (years later, in the twenty-first century, this achievement was still being praised by Kepston on its website), but he was such a poor businessman that the business still teetered constantly on the verge of bankruptcy (Lewis, 2010: 377).

As the years went by, he became obsessively convinced that he had been seriously wronged in relation to his pre-war and wartime activities, having by now persuaded himself that he had never in any respect been pro-Nazi. He was also aware of the harm that had been done to his reputation. (As Beckett pointed out in 1945, 'Ben Greene will never get anywhere in public life with the reputation he has') (TNA KV 1518). His family believed him to be suffering from a form of persecution mania, always seeing plots against himself, and blaming it all on his imprisonment under DR 18B.

In this situation, the appearance in 1977 of Ben Pimlott's book *Labour and the Left in the 1930s* caused him exquisite anguish. In it Pimlott, while praising Greene's activities in the Labour Party in the 1930s, had added the phrase, 'In the end, Greene's pro-Nazi sympathies destroyed him' (Pimlott apparently had no idea that Greene was still alive). When a review appeared in the *Sunday Telegraph* describing Greene as 'a Nazi sympathiser later sent to Brixton under Regulation 18B', Greene was incensed, and threatened libel proceedings against Cambridge University Press (CUP), saying that he had never been a Nazi sympathiser.

His solicitor, while raising a word of warning about the expenses involved and the inevitable uncertainty of the outcome, did initially advise that he considered the statements to be defamatory. Ben Greene thereupon sent him a considerable amount of contemporary material in support (as he thought) of his case. This material raised warning signals, however, to the lawyer, who now wrote to Greene to warn that they might well in the course of proceedings be forced to reveal these documents to CUP. In that case, he felt that CUP's hand would be considerably strengthened, in that Pimlott's words might be considered to be justified. Not only this: he had now seen the record of the 1944 proceedings by Greene against the former Home Secretary Sir John Anderson, and particularly the Attorney General's cross-examination of Greene, in which he felt that the Attorney General had been successful in demolishing Greene's case. On both these counts, he would not advise Greene either to go into court or to proceed with his litigation. There was one ray of hope, however: he sensed that CUP were scared by the prospect of libel proceedings, and he therefore proposed that they should wait and see what CUP's response was to his last letter, before deciding to give up the case (Greene papers, and Lewis, 2010: 469–71).

In the event, amazingly, CUP capitulated without a further shot being fired, and agreed to alter the text, freeze existing stock till this was done, have the existing stocks returned by booksellers, and pay legal costs and compensatory damages, with Pimlott writing an apology in suitable terms to a wide selection of journals. Greene died in the same month as these proceedings came to an end. Pimlott, who knew that he himself was in the right, nevertheless toed the line, accepted the changes and wrote the apology. Years later, he was still smarting at what he had been asked to do (Pimlott, 2001).

Lord Sempill's further financial ventures

It is hardly surprising that Lord Sempill should have continued after the war to pursue various financial ventures, often apparently without thought as to their implications. Some of these were in the media world. For example, he was a director, in 1946, of a film company called Anta Film Productions Ltd. It is interesting that for this directorship he was listed as also being a director of the Anglo-Yugoslav Commercial Syndicate Ltd, because it was involvement in south-eastern Europe that brought him once more to the attention of MI5 – this time, amazingly, because of potential pro-Soviet activity.

For his south-eastern Europe activities Sempill had enlisted the help of his fellow CRA member Major Harry Edmonds. In 1946 on a number of occasions they visited Paris in connection with Sempill's newly founded newspaper there, the *South-East European Observer*, of which the editor was a certain Marcel Mann, and a prominent adviser a certain Stankovitch, both known to MI5 as rather dubious figures on the international political scene. By 1947 it had become clear that this newspaper was producing transparently pro-Soviet propaganda. When challenged about this, Sempill explained that 'the apparent pro-Russian bias observed in the initial numbers of the *South European Observer* [*sic*] was due to the necessity for enabling the paper to be introduced into the Russian zone'. He referred to an earlier conversation he had had with Stankovitch in which the latter 'had pointed out the necessity of starting the paper in this fashion and then, at a later date, toning down the pro-Russian attitudes and gradually introducing the ideas for which the proprietors stood'.

MI5 was puzzled by these developments. What exactly *were* Lord Sempill's current political opinions? How did the known views of the CRA coincide with such a venture? What *were* the 'ideas for which the proprietors stood'? Could it be that a pro-Russian line was being taken in order covertly to launch a new right-wing newspaper? Or were other people responsible for the pro-Russian line, and using Sempill's name as cover?

The reality of the situation seems to have lain in what we have seen as a constant in Sempill's behaviour. An MI5 operative, expressing scepticism with regard to the 'means to an end' argument, pointed out that 'Lord Sempill's only concern was to obtain money from Messrs Benes or Masaryk, and in order to do so it was conceivable that he might try to use the Soviets in some way' (TNA KV 2/874).

Whatever the truth of this interpretation, there is little doubt that, while he held strong political views, Sempill was prepared to adapt them to commercial interests. His post-war activities thus differ little from those he had undertaken earlier.

Life goes on

By the nature of things, most previously pro-Nazi figures were lost from sight in the post-war situation, to the extent that any attempt to examine their reactions to the failure of their previous hopes is bound, as in this chapter, to be fragmentary. What is truly amazing, however, even from this limited selection (to which one can add those we have dealt with elsewhere, such as McKie and Coast) is the wide variety of reactions they had.

The emerging post-war extreme Right on the whole attracted a new clientele, and of the pre-1945 activists, it was only a number of lesser figures who played any significant role in the new movements. Some of the more prominent pre-war figures did remain true to their original colours, but with little success. Most other former activists kept a very low profile in the 'anti-fascist' post-war world, eschewing right-wing politics, and devoting themselves to their work or to other interests. George Drummond decided to stay in his exile in the Isle of Man, living in his mansion there, Mount Rule, and selling Pitsford Hall. Lord Sempill continued blithely on his way, trying various moneymaking schemes. Major Harry Edmonds retired into political obscurity once the Constitutional Research Association had faded out, but became influential in a new field when in 1953 he founded the Wagner Society, which still flourishes. Ben Greene devoted himself to his work at Kepston, and tried to forget the past. McKie, and a number of other former Right Club members, continued their parliamentary and political careers, though rarely achieving any distinction. Various landowners returned to running their estates, whether well or badly. The agriculturalists continued their ecological work, and some of them turned to farming in Africa.

These people showed a wide variety of reactions, filling the whole range from being in denial (like Greene) to being unrepentant and unashamed (like Ramsay, Domvile and Gordon-Canning). Some sincerely changed their views; others denied their former activities and lashed out against their former colleagues; others, while retaining their former principles, concentrated on their other related interests. That their pre-1945 experiences had affected almost all of them, there is no doubt. There were of course some, full of self-confidence and conviction of their own worth, who ploughed on with their lives regardless. For others, the experience had been a far more traumatic one.

Bibliography

Books, articles and interviews

Beckett, Francis (1999), *The Rebel Who Lost his Cause: The Tragedy of John Beckett MP* (London: London House).

Campbell, Chloe (2007), *Race and Empire: Eugenics in Colonial Kenya* (Manchester: Manchester University Press).

Carlson, John Roy [Avedis Boghos Derounian] (1951), *Cairo to Damascus* (New York: Alfred Knopf).

Cesarani, David (1989), 'Anti-Zionist Politics and Political Antisemitism in Britain, 1920–24', *Patterns of Prejudice*, 23, 1 (Spring), 28–45.

Domvile, Admiral Sir Barry (1947), *From Admiral to Cabin Boy* (London: The Boswell Publishing Company).

Farson, Daniel (1958), 'People in Trouble: Mixed Marriages' (ITV television programme, featuring James Wentworth Day).

Griffiths, Richard (1998), *Patriotism Perverted: Captain Ramsay, the Right Club and British Anti-Semitism 1939–40* (London: Constable).

Henderson, Hamish (2000), 'Ballad of the Men of Knoydart', in *Collected Poems and Songs*, ed. Raymond Ross (Edinburgh: Curly Snake Publishing), pp. 128–30 (reprinted by permission of the Estate of Hamish Henderson).

Jefferies, Matthew and Tyldesley, Mike (2011), 'Introduction', *Rolf Gardiner: Folk, Nature and Culture in Interwar Britain* (Farnham: Ashgate).

Lees-Milne, James (2006), *Diaries 1942–1954* (London: John Murray).

Lewis, Jeremy (2010), *Shades of Greene: One Generation of an English Family* (London: Jonathan Cape).

Macklin, Graham (2007), *Very Deeply Dyed in Black: Sir Oswald Mosley and the Resurrection of British Fascism after 1945* (London and New York: I.B. Tauris).

Macklin, Graham (2009), 'A Fascist "Jihad": Captain Robert Gordon-Canning, British Fascist Antisemitism and Islam', *Holocaust Studies*, 15, 1, 78–100.

Miller, Rory (2008), 'British Arabists, Jewish Refugees and Palestine', in Efraim Karsh and Rory Miller (eds), *Israel at Sixty: Rethinking the Birth of the Jewish State* (London: Routledge).

Moore-Colyer, Richard (2001), 'Rolf Gardiner, English Patriot and the Council for Church and Countryside', *Agricultural History Review*, 49, 2 (2001), 187–209.

Moore-Colyer, Richard (2011), 'Rolf Gardiner, Farming and the English Landscape', in Matthew Jefferies and Mike Tyldesley, *Rolf Gardiner: Folk, Nature and Culture in Interwar Britain* (Farnham: Ashgate, 2011), pp. 95–120.

Pimlott, Ben (1977), *Labour and the Left in the 1930s* (Cambridge: Cambridge University Press).

Pimlott, Ben (2001), conversation with Richard Griffiths.

Pitchford, Mark (2011), *The Conservative Party and the Extreme Right, 1945–75* (Manchester: Manchester University Press).

Portsmouth, The Earl of (1965), *Knot of Roots: An Autobiography* (London: Geoffrey Bles).

Ramsay, A.H.M. (1952), *The Nameless War* (London: The Britons Publishing Society).

Thurlow, Richard (1987), *Fascism in Britain: A History, 1918–1985* (Oxford: Blackwell).

Trzebinski, Errol (2000), *The Life and Death of Lord Erroll: The Truth Behind the Happy Valley Murder* (London: Fourth Estate).

Waugh, Evelyn (1982), *The Letters of Evelyn Waugh*, ed. Mark Amory (London: Weidenfeld and Nicolson, 1980; London: Penguin Books, 1982).

Documents

The National Archives (TNA)

CO 733/372/11, CO 733/3398/9
FO 1022/4
KV 2/837, KV 2/838, KV 2/874, KV 2/1518, KV 2/1519, KV 2/2245

National Maritime Museum (NMM)

Admiral Domvile's Diary, DOM 58

In the possession of Mr Edward Greene

Papers of Ben Greene (Greene)

Newspapers and journals

Gothic Ripples (GR)
National Weekly (NW)
Sunday Pictorial (SP)
The Times

CONCLUSION

'Ah yes! I remember it well.' The whole point of this song of Maurice Chevalier's, in the film *Gigi*, was that he in fact remembered everything inaccurately. We all do, at times. It is a feature of human existence that our memories of the past tend to be misleading. Our minds have ordered what was disordered, and in the process have changed the original reality. How often does one discover, when reading old letters, that the past is not just a 'foreign country', but also one in which the landscape has over the years become purely imaginary.

In the case of a number of the pre-war enthusiasts for Nazi Germany, their apparent obfuscation of their past may of course have been caused by this innocent process, of which one of the best examples is the change in people's perceptions of Hitler. The Hitler myth had changed so radically between the Thirties and the post-war period that it is hardly surprising that people should find themselves believing that they had held the same views in the Thirties as they now did in the post-war world. Those who, bowled over by Hitler's charisma, had in the Thirties described him as having had a 'human, pleasant personality' with 'artistic, visionary tendencies' and 'a strong strain of sadness and tenderness in his disposition' were by 1957 convinced that they had always been aware of 'his neurotic character and limited perceptions'. Many of those who had enthusiastically attended Nuremberg rallies, and who had extolled at the time 'the human side of Hitler', were convinced, after the war, by the new stereotype of 'the mad Hitler', and wrote their memoirs accordingly, describing 'those strange mad eyes, lit up by a fanatical glare', which made 'a cold shudder' run over them.

Many of the people we have been studying in this book seem to have suffered from similar amnesia. But was this the result of a similar natural process? Did, for example, John Hamilton McKie really believe, in 1945, that he had always been a supporter of Winston Churchill? And did Ben Greene truly believe that he had never undertaken pro-Nazi activities? In both these cases there may indeed have been a certain element of self-delusion. But one must bear in mind that such beliefs could also serve a purpose, that of self-exculpation. One finds a similar syndrome in France, where it was amazing to discover, from 1944 onwards, how many people had been members of the Resistance 'dès la première heure'.

In most cases it is clear that later accounts were consciously intended to muddy the waters. This was particularly true of those who had broadcast for the Nazis, whose later explanations for their actions tended to be specious and detailed, but were often belied by the actual contemporary documents. Part of the enjoyment of writing this book has consisted in the unravelling of the truth from a tangle of often misleading information.

This study has also given us some insight into the wide range of motives that had originally brought so many of these people to their pro-Nazism in the pre-war period. At the one extreme we have those whose mental background predisposed them to extreme views: Henry Wicks, for example, whose persecution mania found an explanation for his woes in the machinations of the Jews; or the Duke of Bedford, whose horrendous upbringing and deprivation of normal human relationships, combined with his ingrained aristocratic belief in the rightness of all he did, produced a single-minded pursuit of his ends despite unpopularity and the danger of imprisonment. Their contemporaries clearly saw a number of such people as being unbalanced: for example, Mosley qualified Aubrey Lees as 'absolutely certifiable', and Ibn Saud described H. St John Philby to the British Government as being 'mentally deranged'. And there were a number of other people whom readers of this book may well have perceived to have suffered from one form or another of psychiatric illness. Alongside these people, however, there were many others whose anti-Semitic and pro-Nazi views were a rational product of their major beliefs, many of which were apparently logical even if severely misguided: the monetarists, convinced of the sinister designs of 'International Money Power', and of Nazi Germany's stand against that force (which had therefore caused the Jews to foment war against Germany); the eugenicists, obsessed with the dangers to the British race of alien blood and miscegenation; the pro-Arabists, many of whom held not just anti-Zionist, but also anti-Semitic views; and the 'back-to-the-landers', wary of the encroachments of that modern industrial society which had been created by 'alien breeds', and looking for the blend of blood and soil which would recreate a healthy society.

Alongside these more extreme figures there had also been a far larger number of basically well-meaning people who were prepared to see merely what appeared to be good in the German experiment, and conveniently to ignore other less savoury aspects. Such figures admired the new 'self-respect' of the German nation, and saw in its 'economic miracle' an example to be followed by our own 'declining' nation. There were, too, many who saw in Nazi Germany the only bulwark against the Bolshevist threat. And, finally, there were those who, after the experience of the First World War, were convinced of the need for peace, and who were prepared to believe in Hitler's goodwill, and in what they saw as the British Government's determination to give Germany a bad name.

Given such a wide range of motives and beliefs, it is hardly surprising that in the wartime situation we should be faced by an equally varied array of reactions to the new circumstances that faced the pro-Nazi Right. Some continued with their original views, and even tried to form groups dedicated to them, though by the nature of things, amid the widespread anti-fascism of wartime Britain they had to be fairly circumspect. Others, while still holding the same ideas as before, found that their pre-war balance between patriotism and pro-Nazism had now tipped firmly on the side of patriotism; they were able fully to support the war effort, though some of them nevertheless still maintained their old views privately. And other figures, such as the 'back-to-the-landers', whose pro-Nazism had been a concomitant of more deeply-ingrained ecological concerns, continued with those basic concerns while in many cases their pro-Nazi views faded into the background. Other people found that events had sincerely made them change their views. And then there were those who, frightened by the prospect of detention or disgrace, tried to hide or even to deny their former views by a variety of subterfuges.

These are, however, merely convenient generalisations which hide a multitude of other variations. If, for example, we take the broadcasters from Germany, they might seem to fit easily into the category of pre-war Hitler fans who continued as pro-Nazi activists. Yet, as we have seen, they had had a wide variety of motives, and their activities mirrored that variety. Similarly, our study of individual 'back-to-the-landers' has shown just how varied their reactions were, from Norman Hay's continued activism to Lymington's initial denials of involvement (followed by tentative reinvolvement in extremist groups), to Yeats-Brown's patriotic stance (coupled with continued admiration for 'what was good' in Nazism), to Rolf Gardiner's sincere reassessment of Nazi Germany, and finally to John Coast's complete reversal of his original attitudes – one of the most remarkable of our case histories.

So the cocktail of motives within each individual was so personal that very few generalisations are possible. What does emerge, however, is that often the same variety of motives and attitudes had existed within these same people from the very start of their infatuation with Nazism, and that the seeds of their wartime behaviour were already within them. In that sense, this book provides us with answers to questions about pre-war pro-Nazism that we had never thought of asking.

One thing that leaps out of this series of case studies is just how different the society of the Thirties and Forties was from our own age. It was a society where class really mattered; where some upper-class figures could behave as though their actions and opinions could not be questioned (and, indeed, believed in their divine right to express such opinions and undertake such actions); where the authorities compounded this by making special allowance for them; where the deprivation of shooting rights on a Scottish estate could be seen as a major punishment; where the lower classes knew their place, and the middle classes were not sure of theirs. It was, of course, a society that was already under threat. The landed classes had come out of the First World War decimated by deaths on the Western Front, threatened by taxation and loss of assets, but above all questioned in many of their assumptions, amid a society in change. The attitudes of a number of them appear to have stemmed from nostalgia for a more perfect past, and from fear of a more uncertain future – the latter fortified by their reactions to the Russian Revolution. The threat of Bolshevism underlay much of the enthusiasm for Nazi Germany in this period.

Society as a whole has now moved on, in a way that is epitomised by the strangeness, to our modern ear, of the 'BBC accents' we hear on old newsreels. It would be foolish, of course, to deny the fact that the arrogance of wealth and position continues to exist. It is, however, not so widely accepted by the public at large as it appears to have been in the Thirties – and there is no longer the deference which led the authorities and the public to kow-tow to aristocrats and millionaires, and which confirmed many of the latter in their own estimate of their worth.

The other major social change that has taken place is in attitudes to race. In the Thirties and Forties a casual social anti-Semitism permeated society. Though seen as innocuous in itself, it formed a social cushion on which far more dangerous anti-Semitic attitudes could flourish. This form of casual racism has now almost entirely disappeared. The example of the Holocaust has brought home to people its dangers. And again, while one cannot deny that racism continues to exist, its main public expression tends now to be restricted to the more disreputable extremist groups. While a considerable number of people may still harbour such feelings, they are rarely put into words for public consumption, as in the Thirties. It is not just our legal system that has tended to outlaw the expression of racist views; it is the tenor of society itself.

One would be tempted to classify pro-Nazism as just one further example of the difference between the Thirties and the post-war world. From our standpoint, such enthusiasm for a vicious, inhumane regime appears incomprehensible. Yet it was widespread. While Fascism as such had little political future in interwar Britain, pro-Germanism, and the concomitant mistrust of French attitudes, were so important a part of public opinion that they did exert some influence upon British foreign policy.

One would be wrong, however, to classify pro-Nazism in this way, as a mere product of the Thirties. As we have seen in so many examples of pre-war and wartime behaviour, political attitudes were on the whole dictated by contingent fears, by knee-jerk reactions to non-existent threats or by admiration for non-existent virtues. Such basic human attitudes are constant, and in no way peculiar to one time or place. As I have said, in my book *Fellow Travellers of the Right*:

> It is easy for us to be superior when looking at the mistakes of the Thirties. We can see the whole picture, and we are far from the emotions which created the block reactions. Yet we have no cause to be smug. It is a constant factor in human nature that we consider personalities rather than events, take one side 'because of the people on the other side', discount features that should dismay us in the behaviour of 'our own side' if other factors appear of more importance. It takes almost superhuman virtue to view each situation as though it were unrelated to any other, and judge it on its merits alone. This may be stating the obvious, but it cannot be said too often.
>
> (Griffiths, 1980: 378)

Taking this into account, what may the future hold for us? Is there any danger of old attitudes recurring here in Britain, or in Europe in general? Some of the spurs to political extremism, which were present in the Thirties, do seem to be with us once more: a general disillusionment with parliamentary government and with professional politicians; severe austerity after an economic crisis; a fear of immigration and of racial minorities; and a search for 'authentic' politics, whether of Right or Left, which can lead to over-simplified and potentially dangerous solutions being proposed for what are essentially complex problems.

Sixteen years ago, writing about fascism and neo-fascism in my book *An Intelligent Person's Guide to Fascism* (Griffiths, 2000: 147), I ventured the view that such movements no longer presented a serious danger, and that 'appeals to racism, and exploitations of fears about mass immigration, which are the main stock-in-trade of movements such as these, do not in most countries touch a large enough percentage of the population to give them any real prospect of power'. In response to this, the Marxist writer Ian Birchall wrote me a thoughtful letter in 2000, in which he prophetically pointed to the way in which changes to the fabric of society, such as economic crisis or climate change, might give rise to a very different situation:

Conclusion **311**

At the moment they [the extreme Right] have mainly a nuisance value, though they give comfort and encouragement to individuals (probably not under their direct control) who want to make physical attacks on blacks or asylum-seekers. But in the event of serious economic crisis and rising unemployment they could grow very quickly. And if global warming produces massive population movements, the appeal of fascist/nationalist rhetoric will be very strong. [...] I think your appeal for 'constant vigilance' is entirely justified.

Ian's warning is, in our present situation, a timely one.

APPENDIX

Rogues' gallery

The principal protagonists in our story are described fully in the chapters concerned with them. There are, however, a number of other figures who regularly recur in the text, and it has seemed worthwhile to give explanatory details on some of them in this Appendix.

Allen, 'Commandant' Mary (1878–1964)

Allen was a leading suffragette in the years before the First World War. In 1914 she joined the Women's Police Service (WPS), later renamed the Women's Auxiliary Service (WAS), of which she became Commandant in 1920. During the 1926 General Strike, the WAS was involved in strike-breaking. Throughout the inter-war period Allen travelled widely abroad, wearing her police uniform, often being taken by the foreign authorities to be a representative of the Metropolitan Police or of the British Government. These activities were frowned on by the British authorities. She met many of the dictators and other fascist leaders: Mussolini, Franco, Hitler, Degrelle, O'Duffy, Goering, and so on. She frequently expressed great admiration for Hitler, from a 1934 visit to Germany onwards, as for example in a speech in late 1934 to the January Club (a front organisation for the British Union of Fascists). Clearly impressed by Mosley, in the late Thirties she wrote for British Union newspapers and spoke at BU peace rallies, though she did not officially join BU until December 1939. In mid-1940 her internment was considered, but not implemented, as she was seen as comparatively harmless.

Amery, John (1912–1945)

A son of the Conservative MP Leo Amery (later Churchill's Secretary of State for India), and brother of the future Conservative minister Julian Amery, John was a problem child and a troubled adult. He attempted a career in film production, but the companies he set up failed. In 1936 he was declared bankrupt, and went to live in France. There he met the fascist leader of the Parti Populaire Français, Jacques Doriot, and worked with him for a while. By now he was a convinced fascist and anti-Semite. After the fall of France, he remained in Vichy France, and then in 1942 went to Berlin, where he gave a series of pro-Nazi propaganda broadcasts beamed to Britain. In 1943 he proposed, in imitation of Doriot's Légion des Volontaires Français contre le Bolchévisme, the setting-up of a 'Legion of St George' of British soldiers who would fight for Nazi Germany against Soviet Russia. To this end, he visited prisoner-of-war camps to gain volunteers, but with limited success. In late 1944, after a short period in Paris, he went to Italy to support Mussolini's 'Salò Republic'. He was captured by Italian partisans in early 1945, and handed over to the British. He was tried for treason on 18 November 1945, pleaded guilty, and was hanged.

Beckett, John (1894–1964)

Becket was an ILP member whose career started on Hackney Council, 1919–22. He worked closely with Clement Attlee in this period. He then became Labour MP for Gateshead, 1924–9, and Peckham, 1929–31. In 1930 he became notorious because of his act in brandishing the Mace in the House of Commons in protest at the suspension of Fenner Brockway. He stood as an ILP candidate against Ramsay Macdonald's National Government in the 1931 election, and lost his seat. He joined the BUF in 1934, becoming Director of Publications. Sacked by Mosley from this paid job in 1937, he left the party, along with William Joyce, with whom he founded the National Socialist League. He left the NSL in 1938 and became involved with Lord Lymington's British Council against European Commitments and with *New Pioneer,* and then co-founded, in 1939, Tavistock's British People's Party. He was prominent, in the first nine months of the war, in the British Council for a Christian Settlement in Europe. Imprisoned under DR 18B in May 1940, he was not released until October 1943. In early 1945 he joined Tavistock – now the Duke of Bedford – in reviving the British People's Party, which gained some support for a while, but folded at the death of Bedford in 1953.

Booth, Dr Meyrick, B.Sc. (Leeds), D.Phil (Jena) (b. 1883)

An eminent British 'sexologist', he wrote *Women and Society* (1929) and *Youth and Sex* (1932), as well as translating various German texts on the subject, including Gagern's *The Problem of Onanism.* He was strongly opposed to women's rights, and also to birth control (believing, as a firm Protestant, that Catholics were gaining a birth-rate advantage because of Protestant use of contraception). In the Thirties he was described as 'one of the most persistent Nazi apologists in this country', producing numerous articles and letters for *The Patriot, Truth,* the provincial press and many other outlets. Booth and his German wife were in close contact with Admiral Domvile and Ben Greene, and helped in the British People's Party's by-election campaign in July 1939. They were both members of the Right Club.

Bowman, Frederick (1893–1969)

Bowman lived in Liverpool. An eccentric figure, he started out as an actor. In the interwar period he founded the anti-Semitic journal *Talking Picture News,* described by him as having 'run in opposition to a number of Jewish owned cinematograph papers'. Strongly pacifist, he became a close contact of the Marquess of Tavistock, and joined the British People's Party in 1939. He was arrested under DR 18B in 1940. The authorities found much evidence of Tavistock's activities in his possession. He was a troublesome prisoner, founding the 'Frederick

Bowman Freedom League' in Brixton in 1942, and at one stage trying to escape disguised as a clergyman. After his recapture, he went on hunger strike and was forcibly fed. He was then offered conditional release, but refused the terms. The authorities, by now fed up with him, gave him unconditional release, whereupon he sued the prison governor and the Home Secretary in relation to his force-feeding. He appeared as his own advocate, and was unsuccessful. After the war he devoted himself to animal welfare, founding the Animal Service Association. He also became a member of the Order of the Crown of Thorns, an order originally founded by the *episcopus vagans* René Vilatte (1854–1929) aka Mar Timotheus I. This Order is not recognised by the Roman Catholic Church.

Brooks, (William) Collin (1893–1959)

Brooks served in Italy during the First World War, gaining the Military Cross for conspicuous gallantry. A right-wing journalist, in the Thirties he worked with Lord Rothermere (of whom he became a close confidant) in the *Daily Mail* group, and edited the *Sunday Dispatch*, 1935–37. He was a strong backer of appeasement and an admirer of the achievements of Fascist governments; he was also a member of the English Mistery. He engaged in abortive discussions in mid-1939 about co-ordinating 'the scattered efforts' of the 'Right Wing Movement' into a coherent whole. He became editor and chairman of *Truth*, 1940–52, a period in which *Truth* 'indulged lavishly' in anti-Semitism. In the later stages of the war he became involved with Godfrey's British National Party, visiting its offices in Trafalgar Square regularly, and allowing it to reprint, as a pamphlet, an anti-Semitic article of his from *Truth*. He also involved himself in Chesterton's National Front after Victory in 1945.

Burgess, Victor

A member of an East Anglian farming family, who joined the BUF at the time of its anti-tithe campaign in that area, he was briefly interned in 1940 under DR 18B, and then served for a very short time in the Army, but was discharged owing to possession and distribution of subversive literature. In 1944–5 he joined Jeffrey Hamm's League of Ex-Service Men and Women, but soon left it to form the Union of British Freedom, taking a major part in the 1947 anti-Semitic riots. In 1948 he brought the UBF into Mosley's Union Movement.

Carroll, Cola Ernest (1896–1957)

Carroll was born in Tasmania. His father was a Briton of Swiss origin, Fritz Joseph Ernst, and his mother Edith Emily (née Carroll). His original name was Fritz Philip Nicola Ronald Ernst. In the First World War, as Cola Ernest Carroll, he served in the artillery and was badly wounded in 1916. He then joined the Royal Flying Corps, was shot down and captured, and escaped. A very capable journalist, after the war he lived in London and edited the British Legion paper. In 1936 he founded the *Anglo-German Review*, a monthly journal devoted to fostering Anglo-German relations, which gradually produced more and more pro-Nazi and anti-Semitic material. In July 1937 he joined Admiral Domvile in founding The Link, and he served on its Council. After the outbreak of war The Link was officially disbanded. Carroll continued his pro-German activity for a short while, but after that lapsed into comparative obscurity. In June 1940 he was arrested under DR 18B and sent to Brixton prison. After the war he farmed in Suffolk.

Chesterton, Arthur Keith (1899–1973)

A cousin of G.K. Chesterton, A.K. had a distinguished career in the First World War, being awarded the Military Cross at the age of twenty. A journalist, he joined the BUF in 1935, becoming in Skidelsky's words 'the BUF's best polemicist'. He was strongly anti-Semitic. In 1937 he produced a very favourable biography of Mosley entitled *Portrait of a Leader*. In 1938, after a disagreement with Mosley, he left BU. By late 1938, after a brief association with the National Socialist League, he became editor of Lymington's *New Pioneer*. In May 1939, on the basis of a speech to the Nordic League in which he recommended using lamp posts as 'the only way to deal with the Jew', he agreed to join the Council of the NL 'to advise on propaganda'. At about the same time he joined the Right Club. After the declaration of war, he followed the call of patriotism, and served in the Army until 1944, when he was invalided out. In 1944–5 he attempted to bring the disparate right-wing groups together into a movement called the National Front after Victory, but with little success. In the post-war era he had more success, however, founding the League of Empire Loyalists in 1954, and the National Front in 1967. In 1953 he had founded the long-lasting right-wing journal *Candour*. He was one of the leading figures on the extreme Right in the post-war era.

Collier, Captain Vincent

National propaganda officer and 'principal northern speaker' of the BUF in the early Thirties, Collier took a large part in the movement's attempt to gain support in the North. Along with Joyce, Beckett and McNab. he left the movement in 1937 and joined them in the National Socialist League. Later, he followed Beckett into the British People's Party, and spoke in its by-election campaign in Hythe in July 1939. Earlier, in May, he had joined the Right Club. We now know that he had probably been infiltrating it and other groups on behalf of the Jewish Board of Deputies. He is also reputed to have worked for MI5 (under the pseudonym Hawke). Beckett, probably incorrectly, presumed him to be infiltrating the NSL on behalf of British Union.

Creagh Scott, Lt-Colonel John (d.1957)

Creagh Scott was an Anglo-Irishman who served in the British Army, first in the South African War, in which he was severely wounded, and then in the First World War, where he received the Distinguished Service Order and the Croix de Guerre avec Étoile d'Or. In the interwar period he became a committed anti-Semitic conspiracy theorist; he later published a book entitled *Hidden Government* (1954), which was closely based on the *Protocols of the Elders of Zion*. He combined with this the usual monetary theories, and during the Second World War formed a body called the Service for Economic Action (SEA) which combined monetarism with anti-Semitism. During the war he at one stage undertook talks on behalf of the SEA with representatives of other right-wing bodies including the English Nationalist Association. He later became a keen member of the Constitutional Research Association. He was, in the Fifties, a backer of A.K. Chesterton's journal *Candour*, serving on its Council, and also joined the League of Empire Loyalists, serving on its Executive Committee.

Domvile, Admiral Sir Barry (1878–1971)

Domvile was Director of Naval Intelligence until 1930, then president of the Royal Naval College, Greenwich from 1932 to 1934. He retired in 1936. He had visited Germany in 1935, where he was greatly impressed by Himmler and by the rest of the Nazi leadership. A strong proponent of Anglo-German friendship, in July 1937 he founded The Link. Gradually he became more and more outspoken against the Jews, and in favour of the Nazis, forging contact with most of those on the pro-Nazi Right in Britain. He spoke for the British People's Party at the Hythe by-election in July 1939. During the 'phoney war' he took a major part in the discussions between the various 'patriotic societies', keeping a detailed diary that has been of great value to historians. He was imprisoned under DR 18B in July 1940, and released in July 1943, having while in prison become convinced of the evil powers exerted by 'Judmas', a Judaeo-Masonic conspiracy. He gradually returned to right-wing activity, particularly within the Constitutional Research Association, and after the war continued with his conviction of the virtues of Nazism and the evils of the Jews, though he took only a minor part in the extremist organisations that had emerged.

Douglas, Major C.H. (1879–1952)

Douglas was a British engineer and monetary reformer who developed the system known as Social Credit, which gained widespread support. A political party, the Social Credit Party, even achieved power in the Canadian state of Alberta. Social Credit was not purely a financial philosophy, but also, as with so many other monetary doctrines, tended towards a belief in the dangerous Jewish forces behind capitalism. Douglas developed his views on the 'Jewish plot' in his many writings, and in particular in his books *Social Credit* (1924) and *The Big Idea* (1942). One commentator, John Irving, has described Social Credit thus:

> A monetary theory which both 'explains' the inner workings of the capitalistic financial system and offers a remedy for its unsatisfactory functioning in periods of depression and inflation, and an interpretation of history in terms of a long-existing Judaic plot or conspiracy to secure control of and dominate the world.
> (Irving, 1959: 4–5)

Interestingly, unlike so many of the anti-Semites who were influenced by him, Douglas himself was not pro-Nazi. He saw Nazism as part of the international Jewish plot, believing that Hitler was a grandson of an illegitimate daughter of Baron Rothschild.

Findlay, Richard

Having served in the Air Force in the First World War, Findlay joined the BUF in 1935, but left almost immediately in order to stand unsuccessfully (as Randolph Churchill's candidate) in the Norwood by-election on the India issue against the official Conservative candidate Duncan Sandys. Remaining closely in contact with Mosley, he also became a member of the Council of the Nordic League, and vice-chairman of the Central London branch of The Link. In 1939 he became a Steward of the Right Club. He was violently anti-Semitic. In a talk to The Link called 'The Hidden Hand in European Affairs' he described 'the influence exerted by the Jews in Europe for many centuries as an evil one', and declared that 'the people of Britain would never fight to uphold usury'. A Scot, and a personal friend of Captain Ramsay, he moved in aristocratic circles not just in Scotland, but also in Sussex and other parts of England, and regarded himself as socially a cut above most of his fellow fascists. He was detained under DR 18B.

Francis-Hawkins, Neil (1903–1950)

A salesman of surgical instruments, in the 1920s Francis-Hawkins was a leading figure in Rotha Lintorn-Orman's British Fascists (BF). In 1932, after attempting unsuccessfully to negotiate a merger between the BF and Mosley's British Union of Fascists (which was rejected by the BF's Council), he joined the BUF, taking many members with him and effectively splitting the BF, which never recovered. In the BUF he swiftly became indispensable to Mosley, who in 1936 appointed him his second-in-command with the title of Director-General of Organisation. In the 'phoney war' he was active in (unsuccessful) attempts to forge the various right-wing groups into a coherent body under Mosley's leadership. Detained under DR 18B in mid-1940, he remained in prison until 1944. Having suffered increasingly bad health, he died in 1950 at the age of 47.

Fuller, Major-General J.F.C. (1878–1966)

Fuller was an outstanding military theorist, whose revolutionary theories of tank warfare were to be of great influence. He was also a strong anti-Semite (believing in a Jewish desire for world domination) and an enthusiast for 'firm government'. On his retirement in 1933, he became a member of the BUF, and was one of Mosley's closest collaborators on the party's Policy Directorate. He also regularly visited Germany, and came to know many of the Nazi party's leading figures. In the run-up to war, he took part in many pro-Nazi activities and meetings, and in April 1939, shortly after the invasion of Prague, he attended Hitler's birthday celebrations in Berlin as an honoured guest. During the 'phoney war' he continued to be conspicuous in pro-Nazi and anti-war circles. He was not arrested under DR 18B, but 'kept his head down' for a while after May 1940. From 1942 onwards, however, we find him once more involved in various subversive movements, including Godfrey's British National Party and the Constitutional Research Association.

Glasgow, 8th Earl of (Patrick James Boyle) (1874–1963)

Glasgow was a prominent Scottish peer, who had a distinguished career in the Royal Navy until his retirement in 1919. He held extreme right-wing views, often ascribed to his experience of Bolshevik atrocities in Archangel in 1917. He joined a number of right-wing movements, starting in the 1920s with Rotha Lintorn-Orman's British Fascists and then General Blakeney's Loyalists. In the 1930s he was a member of the January Club (a front for the BUF), the Anglo-German Fellowship and other similar bodies. He was president of the Christian Defence Movement, an extremist anti-Bolshevik group, and was obsessed with the virtues of Hitler and the Nazis as a bulwark against communism. In 1938, after a visit to Germany, he made a number of speeches in which he strongly praised the regime.

Gordon-Canning, Captain Robert (1888–1967)

Born of a landed family in Hartpury, Gloucestershire, and a grandson on his mother's side of the South Wales entrepreneur Crawshay Bailey, Gordon-Canning was a very rich man and generous to his associates. In the First World War he served in the cavalry, and was awarded a Military Cross for gallantry. In the early 1920s he revealed himself as a committed pro-Arabist, and a supporter of Abd-el-Krim's cause in the Riff War. In 1934 he joined the BUF, and soon became its expert on foreign affairs. In October 1936 he was best man at Mosley's secret wedding to the Hon. Diana Guinness, held at Joseph Goebbels's Berlin home in the presence of Adolf Hitler. In 1939, after a disagreement with Mosley, he left the movement, and in May joined the British People's Party. During the 'phoney war' he was a leading figure in the British Council for a Christian Settlement in Europe. He was arrested under DR 18B in July 1940, and remained in custody until 1943. Both before and after the Second World War he showed a strong interest in Palestine, his pro-Arabism being combined with strong anti-Semitism.

Hamilton, Gerald (1890–1970)

'A viscerally anti-Semitic, antediluvian die-hard Conservative, Roman Catholic and occultist' (Macklin, 2007: 98), Hamilton was the original for Mr Norris in Christopher Isherwood's *Mr Norris Changes Trains* (1935). In 1940 he had, with the complicity of Monsignor Barton Brown, attempted to get to Dublin, the aim being to arrange Anglo-German negotiations, possibly through the Vatican. After being refused an exit permit, he set off disguised as a nun in a party of French nuns. He was, however, arrested at Euston station before he could depart, and spent six months in Brixton prison. He was introduced to Mosley in 1946 by Enid Riddell. In 1948 he acted as Mosley's emissary to various potential funders of the Union Movement in the United States.

Hamm, Jeffrey (1915–92)

A schoolteacher who joined the BUF in 1935, in 1939 Hamm took a teaching job in the Falkland Islands. There, because his teaching and other activities were seen as subversive, he was arrested in 1940 under DR 18B, and sent to prison in South Africa. He returned to the UK in 1941 and joined the Tank Regiment, but owing to disruptive behaviour he was discharged in 1944. The same year he took over, and transformed, the British League of Ex-Service Men and Women. The League saw much street-fighting, and played a major part in the anti-Semitic riots of 1947. In 1948 Hamm incorporated it into Mosley's Union Movement (UM). He became Mosley's right-hand man, and when Mosley retired in 1973 he took over the UM, relaunching it as the Action Party.

Houston, Richard A. ('Jock') (b. 1903)

A house painter and street bookmaker with a criminal record, he joined the BUF in the early Thirties, becoming a very popular speaker to East End audiences, mixing Cockney humour with crude political anti-Semitism. The resultant increase in East End membership caused him to be appointed to the paid staff of BUF speakers. In 1936, when police proceedings against him led to publicity being given to his criminal record, the movement attempted to move him to Manchester, but after pressure from the Manchester police and the local Jewish community he was redeployed to South Wales. He was expelled from British Union in October 1936. He continued, however, to be active wherever the public expression of violent sentiments might be needed. In 1939 he founded the Nationalist Association, whose street activities continued well after the outbreak of war. In mid-1939 he became a member of the Right Club. After the outbreak of war he continued as one of the few remaining active members of the Right Club, and also took part, as a representative of Captain Ramsay, in a number of the discussions between right-wing movements that took place at that time. In May 1940 a warrant was issued under DR 18B for Houston's arrest. He evaded capture for some time, but was arrested in December.

Jenks, Jorian (1899–1963)

Born in Oxford, the son of an academic lawyer, Jenks trained as a farmer. He went to New Zealand in the 1920s, then returned to England, where he farmed in Sussex, but eventually had to give up the farm owing to the slump in agricultural prices. He attempted to earn a living as a writer, and joined the BUF, becoming its leading agricultural adviser and speaker. He saw the BUF as a force for forward-looking agricultural policies, but also subscribed fully to its vision of a need for strong government, sharing its view of the Jews as a force for evil in society. During the 'phoney war' he continued to rail against Britain's involvement in a 'Jews' War'. He was imprisoned under DR 18B, and released in 1941, returning to farming in Sussex. After the war he became a leading light in the Soil Association and the Rural Reconstruction Association, continuing to campaign for organic methods of farming.

Joyce, William (1906–46)

Joyce was born in New York of Irish parents, the family returning to Ireland a few years later. Strongly Unionist, as a teenager he aided the Black and Tans, and became a target of the IRA. He left hastily for England, where he eventually studied at Birkbeck College, gaining First Class Honours. In the 1920s he worked for a time for the British Fascists, and stewarded Conservative Party meetings (his face being severely scarred as a result of a fracas at one such meeting). In 1932 he joined the BUF, and swiftly became one of the movement's most accomplished (and violent) orators. In 1934 he became the BUF's

Director of Propaganda. In 1937 he was sacked from this post by Mosley. He and John Beckett left Mosley's movement, and formed, with Scanlon, McNab and others, the National Socialist League. He and Beckett also joined Lord Lymington's British Council against European Commitments, Joyce as vice-president and Beckett as secretary. In 1939 Joyce and his wife left for Germany just before war broke out. There he became, as 'Lord Haw-Haw', the leading Nazi broadcaster to the British public. He was captured by Allied troops on 28 May 1945, and brought to trial at the Old Bailey later that year for high treason. Though his defence stressed the fact that he was not a British citizen, he had fraudulently applied for a British passport in the Thirties, and this sealed his fate, He was hanged on 3 January 1946.

Kitson, Arthur (1859–1937)

Kitson was a monetary theorist, who believed that control of money was the key to power, and that the Jews held control of money. He became a member of the far-Right movement the Britons, and had a profound influence on a neighbour of his in Lincolnshire, Arnold Leese, whom he introduced to *The Protocols of the Elders of Zion*. Leese was later to found the Imperial Fascist League.

Laurie, Arthur Pillans (1861–1949)

An academic chemist who pioneered the use of chemical analysis on paintings to reveal deeper layers of paint, Laurie was Principal of Heriot-Watt College, Edinburgh, from 1900 to 1928. In the late Thirties he became a keen pro-Nazi, joining The Link (of which he was a member of the Council). He published in 1939 *The Case for Germany*, a paean of praise for Nazi Germany, to which Admiral Domvile (a close friend of his) wrote an introduction. It was published in Berlin, and was used by Nazi propagandists, who sent copies to British supporters. An article he published in *Action* on 2 September 1939, inciting British troops to desert rather than fight the Germans in a 'Jews' War', caused embarrassment to Mosley and BU once war was declared. During the 'phoney war' he attended a number of the meetings that brought together representatives of the various 'patriotic societies'.

Leese, Arnold (1878–1956)

A veterinary surgeon specialising in the diseases of camels, after twenty years in India and Africa Leese settled down to a practice in Stamford, retiring in 1927. In Stamford, he came under the influence of Arthur Kitson, who introduced him to *The Protocols of the Elders of Zion*. After a short period in the British Fascists (which he described as 'merely Conservatism with Knobs on' (Leese, 1951: 50)), he founded in 1929 the Imperial Fascist League (IFL), which was initially on the Italian model, though by 1931 it had rejected Mussolini (whom it considered to be under Jewish control), and had turned to the Nazis for inspiration. Leese developed a close friendship with the Nazi anti-Semite Julius Streicher. The IFL tried unsuccessfully to compete with Mosley, whom Leese described as a 'Kosher Fascist' because he 'did not attempt to face the Jewish issue'. The IFL, though its membership was small, was perhaps the most extreme of the extremist movements in this period, and was devoted to the doctrines of Nazi Germany (Mosley described it as 'one of those crank little societies […] crazy about the Jews'). During the war, however, Leese differed from a number of his supporters in that he denounced the Nazi–Soviet Pact and Hitler's invasion of Norway. A warrant was issued for his arrest under DR 18B in June 1940, but, protesting his patriotism, he succeeded in evading capture, through various hide-outs, until November of that year. He was released in 1944.

Lintorn-Orman, Rotha (1895–1935)

Lintorn-Orman came of a military family, and during the First World War served in an ambulance unit in Serbia. In 1923, at the age of twenty-eight, she founded the 'British Fascisti', later to be called the 'British Fascists' (BF). While her instincts were essentially Conservative, she had a great admiration for Mussolini and his methods, and was acutely aware of a danger from Communism, against which she wanted the BF to be a bulwark. The BF gained quite a lot of support from Military, Naval and 'County' figures, while also tapping in to working-class loyalists, and had a considerable amount of support in the late Twenties. British Fascism was in no way revolutionary, however, and was soon supplanted by more radical movements, the most successful of which was Mosley's British Union of Fascists (BUF). In early 1932 the New Party (predecessor of the BUF) approached the BF with a view to a possible merger. Though many of the leading BF members were in favour, Lintorn-Orman and others voted them down. Some of the most active members left to join what was to be launched as the British Union of Fascists in October. The BF battled on for a further three years, but was hampered by Lintorn-Orman's growing alcoholism and reliance on drugs. In May 1935 she died at the age of forty, and in September 1935 the BF was finally wound up.

Ludovici, Captain Anthony (1882–1971)

Born in London of a naturalised British father, Ludovici was a keen Nietzschean who wrote extensively on Nietzsche, and was imbued with the vision of a master race that must be maintained and enhanced through the 'science' of eugenics. In the First World War he served as an artillery officer from 1914 to 1916, and then on the Intelligence staff at the War Office, becoming in 1918 Head of the Department MI6 A. He was known to his acquaintances as 'the Captain' and to his friends as 'Ludo'. In the interwar period, he acted as a kind of guru for the eugenically-minded 'back-to-the-landers', and in particular Lymington and Hay. He was a founder member of Sanderson's English Mistery (Sanderson stressing how much was owed to his 'inspiration'), and later followed Lymington into the English Array. In 1938 he published, under the pseudonym of 'Cobbett', a strongly anti-Semitic book entitled *Jews, and the Jews in England*. In the first months of the Second World War, he was amazingly taken on again to work in Intelligence, but was dismissed in August 1940. His house was raided, and on 9 October he was interviewed, but then released as, despite his extreme views, no evidence could be found of any actual untoward activities. Far more hurtful to him was his blackballing that year when applying for membership of the Travellers' Club. He retired in 1941 to farm in Suffolk, where he remained thereafter. At his death in Ipswich in 1971 he bequeathed £70,000 to Edinburgh University for research into miscegenation.

McGovern, John (1887–1968)

McGovern became ILP MP for Glasgow Shettleston at a by-election in 1930. With his fellow ILP members, he withdrew from the Labour Party in 1931. He was a strong proponent of the ILP's pacifist policy. This occasionally led him, in the late 1930s, into strange company. After the outbreak of war, he became a keen member of Tavistock's British Council for a Christian Settlement in Europe, and spoke at its meetings, appearing to share in the pro-Nazi tenor of some of its policies. He was intimately connected with Tavistock's Peace Plan in early 1940, and it was he who broke its details to the press. At about the same time he and his fellow ILP members James Maxton and Campbell Stephen were involved with Lord Beaverbrook in plans for a 'peace campaign' which would put a peace candidate into each of the British constituencies, funded by Beaverbrook. McGovern was undoubtedly a sincere pacifist, who appears to have been 'used' by people more extreme than himself.

McNab, Angus (1906–77)

McNab was a close personal friend of William Joyce, with whom he shared a flat. A member of the BUF, he served in the propaganda department and edited the *Fascist Quarterly*. He left the movement at the same time as Joyce and Beckett in 1937, and joined them in the National Socialist League. He was imprisoned under DR 18B in 1940, and, after the war, settled in Spain.

Mar, 12th Earl of (Walter John Francis Erskine) (1865–1955)

The Earl of Mar was a prominent Scottish peer, and Chancellor of the Order of the Thistle from 1932 to 1949. In the late Thirties he became a keen adherent of Mosley's BU, and a supporter both of Nazi Germany and of the cause of peace. His dual allegiance was typified by Special Branch reports that he went about wearing the Peace Pledge Union badge and at the same time giving the Nazi salute (TNA HO 45/25392). During the 'phoney war' he was an attender at, and a keen participator in, meetings of Norman Hay's Information and Policy group, and also attended a number of the secret meetings of members of the various right-wing groups which sought some kind of joint action.

Mills, H.T. ('Bertie') (b. 1898)

Born in Dublin, educated at Charterhouse and the London School of Economics, Mills was omnipresent in pro-Nazi and anti-Semitic movements, being chairman of the Central London branch of The Link, a Steward of the Right Club and a member of the Imperial Fascist League, the Nordic League and the British Council against European Commitments. He was a regular contributor to *New Pioneer*, and headed the People's Campaign against War and Usury. He was present at most of the gatherings of right-wing activists in the 'phoney war' period.

Oddie, Air Commodore Gerard S. (1896–1985)

Oddie retired from the RAF in 1944. He became chairman of the revived British People's Party in 1945, standing as the British People's Party candidate in the by-election for the Combined British Universities seat in 1946 (obtaining just over one per cent of the vote). He wrote a foreword to Ilse Hess's book *Rudolf Hess: Prisoner of Peace* (translated by Meyrick Booth). He joined the League of Empire Loyalists in 1954.

Philby, H. St John (1885–1960)

Having been a member of the British administration in Baghdad, in 1917 Philby headed a mission to Ibn Saud. He became a strong supporter of Ibn Saud against the claims of the Hashemites. In 1921 he became Head of the Secret Service for the Palestine Mandate, resigning in 1924 over the government's policy in Palestine. He became a major adviser to Ibn Saud, explored much of the interior of the Saudi peninsula and in 1930 converted to Islam. As war approached, he undertook secret negotiations with Germany and Spain, whereby if war came, Saudi Arabia would be able to sell oil to neutral Spain, which would then send it to Germany. In 1939 he returned to Britain, joined the British People's Party and stood at the Hythe by-election on an anti-war (and anti-Jewish) ticket. On 3 August 1940 he was arrested under DR 18B when travelling from Saudi Arabia to Bombay (Ibn Saud having informed the British that Philby, whom he considered to be 'mentally deranged' and violently anti-British, 'wished to travel to India and the USA for the purpose of conducting anti-British propaganda' (TNA FO 371/27270)). Philby was deported to England, where he was briefly interned. He took part in various right-wing activities after his release. His son was the Communist spy Kim Philby.

Ramsay, Captain Archibald Maule ('Jock') (1894–1955)

Ramsay was a Scottish aristocrat, a close relative of the Earl of Dalhousie. He served with distinction in the First World War. In 1931 he became Unionist MP for Peebles. Until around 1937, his parliamentary career was obscure and uneventful. In 1937–8, however, affected by the Spanish Civil War, he formed the United Christian Front, a strongly pro-Franco movement. By now he was obsessed by what he saw as an international Bolshevik plot, and by a belief that it was 'secretly operated and controlled by World Jewry, exactly on the lines laid down in the Protocols of the Elders of Zion' (Ramsay, 1952: 95). As war approached, he became convinced of the virtues of Nazi Germany, and of the Jewish plot to bring Britain to war with that nation, and made a number of public pronouncements on the matter. He belonged to a number of violently anti-Semitic movements, and in particular was a prominent member of the Nordic League. In May 1939 he formed the Right Club, a secret society to co-ordinate the activities of such bodies. After the outbreak of war, he and what was left of the RC undertook a number of fairly innocuous subversive activities, but in May 1940 he was discovered, with Anna Wolkoff, to be implicated in more serious activity, that of the Tyler Kent affair. He was detained under DR 18B on 22 May 1940 (the only Member of Parliament to be imprisoned) and remained in Brixton Prison until 26 September 1944. In 1945 the Peebles constituency deselected him.

Riddell, Enid (1904–80)

Riddell was a woman racing driver and a smart woman-about-town who, like her fellow woman driver Fay Taylour, was attracted to fascism. She took part in the 1937 Le Mans Rally and the February 1939 Paris–San Raphael Rally. A leading member of the Right Club, she was heavily involved with Anna Wolkoff in the Tyler Kent affair in London in 1940. She was interned under DR 18B, and released in 1943. After the war, she continued to mingle in right-wing circles, and took part in private meetings concerning the Palestine situation. She then moved to Malaga, where she opened a club. She competed, with Betty Haig, in the 1954 25th Jubilee of the Paris-San Raphael Rally. In 1973 she had a driving accident in Malaga, in which her passenger Anna Wolkoff was killed. Riddell survived, and died in 1980, aged 76.

Rogers, Captain Arthur

Rogers was a leading figure in the Liberty Restoration League, an association whose commitment to civil liberties masked its underlying anti-Semitism. Special Branch noted that it had close connections with the Nordic League. Rogers wrote a series of anti-Semitic pamphlets, including *The Real Crisis* (1938). Like a number of other anti-Semites, he saw the Palestine situation as a focus for his hatred, as is shown in his pamphlet *The Palestine Mystery: Sidelights on Secret Policy*. During the war he became chairman of the DR 18B Publicity Council. He later joined the Constitutional Research Association.

Scanlon, John

A journalist, formerly member of the ILP, Scanlon joined the BUF in the early Thirties. He later broke with the movement at the same time as John Beckett and William Joyce, and joined their National Socialist League. In 1939 he became a founder member of the British People's Party, alongside his fellow ILP companions Beckett and Ben Greene.

Soddy, Professor Frederick (1877–1956)

Soddy was an eminent academic chemist, recipient of the Nobel Prize in 1921 for his work on the chemistry of radioactive elements, and was Professor of Physical and Inorganic Chemistry in Oxford until his retirement in 1936. In the interwar period he became strongly influenced by Social Credit, eventually producing his own theory of monetary reform, which was dismissed by many as the work of a 'crank'. In 1943 he founded the Honest Money Association, which soon revealed itself as having a right-wing agenda, linking itself with other questionable bodies of pro-Nazi and anti-Semitic nature. His monetary obsession led him, in the immediate post-war period, into prominent membership of the revived British People's Party.

Verdon Roe, Sir Alliott (1877–1958)

Roe was an aircraft engineering pioneer before the First World War, setting up his own aircraft production company, Avro, in 1910. He was knighted for services to aircraft production in 1929. In the interwar period he became more and more disenchanted with democracy and with the capitalist system, and enthusiastic for monetary reform on the model of Kitson and Douglas. He became one of the BUF's most generous financial supporters. During the war he was not interned, and his company was of great value to the war effort. This did not deter him, however, from lending his support to a number of the shady movements that gradually emerged in the later stages of the war, including the British National Party. After the war he became a discreet supporter of Mosley's Union Movement.

Williamson, Hugh Ross (1901–78)

A prolific writer of popular history, in the late Thirties Williamson became a prospective Labour parliamentary candidate. With the approach of war, however, he became convinced that Britain should not go to war. He became associated with British Union, wrote for *Action* and addressed numerous BU meetings, and in 1939 became one of the founder members of the British People's Party. His public expression of his views led to him being obliged to resign his parliamentary candidature. After the outbreak of war he continued to write regularly for *Action*, and addressed public meetings organised by the British People's Party's offshoot the British Council for a Christian Settlement in Europe, as well as speaking to BU groups during the BU Women's Campaign of early 1940. In 1943 he became an Anglican priest. In 1955 he converted to Roman Catholicism, later becoming a strong opponent of the Vatican II reforms.

Wolkoff, Anna (1902–73)

Anna Wolkoff was the daughter of Admiral Nikolai Wolkoff, the Tsar's last Russian naval attaché in London, who remained in Britain with his family after the Revolution, opening the Russian Tea Rooms in South Kensington in 1923. Father and daughter were both strongly anti-Semitic, and in the Thirties became very pro-Nazi. Anna, who had visited Germany in the late Thirties, meeting major Nazi figures, became in 1939 one of those dedicated members of the Right Club who undertook various subversive activities during the 'phoney war' period, and who met regularly at the Russian Tea Rooms. When Tyler Kent started removing important documents from the American Embassy, Anna and Captain Ramsay were both heavily involved. An MI5 'sting' showed Anna to be in contact with William Joyce (now broadcasting from Germany), and also involved in passing documents to the Italian Embassy. She and Kent were arrested on 20 May 1940; she was tried *in camera*, and sentenced to 7 years' imprisonment. Meanwhile her father had been arrested under DR 18B, and spent a large part of the war in Brixton prison alongside Ramsay, Domvile, and so on. Anna was stripped of her British citizenship in 1943, and left prison in 1947, moving to Spain, where she renewed her friendship with Enid Riddell. In 1973 she died in an accident, in a car driven by Riddell.

BIBLIOGRAPHY

Unpublished sources

The National Archives, Kew (TNA)

Cabinet Papers: classes CAB 65, CAB 66
Central Criminal Court Records: class CRIM 1
Colonial Office Files: class CO 733
Foreign Office Files: classes FO 371, FO 800, FO 1022
Home Office Files: classes HO 45, HO 144, HO 262, HO 283
Metropolitan Police Office Files: class MEPO 3
Ministry of Information Files: class INF 1
Prime Minister's Files: classes PREM 1, PREM 5
Special Operations Executive Files: class HS 9
Treasury Solicitor's Files: class TS 27
MI5 Files: classes KV 2, KV 4

Caird Archive and Library, National Maritime Museum (NMM)

The papers of Admiral Sir Barry Domvile:
DOM 56, 57, 58 (Diary)
DOM 84 (Typescript of *From Admiral to Cabin Boy*)

Liddell Hart Centre for Military Archives, King's College London (LHCMA)

The papers of Sir Arthur Bryant:
C/63 (Correspondence, Duchess of Atholl)

C/66 (Appeasement correspondence, 1938–9)
C/69 (Correspondence: R.A. Butler, Lord Brocket, Duke of Westminster, Lord Halifax)
C/96 (Correspondence with Macmillan)
C/111 (General Correspondence: Duke of Buccleuch, etc.)
E/10 (Correspondence with individuals)
E/18 (Correspondence with individuals)
E/19 (Correspondence: Rolf Gardiner)
E/39 (Correspondence: Yeats-Brown)
E/51 (Kinship in Husbandry, Anglo-German Fellowship, etc.)
E/60 (Correspondence with individuals)
F 3/a (Correspondence about *Unfinished Victory*)
vf3e
The papers of A.T.O. Lees
The papers of Sir B. Liddell Hart

Selwyn College, Cambridge Library (SCC)

The papers of Henry William Wicks

Trinity College, Cambridge Library (TCC)

The papers of R.A. Butler

Hampshire Record Office (HRO)

The papers of the 9th Earl of Portsmouth

Bodleian Library (Bod.)

The papers of Richard Rapier Stokes MP

In the possession of Mr Edward Greene

The papers of Ben Greene

Newspapers and periodicals

National dailies, weeklies and Sundays

Daily Despatch
Daily Express
Daily Sketch
Daily Telegraph

Evening Standard
Fortnightly Review
Illustrated London News
Manchester Guardian
National Weekly
New English Weekly
New Statesman and Nation
News Review
The Observer
The Spectator
Sunday Express
Sunday Pictorial
Sunday Times
Time and Tide
The Times
Times Literary Supplement

Specialist journals (including religious and political)

Action
Anglo-German Review
Ashridge Journal
The Blackshirt
British News and Views
Catholic Herald
Church of England Newspaper
Everyman
The Free Press
Gothic Ripples
Information and Policy
Jewish Chronicle
Mother Earth
Nature
New Leader
New Pioneer
The Patriot
Peace and Progressive Information Service
Peace Focus
Peace News
People's Post
Public Opinion
Quarterly Gazette of the English Array

Rural Economy
St Martin's Review
Springhead Ring News Sheet
Talking Picture News
Truth
The Week
The Word

Scottish, Welsh and Irish papers

Aberdeen Press and Journal
Galloway Gazette
Galloway News
Glasgow Herald
Irish Independent
The Irish Press
Peeblesshire Advertiser
Perthshire Constitutional
Western Mail

English local newspapers

Birmingham Post
East Anglian Daily Times
Hythe and Sandgate Advertiser
Morecambe and Heysham Visitor
Northampton Chronicle and Echo
Northampton Independent
Northamptonshire Evening Telegraph
The Star (Sheffield)

Foreign newspapers

Der Angriff
New York Times

Books and articles (up to 1945)

Bell, Clive (1938), *Warmongers* (London: PPU).
Booth, Meyrick (1937), *Peace and Power* (Letchworth: Wardman).

Bothamley, Margaret (1937), *A Statement by an Englishwoman about National Socialist Germany (as broadcast from Berlin, October 22nd 1936)* (republished by Steven Books, London, March 2010).

Bothamley, Margaret (1938), 'The Austrian Plebiscite', *The Patriot*, 21 April.

Bryant, Arthur (ed.) (1934), *The Man and the Hour: Studies of Six Great Men of Our Time* ((London: Philip Allan).

Bryant, Arthur (1940), *Unfinished Victory* (London: Macmillan).

'Cobbett' [Anthony Ludovici] (1938), *Jews, and the Jews in England* (London: Boswell Publishing Company).

Cobbold, Lady Evelyn (1934), *Pilgrimage to Mecca* (London: J. Murray).

Edmonds, Major H. (1934), 'Behind Democracy', *Information and Policy*, 9 May.

Galloway, 9th Earl of (1854), *Observations on the Abuse and Reform of the Monitorial System of Harrow School, with Letters and Remarks by the Earl of Galloway* (London: Hatchard).

Gardiner, Rolf (1932), *World Without End: British Politics and the Younger Generation* (London: Cobden-Sanderson).

Gardiner, Rolf (1933), 'Die deutsche Revolution von England gesehen', in Rolf Gardiner, Arvid Brodersen and Karl Wyser (eds), *Nationalsozialismus vom Ausland gesehen: an die Gebildeten unter seinen Gegnern* (Berlin: Die Runde).

Gardiner, Rolf (1938), Review of Lord Lymington, *Famine in England* in *Quarterly Gazette of the English Array*, April).

Gardiner, Rolf (1939), 'Germany and the Baltic States', *New Pioneer*, May.

Greene, Ben (1939), *The Truth about this War*, with an Introduction by John Beckett (London: Research Department of the British People's Party, December). German translation, *Die Wahrheit über diesen Krieg*, 1940.

Grenfell, Captain Russell, RN (1954), *Unconditional Hatred: German War Guilt and the Future of Europe* (New York: Devin-Adair).

Jerrold, Douglas (1933), 'The Corporate State in England', *Everyman*, 13 October.

Joyce, William (1936), *Fascism and Jewry* (London: BUF Publications).

Joyce, William (1937), *National Socialism Now* (preface by John Beckett) (London: National Socialist League).

Joyce, William (1942), *Dämmerung über England* (Berlin: Internationaler Verlag).

Kitson, Arthur (1933), *The Bankers' Conspiracy which Started the World Crisis* (London: Britons).

Laurie, Arthur P. (1939), *The Case for Germany: A Study of Modern Germany* (preface by Sir Barry Domvile) (Berlin: Internationaler Verlag).

Lymington, Viscount (1938), *Famine in England* (London: The Right Book Club).

Morton, J.B. (1933), 'Sleeping England', *Everyman*, 3 November.

Pitt-Rivers, Captain George Lane-Fox (1920), *The World Significance of the Russian Revolution* (Oxford: Blackwell).

Pitt-Rivers, Captain George Lane-Fox (1938), *The Czech Conspiracy: A Phase in the World-War Plot* (London: Boswell Publishing Company).

Pitt-Rivers, Captain George Lane-Fox (1939), *Czecho-Slovakia: The Naked Truth about the World-War Plot* (London: Boswell Publishing Company).

Portsmouth, The Earl of (1943), *Alternative to Death: The Relationship between Soil, Family and Community* (London: Faber and Faber).

The Protocols of the Learned Elders of Zion (n.d.), translated by Victor E. Marsden (London: The Britons Publishing Society).

Rogers, Captain Arthur (1938), *The Real Crisis* (London: Liberty Restoration League).

Rogers, Captain Arthur (n.d.), *The Palestine Mystery: Sidelights on Secret Policy* (London: Sterling Press).

Sanderson, William (1927), *Statecraft* (London: Methuen).

Sempill, Colonel the Master of (1924), 'The British Aviation Mission to the Imperial Japanese Navy', *Journal of the Royal Aeronautical Society*, XXVIII, 553–84.

Tavistock, Marquess of (1940), *The Fate of a Peace Effort* (High Wycombe).

Wicks, Henry William (1940), 'The Distinguished British Patriots, Sir Barry Domvile and Captain G. E. Pitt-Rivers', *British News and Views*, 6 September.

Williamson, Henry (1937), 'Lawrence of Arabia and Germany', *Anglo-German Review*, January.

Williamson, Henry (1941), *The Story of a Norfolk Farm* (London: Faber and Faber).

Yeats-Brown, Francis (1932), 'Why I Believe in War', *The Spectator*, 30 December.

Yeats-Brown, Francis (1934), *Dogs of War!* (London: P. Davies).

Yeats-Brown, Francis (1939a), *European Jungle* (London: Eyre and Spottiswoode).

Yeats-Brown, Francis (1939b), 'Listen, Tommy!', *New Pioneer*.

Books and articles (post-1945)

Aldrich, Richard J. (2000), *Intelligence and the War against Japan: Britain, America and the Politics of Secret Service* (Cambridge: Cambridge University Press).

Anon. (n.d.), 'History of Kepston', www.kepston.co.uk/history.htm.

Bauerkämper, Arnd (1991), *Die 'radikale Rechte' in Grossbritannien* (Göttingen: Vandenhoeck & Ruprecht).

Bearse, Ray and Read, Anthony (1991), *Conspirator: The Untold Story of Churchill, Roosevelt and Tyler Kent, Spy* (London: Macmillan).

Beckett, Francis (1999), *The Rebel who Lost his Cause: The Tragedy of John Beckett MP* (London: London House).

Bedford, Hastings, Duke of (1949), *The Years of Transition* (Edinburgh: Dakers).

Bedford, John, Duke of (1959), *A Silver-Plated Spoon* (London: Cassell).

Bergmeier, Horst and Lotz, Rainer (1997), *Hitler's Airwaves: The Inside Story of Nazi Radio Broadcasting and Propaganda Swing* (New Haven and London: Yale University Press).

Berthezène, Clarisse (2011), *Les conservateurs britanniques dans la bataille des idées: Ashridge College, premier think tank conservateur* (Paris: Sciences Po).

Bolitho, Hector and Peel, Derek (1967), *The Drummonds of Charing Cross* (London: Allen & Unwin).

Bowra, C.M. (1966), *Memories 1898–1939* (London: Weidenfeld and Nicolson).

Boyes, Georgina (2011), 'Potencies of the Earth: Rolf Gardiner and the English Folk Dance Revival', in Matthew Jefferies and Mike Tyldesley (eds), *Rolf Gardiner: Folk, Nature and Culture in Interwar Britain* (Farnham: Ashgate).

Brooks, Collin (1998), *Fleet Street, Press Barons and Politics: The Journals of Collin Brooks, 1932–1940*, ed. N.J. Crowson (London: Royal Historical Society).

Campbell, Chloe (2007), *Race and Empire: Eugenics in Colonial Kenya* (Manchester: Manchester University Press).

Carlson, John Roy [Avedis Boghos Derounian] (1951), *Cairo to Damascus* (New York: Alfred Knopf).

Carpenter, Louise (2004), *An Unlikely Countess: Lily Budge and the 13th Earl of Galloway* (London: Harpercollins).

Ceadel, Martin (1980), *Pacifism in Britain 1914–1945* (Oxford: Clarendon Press).

Cesarani, David (1989), 'Anti-Zionist Politics and Political Antisemitism in Britain, 1920–24', *Patterns of Prejudice*, 23, 1 (Spring), 28–45.

Cesarani, David and Kushner, Tony (eds) (1989), *The Internment of Aliens in Twentieth Century Britain* (London: Routledge).

Clark, Kenneth (1974), *Another Part of the Wood: A Self-Portrait* (London: John Murray).

Coast, John (1946), *Railroad of Death* (London: Hyperion, and ed. Laura Noszlopy, Newcastle upon Tyne: Myrmidon, 2014).

Coast, John (2015), *Recruit to Revolution: Adventure and Politics during the Indonesian Struggle for Independence*, ed. Laura Noszlopy (Copenhagen: NIAS, first published 1952, by Christophers, London).

Cole, J.A. (1964), *Lord Haw-Haw – and William Joyce: The Full Story* (London: Faber and Faber).

Colville, John (1985), *The Fringes of Power: Downing Street Diaries 1939–1955* (London: Hodder & Stoughton).

Conford, Philip (2005), 'Organic Society: Agriculture and Radical Politics in the Career of Gerard Wallop, Ninth Earl of Portsmouth (1898–1984)', *Agricultural History Review*, 53, 1, 78–96.

Cooper, Lady Diana (1953), *The Light of Common Day* (London: Hart-Davis).

Copsey, Nigel and Olechnowicz, Andrzej (eds) (2010), *Varieties of Anti-Fascism: Britain in the Inter-War Period* (Basingstoke: Palgrave Macmillan).

Coupland, Philip (2000), 'The Blackshirts in Northampton, 1933–1940', *Northamptonshire Past and Present*, No. 53.

Dalley, Jan (1999), *Diana Mosley: A Life* (London: Faber & Faber).

Dalton, Hugh (1986), *The Second World War Diary of Hugh Dalton 1940–45*, ed. Ben Pimlott (London: Jonathan Cape).

Dickson, Lovat (1963), *The House of Words* (London, Macmillan).

Doherty, M.A. (2000), *Nazi Wireless Propaganda: Lord Haw-Haw and Public Opinion in the Second World War* (Edinburgh: Edinburgh University Press).

Domvile, Admiral Sir Barry (1947), *From Admiral to Cabin Boy* (London: The Boswell Publishing Company).

Dorril, Stephen (2007), *Blackshirt: Sir Oswald Mosley and British Fascism* (London: Penguin Books).

Eckersley, Myles (1998), *Prospero's Wireless: A Biography of P.P. Eckersley* (Romsey: Myles Books).

Farndale, Nigel (2005), *Haw-Haw: The Tragedy of William and Margaret Joyce* (London: Macmillan).

Farson, Daniel (1958), 'People in Trouble: Mixed Marriages' (ITV television programme, featuring James Wentworth Day).

Forde, Daphne (1998), *A Stick Called Will* (Henley Beach, South Australia: Seaview Press).

Fowler, David (2011), 'Rolf Gardiner: Pioneer of British Youth Culture, 1920–1939' in Matthew Jefferies and Mike Tyldesley (eds), *Rolf Gardiner: Folk, Nature and Culture in Interwar Britain* (Farnham: Ashgate).

Gardiner, Rolf (1972), 'Can Farming Save European Civilisation', reprinted in A. Best (ed.), *Water Springing from the Ground: An Anthology of the Writings of Rolf Gardiner* (Fontell Magna: Springhead Trust).

Gilbert, Mark (1992), 'Pacifist Attitudes to Nazi Germany, 1936–45', *Journal of Contemporary History*, 27, 3, 493–511.

Gilbert, Martin (1966), *The Roots of Appeasement* (London: Weidenfeld and Nicolson).

Goldman, A. (1984), 'The Resurgence of Anti-Semitism in Britain during World War Two', *Jewish Social Studies*, 46, 1, 37–50.

Gottlieb, Julie (2000), *Feminine Fascism: Women in Britain's Fascist Movement 1923–1945* (London and New York: I.B. Tauris).

Green, E.H.H. (2002), *Ideologies of Conservatism* (Oxford: Oxford University Press).

Griffiths, Richard (1980), *Fellow Travellers of the Right: British Enthusiasts for Nazi Germany, 1933–39* (London: Constable).

Griffiths, Richard (1998), *Patriotism Perverted: Captain Ramsay, the Right Club and British Anti-Semitism, 1939–40* (London: Constable).

Griffiths, Richard (2004), 'The Reception of Bryant's *Unfinished Victory*: Insights into British Public Opinion in Early 1940', *Patterns of Prejudice*, 38, 1, 18–36.

Griffiths, Richard (2005), 'A Note on Mosley, the 'Jewish War' and Conscientious Objection', *Journal of Contemporary History*, 40, 4, 675–88.

Griffiths, Richard (2010), 'Anti-Fascism and the Post-War British Establishment', in Nigel Copsey and Andrzej Olechnowicz (eds), *Varieties of Anti-Fascism: Britain in the Inter-War Period* (Basingstoke: Palgrave Macmillan).

Griffiths, Richard (2011), 'The Dangers of Definition: Post-Facto Opinions on Rolf Gardiner's Attitudes towards Nazi Germany', in Matthew Jefferies and Mike Tyldesley (eds), *Rolf Gardiner: Folk, Nature and Culture in Interwar Britain* (Farnham: Ashgate).

Griffiths, Richard (2012), 'G.A.W. Tomlinson and H.W.J. Edwards: Two Tory Writers and the "People's Literature" Movement of the Late Thirties', *Llafur*, 11, 1, 83–108.

Griffiths, Richard (2014), 'Antisemitic Obsessions: The Case of H.W. Wicks', *Patterns of Prejudice* 48, 1, 94–113.

Hamilton, Alastair (1971), *The Appeal of Fascism* (London: Anthony Blond).

Hart, Jenifer (1998), *Ask Me No More: An Autobiography* (London: Peter Halban).

Henderson, Hamish (2000), 'Ballad of the Men of Knoydart', in *Collected Poems and Songs*, ed. Raymond Ross (Edinburgh: Curly Snake Publishing).

Holmes, Colin (1979), *Anti-Semitism in British Society 1876–1939* (London: Edward Arnold).

Holmes, Colin (2016), *Searching for Lord Haw-Haw: The Political Lives of William Joyce* (Abingdon: Routledge).

Irving, John (1959), *The Social Credit Movement in Alberta* (Toronto: Toronto University Press).

Isherwood, Christopher (2000), *Lost Years*, ed. Katherine Bucknell (London: Chatto and Windus).

Jefferies, Matthew (2011), 'Rolf Gardiner and German Naturism', in Matthew Jefferies and Mike Tyldesley (eds), *Rolf Gardiner: Folk, Nature and Culture in Interwar Britain* (Farnham: Ashgate).

Jefferies, Matthew and Tyldesley, Mike (2011), 'Introduction', in *Rolf Gardiner: Folk, Nature and Culture in Interwar Britain* (Farnham: Ashgate).

Kenny, Mary (2003), *Germany Calling: A Personal Biography of William Joyce/Lord Haw-Haw* (Dublin: New Island).

Kushner, Tony (1989), *The Persistence of Prejudice: Anti-Semitism in British Society during the Second World War* (Manchester: Manchester University Press).

Kushner, Tony (1994), *The Holocaust and the Liberal Imagination: A Social and Cultural History* (Oxford: Blackwell).

Kushner, T. and Knox, K. (1999), *Refugees in an Age of Genocide* (London: Frank Cass).

Kushner, T. and Lunn, K. (eds) (1989), *Traditions of Intolerance: Historical Perspectives on Fascism and Race Discourse in Britain* (Manchester: Manchester University Press, 1989).

Kushner, T. and Lunn, K. (eds) (1990), *The Politics of Marginality: Race, the Radical Right and Minorities in Twentieth Century Britain* (Special number of *Immigrants and Minorities*, London: Frank Cass).

Lees-Milne, James (2006), *Diaries 1942–1954* (London: John Murray).

Leese, Arnold (1951), *Out of Step: Events in the Two Lives of an Anti-Jewish Camel Doctor* (Guildford).

Lejeune, Anthony (1984), *The Gentlemen's Clubs of London* (London: Bracken Books).

Lester, Normand (2002), *The Black Book of English Canada* (Toronto: McClelland & Stewart).

Lewis, Jeremy (2010), *Shades of Greene: One Generation of an English Family* (London: Jonathan Cape).

Liddell, Guy (2005), *The Guy Liddell Diaries, Vol. I: 1939–1942*, ed. Nigel West (Abingdon: Routledge).

Linehan, Thomas P. (1996), *East London for Mosley: The British Union of Fascists in East London and South-West Essex 1933–40* (London: Frank Cass).

Linehan, Thomas P. (2001), *British Fascism 1918–1939: Parties, Ideology and Culture* (Manchester: Manchester University Press).

Lukowitz, David C. (1974), 'British Pacifists and Appeasement', *Journal of Contemporary History*, 9, 1, 115–27.

Macklin, Graham (2007), *Very Deeply Dyed in Black: Sir Oswald Mosley and the Resurrection of British Fascism after 1945* (London and New York: I.B. Tauris).

Macklin, Graham (2009), 'A Fascist "Jihad": Captain Robert Gordon-Canning, British Fascist Antisemitism and Islam', *Holocaust Studies*, 15, 1, 78–100.

Maisky, Ivan Mikhaelovich (2015), *The Maisky Diaries: Red Ambassador to the Court of St James's 1932–1943*, ed. Gabriel Gorodetzky (Newhaven, CT and London: Yale University Press).

Miller, Rory (2008), 'British Arabists, Jewish Refugees and Palestine', in Efraim Karsh and Rory Miller (eds), *Israel at Sixty: Rethinking the Birth of the Jewish State* (London: Routledge).

Moore-Colyer, Richard (2001), 'Rolf Gardiner, English Patriot and the Council for Church and Countryside', *Agricultural History Review*, 49, 2, 187–209.

Moore-Colyer, Richard (2011), 'Rolf Gardiner, Farming and the English Landscape', in Matthew Jefferies and Mike Tyldesley (eds), *Rolf Gardiner: Folk, Nature and Culture in Interwar Britain* (Farnham: Ashgate).

Mosley, Sir Oswald (1968), *My Life* (London: Nelson).

Muir, Kate (1991), 'The Englishman who Felt Nazi Germany Calling', *The Times*, 3 May.

Newton, Scott (1991), 'The "Anglo-German Connection" and the Political Economy of Appeasement', *Diplomacy and Statecraft*, 2, 3 (November), 178–207.

Newton, Scott (1995), 'Appeasement as an Industrial Strategy, 1938–41', *Contemporary Record*, 9, 3, 485–506.

Newton, Scott (1996), *Profits of Peace: The Political Economy of Anglo-German Appeasement* (Oxford: Clarendon Press).

Noszlopy, Laura (2014), Introduction to John Coast, *Railroad of Death* (Newcastle upon Tyne: Myrmidon).

Orwell, George (1968), *The Collected Essays, Journalism and Letters of George Orwell* (London: Secker and Warburg), Vol. 2.

Padfield, Peter (2013), *Night Flight to Dungaavel: Rudolf Hess, Winston Churchill and the Real Turning Point of WWII* (Lebanon, NH: ForeEdge).

Pimlott, Ben (1977), *Labour and the Left in the 1930s* (Cambridge: Cambridge University Press).

Pitchford, Mark (2011), *The Conservative Party and the Extreme Right, 1945–75* (Manchester: Manchester University Press).

Portsmouth, The Earl of (1965), *Knot of Roots: An Autobiography* (London: Geoffrey Bles).

Pugh, Martin (2005), *Hurrah for the Blackshirts! Fascists and Fascism in Britain between the Wars* (London: Jonathan Cape).

Ramsay, A.H.M. (1952), *The Nameless War* (London: Britons Publishing Society).

Roberts, Andrew (1991), *The Holy Fox: A Life of Lord Halifax* (London: Weidenfeld and Nicolson).

Roberts, Andrew (1994), *Eminent Churchillians* (London: Weidenfeld and Nicolson).

Roberts, C.E. Bechofer (1946), *The Trial of William Joyce* (London: Jarrolds).

Saikia, Robin (2010), *The Red Book: The Membership List of the Right Club, 1939* (London: Foxley Books).

Selwyn, Francis (1987), *Hitler's Englishman: The Crime of Lord Haw-Haw* (London: Routledge and Kegan Paul).

Sharf, Andrew (1964), *The British Press and Jews under Nazi Rule* (Oxford: Oxford University Press).

Simpson, A.W. Brian (1992), *In the Highest Degree Odious: Detention without Trial in Wartime Britain* (Oxford: Oxford University Press).

Skidelsky, Robert (1975), *Oswald Mosley* (London: Macmillan).

Spencer, John (1979), 'Criminal Libel in Action – The Snuffing of Mr Wicks', *Cambridge Law Journal*, 38, 1, 60–78.

Stent, Ronald (1980), *A Bespattered Page? The Internment of His Majesty's Most Loyal Enemy Aliens* (London: André Deutsch).

Stingel, Janine (2000), *Social Discredit: Anti-Semitism, Social Credit, and the Jewish Response* (Montreal: McGill-Queen's University Press).

Stone, Dan (2002), *Breeding Superman: Nietzsche, Race and Eugenics in Edwardian and Interwar Britain* (Liverpool: Liverpool University Press).

Stone, Dan (2003), *Responses to Nazism in Britain, 1933–1939: Before War and Holocaust* (Basingstoke: Palgrave Macmillan).

Stone, Dan (2003), 'The British Far Right and the Back-to-the-Land Movement', in Dan Stone *Responses to Nazism in Britain, 1933–1939* (Basingstoke: Palgrave Macmillan).

Stone, Dan (2011), 'Rolf Gardiner: An Honorary Nazi?', in Matthew Jefferies and Mike Tyldesley (eds), *Rolf Gardiner: Folk, Nature and Culture in Interwar Britain* (Farnham: Ashgate).

Stone, Dan (2012), 'Ruralisme et droite radicale en France et en Grande-Bretagne dans l'entre-deux-guerres', in Philippe Vervaecke (ed.), *A droite de la droite: droites radicales en France et en Grande-Bretagne au XXe. Siècle* (Lille: Septentrion).

Thurlow, Richard (1987), *Fascism in Britain: A History, 1918–1985* (Oxford: Blackwell).

Trzebinski, Errol (2000), *The Life and Death of Lord Erroll: The Truth Behind the Happy Valley Murder* (London: Fourth Estate).

Uhlman, Fred (1998), *The Making of an Englishman: Erinnerungen eines deutschen Juden* (Zurich: Diogenes).

Vaughan, Hal (2011), *Sleeping with the Enemy: Coco Chanel's Secret War* (New York: Vintage Books).

Waugh, Evelyn (1952) *Men at Arms* (London: Chapman and Hall).

Waugh, Evelyn (1980), *The Letters of Evelyn Waugh*, ed. Mark Amory (London: Weidenfeld and Nicolson; London: Penguin Books, 1982).

Weale, Adrian (1994), *Renegades: Hitler's Englishmen* (London: Weidenfeld and Nicolson).

West, Rebecca (1949), *The Meaning of Treason* (London: Macmillan).

Williamson, Anne (1995), *Henry Williamson: Tarka and the Last Romantic* (Stroud: Sutton Publishing).

Williamson, Henry (1965), *The Phoenix Generation* (London: Macdonald).

Williamson, Henry (1967), *A Solitary War* (London: Macdonald).

Wrench, J. Evelyn (1948), *Francis Yeats-Brown 1886–1944* (London: Eyre and Spottiswoode).

INDEX

Abd-el-Krim 321
Aberdeen Press and Journal 40
Action 14, 21, 29, 64, 81, 210, 324, 332
Acworth, Capt. Bernard 116
Admiral Graf Spee (battleship) 259
Advisory Committee 19–24, 26–8, 30–1, 98–9, 101, 178, 264, 266–8
Africa 292–5
Agnew, Sir Peter MP 190
Aldred, Guy 69, 88
Alien Money Power in Great Britain 60
Allen, 'Commandant' Mary 108, 312–3
Alternative to Death 240
Amery, John 142, 163, 313
Amery Julian 313
Amery, Rt Hon. Leopold MP 50, 313
Anderson, Rt Hon. Sir John MP (Home Secretary) 15, 97, 106, 208, 299
Anglo-Arab Friendship Society 286
Anglo-German Fellowship 3, 144, 150, 177, 188, 193, 214, 222, 321
Anglo-German Review 3, 316

Angriff, Der 157–9
Anti-Jewish Riots (1947) 285, 322
Anti-Semitism 33–6, 81, 87–8, 118, 120, 122–3, 127, 144, 148, 155, 201, 207, 212–3, 217, 222, 235–40, 243–8, 262–9, 285, 288, 314; ambivalent attitudes to 252, 255, 259–60; eugenics 233, 235–7; excuses for Nazi anti-Semitism 236–77, 239, 243, 249; 'International Money Power' 62–3, 105, 235–6, 241, 250, 281–2, 307; 'Jewish domination of the Press and media' 2, 147, 238, 314; 'Jewish War' 2–3, 15–16, 19, 21, 24, 27, 63, 69–70, 86, 101, 213–14, 236–7, 239, 249; Jews brought persecution on themselves 34–6, 84, 188; lack of concern at Nazi anti-Semitism 38–9, 44–6, 49, 54; Arcand, Adrien 125
Ashridge (Bonar Law Conservative College) 36, 43
Ashridge Journal 36, 43, 54
Atholl, Duchess of (Katharine Marjory) 43

Index

Attlee, Rt Hon. Clement MP 103, 105, 313
Azzam Pasha 288

Bachelors' Club 173–4
'back-to-the-land' movement 4, 118, 120, 232–73, 289–92, 302, 307, 326
Bailey, Crawshay 321
Bailey, James A. ('Bill') 268
Baker, Arthur E. 156
Bali 264, 271–2
Ballad of the Men of Knoydart 297–8
Banning, Leonard 164
Bargaly 172–3, 185
Barker, Professor Ernest 109
Barton Brown, Monsignor 109, 321
Bates, Cyril 112
Bates, Percy 112
Beavan, Arthur Robert 109, 117
Beaverbrook, 1st Baron (William Maxwell Aitken) 86, 327
Beckett, Francis 13
Beckett, John Warburton 4, 63–6, 83, 91, 103–5, 142, 156, 181, 236, 266, 284, 299, 313–4, 317, 324, 327, 331; arrest and detention 68, 97–8; revival of BPP 121–3, 282–3
Bedford, 11th Duke of (Herbrand Arthur Russell) 60–1, 68
Bedford, 12th Duke of (Hastings William Sackville Russell, formerly Marquess of Tavistock) 4, 7, 9, 59–71, 91, 105, 126, 218–9, 229, 235, 259–60, 306, 327; BNP and ENA 115–20; death 70, 283; PPU 84, 87–9; revived BPP 121–3, 242, 282–3, 314; Scottish neighbours 171–4, 179–86, 188–9, 191; 'Tavistock peace proposal' 65–7, 179, 238, 327

Bedford, 13th Duke of (John Ian Robert Russell) 62
Bedford, Duchess of (Louisa, spouse of 12th Duke) 61–2
Bedford, Duchess of (Mary, spouse of 11th Duke) 60
Bedford Newsletter 122
Belgium *see* Low Countries
Bell, Clive 76
Bell, the Rt Revd George, Bishop of Chichester 247, 282
Bellamy, R. R. 208
Bene, Otto 243
Benes, Eduard 301
Bengal Lancer 253
Bennett, 1st Viscount (Richard Bedford Bennett) 125–6
Bennett, Sir Ernest MP 108, 179
Berg, Bengt 53, 198
Berger, Elizabeth 123, 288
Bevin, Rt Hon. Ernest MP 226
Biggs, Howard 112
The Big Idea 319
Birchall, Ian 310–11
Birkett, Sir Norman, KC 26, 99, 31, 98
Blakeney, General R. B. D. 321
Bletchley Park 224
Booth, Dr Meyrick 64, 76, 84, 314
Boswell Publishing Co. 287
Bothamley, Margaret 3, 100, 144, 156, 162–3, 165; broadcasting 142–50, 154
Bowman, Frederick 67–8, 70, 314–5
Bowra, Sir Maurice 149
Boyd-Carpenter, John 235
Boyle, Air Commodore Archie 227
Bracken, Rt Hon. Brendan MP 87
Brenan, Gerald 42–3
Bretton Woods Agreement 281
Bridge on the River Kwai, The 270

British Council Against European Commitments (BCAEC) 4, 77, 236, 263, 266, 313, 324, 328
British Council for a Christian Settlement in Europe (BCCSE) 4, 64, 66, 83–4, 104–5, 179, 205, 314, 321, 327, 332
British Democratic Party 108
British Fascists (British Fascisti) 209, 320–1, 325–6
British League of Ex-Servicemen and Women 121, 283, 285, 316, 322
British Legion 121, 251, 316
British Legion of St George 142
British Movement 217
British National News 118
British National Party (BNP) 70, 88, 114–20, 283, 315, 320, 331
British National Party (post-war party) 283
British News and Views 159
British People's Party 4, 63–5, 70, 77, 97, 100, 104–6, 205–7, 217, 314, 317–8, 321; infiltrating peace movement 78, 80, 83; revival of the party (from 1944) 70, 91, 103, 121–3, 127, 281–3, 288, 298, 328, 331–2
British Union 2–4, 6–7, 13–17, 24–31, 63–7, 77, 105–7, 141–2, 149, 249–53, 260, 262, 268–9, 293, 312–7, 319–24, 326–8, 330–2; 18B detention of members 95–7, 107, 11; 'conscientious objection' 17–24; East Anglian agricultural campaign 121, 249, 316; infiltration of peace movement 81–3, 86, 100–2; peace campaign 3, 77; post-detention 112–13, 115–17, 120; women's campaign 332

British Union of Fascists *see* British Union
Britons Publishing Society 287
Brixton Prison 97, 100, 106–9, 299, 315–16, 322
Brocket, 2nd Baron (Arthur Ronald Nall Nall-Cain) 9, 193–200, 203, 295–8
Brockway, Fenner MP 313
Brooks, (William) Collin 89, 108, 116–18, 315
Brooks's Club 199–200
Bryant, Arthur Wynne Morgan 8, 33–54, 70, 198, 203, 244–5, 257–8, 261
Buccleuch, 8th Duke of (Walter John Montagu-Douglas-Scott) 9, 50, 193–7, 202, 207, 213; contacted by Lonsdale Bryans 199–202; Lord Steward 194, 196, 198–9
Bülow, Idabelle von 152
Burgess, Victor 121, 285, 315–16
Burgin, Rt Hon. Edward Leslie MP 156–9, 163
Butler, Rt Hon. Richard Austen MP 195–7, 200–2, 235
Byles, Charles 39

Cadogan, Hon. Sir Alec 196–8, 200–3
Cairnsmore 60, 68, 173, 183, 185–6
Cambridge University Press (CUP) 299–30
Canada 125 227–9, 253, 318
Candour 317–8
Carlton Club 173
Carlyle Club 150
Carnegie, Lord (Charles Alexander Carnegie, later 11th Earl of Southesk) 178
Carol, King of Romania 223
Carroll, Cola Ernest 79, 84, 91, 97, 217, 316

Carton House Estate 297
Case for Germany, The 324
Catholic Herald 39
Chadwick, the Revd Professor Sir Owen 10
Chamberlain, Rt Hon. Sir Austen MP 222
Chamberlain, Rt Hon. Neville MP 37, 42–4, 49, 53, 64–5, 82, 104, 188, 194, 237, 244
Chanel, Coco 214
Chapman 156
Chesterton, Arthur Keith 123, 236, 241, 251, 283, 315–8
Chesterton, Gilbert Keith 316
Chevalier, Maurice 305
Christian Defence Movement 321
Christian National Party (Canada) 125
Chronicle of Ancient Sunlight, A 251
Churchill, Clementine 262
Churchill, Randolph 319
Churchill, the Rt Hon. Sir Winston Spencer MP 53, 126, 197, 207, 214, 219, 306; becomes PM 7, 97, 198; Galloway election 188, 190–1; general insults levelled at him 114, 159, 178, 213, 260; introduces 18B 7, 97; Sempill case 223–5; 'warmonger' 66–7, 70, 76, 86
Clark, Edward 149
Clark, James 142, 150–55, 162–3
Clark, Sir Kenneth 149
Coast, John 233, 264–73, 301, 308
'Cobbett' 326
Cockburn, Claud 196
Cole, Commander E. H. 156, 177
Colonna, Bertram de 76
Collier, Captain Vincent 64, 317
Conford, Philip 235–6

Conservative Party 36, 42–3, 44, 47, 194, 209–10, 221, 234, 329; *see also* Galloway Unionist Association
Constable, Rosalind 253
Constitutional Research Association (CRA) 89, 120, 124–7, 229, 241–2, 282–3, 298, 300–2, 318, 320, 330
Conwell-Evans, Philip 197
Cooper, Lady Diana 213
Cooper, Rt Hon. Alfred Duff MP 159, 213
Coupland, Philip 218
Cowdray, 1st Viscount (Weetman Pearson) 207
Creagh Scott, Lt.-Col. John 120, 281, 317–18
Cripps, Sir Stafford MP 76
Criterion Restaurant meetings 24, 63, 207, 216, 258
Croft, Diana 207
Croft, Sir Henry Page MP (later Lord Croft) 207–8
Croix de Feu 254
Cross, James Carlton 5
Cross, Rt. Hon. Sir Ronald MP 5
Crossman, Richard 41
Cry Havoc 254
Currey, Muriel 260–1
Czechoslovakia 43, 75–6, 104, 143, 174, 194, 197, 262; Prague coup 76, 86, 194–5, 237, 256

Daily Express 66, 183–4, 210
Daily Mail Group 315
Daily Sketch 158, 258
Daily Telegraph 80
Dalton, Rt. Hon. Hugh MP 104, 202–3
Danzig *see* Poland
Darnley, 9th Earl of (Esme Ivo Bligh) 66

Day, James Wentworth 290
Defence Regulation 18B (DR 18B) 7–9, 53, 59, 68, 111, 114, 159, 180, 264, 299, 314–6, 319–23, 327, 329–30; exceptions 208, 218; May 1940 arrests 67, 95–9, 101–9, 180–1, 210
Degrelle, Léon 262, 312
Delamere, 3rd Baron (Hugh Cholmondely) 293
De Ligt, Bart 85
Denmark 158
Derounian, Avedis Boghos (John Roy Carlson) 286–7
Deutsch-Englische Gesellschaft 257
Devonshire, 11th Duke of (Andrew Cavendish) 214
Dickson, Lovat 46–7, 53
Diettrich, Dr Harald 160
Dincklage, Hans Günther von 214
Dogs of War! 254
Domvile, Admiral Sir Barry 3, 7, 64–6, 77, 89, 101, 103, 115, 144, 148, 156, 159, 207, 213, 217, 237, 259, 263, 266–7, 314, 316, 318, 324; after release, 108–9, 318; arrest and detention, 97–8, 205, 318; membership of groups 125–6, 236, 238–9, 241, 281; post-war 242, 284, 286–8, 302
Donovan, Brian 24–5, 112
Donovan, Heather 112
Doriot, Jacques 313
Dorset, Chief Constable of 247, 266
Douglas, Major C. H. 61, 124, 318–19, 331
Downe, 9th Viscount (John Dawnay) 209
Downe, 10th Viscount (Richard Dawnay) 209
Downe, Dorothy, Dowager Viscountess 206, 209–12, 249
Dowsett, John Arthur 155, 158
DR 18B Detainees (British) Fund 113, 212
DR 18B Publicity Council 144, 260, 330
Drummond, George 217, 301–2
Dublin 65–6, 88–9, 183, 321
Dundas, Ian Hope 293
Dunlop, Robert 109, 113
Dutch East Indies *see* Indonesia

East Anglian Daily Times 41
Eckersley, Dorothy 142, 149–55, 162–3, 165
Eckersley, Peter 149–50
Economic Consequences of the Peace, The 48
Eden, Rt Hon. Anthony MP 159, 224–5
Edmonds, Major Harry 89, 116, 120, 124–7, 229, 241; post-war 281, 300, 302
Edward VIII, King 217
Eire 65–7, 89, 182–3, 226
Elliott, Nina 100
Eisner, Kurt 34
Elizabeth, Queen (consort of George VI) 53
Elton, 1st Baron (Godfrey Elton) 39, 256
English Array 4, 235, 239, 243–4, 267, 326
English Legion 120
English Mistery 4, 222, 234–5, 315, 326
English Nationalist Association (ENA) 70, 107–8, 119–20, 123, 283, 318
English Saga 36, 54

Erroll, 22nd Earl of (Josslyn Hay) 293
Essenleigh, Judge R. C. 20
Eton College 60, 108, 199
eugenics 232–8, 240–1, 243, 262, 290, 293, 307, 326
European Jungle 255–6
Everyman 253

Famine in England 235–6, 243
Featherstone-Hammond, C. 259
Fergusson, Colonel 187, 190
ffolkes, Sir Francis, 5th baronet 209
ffolkes, Sir William, 3rd baronet 209
Findlay, Richard 3, 98, 216–7, 319
Fish, Detective-Inspector Donald 155
Flax of Dream 265
Flockhart, Lawrence W. ('Alf') 109, 113
Foot, Major Hammond 108, 117
Forde, Daphne 265
Fortnightly Review 40
France 76, 162, 254, 313; invasion of 7, 25–8, 250; Vichy Government 86–7, 199, 313
Francis-Hawkins, Neil 17–18, 238, 320
Franco, Generalissimo Francisco 262, 282, 312, 329
Free Press, The 179
From Admiral to Cabin Boy 287
Fuller, Major-General J. F. C. 4, 65, 89, 217, 263, 241, 259, 288, 320; attends subversive movements 116–7, 125–6, 135, 193, 236, 238–9

Galloway, 12th Earl of (Randolph Algernon Stewart) 171–4, 177–9, 186–9, 191
Galloway News 178, 184–7, 190

Galloway Unionist Association 172, 177–8, 186–8, 190
Gandhi, Mahatma 90, 295
Gardiner, Rolf 233, 239–40, 242–8, 250, 252, 254, 261, 267, 273, 308; post-war, 289–91
Gibbon, the Revd Henry 60
George V, King 209
George VI, King 53, 147, 194, 198–9
Germany *passim; see also* Nazi Germany
Geyr, Baron 196
Gibbs, Sir Philip 213
Gilbert, Mark 76
Gill, Eric 84
Girvan, Waveney 282
Gittens, Anthony 288
Glasgow, 8th Earl of (Patrick James Boyle) 190, 320–1
Glasgow, S. 116
Gloucester, Duchess of (née Lady Alice Montagu-Douglas-Scott) 194, 196
Gloucester, Duke of (Prince Henry William Frederick Albert) 194
Goad, Harold 260–1
Godfrey, Edward 115–20, 315, 320
Goebbels, Josef 42, 81, 153, 238, 321
Goering, Hermann 198, 263, 312
Goldman, A. 38
Good, Ann 115
Gordon-Canning, Robert 64–5, 84, 91, 144, 157, 321; detention 98, 108–9, 205; post-war 284–8, 302
Gort, 6th Viscount (John Standish Vereker) 197, 203
Gothic Ripples 288
Graham, Lord Ronald 5, 100, 144, 216
Graham, Marquess of (James Angus Graham) *see* 7th Duke of Montrose
Greece 222

Green Movement 290–1
Greene, Ben 4, 9, 63–5, 89, 103–7, 241, 253, 314; activities in wartime movements 117–20, 123, 126–7; arrest 68, 97, 99; Brixton 107–8; Peace Pledge Union 77–8, 80, 83; post-war 298–300, 302, 306
Greene, Edward 105, 116, 281
Greene, Graham 103
Greene, Katharine 105, 123
Greene, Leslie 105
Grenfell, Captain Russell 116, 125–6
Grigg, Sir Edward MP 224
Guinness, Alec 270
Gurney 156

Halifax, 3rd Viscount (Edward Frederick Wood) 48, 53, 63, 65–6, 194–6, 198
Hamilton, 14th Duke of (Douglas Douglas-Hamilton) 198, 203
Hamilton, Gerald 109, 321–2
Hamm, Jeffrey 121, 284–6, 316, 322
Hankey, 1st Baron (Maurice Hankey) 52, 125–6
Harrow School 172–3, 292
Hassell, Ulrich von 200
Hattersley, Charles Marshall 61
Hay, Norman 7, 66, 89, 101, 108, 120, 124, 229, 233, 237–42, 244, 259, 273, 284, 308, 326, 328; membership of subversive bodies 117, 126, 234–6, 237–9, 241–2
Hayes, Flo 115
Henderson, Hamish 297–8
Henderson, Rt Hon. Sir Nevile 200
Hepburn, Audrey 98
Hepburn-Ruston, A. T. V. 98
Hess, Ilse 328
Hess, Rudolf 203, 328
Hetzler, Dr Erich 79
Hickson, Oswald 30, 211–2

Hidden Government 317
Himmler, Heinrich 318
Hinsley, His Eminence Cardinal Arthur 87
Hitler, Adolf 2, 34, 52, 54, 70, 83, 86, 199–200, 237, 241, 256, 265, 319; changing perceptions of 54, 245–6, 305–6; excuses for, 64–66; fiftieth birthday celebrations 195, 320; hero-worship of 36, 70, 77, 84, 149, 214, 244, 249, 253; portraits, and bust 147, 210, 284; praise for 67, 78, 105, 114, 124, 175, 201, 213, 250, 263, 288
Hoare, Rt Hon. Sir Samuel 161
Hoare-Laval Pact 189
Hobhouse, Christopher 42–4
Hoffmann, H. R. 78, 144, 156–9
Holland *see* Low Countries
Holmes, Colin 38
Home Defence (Security) Executive 69
Honest Money Association 120, 331
Hore-Belisha, Rt Hon. Leslie MP 158
Housman, Laurence 84
Houston, Jock 217, 267–8, 322–3
Howard, Pat 115
Huggard, Ronald McEwan 120, 126
Hughes, Raymond Davies 164
Hungary 143, 152
Hythe by-election 64, 104, 207, 317–8, 329

Ibn Saud 306, 328–9
Iddesleigh, 3rd Earl of (Henry Stafford Northcote) 234
Illustrated London News 36, 39
Imperial Fascist League (IFL) 4, 67, 100, 123, 144, 150, 156, 236, 282, 288, 324–5, 328

Independent Labour Party (ILP) 63, 67, 84, 103, 313, 327, 330
Independent Nationalists 282
India 252–3, 261
Indonesia 270–2
Information and Policy 7, 53, 124, 238–9, 244, 328
Interradio 160
Isherwood, Christopher 321
Italy 26, 197, 200, 252–3, 261

Jackson, Derek 215–6
January Club 253, 312, 320
Japan 87, 221–2, 224–7, 229–30
Jarvis, Mrs 23–4
Java 264, 271–2
Jefferies, Richard 248–9
Jenks, Jorian 27, 210, 233, 249, 273, 289–90, 323
Jerrold, Douglas 253
Jerusalem, Grand Mufti of 288
Jewish Chronicle 41–6
Jews, and the Jews in England 326
Jordan, Colin 288–9
Joyce, Margaret 142, 164, 324
Joyce, Quentin 108
Joyce, William ('Lord Haw-Haw') 4, 42, 63, 66, 103, 150, 177, 236, 262–6, 313, 317, 323–4, 327, 331; broadcasting 142, 147, 151, 163–4, 263, 267, 324

Kennedy, Major-General Sir John 126
Kent, Tyler 7, 96–7, 180, 330, 332
Kenya 293–5
Kenyan Society for the Study of Race Improvement 293
Kepston Ltd 121, 298, 302
Keynes, John Maynard 48
Kinship in Husbandry 240, 246
Kitson, Arthur 61, 324–5, 331

Knights of Columbus 227–8
Knoydart Land Seizures 295–8
Kondo, Captain 225
Kristallnacht Pogrom 76, 176
Kruger, Lisa 145
Kurtz, Harald 106
Kushner, Tony 38, 119, 127

Labour and the Left in the 1930s 299
Labour Party 103–4, 182, 299, 327, 331–2
Land Settlement Act 296
Lander, Kenneth 165
Laurie, Arthur Pillans 15–16, 324–5
Laval, Pierre 86–7, 189
Lawrence, T. E. 249, 251, 255
Lawton, Lancelot 237–9
League of Empire Loyalists (LEL) 283–4, 287–8, 317–18
Lees, Aubrey 9, 99–103, 108, 123, 144, 157, 216–7, 259, 267–8
Lees-Milne, James 199, 203, 215
Leese, Arnold 98, 100, 108, 156–7, 236, 282, 288–9, 306, 324–5
Légion des Volontaires Français contre le Bolchévisme 313
Legion of St George 313
Lennep, Anne van 108, 144, 146
Liberty Restoration League 4, 114, 120, 205, 330
Liddell, Guy 83, 114
Liddell Hart, Sir Basil 119
Link, The 3–4, 42, 65, 77, 97, 100, 108, 112, 144, 150, 205–7, 213–4, 217, 223, 238, 263, 316–19, 324, 328; relationship with PPU 79–80, 82–3
Lintorn-Orman, Rotha 209, 320–1, 325–6
Lloyd, 1st Baron (George Ambrose Lloyd) 102, 223
Lloyd George, Rt Hon. David MP 194
Lockwood, H. H. 123, 288

Lonsdale Bryans, James 199–202
Lorimer, Emily 41
Lovely, Percy 120
Low Countries 76; Belgium 145–6, 254; Dutch 'Fifth Column' 77, 20, 96; Holland 146; invasion of 7, 20, 26–7
Loyalists, The 321
Ludovici, Anthony 64, 232–4, 236, 326–7
Lunn, K. 38
Luttman-Johnson, Captain H. W. 205
Lymington, Viscount *see* Portsmouth, 9th Earl of

Macaulay, Rose 78, 80
MacDiarmid, Hugh 296
McGovern, John MP 66–7, 84, 182, 327
McGrath, Commander 224
McKie, John Hamilton MP 171–82, 185–91, 301–2, 306
Macklin, Graham 290
Maclean, Thomas 115
Macmillan, Daniel 52
Macmillan, Harold MP 46–53
McNab, Angus 317, 324, 327
Makins, Lady 286
Manchester Guardian 41, 74
Mander, Geoffrey MP 182
Mann, Marcel 300
Mannin, Ethel 80–1, 87
Mar, 35th Earl of (Lionel Walter Erskine) 65–6, 84, 109, 212, 327–8
Martial India 261
Mary, Queen (consort of George V) 209
Masaryk, Jan 301
Maxton, James MP 327
Maxwell, Sir Alexander 210
Meaning of Treason, The 148

Mellotte, Dr J. H. 179
Men at Arms 252
Metcalfe, Lady Alexandra 29
Militant Christian Patriots 4
Mills, H. T. ('Bertie') 3, 101, 108, 123, 126, 236, 241, 259, 328
Mitchell, Sir Harold Paton MP 190
Mitford, Deborah (later Duchess of Devonshire) 214
Mitford, Tom 215
Mitford, Unity 149, 214–5
Mitsubishi 222, 224
Monetarism 61, 63, 69–70, 118, 120, 124–5, 228, 240–1, 243, 248, 282, 307
Montrose, 7th Duke of (James Angus Graham) 216, 293
Moore, Humphrey 74–6, 80–1, 85
Moran, Tommy 107, 109, 114–7
Morris, Canon Stuart 79–80, 82, 90–1
Morrison, Rt Hon. Herbert MP (Home Secretary) 114, 182–3, 212
Morton, J. B. 259
Mosley, Lady (The Hon. Diana, née Mitford) 26–31, 98, 214–5, 262, 321
Mosley, Sir Oswald Ernald, 6th Bart. 3, 7, 8, 37, 63–5, 82, 100–1, 112, 207, 210–2, 217, 237, 249–54, 258–9, 262–3, 290, 293, 306–7, 312–3, 319–28, 331; before Advisory Committee 29–32; 'conscientious objection' 17–24; detention 98, 205, 215; Earls Court Rally 257; later reinterpretation of events 13–17, 21, 24–31; post-war 212, 283–4
Mother Earth 289
Mottistone, 1st Baron (Maj.-Gen. John Edward Bernard Seely) 213
Moyne, Moyne, 1st Baron (Walter Edward Guinness) 126

Mr Norris Changes Trains 321
Murry, John Middleton 85–6, 88–9, 91, 116–7, 126
Mussolini, Benito 76, 78, 253–4, 312–3, 325
My Life 13

Nagy, Ivan 76
Nameless War, The 287
National Book Association 36
National Front 283–4, 288, 317
National Front after Victory 103, 123, 241, 251, 315, 317
National Socialist League 4, 63, 150, 236, 313, 316–7, 324, 331
National Weekly 296
Nationalist Association 268, 322
Nazi Germany *passim*; 'anti-German propaganda' 38, 77, 81–2, 146, 213–4; 'attacked because challenging Jewish financial domination' 2, 63, 69–70, 84, 118, 125, 144, 147, 214; 'economic miracle' 2, 175, 245; 'effects of Versailles treaty' 2, 198; protection against bolshevism 2, 143, 175, 244, 257; 'regenerated, with new self-respect' 2, 124–5, 243, 245; to be trusted 63, 70, 75, 195, 244
New British Broadcasting Service 102
New Club, Edinburgh 173
New English Weekly 40
Newenham, Mrs 268
New Leader 84
New Party 326
New Pioneer 4, 65, 236, 238, 244, 255, 314, 316, 328
New Statesman 41
New York Times 181, 198–9
News Chronicle 82
News from Germany 78, 144
Newton, Frances 286–7

Nichols, Beverley 254
Nietzsche, Friedrich 326
Nordic League 4, 65, 82, 100–1, 144, 156, 177, 193, 223, 237, 316, 319, 328–30
Norfolk, Chief Constable of 251
Noszlopy, Laura 269, 272–3
Nuremberg Trials 263
Nyasaland 291–2

Observer, The 254
Oddie, Air Commodore Gerard 282, 328
O'Donohue, Brian 112
O'Duffy, Eoin 312
Ordeal by Battle 52
Orwell, George 86

Paget, Reginald, KC, MP 282
Pakenham, Hon. Frank (later 7th Earl of Longford) 282
Palestine 76, 78, 81, 87, 99–101, 255, 283, 285–8, 321, 329–30; London Palestine Conference 99; Palestine Information Centre 246
Palestine Mystery, The 330
Parti Populaire Français 313
Patriot, The 144, 314
Peace and Progressive Information Service 77–8, 80, 104
Peace Focus 41
Peace News 70, 74, 75–91
Peace Pledge Union 7, 17, 67, 70, 75–91, 104, 328
Peace Service Handbook 79–80
Pearson, Sir Edward 207
Pearson, Lady 64, 109, 206–9
Peeblesshire Advertiser 108
People's Campaign Against War And Usury 328
People's Post 122
Pepys, Samuel 36

Perthshire Constitutional 40
Pétain, Marshal Philippe 87
Peter Joseph Lenné Gold Medal 292
Peveril Camp, Peel (Isle of Man) 98
Philby, H. St John 17, 63–4, 84, 207, 306, 328–9
Philby, Kim 329
Phoenix Generation, The 265
Pimlott, Ben 103–4, 299–300
Pitt-Rivers, Captain George Lane-Fox 94, 156, 159, 205, 232–3, 236, 259, 261–4, 266, 268
Pitt-Rivers, General Augustus 261
Pius XII, Pope 161
Poland 64, 76, 86, 104, 150, 152; Danzig 156–7, 196; guarantee to 77, 194–5, 197, 249
Portrait of a Leader 316
Portsmouth, 9th Earl of (formerly Viscount Lymington) 4, 7, 63, 65, 77, 89, 101, 116, 123, 243–4, 252, 259, 263, 266, 308, 313, 316, 324, 326; association with John Coast 266–8; 'back-to-the-land' activity 233–5, 237–40, 241–3; membership of wartime bodies 125–6, 241, 251; post-war activity 289, 293–5
post-war sentencing 142, 148, 154–5, 162–5
pro-Arabism 99–101, 255, 285–8, 307, 321
Pro-British Association 216
pro-Nazism *passim*
Propaganda Ministry (German) 153, 160
Protocols of the Elders of Zion, The 262, 317, 324–5, 329
Prytz, Björn 227
Pugh, Martin 198
Purdy, Walter 164

Radio Metropol 160–1, 164
Railroad of Death 270
Ramsay, Captain Archibald Henry Maule MP 4–5, 7, 31, 65, 101, 109, 121, 207, 217, 223, 238, 242, 255, 259, 267–9, 319, 323, 329–30, 332; arrest and detention 67, 97–8, 107–8, 180, 205; post-war activity 285–7, 302; views on 176–9, 181, 186, 188–9
Ramsay, the Hon. Mrs Ismay 108, 223
Ramsay Macdonald, James MP 103, 313
Ratcliffe, Alexander 118
Real Crisis, The 330
Recruit to Revolution 272
Red Book (membership, list of Right Club) 5–6, 180–2
Redesdale, 2nd Baron (David Bertram Ogilvy Freeman-Mitford) 177, 214–5
Redesdale, Lady 211, 215
Reed, Douglas 286
Reichsrundfunk 142, 146–7, 150–4, 158
Reith, Sir John 53
Return to the River Kwai 270
Rexism 254, 262
Ribbentrop, Joachim von 79, 195, 200
Riddell, Enid 286, 322, 330, 332
Ridout, P. J. 236, 288
Riff War 321
Right Club 4–7, 65, 96–7, 100–2, 144, 150, 174–9, 188, 190, 205, 214, 217, 238, 255, 259, 286, 314, 317–9, 322, 326; membership list 5–6, 180–2; wartime activities 7, 101, 108, 146, 178, 216, 222, 268, 332

Roberts, Andrew 37, 43, 52–3, 198, 258
Rogers, Captain Arthur 4, 114, 281, 330
Romania 224
Roosevelt, President Franklin D. 70
Rösel, Dr Gottfried 78
Rosenberg, Laura 273
Rothermere, 1st Viscount (Harold Sydney Harmsworth) 315
Rowse, A. L. 37
Rudmore-Brown, Professor Thomas 88
Rudolf Hess: Prisoner of Peace 3228
Rural Economy 289
Rural Reconstruction Association (RRA) 289–90, 294, 323
Rushcliffe, 1st Baron (Henry Betterton) 213

Salò Republic 313
Sanderson, William 234–5, 326
Sandys, Duncan MP 319
Saunders, Robert 121, 233, 273, 289–90
Scanlon, John 63, 236, 281, 324, 330–1
Schlottmann 257
Schmidt, Dr Karl 157–8
Schmidt-Hansen, Johannes 146, 150, 153
Schoeberth, Dr Friedrich 145
Sempill, 19th Baron (William Francis Forbes-Sempill) 5, 218, 221–30; Canadian visit, 227–9; Japanese connections 221–2, 224–6, 229–30; membership of right-wing and pro-Nazi groups 116, 125–6, 177, 179, 229, 235, 241, 281; post-war activities 289–302
Sencourt, Robert 39, 66
Sharf, Andrew 38

Sheffield Star 40
Sheppard, the Revd Dick 74, 86
Simon, 1st Viscount (Sir John Simon) 71
Simpson, W. Brian 106
Skardon, Captain W. J. 162
Skidelsky, Robert 316
Smith (architect and possible MI5 informant) 125
Snowden, Viscountess 226
Social Credit 61, 83, 118, 122, 124, 228, 243, 318–9, 331
Society of Friends (Quakers) 74, 103
Soddy, Professor Frederick 282, 331
Soil Association (SA) 289–91, 294, 323
Soper, the Revd Donald 84
South-East European Observer 300
Southern Rhodesia 292–3
Spain 156, 161
Spanish Civil War 254, 262, 329
Spears, Brigadier-General Edward MP 15
Spectator, The 41–3, 45, 253
Spooner, Major Reginald 147–8, 153–4
Spranklin, Philip 238
Squire, the Revd Cecil 62
Stanford, Mary ('Mollie') 102, 144–6, 156
Stankovitch 300
Stapledon, Professor George 234
Statecraft 234
Statement on the European Situation, A 84
Stent, Ronald 180
Stephen, Campbell MP 327
Stern Gang 126
Stewart, Andrew 81–2
Stewart, General Sir William 172
Stokes, Richard Rapier MP 66, 84, 210–1, 282
Stokes, Ron 155–7

Stone, Dan 38, 232–3
Streicher, Julius 157, 325
Strong, Harold Vesey 126
Stuckey, Derek 20–4, 111–13, 273, 289–90
Stuckey, Gladys 111
Stürmer, Der 157
Sukarno, 1st President of Indonesia 272
Sunday Dispatch 313
Sunday Telegraph 299
Sunday Times 39
Sun Life Assurance Company of Canada 155–6
Suspect List 69, 102, 112, 230, 247, 264
Swinton, 1st Viscount (Philip Cunliffe-Lister) 69, 211–12

Talking Picture News 70, 314
Tarka the Otter 272
Tavistock, Marquess of *see* Bedford, 12th Duke of
Taylor, A. J. P. 41
Taylour, Fay 330
Temple Cotton, Ralph 112, 289–90
Thailand-Burma Railway 269–71
This Age of Plenty 321
Thomsen, Henning 65
Thurlow, Richard 283
Time and Tide 41
Times Literary Supplement 39
Times, The 211
Tost Internment Camp 160
Toyoda, Captain 222
Travellers' Club 327
Tremlett, Rex 116, 125–6, 289
Trevor-Roper, Hugh (later Lord Dacre) 53
Truth 40, 64, 118, 314–5
Truth about the Jews, The 118
Truth about This War, The 105

Uhlman, Fred 207
Ukraine 237
Unconditional Hatred 125
Unfinished Victory 8, 33–54, 258
Union and Reconstruction 53, 258
Union Movement 121, 212, 283–4, 316, 322, 331
Union of British Freedom 121, 285, 316
Unionist Party *see* Conservative Party
United Christian Front 329
United States of America (USA) 198, 201, 219, 253; American opinion 199, 219, 229; embassy 7, 96, 229

Vaneck, John 268
Vardon, Pearl 141
Vatican 322
Verdon Roe, Sir Alliott 84, 117, 331
Vilatte, Paul *(episcopus vagans)* 315
Vittel Internment Camp 162
Vivian, Dr Margaret 117

Wagner Society 302
Walker, Alfred Graham 20
Walker-Smith, Derek 235
Warburg, G. 45–6
Ward, John Alexander 161, 164–5
Watts, Charlie 107, 109, 114–7
Waugh, Evelyn 252, 292
Weale, Adrian 148
Week, The 196
Wellington, 5th Duke of (Arthur Charles Wellesley) 4–5, 177, 212–3
West, Rebecca 41, 148
Western Mail 41
Westminster, 2nd Duke of (Hugh Richard Arthur Grosvenor, 'Bendor') 197, 212–4
What Hitler Wants 91
Whinfield, Mrs Muriel 108, 145

Whitham, Mrs de Grey 208
Whittleton, Eric 112, 289–90
Whitwell, Robert 61
Wicks, Caroline 157
Wicks, Derek Malcom 155, 157
Wicks, Henry William 142, 155–65, 306
Wicks, Margaret *see* Margaret Wodrich
Williams, Thomas 90
Williamson, Anne 251
Williamson, Henry 210, 233, 248–52, 255, 259–60, 265–6, 272–3
Williamson, Hugh Ross 19, 64, 66–7, 84, 86, 89, 331–2
Wilson, Sir Arnold 6
Wilson, Sir Horace 37, 49
Wodehouse, P. G. 173
Wodrich, Margaret (née Wicks) 142, 155, 157–8, 160–5
Wodrich, Willi 1661–2

Wolff, Henry Drummond MP 213, 258
Wolkoff, Admiral Nicolai 332
Wolkoff, Anna 217, 268, 329–30, 332
Women's Auxiliary Service 312
Woodham, H. S. 40
Woolf, Virginia 149
Woollard, Caaptain 108
Word, The 69–70, 88
Wrench, Sir Evelyn 253, 261
Wülzburg Internmant Camp 159–60

Years of Endurance 1793–1802, The 36
Years of Victory 1802–1812, The 36
Yeats-Brown, Francis 114, 179, 252–61, 273, 308
YMCA 52
Young, G.M. 52

Zeppelin, Count and Countess von 152